16.50

George-Etienne
CARTIER

George-Etienne Cartier, 1871 (Notman).

George-Etienne CARTIER

A Biography

Alastair Sweeny

McClelland and Stewart

Photographs © Notman Photographic Archives, McCord
Museum, McGill University; Public Archives of Canada;
Public Archives of Manitoba.

Maps by Courtney C.J. Bond.

ISBN: 0-7710-8363-7

McClelland and Stewart Limited
The Canadian Publishers
25 Hollinger Road
Toronto, Ontario
M4B 3G2

Printed and bound in Canada

For Andrew and Malcolm.

CONTENTS

6   FOREWORD

7   INTRODUCTION

15   PART ONE
From the House of the Seven Chimneys
(1735-1854)

93   PART TWO
Siamese Twins (1854-1868)

177   PART THREE
All Aboard for the West (1867-1871)

237   PART FOUR
Pandora's Box (1871-1873)

331   BIBLIOGRAPHY

342   REFERENCES

349   INDEX

FOREWORD

It is well known that there is a great obstacle to overcome in the writing of a fully documented life of George-Etienne Cartier. His personal papers are thought to have been destroyed; even the scholarly study of Cartier by Dr. Henry Best firmly admits what we cannot know. Our knowledge of Cartier as a person must remain fragmentary or shadowy.

Alastair Sweeny in this bold and zestful life accepts that limitation, and transcends it. He does so by dealing fully with Cartier as a public man, the well known and dynamic Cartier. He seizes on the central fact that Cartier – the poet of the rebellion of 1837 – became the central figure, latterly the human dynamo, to use a for once justified metaphor, of railroad development in Canada from 1847 till his death in 1873. His passions – to give Canada an ice-free winter port and unite British North America by the new magic of the iron horse, to win the Northwest and British Columbia by a railroad to the Pacific, and above all, to ensure the survival of the French Canadians in a federal state – were the fiery themes of Cartier's life. By developing this focus, Alastair Sweeny not only gives us Cartier as the great-hearted, never beaten terrier of Canadian politics, but also gives us, as it were by reverberation, the personality of the man and makes coherent what is known of his private life. The result is very much a "life" of Cartier, vivid, spirited and dramatic.

In the accomplishment of Confederation, Cartier was the ever-loyal, mutually recognized equal, of John A. Macdonald. Cartier exemplified, as the author well demonstrates, the full partnership, dynamic and invigorating, of English and French in the Canada of Confederation. Cartier needed Macdonald's easy sagacity as much as Macdonald needed his fiery resolution. Yet, it is above all to be noted Cartier remained at the same time, in his style, his energy, his tastes, French – French, all wool and a yard wide, *français pure laine, pur-sang*.

W.L. Morton

INTRODUCTION

**"After all, the life of an individual has, in its
silent passage to the end, the same unfath-
omed meaning as the life of a nation."**

Stephen Leacock

Cartier and his Ontario Lieutenant

To write a biography of George-Etienne Cartier is in itself to illustrate
the political life and times of Canada's critical half century, of those
fascinating years between the Rebellions of 1837 and the accomplishment of a transcontinental dominion. More than any other man, Cartier
was at the centre of those events that led to our awakening as a nation.
Cartier's desires were the clear mirror of the wishes of those scattered
communities who came together to create a political state; his will-
power was a whip that drove the nation into being. As the chief voice of
the French Canadian community, the pivotal point of the union, Cartier
was the kingpin of Confederation.

Sir Joseph Pope, John A. Macdonald's secretary and biographer, did
nothing to diminish his chief's reputation when he declared that, "Had
it not been for Sir George Cartier, it is doubtful whether the Dominion
of Canada would exist today." Yet this negative, almost regretful compliment merely begs the question. What Pope surely meant, yet re-
strained himself from saying, was that George-Etienne Cartier deserves
to be regarded as the first among the Fathers of Confederation.

What a forgetful nation we are! The legal and constitutional acts this
man drew up and pushed through into legislation were, and still are, the
cornerstones of our country. It was Cartier who fathered the Grand
Trunk, Intercolonial, and Canadian Pacific Railways; Cartier who, as
Prime Minister of the Union of the Canadas, initiated discussions which
led to the passage of the British North America Act, who ensured the
choice of Ottawa as the Capital City; Cartier who negotiated the transfer of the Hudson's Bay Company territories to the Dominion; Cartier
who was largely responsible for legislation creating the new provinces of
Manitoba and British Columbia; Cartier who, as Canada's first Minister of Militia and Defence, flexed the young country's muscles against
American expansionism, personifying Harold Innis' witty dictum that
"We can only survive by taking persistent action at strategic points
against American imperialism in all its attractive guises"; Cartier, arguing that "we can and will build up a northern power," who persuaded

the politicians of British Columbia to press for a transcontinental railway as their price for admission into Confederation; and Cartier – with his last breath outmanoeuvring the American railway barons – who laid the groundwork for the success of the Canadian Pacific Railway, and fixed our national nervous system.

Yet Cartier is the mystery man of Confederation, long overshadowed in the popular mind by his great colleague, his "Siamese Twin,"*John A. Macdonald. The pair worked brilliantly together, with rarely a difference of opinion. Cartier once remarked that "My colleague is a happy man. He is so marvellously endowed that it is unnecessary for him to work. In important debates he makes me speak first, so that I may study to the bottom the subject of discussion and do all the required research. When I have made my speech, and replied to objections, he remarks: 'All right, I am now thoroughly posted, and in a position to reply to all.'" They complemented each other perfectly, yet up to Confederation, it is apparent that Cartier (called "the Lightning Striker" by his Parliamentary colleagues) wielded more direct political power. Macdonald's genius manifested itself largely after 1867, in the consolidation of the great work, yet from our Pantheon of Gods, we needed a single Father and relegated Cartier to the back of our minds. He is primarily thought of as the Quebec lieutenant of Macdonald, someone Macdonald needed for his own ends, and wooed like a shrewd lover to his side. It has suited some English Canadians to think that, like Quebec, Cartier was won over, and then forgotten; or some French Canadians to argue that, like a "Negro King" or puppet of the English, Cartier was rewarded for selling out his people.

Macdonald did little to correct the impression, not necessarily because he wanted to ensure for himself a higher place in history, but because, realistically, it was to his political advantage in English Canada to enhance his own stature. "Cartier," he said to Pope, "was as bold as a lion. He was just the man I wanted. But for him confederation could not have been carried."

In fact, the present nature and shape of Confederation owe the most to Cartier's demands for French Canada; and Macdonald, with an eye on Cartier's steadfast and powerful bloc of votes, did not need much urging to be won over. His own political survival before Confederation was predicated on these votes and Cartier's support. But Cartier did not merely supply the political capital for the enterprise of Confederation; he set the wheels in motion over the track he himself had laid. Macdonald was just the man he wanted.

The Missing Cartier Papers

Our ignorance of Cartier perhaps stems from the fact that there is no

---

* A term first applied to Cartier and Galt, later to Cartier and Macdonald.

clearly defined body of Cartier Papers available to scholars. There are stories that much of his correspondence was destroyed to protect the Ministry during the Pacific Scandal, or that he left secret memoirs – possibly telling the *real* truth about John A. Macdonald – to be published ten years after his death. Cartier's only comment on the matter was an offhand remark made in the Commons in 1864, with regard to a Grit motion: "I will treasure it as an historical document, just as I have done with so many others since 1848, the year I entered public life. None of these papers will leave my hands until long after my return to private life."

But Cartier died in harness, and his papers were dispersed. Apart from the meagre collection of Cartier Papers in the Public Archives of Canada, there is quite a surprising amount of Cartier material in the Macdonald Papers, and in the Langevin Papers at Quebec City. It is apparent, from the 1874 testimony of Cartier's Deputy Minister of Militia, Major Georges Futvoye, that his papers fell into these hands:

After Sir George's death all the papers in his official room were minutely examined by myself and Mr. Sulte, one of the clerks in the office. He was in the habit of keeping everything. We destroyed everything which was of no importance. As to the rest, they were packed in separate parcels and delivered to such persons as we supposed to be most interested in them. All in any way relating to the North-West were placed in a large envelope, sealed and sent to Sir John Macdonald in his capacity as First Minister.

The papers he used to keep at his office were relatively unimportant. He always took home with him, to a room or office in his own house, the important papers. What became of these I know not, save that Mr. Langevin told me he had taken possession of everything.

Macdonald added that, "As to Sir George Cartier's papers at his residence, I understood that Sir George's executors and Mr. Langevin had examined them all and destroyed such as they thought were unimportant or ought to be destroyed. What became of the rest I do not know."

There is a story that most of Cartier's papers were destroyed in a fire, and this may have some basis in truth. His Professional Fees and Accounts Book, with legal entries dating from 1836 to 1853, is charred around the edges. There are a few later entries dated 1879 in a different hand, which might suggest that, after Cartier's death in 1873, the book was removed from his house and delivered to his law partner and executor Pominville as a souvenir. It was saved from a fire and eventually found its way into the collection of the Château de Ramezay.

In spite of the correspondence that remains, it has been quite difficult to reconstruct the same sort of picture of Cartier's life and opinions as has been done so brilliantly by Professors Creighton and Careless in their biographies of John A. Macdonald and George Brown. Unlike

Brown and Macdonald, Cartier did not pour out his soul in letters to his wife, so we have no intimate view of his impressions of politics, scenery, friends or enemies. Yet it is clear that Cartier wished to be remembered by his accomplishments, and not through written sentiments. He was a man of actions more than words. His speeches, the largest body of textual information remaining, were calls to action. Few Canadians have seen better into the future – reading them is like reading prophecy.

His Character

On the surface, Cartier appears as a single-minded, almost characterless political machine, an historical deity, a law-maker like Moses or a civilizer like Napoleon. However, by a study of anecdotal information and newspaper accounts, it is possible to glimpse the man through the maze of his acts. His character was not complex, like Macdonald's, but then he had not endured the same personal sufferings as his great political ally. He was basically a one-dimensional, tough-minded pragmatist, an uncomplicated man who knew exactly what he wanted, and buried himself in working for it with a dedication no one could match.

Yet like his *bon vivant* father, he could enjoy good company. In Ottawa he would surface socially at his famous Saturday afternoon get-togethers, or *conversationes*, where cabinet ministers mingled with junior clerks, and partisans met on neutral ground and let their guards down, where guests were treated to the latest operatic aria or urged to sit in a row of chairs, swing their arms in unison, and sing voyageur songs at the top of their lungs.

Cartier's assistant Benjamin Sulte has left us with a detailed physical description of his chief:

> Of medium stature, even small, about five feet six inches in height, he was of strong and robust build . . . Without being fat, he was what may be described as rotund, and his limbs were so well proportioned as to give an appearance of uncommon vigour to the entire frame. His hands and feet were small but finely modelled. His well-proportioned figure was surmounted by a massive head – the most striking portion of his whole physical make-up. An expansive brow denoted intellectual power, the eyes were keen and piercing, the nose prominent, and the under part of the face strongly developed, denoting great strength of character and will power . . .
>
> In his personal attire George-Etienne Cartier was always neat, even to fastidiousness. His customary attire in public was the long black Prince Albert which public men of that period almost habitually wore. An expansive collar with a bow tie, a light vest, and a plain or striped pair of trousers completed his wearing apparel. Generally in public he wore the silk hat which statesmen of a former day always affected.

George-Etienne Cartier's features were generally animated, the whole face lit up with that intelligence which denoted the spiritual force within. His gestures have been well compared to those of a lion, powerful and supple, but not rough . . . Quick, alert, and at times even abrupt, he was the embodiment of nervous force and energy. He thought quickly, and acted quickly. *Ever on the alert, he perceived everything, and provided for every contingency.* Force, energy, determination, were in fact the leading features of his character.

He was a nervous, restless, almost possessed man, who worked fifteen hours a day, and bore on his shoulders all the aspirations of the French Canadian nation. Cartier was the personification of his people, mirroring all their struggles and their greatness. Wolfe's victory on the Plains of Abraham had set in motion their nationality, Papineau's rebellion wakened it, LaFontaine's union with Baldwin took it safely through adolescence, but it was Cartier who ensured its survival, through the establishment of the Province of Quebec, within Confederation.

Cartier realized that a union of all the provinces of British North America would ensure this survival. A federal union, with provincial legislatures, and in Quebec's case, an Upper House, would give the French Canadians a forum for their own particular cultural needs. Moreover, a strong central government would help prevent an American takeover of all of North America, in which his people would surely be lost.

The culture Cartier represented, a truly national, deep-rooted and vital way of life, was already well-developed at the time of Confederation. The Maritime Provinces were young, and Upper Canada scarcely out of the cradle, when a mature Quebec led them by the hand into nationhood. The personality that Cartier gave to the political life of his day is the same personality the French Canadians have given to Canada. Their independent sentiments and their cultural and social desires are the microcosm of our greater sense of nationality. That we are not entirely northern provinces of the United States is due largely to Cartier and the French Canadians.

Cartier and Canadian Nationalism

In recent years, there has been some confusion in this country over the definition of the word, "nationalism," as well as a great desire among certain of our intellectuals to force an evolution of "nationalism," which is an affair of the instincts, into "statism," which is an affair, if so it can be termed, of the mind. Some have called nationalism "an emotion which hides real problems behind an abstraction," or have suggested that "the nationalist interpretation lives on mere abstractions and projections." One Right Honourable gentleman, reflecting the advanced opinions of his contemporaries in the heady days of the early 1960s, sharpened his pen and wrote,

> nationalists – even those of the left – are politically reactionary because, in attaching such importance to the idea of a nation, they are surely led to a definition of the common good as a function of an ethnic group, rather than of all the people, regardless of characteristics. This is why a nationalist government is by nature intolerant, discriminatory, and when all is said and done, totalitarian. A truly democratic government cannot be "nationalist," because it must pursue the good of all its citizens, without prejudice to ethnic origin. The democratic government, then, stands for and encourages good citizenship, never nationalism.

Other thinkers have zeroed in on Canadian nationalism in particular, suggesting that "far from contributing to the growth of a stronger, more independent, and identity-conscious nation, Canadian nationalism as it has developed in recent years has been diverting Canada into a narrow and garbage-cluttered *cul-de-sac*."

While not wishing entirely to disagree with the above opinions, I would merely suggest that we should be careful how the word is used. Nationalism is a sociological problem, as Michel Brunet suggests when he asks, "What is nationalism? It is simply the manifestation of a natural solidarity that exists among members of a human group who possess an historical and cultural past . . . Nationalism is not an artificial movement or sentiment. It is the result of the need which forces men to live in society." Perhaps the quality of a people's nationalism is the important thing, as Donald Creighton suggests when he says that "It is imperialism, not nationalism, which poses the greatest threat to the peace of the world."

George-Etienne Cartier is the foremost nationalist ever to appear on our political stage. If anything, he can be described best as a Canadian expansionist, a forceful, dynamic proponent of the creation and survival of a workable political nationality. His success was hard-fought and hard-won. His conduct during what was called "the Pacific Scandal" has always been a question mark in Canadian history, and Cartier's reputation has always been somewhat under a cloud, yet by a thorough examination of the facts of the case, it can be seen that his motives and actions during the affair mark him as a great national hero. Faced with what he perceived as a national disaster, and a betrayal of Canada's future, he fought for his young country with the bravery of a lion and the cunning of a fox. More than any other figure of that era, he was the embodiment of what Pierre Berton has so aptly called "the National Dream."

Like his distant ancestor Jacques Cartier, the European discoverer of Canada, Cartier was a man whose actions changed the course of history. Like Napoleon – a man of the same physical stature and presence –

Cartier was a catalyst of events, and gloried in his role. He was fond of calling his railway bills – the Grand Trunk, Intercolonial, and Canadian Pacific – after Napoleon's victories at Jena, Wagram, and Austerlitz. Yet he outdid Napoleon. Cartier did not retreat from Moscow – the winning of the Canadian Northwest was his most significant victory. Cartier's Waterloo – the election of 1872 – was no real political defeat, but rather much like the finale of a tragicomic opera. He was propped up on the platform, his wounded legs useless beneath him, like a puppet rebelling against the strings that held him, to promise his constituents a railway. Napoleon's glory, his empire, was shattered overnight. Cartier's survived, and Jacques Cartier's dream of a passage to China fulfilled by the building of the Canadian Pacific Railway.

Cartier is responsible for the most severely nationalistic pronouncement ever uttered by a prominent Canadian politician: *"It is necessary to be anti-Yankee . . . we can and will build up a northern power."* To be a partisan of Cartier is to be a partisan of this statement, and to have the belief that the work of the Fathers of Confederation was not in vain. It is a clear enough credo, and quite adequately fixes the horns of our national dilemma, but it was not meant to inspire us to close the border or violate the Golden Rule. For Cartier, it was a question of good political nationalism versus bad political nationalism, however one defines it. Nations are by nature competitive. Competition is a healthy thing. In Canada's case, he felt, it was more necessary to be more competitive.

The date May 20, 1973, passed without recognition in Canada: the centenary of Cartier's death was scarcely noticed by a forgetful nation. I determined to begin work on this book that day, in hope that Cartier's love for Canada, his work for her future, and his desire to ensure her survival, might be an inspiration and challenge to English-speaking Canadians, now as long natives of his country as the French-Canadians were at the time of Confederation; to new Canadians, interested in the forces and human wills that brought this country into being; and to the citizens of Quebec, whose constitution comes from Cartier, and whose present predicament would have challenged him. Cartier was fortunate – he lived at a time when clear and new issues could be grasped and won. But Cartier is not so far from us, and the work he began is far from complete.

Bleu-Coloured Glasses

Frank Underhill once wrote that "a biography only becomes interesting and alive when the biographer is a partisan." Hopefully, this is a partisan biography.

The Cartier years have been chronicled elsewhere, particularly in the brilliant work of J.M.S. Careless, Donald Creighton, W.L. Morton and P.B. Waite, and like any student of the period, I must gratefully acknowledge their influence. In attemping to focus on these years through the different eyes of George-Etienne Cartier, one cannot help but borrow their historical spectacles. Nevertheless, to change perspective and look at that world through, as it were, *bleu*-coloured glasses, to be an apologist for Cartier's role is, I think, an illuminating exercise.

The last full-scale biography of Cartier, by John Boyd, a Montreal journalist, appeared in 1914, on the centenary of Cartier's birth. It was an immense, pioneering work, but sixty years have passed, and some of its conclusions are inadequate in the light of more recent discoveries, particularly in the work of Messrs Bonenfant, Cooper, Hamelin, Monet, Ouellet, Rumilly and Wade on nineteenth century French Canada, and Morton and Stanley on Victorian Canada and the Red River Insurrection. Dr. Henry Best's 1969 thesis on Cartier, submitted to Laval University, is an impressive work, particularly with regard to family history and Cartier's relationship with the Catholic Church, and is gratefully acknowledged.

A number of individuals across the country have expressed some reservations about the possibility of a biography on Cartier, since there is no large and clearly defined set of Cartier papers. However, they have accepted my argument that this was to be a seminal work rather than a definitive one, and cooperated magnificently. Particular thanks are due to R.S. Gordon, Carl Vincent, Bill Yeo and Pat Kennedy of the Public Archives of Canada; John Crosthwaite of the Toronto Public Library (Baldwin Room); F.H. Armstrong, Henry Roper, Edward Phelps and H.J.M. Barnett of the University of Western Ontario; J. Norman Lowe, Curator of the CN Archives; Omer Lavallée, of the CP Archives; Stanley Triggs ("On! Stanley On!"), of the Notman Photographic Archives; Lionel Dorge of the Saint-Boniface Archives; Robert Prud'homme of the Château de Ramezay; and the staff of the Archives Nationales de Québec, the John P. Robarts Research Library at the University of Toronto; and the Public Archives of Manitoba.

Mindful of the growl of Napoleon Bonaparte – "Complaints have been made that we have no literature; this is the fault of the Minister of the Interior" – I hereby give thanks to the Ontario Arts Council for their generous support.

My immense gratitude to Anna Porter and the staff of McClelland and Stewart, whose kind and shrewd impatience kept me on the rails, and to Professor W.L. Morton, who I hope will accept this volume as a supplement to his recently published *festschrift*. Above all, thanks to Jennifer, critic, catalyst and companion.

Toronto, April, 1976

PART ONE

FROM THE HOUSE
OF THE SEVEN CHIMNEYS
(1735-1854)

"You may perhaps *americanize*, but, depend
on it, you will never *anglicize* the French inhabitants of the Province, – let them feel on
the other hand that their religion, their customs, their prepossessions, their prejudices,
if you will are more considered and respected
here than in other portions of this vast continent which is being overrun by the most
reckless, self-sufficient and dictatorial section of the Anglo-Saxon race, and who will
venture to say that the last hand which
waves the British flag on American ground
may not be that of a French Canadian?"

**Lord Elgin to Lord Grey,
May 4, 1848**

> **"Life went on in spite of the devastation of war, in spite of an occupying army, in spite of an uncertain future. The clash of arms was over, and the French-Canadians asked nothing more than to live. If living meant collaboration with the English, then they would collaborate, all of them."**
>
> **Michel Brunet**

In the year 1535, a French seaman named Jacques Cartier set sail to claim Canada for his King. In June of 1735, exactly two hundred years later, three young men, quite probably descendants of Cartier's brother, packed up their belongings, travelled north from Angers to Saint-Malo, and boarded a small, leaky trading vessel bound for New France. The brothers were proud, and full of their adventure, and they watched the Breton coast disappear with few regrets. After seven weeks, they made land at Gaspé, then sailed slowly up the long funnel of the lower St. Lawrence, watching the shores of that great river close, like a mother's arms, around the water that bore their little ship. During the days that followed, they tacked north and then west past mammoth cliffs and low rounded mountains, while white belugas and porpoises played around them.

At night, they anchored and smelled the spruce and pine over the water, and from far upriver, smoke from the fires of New France. Then the land softened along the south shore, and settlements appeared, bright little villages with whitewashed houses, and churches with silver spires. At sunset one early September evening, they rounded the Ile d'Orléans, passed the great white beard of Montmorency Falls, and looked for the first time on Quebec – the Gibraltar of the North – its Citadel rearing before them like the Sphinx.

The brothers had never seen such a sunset in France! The basin of Quebec seemed to be on fire, shades of orange and purple playing across its calm surface. They blinked into the sun as it fell slowly over the city, glinting dully off the spires of the Cathedral, and the churches of the Ursulines, the Recollets, and the Jesuits, glowing over the grey stone houses, the convents, warehouses, and the darkening green poplars of the seminary garden. The tide began to ebb, driving their ship back behind Orléans as the sun finally set. Early next morning they went up again with the flow, and at dawn, put into the estuary of the St. Charles River.

At noon, in the mariners' chapel at Beauport, three young Frenchmen thanked God for the blessing of a new land.

Two of the brothers, François and Louis Cartier, were skilled carpenters, whose talents were soon appreciated and put to use. The third, Jacques Cartier, was more enterprising than his artisan brothers; while they settled down along the Beauport shore, he established himself in the lower town of Quebec and began trading in fish and salt between New France and Old. The three brothers prospered, and one after the other married the three Mongeon sisters, nieces of Monseigneur Signan, the first Archbishop of Quebec.

They soon found that the stories they had heard about New France were true, that here was a raw, vain, hypocritical, friendly country, where peasants had become lords and lords little better than peasants; a land of incredible contrasts, of searing summers and numbing winters; a little kingdom run by pious prelates and corrupt administrators; a class-ridden dead end like Old France, but with an avenue of escape – upriver, up-country – a state-of-mind opening up behind Quebec into a careless, unbroken future.

But the world outside was changing, and their future, once so bright, seemed less and less secure. In 1758, the great fortress of Louisbourg fell. By September of the next year, the guns of Wolfe had blasted Quebec into ruins. Jacques Cartier watched – through mixed tears of bitterness and relief – as the first big snow began falling on an early December afternoon, falling over a defeated Quebec, blotting out the view first to Mont Ste-Anne, then Beauport and Orléans, then Lévis and the town itself, blanketing the meadows beyond the walls, smothering the grey rocks, shale and moss still spattered brown with dried blood, sifting through the naked rafters of shelled-out houses and sinking in the gunmetal grey St. Lawrence.

New France was dead, and Jacques Cartier took stock. He had two sons and four daughters. What would their future hold? His house in the Lower Town had been blasted to pieces. But the Cartiers were builders, and out of the rubble of defeat he and his brothers patched, plastered and roofed what remained, and in the spring, set about building anew.

As one of the few merchants who chose to remain in Quebec after the Conquest, Jacques Cartier found himself in a favourable position. A victorious army had to be provisioned, British demand for salt fish soon filled the vacuum left by the French, and the parasitical civil administrators of France were replaced by the more enlightened military governors of Great Britain, who encouraged the restoration of commerce. Jacques was an intelligent and industrious man. As his interests rapidly diversified into wheat, potash and hard goods, Cartier's growing family shared in his prosperity. One of his four daughters was the first French Canadian woman to marry an English merchant, Murdock Stewart, the builder of the new Saint-André docks.

To take advantage of British demand for wheat and flour, Cartier sent his two sons Jacques II and Joseph to open up trade with settlers in the lush and fertile Richelieu valley, just east of Montreal. Jacques II, the elder brother, had been to school in Montreal, and knew of the potential of the region. In about 1760, after a family conference, the two young men decided to settle in the valley as commercial agents of their father, dealing in grain and wholesale merchandise. Jacques II made his home at Saint-Antoine, and Joseph moved across the river to the larger village of Saint-Denis, where they built their first storehouses and docks.

By the time the patriarch Jacques Cartier died in 1763, the family had built two large flour mills, with seven pairs of grindstones – imported from France – capable of milling 70,000 bushels a year, as well as two huge stone houses with vaults for storing grain, facing the Saint-André docks. After 1763, Madame Cartier joined Jacques II at Saint-Antoine with the three unmarried sisters, but the family continued to operate the mills at Quebec, and feed them and the British ships with the wheat that was beginning to pour out of the Richelieu valley. In 1785, a bumper year, they sent 500,000 bushels to Quebec. By the end of the eighteenth century the Cartiers dominated the province's grain and flour trade, exporting about a third of Quebec's total production to England.

On September 27, 1772, Jacques Cartier II married Cécile Gervaise, niece of the first parish priest of the village and a cousin of the great Bishop Plessis of Quebec. Two years later his wife gave birth to a son, also named Jacques. The brothers' future seemed bright, but no sooner had they settled into family life, when rumblings of dissent and revolution were heard from the Thirteen Colonies of England far away to the south. Since they were well-connected with the Church hierarchy, the Cartiers understood the fear held by the bishops and priests toward the Protestant south. New England was an ancient enemy of Quebec, the devil that had armed the Iroquois to terrorize New France. Most important of all, they had been given to understand, through their father and cousins, that Britain's strategy, to tap the riches of the continent through the Great Lakes, depended upon their loyalty, and on this loyalty hung the survival of their language, their religion and their way of life. As merchants – a rare breed in this new land – they suspected that their fortunes lay with Britain, that although the average *habitant* preferred to be left in peace, he could be roused to defend his way of life. They understood instinctively that a loyal Quebec might survive – French roots had dug too deeply into the banks of the St. Lawrence to be shaken out by anything other than mass slaughter or deportation.

When the American Revolution broke out in 1775, the Cartiers pledged allegiance to His Majesty King George III and joined the militia, a choice that was to help guarantee not only their survival, but eventually lead to the creation in North America of an alternative to the political system of the American Republic.

Even before the harvest of 1775 had been gathered in, two motley rebel armies, dressed in every conceivable costume and uniform, from buckskin to riding breeches, wearing caps inscribed with the words, "Liberty or Death," left their towns and settlements, hauled themselves and their boats up the Appalachians, and poured down the Richelieu and Chaudière valleys toward Quebec. They carried with them copies of a proclamation from their Commander-in-Chief, George Washington, asking the French-Canadian *habitant* to rise and follow the "standard of general liberty, against which all the forces of artifice and tyranny will never be able to prevail." [1]

Few French Canadians were moved by the Americans – Bishop Briand suggested that no more than 500 joined the invaders – and a general state of apathy prevailed in the province, except in the Richelieu valley. Faced with American propaganda, the Cartiers were probably the chief movers behind a proclamation of loyalty from six Richelieu parishes to Governor Carleton. [2] In response, Carleton sent a loyal merchant, Sieur Jean Aurillac, to Saint-Denis, but the Americans in the neighbourhood got wind of his presence in the priest's house and decided to attack it. At dawn on September 18, 1775, Aurillac, the priest, and his servant girl were wakened by the sound of troops outside the rectory. When the girl showed her face at an upstairs window, a jittery soldier shot her dead. Aurillac and the priest were taken away to the States. [3]

Possibly on British advice, most French-Canadian militiamen did not actively resist the American invasion. Jacques and Joseph Cartier were quite prepared to sit tight, feeling out the strength and intentions of the invader. They knew from the British that the American Congress had declared itself against their religion; they had seen how some priests and active loyalists were mistreated or sent south; they had watched with dismay as some of their fellows were bribed by a promise of pillage and free land.

By October 24, 1775, General Richard Montgomery's soldiers were masters of the valley; by November 12, they had captured Montreal. Although the Americans were able to band together two French-Canadian regiments, the *habitant* generally ignored Washington's proclamation and the urgings of American agents. Why should he meddle in a British quarrel?

During a lull in the action, Jacques Cartier was given a passport to travel downriver to Sorel to pick up some trade goods. It was granted, in Montgomery's name, by Jean-Baptiste Ménard, Cartier's militia captain, whose head had been turned by the word, "Liberty." Sorel was still in the hands of the British, and Cartier may have given them information on the troop strength of the Americans. His return pass was signed by Colonel Maclean of the British Army.

The American operation was a failure. Carleton had slipped through their fingers and was now safe behind the walls of Quebec. Some loyal *seigneurs* had raised troops to defend him, and on December 1, he served notice that all those who refused to "serve in arms" would be treated as rebels and spies. Among those mentioned as being forced to leave for refusing to serve was Cartier's brother-in-law Murdock Stewart.[4]

Smallpox and dysentery conspired to defeat the Americans, but a severe winter and an early one – the worst in living memory – piling drifts thirty or more feet deep before the walls of Quebec, administered the *coup de grace*. Montgomery, an Irishman who had served with Wolfe in 1759, tried to emulate his old commander, but was shot dead at the first barricade, trying to storm the Lower Town in a New Years Eve blizzard. Benedict Arnold, coming around from the north, fought his way halfway up the slope road before being driven back.

With the arrival of the British fleet the following spring, the beaten remnants of the Army of the Continental Congress trudged home, through ice and mud, back to their own new nation. Jacques Cartier watched them as they passed up the valley, noting with wry amusement that Captain Jean-Baptiste Ménard joined the exodus – his son eventually became Governor of the State of Illinois – and when British troops arrived on the tail of the Americans, Cartier threw open his house, broke open a cask of rum, and toasted the advent of peace. The Fourteenth State, provided for in the Declaration of Independence, was assuredly not to be.

Prosperity returned with peace, and the wheat trade flourished. In 1782, Cartier built a large house, about a mile south of the village, known as the House of the Seven Chimneys.* It stood close to the river, and was a landmark for boatmen. Down the steep bank, the family had a private wharf, in sight of the storehouses and barge docks at Saint-Denis. The house itself served as a storehouse for grain. It was nearly one hundred feet in length, with basement, ground floor and attic. At each end were fireproof apartments, stores, vaults and servants' quarters.

However, prosperity also brought new dangers. A military conquest had been hard enough to bear, and a civil war between Americans and British fought on Quebec soil had been an imposition; now the Yankee traders and Scots adventurers who arrived in the wake of the troops wanted more, wanted a real Conquest, wanted the expulsion of Cartier and his people from Quebec.

---

* The House of the Seven Chimneys stood for 124 years, until 1906, when it was demolished by the family because of the high cost of maintenance. A wood frame farmhouse was built in its place. All that remains is the well, and a plaque on the road.

2 "The handing-over of Canada to England neither broke the psychological equilibrium of the French-Canadian cultural group, nor resulted in a general substitution of economic, social or ideological institutions. Changes of this kind began to appear only by the beginning of the Nineteenth Century."

Fernand Ouellet

Even after the Conquest, the great commercial enterprise of Quebec was still the fur trade, although merchants like the Cartiers were beginning to challenge its dominance. Its profits, so long French, made an easy transition into the pockets of the New Englanders and Scots who swarmed into Quebec. The new merchants – some little more than carpetbaggers – soon clashed with the military government, whose paternalism insulted them, whose governors – Carleton, Murray, Haldimand – embodied the authoritarianism and aristocracy they had escaped from. Their organ, the *Quebec Mercury*, whined that "this province is already too French for a British colony," Indeed, the colonial governors easily sided and sympathized with the French and their Church, Murray declaring to the Lords of Trade that "Nothing will satisfy the licentious fanaticks trading here, but the expulsion of the Canadians, who are perhaps the bravest and the best race upon the *Globe*."

This new mercantile class complicated the life of the average French Canadian, for now a new enemy, "progress," was within the gates. Now there was a future to build, a prize to be won. These *arrivistes*, more opportunist than loyalist, alerted the *habitant* to different dangers, gave him a new Iroquois to fight against. The mercantile spirit these newcomers brought with them threatened his language and the very fabric of his existence. Their economic power, far out of proportion to their numbers, led to racial, religious and class strife, that forced the *habitant* to waken from his slumber, take up his law books and absorb the tools of the usurper, as the only means of survival. The story of the Cartiers is the story of that survival: they were members of a small minority of the French Canadian population who understood the new conquerers, who, as part of the mercantile class left after the Conquest, could compete on equal terms with them, and make the little flame of French Canadian nationality quicken and grow.

While New France grew in peace under more enlightened masters, Old France trembled with civil war. Britain had had her revolution: her Parliament was supreme, her doors open to men of ability, never more so than during the brief renaissance led by Pitt, while across the Channel at Versailles, Louis the Fifteenth, shining in phosphorescent decay, strutted before his court and concubine.

In 1789, Old France fell; the Sun Kingdom was eclipsed by the guillotine. A still nostalgic Quebec was deeply shocked by reports telling of the murder of priests and of a Reign of Terror in the Mother Country. When it was over, the French Canadians breathed a collective sigh of relief at having been spared the bloodshed of revolution. At the funeral of Bishop Jean-Olivier Briand in 1794, Abbé Joseph-Octave Plessis, later Bishop of Quebec and a cousin of the Cartiers, expressed the sentiments of the majority of his countrymen in an extravagant hymn of praise for Great Britain:

> . . . charitable nation, which has just rescued with such humanity the most faithful and maltreated subjects of the kingdom to which we formerly belonged; kind nation, which gives each day new proofs to Canada of your liberality; no, no, you are not our enemy, nor of our holy religion, which you respect. Pardon this early distrust of a people who had still not the happiness to know you.[5]

The aftermath of the French Revolution saw about fifty *émigré* French clergy arrive in Quebec. Of far greater influence than their number would indicate, these men helped to promote the culture and learning of Old France, and the establishment of some seven classical colleges, founded between 1802 and 1832. They effectively headed off any attempts by the British to anglify the Province, and by the 1830s, were turning out from their colleges two to three hundred well-educated, professional men a year, far more than the country could absorb without radical social change.

In 1791, as a reward for French Canadian loyalty, a concession to the new merchants, and to prevent the Canadians from imitating the revolutions of America and France, the British government passed the Constitutional Act, splitting Canada into Upper and Lower, each with its own Assembly. In Parliament, Pitt suggested that "In Lower Canada, since the inhabitants are principally French-Canadian, their assembly, etc. will be adopted to their customs and to their particular ideals. This will be an experience that ought to teach them that English laws are superior."[6]

By 1800, Canada was still a small backwater of 200,000 people. Quebec, with only 14,000 inhabitants, was scarcely more than a big town. Montreal was larger, with a population of 18,000. As the nineteenth century dawned, it became apparent to the British that to keep and defend this gateway to the continent would prove an enormous drain on the treasury; yet Britain needed the resources, first wheat, then timber, that were beginning to flow in such quantities from Canada. The trappings of representative government were granted to the French Canadians to keep them satisfied, and more militia responsibility developed to involve local regions in the financial and moral burden of defence.

In 1805, Jacques Cartier II was elected to the Lower Canadian Assembly as the Member for Surrey (Verchères). He soon allied himself to a group of lawyers and merchants described by Governor Craig as "a new order of men,"[7] men who, whether Craig liked it or not, had begun to understand the workings of the British system of parliamentary democracy. They founded a newspaper, *Le Canadien*, to counter the scurrilous attacks of the *Quebec Mercury*, and began the uphill task of educating the people in an understanding of that "generous gift,"[8] that "rare treasure"[9] that was their new constitution. They soon showed themselves to be dedicated and enthusiastic parliamentarians, quoting Blackstone, Locke, and other British constitutional authorities, regarding themselves as "free British subjects,"[10] worthy of all the rights and privileges consistent with their new status. Yet they were proud nationalists, anti-Yankee and hotly opposed to anyone who would assimilate them in an English-speaking melting pot. Cartier was an active member of the Assembly; on April 1, 1806, he seconded a motion asking that the minutes of the proceedings of government be translated into French.

While at Quebec, Cartier took account of a succession of bad harvests, inflation and American competition – in 1802, 1,010,033 bushels of wheat left the port of Quebec; by 1805, the figure had dropped to 22,016 bushels.[11] He decided to dismantle the flour milling business his father had set up; all the family assets would now be concentrated in the Richelieu valley, close to the growing market in Montreal. The Quebec City area had become overpopulated, and he was able to bring a large number of settlers upriver to pioneer in the valley. He and his brother started a mail service for the area and, in anticipation of a new American invasion, both continued their militia work. In 1808, Jacques Cartier became first Lieutenant-Colonel of the Verchères division, and this task took up so much of his time that he declined to run in the elections of 1809.

Jacques Cartier II had many children, but only two survived, a daughter, and a son, also named Jacques, born on August 29, 1774. Cartier discovered to his dismay that his boy had the temperament of a voyageur, and so decided to establish his nephew Joseph II, who had shown more aptitude for business, in Saint-Antoine. Cartier built a large house for Joseph, similar to his own (which is still standing). Yet the son Jacques Cartier III was to show an aptitude for other things – by his wife Marguerite, daughter of Joseph Paradis, a local merchant, he sired five sons and three daughters.

As the Cartier family grew and prospered on the peaceful banks of the Richelieu, the balance of world power began to shift. The rise of Napoleon Bonaparte in France left the French Canadians with mixed feelings, but the Cartiers, participating in the forging of their own nationality, must have been impressed by his forcefulness and the way he gave back to the French the nerve and pride they had lost in the Reign of

Terror. Napoleon's bold leap into power affected Canada in two very significant ways. The danger of a war with Napoleonic France had strained Britain's military resources to the breaking point, and the Canadian militia were given much more responsibility for the defence of their country. In addition, Napoleon's Continental Blockade forced Britain to look to Canada instead of the Baltic for her timber, which began to flow down the Ottawa and St. Lawrence in vast quantities, taking the place of wheat as Canada's principal export.

With Britain's strength weakened and overextended, there arose dangers closer to home. On June 18, 1812, President James Madison of the United States declared war on Great Britain. On September 12, during one of the worst harvests in memory, Lieutenant-Colonel Cartier ordered the Saint-Denis and Verchères militia mobilized, and six months later induced his devil-may-care son to take some part in the conflict. Jacques Cartier III, aged thirty-nine, joined the 5th Battalion of Militia as an Ensign.

Two genuine Canadian heroes emerged from the War of 1812: the national martyr Sir Isaac Brock, shot at Queenston Heights, and a French Canadian *seigneur*, thirty-three-year-old Lieutenant-Colonel Charles Michel de Salaberry, whose night attack at Châteauguay, with only 800 men, mainly French Canadian militia, against General Hampton's 4,000 American troops, made the Americans think twice about conquering Canada. Only two companies from the 5th Battalion, under Captains Debartzch and Levesque, were at Châteauguay in time for the battle, so Jacques Cartier III missed his chance for glory. In April of 1814, however, he joined de Salaberry's *Chasseurs*, and was with him that September as First Lieutenant and Paymaster during the aborted attack on Plattsburgh, New York. He returned home a Major, buried his father in the parish church of Saint-Antoine, and settled back into doing what he knew best – living well.

The year before the Battle of Waterloo, and six months after the death of his father, Cartier's seventh child and youngest son was born in a small room on the ground floor of the House of the Seven Chimneys. On the day of his birth, September 6, 1814, the boy was taken to the parish church and baptized Georges-Etienne Cartier, after the reigning monarch, King George III.*

---

* Although he was baptized "Georges" with an "s", Cartier came to prefer the spelling "George" in the later years of his life, perhaps because it simplified matters. The English called him "Sir George," the French "Georges-Etienne." Although a convention seems to have been established regarding the orthography of "George(s)", the problem is purely academic, depending on whether the name is pronounced in English or French. "George-Etienne" seems to solve the problem nicely.

3 "The country's resources are devoured by the newcomers, and although I may have the pleasure of meeting among them some educated and estimable men who meet me with equal pleasure, the thought that my compatriots are unjustly excluded from participation in these same advantages saddens me even in their company and makes the visit to Quebec disagreeable."

Louis-Joseph Papineau to his wife, 1828

Although not a *seigneur*, Jacques Cartier III lived like one. The House of the Seven Chimneys was the centre of the social and commercial life of the district, Cartier directed his declining business operations from the house, and stored his goods in the basement vaults. He was a *bon viveur*, an entertainer, who loved to see the guest rooms filled with his cronies, the fiddles playing, roasts and meat pies loading down the table and the brandy flowing. He had a fine voice – when the church choir sang off-key, he would sing out loudly to give them the correct pitch – and he never lost an opportunity to lead his friends and associates in old French airs or voyageur paddle songs. In the early morning, his guests were sure to be wakened with a loud knock, a rousing song, and a dram of the very best Fine Old Jamaica rum.

Madame Cartier was known as a saintly, intelligent, charitable and long-suffering woman, who often opened her doors to the travelling Recollet friars who roamed the countryside teaching the catechism. It is said that her husband's jovial hospitality clashed with her more serious nature, and in spite of her strength of character, she could not prevent him from running to seed, from dissipating most of the fortune his father and grandfather had built up.

This was still *le bon vieux temps*, the "good old days" of French Canada, and the valley of the Richelieu was still a garden of plenty; yet there were ominous signs that the end of those days was at hand. Beginning in about 1802, the wheat yield in the valley began to fall. The wheat fly had appeared. Its worm burrowed into the roots of the plant, leaving shrivelled or empty grains. Wheat rust also took its toll, rotting the head of the wheat with a dirty orange fungus. But most important of all, the land was exhausted from going for three generations without fertilization. It was no longer the virgin soil of the old forest, blessed with the pot ash from burning stumps. The Richelieu *habitant* had grown accustomed to dumping manure in the river; he had ignored good husbandry, avoided crop rotation, and concentrated on the one yield he knew the Cartiers would pay a good price for – wheat.

As George-Etienne Cartier grew up in this Eden-going-to-seed, he never lacked for adventure. As the youngest boy, he had the run of the huge house and spent many hours watching the grain being delivered, weighed and stored, or taken down to the dock on the river to be loaded on barges bound for Sorel, Montreal, and Quebec. He would scramble up the enormous willows for a view of enemy encampments, or pretend to be a voyageur and paddle across the river to visit his uncle and cousins. He would try to listen carefully as the visiting friars recited the dogma of the church. Some nights, he and his brother Damien would wake, tiptoe down stairs and watch, wide-eyed, as their father's friends joked and argued, or lined up the dining room chairs one behind the other, seated themselves, and roared off into a voyageur song, swinging their arms in unison as though paddling a big canoe. Yet there were bad times, when his parents began to quarrel, or when he could see misery and despair written on his father's face.

Perhaps because of the contrast between his parents, or possibly because he was the youngest of five sons, George-Etienne Cartier developed a belligerent personality that never left him. Still, his young years were full of spirit and fun, and a feeling for good times and hospitality, nurtured in the house of his free-spending and jovial father, always remained in him, bubbling just under the surface. The more serious side of his nature, inherited from his mother, began to come to the fore when, in 1824, at the age of ten, he was rudely plucked from the garden of the Richelieu and sent to study with his brother Damien at the Collège de Montréal, run by the Sulpician Order. The so-called "Gentlemen of Saint-Sulpice" were the *seigneurs* of Montreal; they owned numerous buildings and tracts of land which were used to support their school, seminary and churches.

The Collège, founded in 1767, was housed in an old four-storeyed stone building on St. Paul and McGill Streets. Cartier's grandfather and uncle were graduates, as well as all his brothers and cousins. His eldest brother Antoine-Jacques had died there in 1801 at the age of sixteen. Recent graduates included Louis-Hippolyte LaFontaine,[12] a young lawyer and family friend, and the fiery politican Louis-Joseph Papineau, the undisputed leader of the French Canadians.

The Collège, with its enormous library, was perhaps the finest seat of learning in the province. It housed 160 boys, with an equal number of day students. To ten-year-old George, used to the freedom of the little village school at Saint-Antoine, it must have seemed like a penitentiary. The brothers maintained strict discipline, and allowed little contact with the outside world. Day began early. A breakfast of barley porridge was followed by mass, lessons, a light lunch of bread and cheese, more lessons, and then recreation in the playground to the west of the main building. The yard was nothing more than dirt bounded by a stone wall – good for knocking a ball against – but had a line of straggling poplars that could be climbed for a glimpse over the wall. Dinner consisted of an endless diet of boiled beef, augmented only on feast days by some butter, and ham or meat pie. While they ate in silence, the students listened and digested words of scripture or morality, read, usually in Latin, by one of their fellows who stood at the head of the dining hall.

Students were required to look after their own laundry. The school uniform was a suit made of navy blue serge. Trousers were held up by a blue woven sash worn around the waist, and the boys wore a round blue cap bearing the college monogram when, on the odd occasion, they were trooped out of the grounds for a parade or a festival.

A wild scamp when he arrived, George-Etienne Cartier was soon moulded by the men of the order into one of their most successful students. He was awarded most of the prizes in all six years of the classical course, which consisted of Latin, grammar, versification, *belles-lettres* rhetoric, sacred and profane history, and philosophy.

In June of 1830, Cartier hauled his bags down the hill to the harbour and boarded the steamboat *L'Union Canadienne* for the trip down the St. Lawrence and up the Richelieu to Saint-Antoine. The following month, he watched proudly at a ceremony appointing his father Lieutenant-Colonel commanding the 5th battalion of Militia of Verchères. When he returned to Montreal that autumn, many of his friends talked excitedly of the French revolution of that July. In November, the students held a mock revolution of their own, putting up barricades, hanging a professor in effigy and draping the French tricolour across the front of the school, all in celebration of the victory of the liberals in Paris. It is not recorded whether Cartier was involved, but considering his later career, he was probably the ringleader. Next spring, he vindicated himself by being chosen as the College Scholar, and at his graduation was given the honour of defending, in public, a Latin thesis propounded by his professors.

The Sulpicians, most of whom had come from France, recognized Cartier's ability early, and trained him well. For his part, he never forgot the debt he owed them, and supported the Order all his life, serving for most of it as their solicitor. On June 10, 1860, as Prime Minister of United Canada, nearly thirty years after his graduation, he returned to be honoured by the Collège and heard the students, among whom was a young Métis boy from the Red River, Louis Riel, sing the patriotic ode he had written before the Rebellion of 1837 – "O Canada, Mon Pays, Mes Amours." In his speech, he praised the Superior of the Collège, Abbé Bayle, for having "instructed, disciplined and enlightened me, who showed me the road to follow, and as I am infinitely pleased to see him today the Superior of Saint-Sulpice, perhaps he on his part rejoices to see me as an advisor and representative of Her Majesty." [13] The Sulpicians had instructed him in more than the classics: they had awakened his interest in the preservation of French Canadian nationality, and he was soon to learn how to fight for it.

In the summer of 1831, just before his seventeenth birthday, a ner-

vous, unsure George-Etienne Cartier left the House of the Seven Chimneys and travelled back to Montreal to begin studying for the bar in the
law office of Edouard-Etienne Rodier, a graduate of the Collège. The
dark, handsome Rodier was a spell-binding orator, adored by the citizens of Montreal, and at the age of twenty-seven, the youngest Member
of the Assembly. Cartier's articling papers were signed by another Assembly member, the elegant, eloquent Louis-Hippolyte LaFontaine,
who, ten years later and with Cartier's help, would become leader of the
Lower Canadian wing of the Reform Party, and co-Premier of Canada.

When they were not at Quebec supporting Papineau and the Reform
Party, Rodier and LaFontaine spent all their energies speaking and organizing resistance to the English-speaking members of the Governor's
Council, the so-called *Château Clique*, or as Rodier contemptuously
termed them, the *Bureaucrats*. These men and their cronies were deliberately and systematically shutting the French Canadians out of civil
office. While supporting the letter of the Constitution of 1791, they
made a mockery of its intent – as expressed by Fox in the British Commons, that the French Canadians be given "those institutions that will
leave them nothing to envy in their neighbours" [14] – and appropriated
the lion's share of government patronage for themselves.

In this period, racial strife between French and English Canadians
reached a peak. Attacks on the French came primarily through the
Montreal *Gazette*, the organ of the Constitutionalists, as they called
themselves. One of the chief aims of this newspaper was a single legislative union of Upper and Lower Canada, or at the very least, the annexation of Montreal to Upper Canada. Chafing under a French majority in
the popular Assembly, the English wanted out. The French, led by Papineau, Rodier and LaFontaine, counterattacked by establishing a
newspaper, *La Minerve*,* edited by a pale, sickly genius, Augustin-
Norbert Morin, brother-in-law of Cartier's godfather.

These were heady days for the young Cartier, thrust from the company of priests into a hotbed of nationalistic fervour, LaFontaine and
Rodier had sized him up well, and Cartier immediately gave evidence of
his enterprising mind, as well as the tremendous fund of energy he would
always be noted for. He studied hard, and soon had a fine grasp of the
nuances of French and English civil and commercial law. Rodier found
that his young clerk could get to the heart of a problem quicker than
most. After a year had passed, he felt confident enough in Cartier to
leave him to mind the firm when he was attending the Assembly at
Quebec. But business was slow, and Rodier gave Cartier other responsibilities. In 1831, Rodier's friend Ludger Duvernay had taken over the

---

* named after Minerva, the Roman goddess of wisdom, art and trade, who
invented musical instruments, and was identified with the Greek Athene as
the goddess of war. A good burgeois deity.

editorship of *La Minerve*. Duvernay, a militant and reckless lawyer from Verchères, was a braggart, a lecher and a drunkard, but he was also a great patriot and the most persuasive journalist in the province. Cartier was asked to serve as confidential messenger between Rodier and Duvernay, and to edit the paper's dispatches from Quebec.

It was a few short paces down the street from the law office to *La Minerve*, and Cartier negotiated them often, to give Duvernay the latest from Quebec, prop him up after he had been on a binge, or even set type on those frantic nights before the paper went to press. He was probably responsible for a letter, signed "A Young Canadian," that appeared in the March 28, 1831 edition:

> I am, it is quite true, a novice in politics, but having often been blessed with conversations on this subject with persons judged as professionals, I hope to risk nothing in confiding to your paper the following observations bearing on the state of our political education . . .
>
> A beautiful dawn is breaking. We now learn with pleasure that, in many of our educational institutions, the students have been inspired to read the public journals and to acquaint themselves with our constitution. On occasion, they have even been given summaries of the great questions that concern us so strongly today . . .
>
> Take courage, my young compatriots. Have you not gazed with respect on the fine men who are working for the well-being of our country and your own happiness? In the eyes of posterity, they will be crowned with laurels! They do not have your resources, but your task will be made easier by the work they are now doing. They have cleared the trail; the field of honour is open to you! the NATION smiles on you; do not refuse to heed its call.

Although expressed in an awkward and flowery manner, Cartier's sentiments were mature and with the times. He was fortunate in having a fine teacher in Edouard Rodier. Two frank letters to Cartier from Rodier survive from this period. They serve to show the trust Rodier placed in his young clerk, and the depth of political education Cartier was receiving from his mentor. The first expressed Rodier's anger at the Solicitor-General, Charles Ogden, for having called LaFontaine a felon on the floor of the Assembly. He advised Cartier in a postscript to

> Be always a patriot; detest Aristocracy: scorn the pride and arrogance of the idiotic nouveau riche and stupid nobility: never have any other ambition than to raise up for yourself a monument in the hearts of all your fellow countrymen: that is the only monument that lasts. Study constantly; read all the journals; read the political history of your country: the survival of our nation depends on the youth of Canada. I would never wish any other inscription on my tombstone than this: A Loving Child of the Nation.

He also seemed concerned to interest young Cartier in the ways of women:

> If you happened to pick any Quebec woman, you would without doubt choose a patriot, for all of them, to some degree, know a good deal about politics. You would be amazed to hear Madame Huot, a young woman of seventeen. She speaks with incredible ease, and in a language as pure and as elegant as Papineau's. Madame Leblanc is more knowledgeable, but she is a *gossip*.
>
> The women here are more zealous patriots than their husbands, but the funny thing is, the most educated ones have no children. I don't understand it at all.

In a letter dated December 11, 1832, Rodier outlined to Cartier some examples of the racial tension that then existed in the Assembly, pointing out that on one occasion he had to restrain himself from shouting "Down with the English" – the Clerk of the Assembly had caught the Montreal member and newspaperman Robert Armour in the act of spying on them. It was a long time before Armour felt able to show his face in the streets of Quebec. Then Rodier relaxed and concluded the letter with some advice to the bachelor Duvernay:

> Tell Duvernay I allow him to go skating with widows, and to behave himself with them just as I did at Quebec . . . I have no lustful desires toward the women of Quebec, although a certain little coquette does her best to console me for the aches of homesickness. But I only annoy her, and when she becomes serious, I talk to her seriously about my wife. This just makes her sulk. Because I am flippant and playful, she imagines that I am touchy about married fidelity. She takes my charades seriously, thinking I am about to take liberties with her. On my return, I'll tell you stories about her that will make you howl. I can't tell you her name because it might jeopardize friendly relations . . .
>
> Tell Duvernay I haven't seen his lady jailer even though I've been here twice . . .
>
> My regards to Mme. Rodier, and give my little girls a hug.[15]

The eighteen-year-old Cartier doubtlessly did as he was told, and communicated the messages to Duvernay.

The 1832 session of the Assembly saw the Reformers harassed, abused and insulted by the *Château Clique*. Duvernay was arrested for libel by the Legislative Council, and while Cartier minded the paper, he was taken to Quebec, charged before the Bar of the House and sentenced to a month in the Quebec jail. Duvernay laughed it off, and returned in glory to Montreal, where his attacks on the government continued unabated. His high spirits soon turned to quiet desperation; it was increasingly apparent to the leaders of the Reform Party that the English oligarchy under Governor Aylmer were conspiring to chase the French

Canadians off the face of the earth. The Montreal Bank and the Quebec Bank, established with fur trade money in 1817 and 1818, were now prospering with the timber trade and augmenting the power of the English; some of the port revenues of Lower Canada were being diverted out of the province to benefit works in Upper Canada; and it seemed that the British American Land Company, chartered in 1832 and granted more than 500,000 acres in the Eastern Townships, was one more deliberate device to denationalize the French, to take away any areas for future settlement and drown them in a sea of English.

In the early 1830s, Montreal was still little more than a large town. Its population of 25,000 was burgeoning with an influx of country people, driven there by overpopulation in the better farm lands, yet when Cartier left the Collège to make his mark, the economy of Montreal was in decline due to the disappearance of the fur trade. The town was full of American traders and outlaws, the latter attracted to Canada by its lack of an extradition treaty with the United States. Huron and Iroquois Indians could still be seen in the streets or down at the wharves, and in the autumn and winter, the town was packed with *habitants* selling their crafts and their produce. An English traveller, John Palmer, described the *habitants* as

> a curious looking set of men, they are short in stature; their dress is trowsers, and mocasins, or large boots of undressed leather, a frock coat or jacket, and greasy red cap; a short pipe is always an accompaniment, whether attending the market, driving a cart, or pursuing any other avocation; many of them wear comfortables, or yarn sashes round their waists, in the manner of the Indians. In their dress the better sort of inhabitants are genteel, and they live expensively. They have few amusements, except in the winter, when all trade, or thought of it, is laid aside, and a round of pleasure ensues: visiting, tea and dinner parties, sleighing (the sleigh is called a cariole) dances; and sometimes a concert, or scenic representation, present their irresistible attractions.[16]

This idyllic situation changed quickly. Urged on by the merchants of Montreal and Quebec, the British government began to encourage emigration of its poor and downtrodden to the Canadas. The timber ships returning to Canada needed ballast, and tens of thousands of penniless and disease-ridden migrants were packed into these "coffin ships" and debarked at Quebec or Montreal. Unable to proceed westward, the newcomers became a drain on the public purse, and in 1832, brought with them an epidemic of Asian cholera, which killed 7,000 people, leading Rodier to exclaim in fury:

> It was not enough to send among us avaricious egotists, without any other spirit of liberty than that which could be bestowed by a simple education at the counter, to enrich themselves at the expense of the

Canadians, and then to enslave them; – they must also rid themselves of their beggars, and cast them by thousands on our shores; they must send us miserable beings, who after eating the bread of our children, subject them to the horrors resulting from hunger and misery; they must do still more, they must send us, as the final outrage, pestilence and death.[17]

It is a wonder that the French Canadians did not resort to open rebellion sooner than 1837, yet many of them, including Cartier, still had some faith that they could survive by constitutional means. That faith was now being rapidly eroded.

"This young nation was beginning to feel the anxieties of adolescence. Papineau found himself at this awakening without being sufficiently equipped to direct it . . . . Providence sent us Cartier at the very moment when our battle was to change our nature."

4

Arthur Dansereau

In 1834, in order to give the French Canadians a national society devoted to the preservation of their language and culture, Ludger Duvernay founded the Saint-Jean-Baptiste Society. He chose John the Baptist as the patron saint of the society in order to restore the pride of the *Canadien*, called "Johnny Batiste" by the derisive *Bureaucrats* and military men of the province. The Maple Leaf was chosen as the emblem of the Association, and its motto was "Nos institutions, notre langue, nos droits."* Cartier, then twenty years old, assisted in the work of organization, was its first Secretary, and later President of the Society. On June 22, at the founding banquet, he showed that he was also the poet of the movement: the gathering rose and sang Cartier's national hymn, "O Canada, mon pays, mes amours," composed especially for the occasion:

Puissent tous les enfants enfin se joindre,
Et valeureux voler à ton secours!
Car le beau jour déjà commence à poindre,
O Canada! mon pays! mes amours!†

Unknown to all but a few of his closest compatriots, Duvernay had founded a secret society to parallel the work of the Saint-Jean-Baptiste Society. It was called simply, *"Aide-toi, le ciel t'aidera"* ("Heaven helps

* "Our customs, language and rights"

† May all your children join together, and valiantly run to your side!
For the great day is beginning to dawn, O Canada! my own beloved land!

those who help themselves"), and Cartier was one of its hand-picked members, sworn to absolute secrecy. To keep themselves busy until the revolution they suspected was inevitable, members were obliged to submit an essay annually on a political or literary topic.

In the battle for majority rule that came to a head in 1837, the name of Louis-Joseph Papineau stands out. Like LaFontaine and Cartier after him, the forceful, eloquent *seigneur* of Montebello was the embodiment of the desires of a whole people. First elected to the Assembly in 1808, Papineau, seven years later, at the age of twenty-nine, was voted into the Speaker's chair, where he sat, with a few rude interruptions, for the next twenty years, frustrated by office-holders who would be neither responsible, nor responsive to the wishes of the majority. In 1828, for example, the Legislative Council threw out no fewer than fifty-seven bills, passed by the majority of the elected members.

A peerless patriot and orator, Papineau tried to make the Constitution work, but in the end, he, and more especially his followers, had to resort to the only solution possible – armed rebellion. He was an erratic genius, and although he later changed his tune, Papineau's principles were at the outset based on the British model. The justice he first claimed for the people of Canada was British justice.

By the end of 1834, as Cartier toiled away in Rodier's office, becoming less lost in the minutiae of mortgages, damages, and claims, less enmeshed in the differences between French and English civil law, the Assembly grew to a mood of open rebellion. That session, Elzéar Bédard, son of one of the founders of *Le Canadien*, placed before the Assembly the Ninety-Two Resolutions, incorporating the ideals of the followers of Papineau, or the *Patriotes*, as they began to call themselves. The Resolutions, voted on and sent to the Parliament of Great Britain, were Lower Canada's version of the declarations that had proceeded the French and American Revolutions, with one important difference, stated at the outset. The first thirteen resolutions reviewed the grievances of the Assembly, but they also contained a strong expression of loyalty to the Crown. Other resolutions summed up in detail the rights of the French Canadians, and demanded for the Assembly all the immunities and privileges of the British Parliament.

In a speech in support of the Resolutions, Papineau made certain statements that were soon to alienate him from his more moderate followers, including Cartier. He accused the clergy of being bought out by the Quebec Act, and declared his wish for a republican form of government, and eventual annexation, or union with the United States: "It is certain that before long all America is to be republican. Meanwhile," he asked, "ought a change in our constitution, if necessary, be guided by this consideration; and is it criminal to raise the question?"[18] To some of his followers, LaFontaine and Cartier among them, anticlericalism and republicanism were irrelevant, practically unthinkable, and might prove suicidal to the French Canadian nation. Why replace one master for another? But for the time being, his followers sat back and applauded his oratory. Papineau was the man of the hour, and commanded tremendous prestige. Even then, when his philosophy showed the first signs of becoming bankrupt, and some of his followers – John Neilson, A.-N. Morin, Amable Berthelot and Elzéar Bédard – split with him, they still found it hard to deny his leadership. He expressed things so well! "The government I long for," he declared to the Assembly in 1835,

> is one composed of friends of legality, liberty and justice, a government which would protect, without discrimination, every proper interest, and accord to all ranks and to each race of the inhabitants equal rights and privileges . . . Briefly, we demand for ourselves such political institutions as are in accordance with those of the rest of the Empire and of the age we live in.[19]

In spite of such rhetoric, the demands of the Assembly fell on deaf ears, and as the Reformers fell back on their only remaining constitutional weapon – the withholding of funds for the administration of government – the situation in both provinces went from bad to worse, from deadlock to open rebellion.

After refusing to vote funds, the *Patriotes* tried to persuade the people to adopt economic coercion. The English-speaking merchants of Montreal, already badly affected by financial panic in the United States and Britain, found their goods boycotted and cash withdrawn in runs on their banks. The Montreal *Gazette* was enraged, and with imperious disdain, described Papineau as "a well-drugged Malay running a-muck."[20]

The day after the presentation of the Ninety-Two Resolutions, the Montreal *Patriotes* established a Permanent Central Committee, to act as an information bureau directing the struggle and coordinating Reform activities. The first Secretary of the Committee was Charles-Ovide Perrault, a brash young lawyer and Member of the Assembly from Vaudreuil. After the establishment of this committee, Rodier set off with Cartier in tow, travelling the length and breadth of the province to set up local sub-committees in the counties and towns which were Reform strongholds. On their return, the meetings of the Central Committee began in earnest, held every afternoon in the St. Vincent Street bookstore of Perrault's brother-in-law, Edouard Fabre, across from the law courts and right next to Rodier's office. As the year wore on, meetings were held in the larger quarters of the Hotel Nelson* on Jacques Cartier Square, just up from the idle port of Montreal.

On the surface, Edouard Fabre was a mild little man, whose bookstore did a good side business in church ornaments and patent medicines, but

---

* The Hotel, with its lively summer beer garden, is, at this writing, still a fine drinking spot for revolutionaries.

he was a tough, shrewd *Patriote*, a good host, and the heart and soul of the movement. Back in 1827, he had paid the expenses of D.-B. Viger, Austin Cuvillier and John Neilson when they went to England to press the demands of the Assembly. He had subsidized Duvernay's purchase of *La Minerve*, and in 1832, founded *La Maison Canadienne*, a banking and import house that grew into *La Banque du Peuple*, which was partly an alternative to the English banks, partly a front for the accumulation of funds for the revolution, funds for arms and ammunition.

Edouard Fabre was later Mayor of Montreal. One of his sons became the Archbishop; the other, Hector, a journalist, was to become a strong political foe of Cartier, and eventually Canadian High Commissioner to Paris. Cartier spent many afternoons in the backroom of the Fabre bookstore, soaking up the rage, the enthusiastic high-blown phrases, the arguments and dialectic of Viger, LaFontaine, Perrault, Fabre, and of course, Papineau. He was scarcely in his twenties – the rest were older men – yet he was able to hold his own, deflating, with his relentless logic, some of the more hare-brained schemes that surfaced. As some meetings went on until late in the night, as coffee became laced with rum and was finally replaced by rum, he felt at the centre, the heart of his country's being. As the conversation and planning sometimes lagged, he could not help but notice the presence of Fabre's young children, running around the table and underfoot. As the youngest, Hector, later remembered,

> There was an open, free and easy atmosphere to those meetings; you felt right off that you were among friends, on the well-understood premise that you were a patriot, never a bureaucrat. The latter opinions were never tolerated. It was necessary to be a patriot, to love only patriots, to meet only patriots; without this one was suspect.[21]

If it was necessary also to love the daughters of patriots, Cartier succeeded. Fabre's little girl Hortense, then just seven years old, must have been played with and told stories more than once – in 1846 she became his wife.

Late in 1835, one hundred years after the arrival of his great-grandfather at Quebec, George-Etienne Cartier was admitted to the bar of Lower Canada. He continued in practice with Rodier for a time, then started the firm of Cartier and Cartier with his brother Damien. But as commercial depression set in, the brothers found little to keep them busy, and Cartier found more and more of his time devoted to the activities of the *Patriotes*.

Some blow-up, some cataclysmic event was in the wind. The only questions for both frustrated sides were when, and how, and would the rebellion succeed? Yet all the amateur strategists of Montreal were in agreement – it would come in the late fall, probably outside Montreal, when the great St. Lawrence and its tributaries were still open in the middle. The thin and treacherous ice growing out from the shores would make any troop movement difficult, and for a time, no one knew how long, the rebels would hold the countryside.

"How times have changed! For the past twenty-five years, the French-Canadians have taken the honour of serving His Britannic Majesty, and spilling their own blood to preserve British supremacy in Canada. Now all is different, yet there is an easy explanation: instead of giving the French-Canadians their rights, the King has let his ministers rob and mistreat them."

5

A veteran of Châteauguay,
to the Editor of *La Minerve*, July 27, 1837

The demands of the Reformers found a sympathetic hearing in the Parliament of Great Britain, where such radicals as Lord Brougham and the "Irish Liberator," Daniel O'Connell, primed by the *Patriotes*' London agent, D.-B. Viger, supported their cause. But generally the desires of Papineau, William Lyon Mackenzie and their followers were thought to be "inconsistent with their status as colonials." During the winter of 1836-37, a disastrous Royal Commission on Canadian grievances led to an aggravation of the situation. Sir Francis Bond Head, Governor of Upper Canada, foolishly disclosed the Canada Commission's instructions, that showed to all the world the British were more concerned with palliatives than remedies.

On March 2, 1837, the Colonial Secretary, Lord John Russell, took account of the Commission's report and presented his Ten Resolutions to Parliament. This British Reformer did not feel himself able to translate his ideals to the colonies, however, and he rejected any proposals to make the Legislative Council elective. In addition, Russell continued to support the work of the British American Land Company, and finally authorized the Governor to bypass the Assembly for funds. A furious Lord Brougham warned the Ministry that "if you attempt to consummate your iniquitous works, the Canadians have a moral duty to resist you. Yes, if the same blood ran in their veins as that which produced Washingtons, Franklins and Jeffersons, they would chase you from their country as you were justly chased from the old colonies." [22]

It was obvious to the *Patriotes* that more direct pressure would have to be put on the authorities before concessions were made, and they therefore began to preach economic revolt in deadly earnest. On April

27, Duvernay laid out their program in *La Minerve*, recommending smuggling as a prime duty:

> Major remedies are needed for major evils. The sources of revenue must be dried up. The vaults will empty; the thieves will find nothing there. Then England will listen to reason. Never has a struggle been more just. We have withheld the subsidies; this weapon is now taken from us and we must seek others more effective.[23]

That summer, serious disturbances began in the Montreal district. Militiamen resigned in droves; Cartier's father refused to take part in any exercises. In fact, the staff of the regular army did not dare to mobilize any of the French Canadian battalions. The Saint-Jean-Baptiste Day celebrations of that June saw some ugly scenes of violence, and "anti-coercive" demonstrations took place constantly. When the Assembly convened that August, Rodier, Dr. O'Callaghan and a newly-elected Duvernay engaged in a little of what is now known as guerrilla theatre. According to the *bureaucrat*-controlled Quebec *Mercury*,

> Mr. Rodier's dress excited the greatest attention, being *unique*, with the exception of a pair of Berlin gloves, viz.: frock coat of granite coloured *étoffe du pays*;* inexpressibles and vest of the same material, striped blue and white: straw hat and beef shoes, with a pair of home-made socks, completed the *outré* attire. Mr. Rodier, it was remarked, had no shirt on, having doubtless been unable to smuggle or manufacture one. Dr. O'Callaghan's 'rig-out' was second only to that of Mr. Rodier, being complete with the exception of hat, boots, gloves, and shirt and spectacles.[24]

The heat in Quebec must have been rather intense that month, for on August 26, the Assembly voted to refuse funds for the maintenance of government. The vote proved to be their last; they were immediately dissolved by a furious Governor, after only eight days sitting. For the next thirty years, until Cartier was able to guarantee the success of Confederation, the French Canadians were without their own 'national' Assembly.

On September 5, 1837, Cartier was involved in the organizational meeting of the paramilitary *Fils de la Liberté*, held at the Hotel Nelson, in the main ballroom. Papineau's son described the room as "elegantly decorated with sprays of maple leaves, a three-dimensional tableau of John the Baptist in the desert, and French-Canadian flags. The table was loaded down, but with nothing imported! There was whisky, cider, beer, but no wine: there was sugar, but it was maple sugar."[25] As the evening wore on, five hundred young and ardent patriots passed a constitution and listened as the hotel's ballroom orchestra played their favourite patriotic songs, including Cartier's. The association, founded in

* home-spun

imitation of the "Sons of Liberty" of the American Revolution, was led by the New Brunswick-born, Loyalist-bred, American-raised journalist Thomas Storrow Brown, a founder of the Montreal newspaper, *The Vindicator*. The delegates chose as their motto the words "*En Avant*" (Forward!), and threatened to become more radical than their leaders. Brown wanted to bring in arms from south of the border, but was dissuaded by Papineau. Other revolutionary leaders besides Brown were not of French origin. Dr. Edmund Bailey O'Callaghan, fiery publisher of *The Vindicator*, had been a follower of Daniel O'Connell in Ireland, and was active in exposing the Assembly's grievances. Dr. Wolfred Nelson, a six-foot four-inch giant of a man with a shock of bushy red hair, was an old family friend of the Cartiers from Saint-Antoine. A cousin of Horatio Nelson, the great English naval hero, the big doctor had served as surgeon to Cartier's grandfather's battalion in the War of 1812, and he was to lead the *Patriotes'* main body in the Richelieu valley, where he was known far and wide as "the Big Red Wolf." Amury Girod, a Swiss, directed the rebels north of Montreal.

As co-secretary of the Permanent Central Committee since May, the twenty-three year old Cartier joined in the organization of the Sons of Liberty with his usual gusto. When they engaged in open military training, drilling with sticks and brooms, Cartier was there, and for his eight or nine hundred fellow fighting cocks, he composed the patriotic marching song, one that would be the text of his life: "Avant tout je suis Canadien."* Called "Petit Georges" as much on account of his height – about five feet, seven inches – as his youth, Cartier contributed greatly to the cause by his energetic and superb organization of the meetings and assemblies in and around Montreal that were a close prelude to rebellion.

The root causes of the Rebellion of 1837 were many and varied, but largely external in origin. During Andrew Jackson's presidency, the people of the United States had speculated wildly in railways, land and commodities. By 1837, the boom had collapsed, and world demand for Lower Canadian produce was seriously affected. The depression was worsened by the already long currency deflation that had lasted since 1815, and would continue until 1850. The deflation left the workers and farmers with lower salaries and less money for their produce. The high birth rate in Lower Canada had resulted in overcrowding, smaller farms, and the beginnings of a trickle of emigration to the mill towns of New England that was soon to grow into a flood. Yet all the while, the British encouraged immigration from the British Isles. They had effectively closed off the Eastern Townships to French Canadians, by means of the British American Land Company's policy of free land grants to British soldiers – grants that were rarely developed.

However, the causes of the Rebellion were not all external. Within

* Before all else I am a Canadian.

Lower Canada, young and ardent French Canadian lawyers – Cartier among them – as well as other professionals, such as doctors, and to a lesser extent, priests were frustrated. Every year the colleges were sending out more of these educated men – revolution fodder – than the country could absorb. The lawyers found themselves underemployed not only because of the economic situation, but also because of the closed shop of government patronage – a situation which enraged them. One Member of the Assembly summed up the problem to an English traveller, Dr. Bigsby:

> There is a grievance which we feel most acutely, that I may be allowed to state: it is that the greatest number, and the most lucrative, of our public offices are given to strangers. Every vacant place almost is filled up by the second cousin of a member of the Imperial Parliament, or by someone who has been useful to the ministry in some obscure county election ... At present, therefore, our own young ambitions are in despair. I can show you a hundred young men of family, with cultivated and honourable minds, absolutely running to seed for want of occupation.[26]

In fact, the Rebellion was primarily of middle class origins; its leaders were the sons of merchants and well-to-do farmers, rising new professionals whose pride had been insulted by the British colonials, sneering at their way of life. The leaders were liberal nationalists of the French variety, in the midst of their own self-discovery, and held ideas quite distinct from the average *curé* or *Anglais*. But now their cultural and economic future, once so bright, was clouding over. The Cartier family felt this malaise as much as any. The bottom had fallen out of their wheat market, and they knew that over in Britain, the Liberals and the Baltic traders were pressing for a change in preferential duties, a diminishing of Canadian protection. What was merely disastrous could become utterly ruinous.

The autumn of 1837 saw yet another disastrous wheat crop, particularly in the valley of the Richelieu. Cartier's father shared in the general depression of all about him. His business had practically evaporated before his eyes, and he had very little to lose. It is not known what Lieutenant-Colonel Cartier, Commander of the local militia, thought of his son's deep involvement in revolutionary activities, but we can be sure that he turned a jaundiced but kindly eye on his other son, Antoine-Côme Cartier, now involved in the family business, who was instrumental in founding a local branch of the Sons of Liberty; and on his daughters, involved in a women's patriotic organization, urging the use of local and not imported goods.

Saint-Denis, so quick to be loyal during the American invasions, was now a hotbed of revolutionary activity. Late in September, the *seigneur* of nearby Contrecoeur, the Honourable Pierre-Dominique Debartzch, had agreed, with some reservations, to serve on the Council at Quebec. He was regarded as a sell-out by the general populace, and hanged in effigy in the Saint-Denis marketplace. However, Madame Saint-Jacques, the widow of one of Jacques Cartier II's militia captains in the War of 1812, was furious, and tore the labels off the effigy, lecturing the rioters on their disrespect. On September 26, her house was attacked by a mob, one of whom was shot dead from an upstairs window. The house was demolished, and although she managed to escape with her three sons and two daughters, she was later charged with homicide. The case, of course, was thrown out of court.[27]

To counter the rising demands and the provocative conduct of the *Patriotes*, the military men and merchants of Montreal, led by such hotheads as Campbell Sweeny and Peter McGill – whom the French called "British Iroquois" – founded the Constitutional Association and held meetings of their own, where they petitioned the Crown to crush the sedition of the radical Reformers and unite the two Canadas under one English-speaking majority. The most radical of the Constitutionalists, regarded as extreme by even a good section of the English minority, was the garrulous and violent Scottish lawyer and schoolteacher Adam Thom. In his savage "Anti-Gallic Letters" to the Montreal *Herald*, Thom argued that "peace and prosperity must be guaranteed to the English, even in spite of the French-Canadians." "But," he said, "to be at peace we must make our own solitude; we must sweep the French-Canadians off the face of the earth."[28]

According to Lord Durham, in a dispatch previous to his famous *Report*, the Rebellion of 1837 in Lower Canada was precipitated by the loyalist British party, who instinctively knew that they would be in greater danger if the *Patriotes* had more time to prepare for the conflict that all knew was inevitable. Therefore, to counter the activities of the Sons of Liberty, the English-speaking youth of Montreal established the Doric Club, and the battle lines were at last drawn.

Toward the end of October, Papineau's cousin, the sickly old Bishop Jean-Jacques Lartigue, issued a pastoral letter declaring that Roman Catholics were duty-bound to obey the established authorities; but the hour was already too late, and this document served only to infuriate the *Patriotes*. Some, like Cartier, undoubtedly felt some sense of guilt about their own provocative actions – more so when he learned that the cash box of the parish priest of Saint-Denis had been rifled to buy arms and ammunition – yet he too was swept along by the inevitable and inexorable current of events that led to one spontaneous explosion of rage.

6   "The term *rebel* is no certain mark of disgrace. All the great assertors of liberty, the saviours of their country, the benefactors of mankind in all ages have been called rebels. We owe the constitution which enables us to sit in this House to a rebellion."

Charles James Fox,
in the British House of Commons

November 6, 1837 saw the first drawing of blood in Canada's Rebellion. Against Papineau's advice, the Sons of Liberty let it be known that they intended to meet on the Place d'Armes, there to begin their version of the French Revolution, to plant the tree, and raise the cap of Liberty. That morning, the Doric Club plastered the English wards with posters urging a mustering of loyalists on the Place d'Armes at noon, "to crush rebellion in the bud." The mob gathered, and at two o'clock moved a few blocks away to where the Sons of Liberty were drawing up. Although Cartier and others warned the younger hot-heads to avoid a battle in which they might be trapped, name-calling soon degenerated into stone-throwing, and for the remainder of the day, fighting raged throughout Old Montreal. Although axe handles and leaded whips were the favourite weapons of the day, no deaths were recorded; however, Thomas Storrow Brown lost the sight of his right eye after being assaulted and left for dead on the steps of the post office. The Royal Regiment was called out, complete with artillery, but they were unable to prevent an attack on Papineau's house, and the sacking of Dr. O'Callaghan's newspaper office, where trays of type were strewn into the street, and every window smashed.

The authorities responded quickly. By November 9, Commander-in-Chief Sir John Colborne had moved his troops from Sorel to Montreal, and, not wishing to involve the militia, had ordered reinforcements sent from New Brunswick. On November 16, the government finally yielded to pressure from the *Bureaucrats*, and warrants were issued for the arrest of a number of *Patriotes*, including Papineau, O'Callaghan, and Nelson, on charges of high treason. It is likely that advance warnings were given, because most of the *Patriote* leaders had by that time slipped away from Montreal to the countryside. Cartier joined the general exodus, and after a short stay with his family, where his mother argued concern for his safety, he crossed the river to Saint-Denis and joined Dr. Nelson, already organizing the defences of the village and fortifying the distillery he owned on the bank of the river. The men helping him were given generous rations of rum, and soon became quite fortified themselves. The rebellion was ready and only a few sparks were needed to ignite it.

Colborne's intelligence network had served him well, and a systematic

The House of the Seven Chimneys (PAC).

Rue Notre-Dame looking west. Engraving by J. Murray (PAC).

roundup of *Patriotes* began. On the night of November 16, a troop of the Montreal Volunteer Cavalry, sent out for this purpose, was ambushed by a rebel force near Longueuil, and two prisoners released. News of this initial success heartened most *Patriotes*, but upset the more moderate Reformers such as LaFontaine, who, fearful of bloodshed against hopeless odds, turned against Papineau and rushed to Quebec, where he begged the Governor to summon the Assembly. This was refused, and in December, fearful for his own safety, LaFontaine escaped to the United States and then on to England, where he hoped to make a last plea for sanity. On arriving in London, LaFontaine was told that he, too, had been charged with high treason; before he could be arrested, he was on a boat bound for France.

The stage was set, and, to the misfortune of the *Patriotes*, Colborne acted swiftly, hoping to dislodge the traitors from their fortified strongholds at Saint-Denis and Saint-Charles before the freeze-up. A week after the Longueuil ambush, Lieutenant-Colonel George Wetherall was sent downriver from Chambly with a battle-hardened infantry regiment, a troop of horse and two field guns. The plan was that Wetherall should meet up with the Waterloo cavalry veteran Colonel Charles Gore, coming eighteen miles up the Richelieu from Sorel with five companies of infantry and the Montreal Volunteer Cavalry to make a night attack on Saint-Denis. A neat pincer movement, but Colborne reckoned without the rain and sleet that bogged down Gore's troops and horses on a muddy back road short of Saint-Denis.

Dr. Nelson, possibly with the help of his former militia chief, Colonel Cartier, had planned the defences of the village well. Women and children were evacuated across the river to Saint-Antoine, and men who could scrape together arms superior to pitchforks were placed in all the houses and in his distillery. But the main force of about a hundred men – Cartier included – was stationed inside the large house of Mme Saint-Germain, on the main Sorel road just at the outskirts of the village. The *Patriotes*' only cannon, a little parade gun made of wood held together with iron bands, was set up in the road before the house.

Nelson had already heard of Gore's arrival at Sorel, but did not expect him to move so quickly. At one o'clock in the morning of November 23, a young British officer, Lieutenant George Weir, not in uniform and carrying no arms, stumbled into Saint-Denis with messages to Gore from Montreal. Noting Weir's surprise at his capture, and fearing the worst, Nelson galloped his horse four miles down the high road, and in the gloom of six o'clock, narrowly missed being captured himself by Gore's advance guard. Back in the village, he ordered the bridges in the vicinity burnt, the church bells rung, and bullets cast.

By about nine o'clock, Gore's Waterloo veterans – their drums beating and their mud-spattered red coats glowing against the grey – reached the outskirts of the village. As Cartier watched the troops set up their field gun down the road and aim it straight at the house, a cold chill ran down his back. Gore hesitated and summed up the situation; but soon the action became hot and furious. The British found their range, and their twelve-pound cannon began a deadly-accurate fire on the upper storeys of the house of Mme Saint-Germain. Most of the shot bounced off the four-foot thick walls, which cheered the men greatly. Suddenly, with a sickening explosion, a shell rocketed through the window and blew up on the far wall, mowing down four defenders, including Mme Saint-Germain's newly married son Charles, whose head was shot completely away.

The defenders moved to the ground floor, and for the next five hours, Cartier took his turn firing, loading, pouring lead and shouting encouragement at the sharpshooters, as the *Patriotes* held off Gore's guns from behind those massive stone walls. There was too much small arms fire to allow the defenders to set off their own little cannon, which stood cold and unused down in the road, dripping dully in the fog and sleet. At around one in the afternoon, Gore tried to storm the house, but a ferocious hail of bullets drove the red coats back. When British fire lagged at about two in the afternoon, Nelson sent out for reinforcements. Twenty-eight year old Charles-Ovide Perrault, a member of the Assembly, and Fabre's brother-in-law, volunteered to go first. He was shot twice as he tried to make a break down the street. Cartier followed, going out the rear toward the river. He ran quickly out of range, reached a boat, and was soon across to the House of the Seven Chimneys. He returned under fire about an hour later – to the cheers of the defenders – bringing nearly a hundred fresh reinforcements and lead for bullets. His bravery may have turned the tide, for the British troops, with only a few rounds left for their big gun, began to group for a retreat.

Dusk fell, and rain and sleet poured down on the battleground. When other *Patriotes* arrived from Saint-Ours and Contrecoeur, Gore's retreat turned into a rout. The rebels, howling in hot pursuit, chased him up the Sorel road, capturing several soldiers. They found the field gun left behind, spiked and useless, and ammunition thrown into the river. All told, 117 British troops were missing from roll call the next day in Sorel. The *Patriotes* had lost thirteen killed, the British thirty, including the hapless Lieutenant Weir, who had been brutally hacked down as he tried to escape. That night, the *Patriotes* took the body of Perrault across to Saint-Antoine, and buried him by torchlight.

The action at Saint-Denis was the *Patriotes*' only real victory of the Rebellion. Up the Richelieu at Saint-Charles, in the commandeered and fortified Debartzch manor house, Thomas Storrow Brown's band of *Patriotes*, outnumbered two to one, reeled before the deadly grapeshot of Wetherall's field guns, and his charges with fixed bayonet. "On entering the town," a British officer related, "there was little quarter given, almost every man was put to death; in fact they fought too long before

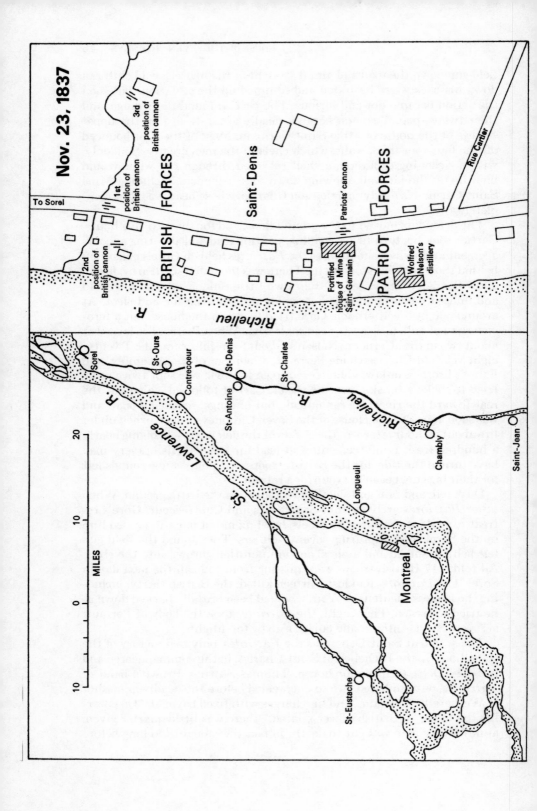

Nov. 23, 1837

3rd position of British cannon

1st position of British cannon

To Sorel

BRITISH FORCES

Saint-Denis

2nd position of British cannon

Richelieu R.

Fortified house of Mme Saint-Germain

Patriots' cannon

PATRIOT FORCES

Wolfred Nelson's distillery

Rue Cartier

St. Lawrence R.

Sorel

St-Ours

Contrecoeur

St-Antoine

St-Denis

St-Charles

Richelieu R.

Longueuil

Chambly

Saint-Jean

Montreal

St-Eustache

MILES

20   10   0   10

thinking of flight. Many of them were burned alive in the houses and barns which were fired as they would not surrender . . . The loss of the rebels was great; their position was strong and they defended it with desperation."[29] *Patriote* losses were as high as 150 killed, and an equal number wounded. The one-eyed Brown was able to escape across the river and ride away from the carnage north to Saint-Denis.

While the battle of Saint-Charles was raging, some of the victorious *Patriotes* of Saint-Denis argued for abandonment of the village. Still flushed from the battle, Cartier was hotly opposed to this, and urged that the road be blockaded with stones and trees, and the Saint-Germain house refortified. This was agreed to by the *Patriotes'* council, and Cartier, ready for another fight, furiously threw himself into the work of digging trenches and throwing up a palisade in front of the house.

When Brown arrived late that night with the horrific news from Saint-Charles, most of the men shouldered their pitchforks and muskets and deserted. Sunday morning dawned clear and bright, on a Saint-Denis that was practically empty of life. The parish priest found few men present at his Mass. After the service, he urged the remaining *Patriotes* to abandon the fight and prevent further bloodshed. Most of them swore to obey him. Across the river at Saint-Antoine, the priest gave his flock the same advice. A spy must have been present in the church, for two days later, the Montreal *Herald* reported the following news:

> On Sunday the congregation of the church of St. Antoine was ad-dressed by Mr. Cartier, a young advocate of this City, who recom-mended that a "liberal regiment" should be immediately formed, which he would lead to death or victory in attempting to release his brave compatriots from the gaol, but he met with little success, as at the muster, his regiment, including himself, numbered only four individuals.[30]

That night the leaders met, and after bitter arguments, regret, and then resignation, they decided to evacuate Saint-Denis. On Monday, Novem-ber 27, Cartier, Nelson, Brown and some other stalwarts, fled east and hid out in a swamp for a day, but with no news of British troop movements, Cartier left for home while Nelson and Brown went up to Saint-Charles to survey the disaster. On December 2, Cartier learned that a price was on his head; he and his cousin Henri said a hasty fare-well to the family, and set off up the Richelieu. After overtaking Nelson and discussing the woeful situation, the pair decided to retrace their steps and go into hiding not far from Saint-Antoine, at the farm of a friend Louis Larose. There they learned that Saint-Denis had been en-tered by a force of troops, sacked, looted and put to the torch.

On December 12, the Bureaucrat newspaper *Le Populaire* carried the following choice piece of information for its readers:

We have learned that the young lawyer Cartier, who was up to his neck in the agitation, has been found dead in the bush by his own father. While fleeing arrest he froze to death.

The report was generally believed, and Etienne Parent's Quebec paper, *Le Canadien*, carried the following obituary:

He was a young man endowed in the highest degree with qualities of heart and mind and before whom a brilliant career opened.[31]

"Now, my dear Henri," said Cartier to his cousin, "we may sleep in peace." But this was not to be, for one day in the spring of 1838, they came in to the farmhouse from Larose's sugaring cabin, where they had spent most of the winter, and Henri was seen briefly by the visiting lover of a servant girl. The lover was a jealous type, and demanded to know who Henri was. That night the two left on foot, and a week later, were taken across the border, shut up in one of Nelson's huge spirit barrels, by a driver going by the curious name of Alexandre Ladébauche. Once across, they were liberated by Ladébauche, who drove them on to Plattsburgh, New York, where they stayed for a few days with two old spinsters, the Misses Gregory, who had given them English lessons when they were boys. Soon they heard that Rodier was in St. Albans; they found him cheerfully tending bar in a local hotel, calling himself the Baron Cuvier, after the famous French zoologist. They learned from Rodier that Nelson had been arrested in a manhunt in December, and led to prison through a gauntlet of jeering, spitting Tories, and their hearts sunk when he told them that six *Patriotes* had been hanged for treason, including Cartier's friend and co-Secretary of the Central Committee, the Chevalier de Lorimier. But Duvernay was safe and sound in Burlington, Vermont, where he had begun to publish a newspaper, *Le Patriote Canadien*, and Cartier set off to visit him. Duvernay told him that the British had been making overtures to the *Patriotes*, and that the United States had signed a Neutrality Treaty with the British, promising not to give any assistance to the rebels. The great republic, the Cradle of Liberty, had betrayed them, Cartier had expected as much, and argued with Duvernay that they should give up the struggle and see what peace offers the British were prepared to make. Duvernay was adamantly opposed to this course of action, and protested that the struggle must be continued, and Lower Canada invaded by a new army of *Patriotes*. The two parted, not on the best of terms.

On February 10, 1838, the Parliament of Great Britain suspended the already collapsed Constitution of Lower Canada, and appointed one of the authors of the Reform Bill, Lord Durham, as Governor General and High Commissioner to investigate the rebellions and suggest solutions to the grievances of the Canadas. Soon after his arrival, "Radical Jack" appointed a special council made up of military men and three of his brilliant young aides to rule the two provinces. The council's first difficulty had to do with the imprisoned *Patriotes*. Wishing to avoid a trial, Durham obtained signed confessions of guilt from eight of the chief *Patriotes*, including Nelson, who then threw themselves on his mercy, begging that the public peace not be endangered by a trial. On June 28 – Victoria's Coronation Day – he exiled the eight to Bermuda, under pain of death if they returned without permission.* Sixteen others, including Papineau, O'Callaghan, Brown, Rodier, Duvernay and Cartier, were indicted for high treason and forbidden to return to Canada, also under pain of death. This matter neatly dealt with, Durham then granted a complete amnesty to the remainder of the Patriotes, and set about gaining the confidence of the exiles.

In the same month, Cartier learned to his great joy that Louis-Hippolyte LaFontaine had returned from France and was now in Saratoga, New York. Here was the man of reason who could restore some direction to the cause! LaFontaine welcomed him warmly, and the two set about planning some sort of return to politics and sanity. On June 17, they had dinner with Papineau, who proved stubborn and unmoveable in face of their arguments for moderation and compromise. Their disappointment with their chief led them to travel down to New York to meet one of Durham's aides, Edward Gibbon Wakefield, who had already sent word to the *Patriotes* that he was ready to have dealings with them.[32] Wakefield was an erratic genius who had himself served a term in jail – not for political reasons, but for abducting a young heiress. He gave LaFontaine and Cartier the welcome news that Durham was kindly disposed toward them, and would work for total amnesty.

Another of Durham's aides, Stewart Derbishire, had tried to win over Papineau, but failed. Derbishire's reports to Radical Jack were brilliantly perceptive. He blamed the English Canadian militia for being the worst offenders in the rebellion, noting that they had burned 297 buildings, including two churches, a convent, twelve granaries, and at Saint-Benoît, where no resistance at all was found, eighty-seven houses. Hardly a brave and glorious feat of British arms! Derbishire's view of the *habitant* was right on the mark:

> With a people thus wedded to their own ways, & thus limited in their views, it may be readily understood that they would look with jealousy upon a race of more active and enterprising *habitants* who came to settle among them . . . When to these feelings of aversion towards the intruder is added the alarm, oft sounded, of an intention on the part of the "foreigners" to abolish the laws & language of the "conquered nation," to "anglicize" the province and destroy every vestige

---

* a young student, Antoine Gérin-Lajoie, later editor of *La Minerve*, wrote the famous song, "Un Canadien Errant," in honour of these exiles.

of a distinctive race in the original settlers, – notions diligently incul-
cated by the revolutionary leaders and ably seconded by the newspaper organs of the English party in the current of contemptuous abuse
they have never ceased to pour down upon the habitants, & in their
frequent demands to keep them down; and when Papineau & his Confederates' appeals to the nationality of this vain people . . . are taken
into account . . . the conduct of the people last Autumn will no longer
appear extraordinary.[33]

Derbishire learned more in his few weeks in Lower Canada than he was
able to make his chief understand. Radical Jack was set upon soon after
his arrival by the *Bureaucrats* and Adam Thom, and not abandoned by
them until his departure five months later. He was to set little store in
his *Report* on the aspirations and desires of the French Canadian people.

7   **"Mr. President, I have just left Canada, and
taken leave of Mr. Cartier, the Prime Minister of that country. The Queen has not a more
loyal subject. Yet, in 1837, he was a rebel in
arms against the Crown. *He* was a secession-
ist. For a while he was a refugee in the
woods . . . . A reward of £ 500 was offered for
his apprehension. But our country removed
grievances, recognized the equality of
French and English Canadians, united the
Provinces, and forgave the rebels. All that
sad contest is now forgotten."**

**Edward Watkin to U.S. President
Andrew Johnson, 1865**

In February of 1838, the split in the *Patriote* ranks became an open gulf.
Against the advice of moderates like Cartier and LaFontaine, Dr.
Wolfred Nelson's brother Robert crossed the border into Lower Canada
with a small guerrilla army of radical *Patriotes* and their American
sympathizers, and proclaimed himself President of the Provisional Republic of Lower Canada. Nelson and his *Chasseurs* or Hunters planned
to govern in style, by taking over the banks, the Lachine Canal and the
Customs, by extracting £ 80,000 in reparations from John Molson, and
by strangling the Jews and confiscating their property. Colborne's troops
had little trouble in keeping this second rebellion from getting out of
hand, and when Nelson tried to steal the weapons of the Indians at
Caughnawaga, most members of his raiding party were captured and
handed over by the people of the Reservation.

In May of 1838, a British officer, Colonel Gascoigne, wrote to a colleague that he had talked to two magistrates in Saint-Denis – one was probably Joseph Cartier – who expressed the opinion that the people of the district were "heartily repentant of their sins . . . ashamed of their conduct" and had a "lively sense of the folly and fruitlessness of rebellion."[34]

That August, a miserable and homesick Cartier ignored the price on his head and made his way across the border, avoiding Saint-Denis and Saint-Antoine, back to Montreal. During the days that followed, he shut himself up in his brother Damien's room to study law and the newspapers. Some evenings, he would leave and stroll east along Rue Notre-Dame out to the suburbs, needing escape as much as fresh air. Walking down lonely roads or along the St. Lawrence under a harvest moon, or caught out late in a thunderstorm, he often imagined that mysterious footsteps dogged him, that every bush concealed a militiaman or officer of the law, eager for the reward. Here he was, nearing his twenty-fourth birthday, a felon in his own country, waiting for a far-away Parliament to come to its senses.

By September 20, he felt collected enough to write Durham's chief aide, Charles Buller, with words that might seem outrageous from a rebel, but basically did not depart from the legal and constitutional principles he had learned from Rodier and Duvernay. "I have never," he declared, "forfeited my allegiance to Her Majesty's Government of the Province of Quebec."[35] Buller replied that, if Cartier conducted himself with discretion, the law would turn a blind eye to his presence in Montreal. Buller and Durham were well supplied with intelligence, and probably knew he was in the city all along, but they did not risk arresting Cartier for fear of rekindling the passions they had so carefully cooled down. The young lawyer happened to be the son and grandson of two Lieutenant-Colonels of the Verchères militia. Although Cartier's father had kept to his house during the battle of Saint-Denis, he probably had supplied the rebels with ammunition, at his son's request. Radical Jack and his chief aides realized that it would be a mistake to alienate further such a prominent and powerful family, one that had loyally upheld the British connection during two American invasions.

With the departure of Durham from Canada, and the continuation of Robert Nelson's own private rebellion, Cartier felt compelled to write to Civil Secretary Goldie:

> Since my return from exile up to the present, I have remained in Montreal to give the authorities a chance to observe my conduct. I left the city for only two days, the 16th and 17th of October last, to see my family in the country, after a year's absence from them.
>
> In spite of my peaceful conduct and my restraint in word and deed, I must tell you that I am far from living without anxiety these days. The many arrests, and the language of several individuals, has kept

me in continual fear of arrest, all of which prevents me from freely attending to business. I would like, if at all possible, to ward off any interference I do not deserve. I must declare, on my word of honour, that I have had no connection with the recent troubles, and that there is no one who deplores and disapproves of them as much as I. I repeat that it is my determination to conduct myself in the most peaceful and irreproachable manner possible. Finally, I would be infinitely grateful if you would communicate the same to His Excellency Sir John Colborne, and inform me whether there is any threat to my personal liberty.[36]

Whatever Goldie's reply to this letter, Cartier was left in peace to re-establish himself in legal practice. He and Damien set up a new office on Rue Saint-Vincent, near the old haunts and the smell of the harbour. Some of their work at this time was free legal advice for the families of those killed, hanged or still in exile.

The nightmare of struggle was over, and Cartier had come through it all relatively unscathed, ready to fight new battles with his friend La-Fontaine. The Rebellion had mirrored in Cartier the clash between his gentle pious mother and his vital, devil-may-care father. The fight was not only between English and French for/constitutional control, but in Cartier's psyche a struggle between the two natures of French Canada, between what might be called the Virgin and the Voyageur, between the conservative, religious, passive, essentially static and organic existence of the *habitant*, and the increasingly vigorous, dynamic, progressive, nationalistic and entrepreneurial nature of the new *Canadien* professional. Both these elements were forged together in Cartier's general makeup in the crucible of Rebellion, so that he was able to be at the same time rebel and loyalist, loyal to his people and their innate constitutional authority, but a rebel against those who would pervert and usurp that authority. Through the chaos of rebellion and civil war, in face of demands from the Church to lay down arms and from the more rabid *Patriotes* to fight on, Cartier carried these principles, with Duvernay, Rodier, Nelson and LaFontaine, like the Ark of the Covenant of the French Canadian people.

Durham's celebrated *Report* was issued at the close of 1838. Unfortunately, Radical Jack saw the problem of Lower Canada as principally racial:

I expected to find a contest between a government and a people: I found two nations warring in the bosom of a single state: I found a struggle, not of principles, but of races; and I perceive that it would be idle to attempt any amelioration of laws or institutions until we could first succeed in terminating the deadly animosity that now separates the inhabitants of Lower Canada into the hostile divisions of French and English.[37]

A politician to the end, Radical Jack blamed the French Canadians for their lack of enlightenment:

> The French appear to have used their democratic arms for conservative purposes, rather than those of liberal and enlightened movement; and the sympathies of the friends of reform are naturally enlisted on the side of sound amelioration which the English minority in vain attempted to introduce into the antiquated laws of the Province.[38]

To be fair to Durham, his whitewash of the problem was for political purposes, to keep the Montreal merchants happy with the British connection. His remedy for the problems of Canada was simple: "I entertain no doubts," he concluded, "as to the national character which must be given to Lower Canada; it must be that of the British Empire, that of the majority of the population of British America, that of the great race which must in the lapse of no long period of time be predominant over the whole North American continent."[39] The spirits of Cartier and his colleagues sunk as they read that everything possible, including a confederation of the provinces of British North America, must be done to assimilate the French Canadians as painlessly as possible, to make them abandon their "vain hopes of nationality."[40] Durham's recommendations were well received in Britain, where the Prime Minister, Lord Melbourne, declared that "it is laid down by all as a fundamental principle that the French must not be reinstated in power in Lower Canada."[41]

On February 10, 1841, by Royal Proclamation, the provincial legislatures were abolished, and the legislative Union of Upper and Lower Canada came into being. The *Bureaucrats* and the merchants now had the union they wanted. It was not a federal system, which would have given the French back their Assembly, but a single union of the provinces with an engineered English majority in the Assembly. This was Durham's recommendation. In February of 1839, Buller had suggested to him that "the great argument against a federal Union is that it does nothing to attain the main end which we ought to have in view. That end is keeping Lower Canada quiet now, & making it English as speedily as possible."[42]

Cartier's spirits were at a low ebb. Rodier had hardly returned from exile when he died of heart failure. So much fire and persuasion and inspiration was snuffed out with that life that it seemed that all had been in vain. So much light had gone. Yet LaFontaine was hopeful that some benefit could be achieved under the new constitution, however much it was weighted in favour of the English. Their Rebellion had been just. Of this, he and Cartier had no doubt. Now they were willing to temporize, and work for the establishment of majority rule, of a government chosen on the basis of representation. The Reformers in Upper

Canada were prepared to cooperate as well: two years earlier, in May of 1839, LaFontaine had shown Cartier a letter from the Toronto banker and journalist Francis Hincks that revived his spirits and gave him new hope. "Though I have not the honour of personal acquaintance with you," Hincks wrote politely and carefully,

> yet entertaining a high respect for your political and private charac-
> ter, I take the liberty of addressing you on the subject of Lord Dur-
> ham's Report . . . I am most anxious to know how that document is
> received by you and your political friends, and your press is at present
> so completely gagged that it is no true index of public opinion. With
> respect to the principles of government recommended by Lord D. I
> presume there cannot be a doubt that they will be as satisfactory to
> you as to us . . . You may be assured that in this promotion of liberal
> and economical government the Reformers of this Province will coop-
> erate with those of Lower Canada. On national questions it is not
> likely that they would. Lord Durham ascribes to you national objects;
> if he is right, union would be ruin to you; if he is wrong, and that you
> are really desirous of liberal institutions and economical government,
> the union would in my opinion give you all you could desire, and an
> United Parliament would have an immense Reform Majority . . . If
> we all combine *as Canadians* to promote the good of all classes in
> Canada there cannot be a doubt that under the new Constitution
> worked as Lord Durham proposes, the only party which would suffer
> would be the bureaucrats.[43]

Hincks elaborated that "*we can not be beat.* Our [Upper Canadian] Tories, particularly Orangemen, are savage at the Union. They talk openly of preferring a Junction with the Yankees to one with you French Canadians . . . You may depend upon it that we shall never con- sent to a Union unless it is founded upon *Justice to all classes.*"[44] This was the kind of hope, the kind of intelligent compromise, that would rebuild the shattered morale of French Canada, that would be the foun- dation stone of Cartier's political career.

On November 6, 1839, Cartier felt comfortable enough to attend the Governor's levee, a fact that did not endear him to Ludger Duvernay, still in exile in Vermont churning out his newspaper *Le Patriote Cana- dien.* As early as May 14, Cartier had written to Louis Perrault in Bur- lington, sending him $30 and advising him to "take no notice of Duver- nay's paper. It is regarded by the people of the country as a vile rag that will do as much harm as good."[45] In this letter – opened by the police magistrate at Saint-Jean – Cartier noted that he was about to travel to Quebec to argue for the amnesty of those still in exile. Duvernay and the others felt that Cartier and LaFontaine were giving up the struggle without a fight, yet much of their resentment probably stemmed from a combination of jealousy and homesickness. A resentful Duvernay em-

barrassed Cartier on a number of occasions by printing Cartier's patriotic songs in his newspaper. Cartier was furious, but turned away from
these stings and darts to concentrate on the great work opening up
before him – the creation of a new and powerful political alliance.

With Papineau in exile in Paris, the mantle of leadership of French
Canada now fell on the shoulders of Louis-Hippolyte LaFontaine, Cartier's mentor, hero and friend. Barely thirty-two, with broad forehead
and a firmly set jaw, Louis LaFontaine commanded respect throughout
the whole of the province; his eloquence rivalled Papineau's. He put
many people in mind of Napoleon, including Lady May Bagot, wife of a
Governor General, who had herself met the Emperor. When she saw
LaFontaine for the first time, she exclaimed to a friend, "If I was not
certain that he is dead, I should say it was Napoleon himself." [46] LaFontaine did nothing to dispel the legend – he even combed his hair down
over his forehead like Napoleon – and Cartier, who was widely regarded
as his *aide-de-camp*, constantly wore a small bust of Napoleon in his
lapel. The story circulated throughout Canada that when LaFontaine
was in exile in Paris, he once visited Napoleon's tomb at Les Invalides,
still guarded by Bonaparte's faithful old soldiers. One ancient veteran,
on seeing LaFontaine, wept with emotion at the vision before him of the
walking image of his dead Emperor.

In September of 1840, Hincks visited Montreal to meet with the
French Reformers and hammer out a philosophy of politics. His visit
was a great success, and at the farewell banquet, Cartier spoke, promising full cooperation and vowing that, after the coming elections, the new
Assembly would be packed with a solid phalanx of Reformers.

In his address to the electors of Terrebonne, LaFontaine protested
that he and his followers had only accepted the new Constitution under
protest:

> The union is an act of injustice and despotism, in that it is imposed
> upon us without our consent, that it deprives Lower Canada of its
> legitimate number of representatives, that it deprives us of the use of
> our language in the proceedings of the legislature, contrary to the
> faith of treaties and the word of the Governor General, in that it
> makes us pay without our consent a debt which we did not contract,*
> in that it permits the executive illegally to employ under the name of
> a civil list and without a vote of the representatives of the people, an
> enormous portion of the revenues of the country. [47]

None the less, LaFontaine saw in the Union the key to the survival of
the French Canadians: with political unity, the strongbox of patronage
could be opened.

* the colossal public debt of a bankrupt Upper Canada was to be shared
equally under the new Union.

On April 29, 1841, Cartier's father died at the House of the Seven Chimneys. LaFontaine had asked him to run in the elections of that year, but Cartier decided to spend some time at Saint-Antoine comforting his mother and helping out with legal matters. He returned to the fray in the summer, and, as the provincial campaign manager, engaged in a whirlwind round of political organizing in the backrooms and meeting halls of Lower Canada. In LaFontaine's riding on election day, he watched with disgust as several hundred strong arm bullies, brought in to support the *Bureaucrat* candidate, chased the Reformers away from the polls. By the time the Reformers could arm themselves with sticks and cudgels for the counter-attack, the intruders had organized themselves into impregnable positions around the polls, and LaFontaine was defeated.

Yet all was not lost for the Reform cause. When the first Parliament of United Canada met at Kingston on June 14, the Upper Canadian Reform leader Robert Baldwin successfully nominated Austin Cuvillier as Speaker, and in September, at Baldwin's suggestion, the farmers of North York, Upper Canada, nominated and elected Louis LaFontaine as their member. The favour was returned a year and a half later by the electors of Rimouski, who sent Robert Baldwin to Parliament. Baldwin was appointed to the Draper ministry, but resigned when the Governor General, Lord Sydenham, refused to give adequate representation in Council to the French Canadian bloc. In fact, Sydenham's first Council had no French Canadian members.

Responsible government in theory came to the Canadas when, in September of 1842, LaFontaine and his colleagues became the first French Canadians since the Conquest to enter into the executive branch of their government. The Governor General, Sir Charles Bagot, still had the power to select whatever ministers he pleased; yet unlike Sydenham he was an impartial man, and respected the wishes of the majority, choosing Robert Baldwin of Toronto and Louis-Hippolyte LaFontaine of Montreal as co-Premiers and Attorneys-General of the two provinces. Responsible government still had to be tested before it became fact, and it was to take six years of see-sawing, a succession of ministries and Governors before the theory could be put into practice.

Cartier was in the countryside when he heard the news of the first breakthrough. He was overjoyed and straightaway wrote to his leader:

Dear Sir: I did not expect to learn on my arrival yesterday from St. Charles the extremely good news, so happily confirmed, of your appointment as Attorney-General. Permit me to offer you my congratulations on your promotion to such an important position . . .

I wish to tell you that all our friends here, and myself in particular, give our complete approval to the conditions which you made before accepting your new office. We recognize your independence, your rectitude and your patriotism. Your appointment has electrified our hearts and our spirits; we begin to revive, to have hope and confidence, things which we had so long abandoned. We seem to rouse ourselves from the torpor and disgust which have weighed us down, and advance toward a more vital politics – for the defence and victory of our legitimate rights . . .

Berthelot and I drink champagne to your health. We put our stomachs in unison with our hearts.

I close by wishing you success and prosperity. Believe me, your very obedient servant and friend,

Geo. Et. Cartier

N.B. I write this letter slowly, so you can read it.[48]

The last refers to Cartier's incredible handwriting; some of it is and will forever remain indecipherable. He said once that he had three writing styles, one that everybody could understand, one that only his assistants could decipher, and one that he alone could understand. Pierre Chauveau, a political colleague, once wrote Cartier that he was "unable to read what you sent in the envelope of the letter you addressed to me. Your handwriting is, however, better than mine, and I thank you for those hieroglyphics – they have a friendly aspect to them."[49]

"In the reasonable construction of that undefined theory, I have avowed my adherence to Responsible Government to the fullest extent which it can be avowed in a Colony, and it must be either Blindness or Disaffection that can desire to get further."

8

**Governor General Metcalfe to Colonial
Secretary Stanley, Feb. 25, 1844**

The period of the 1840s was a time of consolidation and political apprenticeship for George-Etienne Cartier. As he neared his thirtieth year of age, he mellowed slightly, and under LaFontaine's influence, grew from a nervous, bristling revolutionary into a brash, debonair professional man. In his early years of law practice, life was difficult, and business aggravated by a depression that began in the late years of the decade. His cases came mainly from relations or friends, and sometimes took the young lawyer out of Montreal. In January of 1842, he undertook one case for the Debartzch family, *seigneurs* of Contrecoeur. Debartzch had four daughters, known throughout the province for their beauty and wit, and Cartier was quite overwhelmed by one of them. When he got up his courage and asked for her hand in marriage, she refused him outright, and he rode back to Montreal with his tail between his legs.[50] She may have told her sisters about "Little George," for soon after Cartier's friends discovered what had happened, and teased him without mercy.

Cartier worked out a very profitable division of labour with his brother Damien. While the elder, more bookish brother remained in the office and prepared cases, George drummed up business and pleaded in court. It would appear that the young former rebel was better at business than legal rhetoric, although the brothers seldom lost a case. It was later said of Cartier that he "lacked the quality necessary to really succeed at the Bar: he was not eloquent; quite the opposite. A man of cultivation and learning, he nevertheless spoke his language with astonishing incorrectness, as if he had a speech defect." [51] Although Cartier's discourse was awkward, his mind was razor-sharp and his opinions well thought out, and he certainly was a terror in the courts. On one occasion, he was hammering away at a point when the judge interrupted him and politely suggested that he was emphasizing the matter too strongly. Cartier was furious, and reminded the judge that he himself was the best judge of what was of value to his case. He further suggested to His Honour that he would plead the case as he understood it, and that he was not a mouthpiece for the judiciary. It is not recorded whether Cartier was awarded that particular judgment.

The account book of the firm of Cartier and Cartier survives, [52] and it reveals a surprising variety of legal work. Apart from the usual business of chasing bad debts and arranging mortgages, wills, separation agreements and bankruptcies, the Cartiers appeared to have acted almost as management consultants. They did accounts or arranged financing and insurance, or simply paid bills for commercial firms, seigneuries and religious orders. As he was to say later, "perhaps I was wrong in not following the profession of my family, instead of the law and politics. But as you can see, I am the kind of lawyer who engages in business and politics. Nothing pleases me so much as a question of business and political economy."

Cartier's social life began to improve toward the middle of the decade, with the return of the *Patriotes* from exile. A chastened but still angry Duvernay came back to rebuild *La Minerve*, and the two made amends for past bitterness. The newspaper was soon its old self, attacking the *Bureaucrats* and educating the Reformers. Dr. Wolfred Nelson* returned after a five year exile in Bermuda and the United States, and was wined and dined and taken everywhere by a delighted Cartier, especially to whist parties, that were then all the rage, and for promenades on the Place Viger, where Nelson greeted all his old friends and political cro-

---

* Nelson was to have a prominent career as Mayor of Montreal, as an expert on civic sanitation and the prevention of cholera. He was the first Canadian physician to use anaesthesia.

nies, with shouts and whoops of joy. In April of 1843, the pair attended a banquet of Montreal Reformers honouring Sir Charles Bagot, then in ill health and about to retire. In a speech to the gathering, Cartier expressed the hope of all present that the newly appointed Governor General, Sir Charles Metcalfe, "would be ready to continue and to extend the liberal and constitutional policies of his predecessor." [53]

Cartier's hopes were shattered in late 1843 when Metcalfe refused a recommendation from Baldwin and LaFontaine with regard to some public appointments. On November 27, the ministry resigned, and only one French Canadian, Denis-Benjamin Viger, could be found to enter into the new ministry led by William H. Draper. Viger was Papineau's cousin, and had been imprisoned in 1838. Now he was considered to be a sell-out.

As the reputation of the firm of Cartier and Cartier grew, they began to concentrate more on real estate and land transfer cases, and developed a very real loyalty toward the prosperity of Montreal. An idle and restless Louis-Hippolyte LaFontaine became a partner in the firm, and returned to the business of law while Draper and Viger tried to run the government.

Parliament had not met for months when, on September 23, 1844, Metcalfe dissolved the legislature and called an election. LaFontaine again asked Cartier to run, and again Cartier refused, wishing instead to build up enough financial security to allow himself to seek office without worry. His family's affairs still needed his attention. That March, his uncle Joseph, the brains of the family business, had died at Saint-Antoine. Cartier agreed, however, to organize the Reform campaign in the province, and go on the election trail with the candidates.

The day after the election was called, Viger stood on the platform at Saint-Denis, seeking re-election as the Member for Saint-Hyacinthe against Dr. Wolfred Nelson. To his great chagrin, he spied Nelson and Cartier in the crowd. After his speech, Cartier got up on the platform and hounded the "*vendu*"* for having agreed to accept power under Metcalfe's terms:

> Sir Charles Metcalfe has refused to follow the advice of his ministers in matters which were within their absolute responsibility, and I am here today to blame him. He has found three Lower Canadian members to approve of his conduct, and Mr. Viger is one of them. Not satisfied with having voted badly, Mr. Viger now has become the chief advisor of the Governor in alliance with our worst enemies. What has become of the man who remained nineteen months behind bars for

---

* "sell-out" – an epithet commonly conferred on those French Canadians who are deemed to have sold out to the English.

not submitting to the dishonour of our country? Surely, the times have changed . . .

Electors of St. Denis, you gave proof of your courage when, on November 22, 1837, armed with a few pitchforks, guns and bludgeons, you repulsed the troops of Colonel Gore. I was with you, and I don't think I showed any lack of courage. Today I demand from you a greater, a better, a more patriotic action. I appeal to you to repel by your votes an army still more formidable – those who would continue to oppress you by depriving you of the advantage of responsible government. Yes, electors of this noble parish, do your duty, give a salutary example, and Lower Canada will be proud of you.[54]

Cartier's words struck home, and Viger was badly beaten, most of all in the French sections of the riding. This victory was followed up by the successful election – one of the wildest in memory – of Hincks' friend L.T. Drummond in Montreal. Cartier and Duvernay managed the election, which saw the use of vast sums of money, gangs of dockworkers, and crowds of 7,000 strong – on both sides. Viger procured another seat, however, and for the next four years, he ruled in lonely splendour – Draper's only French Canadian – while the Reformers stewed out of office.

With LaFontaine as a legal partner, Cartier's firm prospered. He soon became involved in a direction that would eventually provide the foundation of his political career – the business and the politics of railways. In March of 1845, the legislature gave assent to a bill establishing the St. Lawrence and Atlantic Railway, a line that would connect Montreal with the ice-free port of Portland, Maine. The newly appointed solicitor of the company, thirty-one year old George-Etienne Cartier, presented its prospectus to the legislature's Standing Committee on Railways.

On June 16, 1846, under the newly completed towers of the Sulpician Church of Notre Dame, Cartier married the girl he had first met at the *Patriotes*' haven in Edouard Fabre's bookshop – Fabre's daughter Hortense, a strong-minded young woman of eighteen. Fabre was delighted, and wrote to his sister that "we have made great sacrifices to have her well-educated, but nevertheless we are marrying her well; we have known the young man for twelve years and he has always been a friend of the household . . . he is certainly one of the best matches in Montreal: an *excellent* lawyer engaged in brilliant pursuits."[55] It was a great political wedding, with practically the entire Reform party in attendance. Morin and LaFontaine witnessed the marriage licence, and after the ceremony in the Hotel Nelson, the pair went on a three-week honeymoon to New York and Washington. On their return, they lived in Joseph Donegana's "palatial" hotel – Cartier defrayed expenses by doing legal work for the landlord – and waited eagerly for the masons and carpenters to finish their nest, a three-storey cut-stone townhouse on then fashionable Rue Notre-Dame.* No sooner had they moved in than a daughter Josephine was born, followed two years later by another daughter, named after her mother.

With the Reformers out of office, two new political factions rose in the Canadas to challenge the conduct of the Governor General. Although they had not yet broken openly with the Reformers, William Lyon Mackenzie and Louis-Joseph Papineau, now both returned from exile, began to attack the moderate ways of the Reform leaders. Exile had changed their ideals in different ways. William Lyon Mackenzie had greatly revised his opinions of American democracy. During the Rebellion, his fellow rebels had been ardent Yankee-lovers, fighting hopefully under a blue flag with two stars in the centre, a flag that symbolized the two Canadian states that would enter the American union on the achievement of their own liberty. Mackenzie's exile disgusted him with American political institutions and he became a British loyalist. In a letter to Hincks' Toronto paper, *The Examiner*, he said that his

> sojourn in the United States had wrought a disillusionment. American democracy as it presented itself in the form of political corruption, crass materialism and human slavery, filled his soul with righteous indignation. He was convinced that the vaunted liberty of the United States was merely a sham; that neither the grandiloquent principles of the Declaration of Independence, nor the unctuous guarantees of the American Constitution assured to the private citizen the same measure of civil and political freedom as was enjoyed by the humblest Canadian subject under the British Constitution.[56]

Although now a loyalist, Mackenzie and his radical friends still loathed Tories with a passion. One crony wrote to him describing Tory loyalism as "the spawn of the puke of the American Revolution."[57]

While Mackenzie had regained a more or less even keel, Papineau returned from Paris a thoroughgoing Red Republican, full of all the revolutionary fervour of France. Soon after his arrival, Cartier went to see him with some news from a bed-ridden LaFontaine. Papineau seemed friendly, and approving of the conduct of the Reformers.[58] But European radicalism had been too glorious for the *seigneur* of Montebello; he settled gloomily back into colonial life, depressed with everything about him, and increasingly attacked by his former disciples as he tried to explain his new principles. "The political state of this country,"

---

* The house is still standing, at #16 Notre-Dame East, on the south side where the street crosses the Berri extension. It overlooks the harbour, and from its windows Cartier could watch the progress of Montreal commerce. He had extra offices on the ground floor to supplement his law office. After his death, the house was sold, and for many years it served as a small hotel for old men and transients. Now empty and boarded up, it has been designated as a federal historical site, and could be a good location for a museum of nineteenth century Montreal.

he moaned, "is more of a stench in my nostrils than it has ever been-
. . . Birthplace, old relations, family interests chain me here like an
oyster on the rock where I was born, but the intellectual life here is so
dead, political life so detestable, that I shall live here in misery."[59]

With Papineau's return by acclamation to the legislature, some of the
young moderate Reformers began a hatchet job on the old chieftain.
LaFontaine's followers had been chafing under Papineau's attacks on
their policies, his exhortations that they should become more radical.
One of the new members, Joseph Cauchon, editor of the new *Journal de
Québec*, who was already a power in the Quebec City area, and later one
of Cartier's ministers, commented:

> For my part, I should be glad to see M. Papineau in the House, because
> his talents, if his opinions were not extreme, could be useful to us. In
> the contrary case, in order to spare blood and the oppression of our
> compatriots, we would be obliged to react against him and isolate
> him. But then he would place us in a false position by making us
> appear men opposed to the democratic ideals which invade the new
> world.[60]

A fair warning: the battle lines were drawing up in new formation, and
as the Lower Canadian Reform Party began moving rapidly to the centre, Papineau's followers set up a new group, the *Parti Démocratique*,
known increasingly as the *Rouges*, and a newspaper, *L'Avenir*, to coun-
terbalance the weight of *La Minerve*. *L'Avenir* was edited by a lean
little dynamo of a man, Antoine-Aimé Dorion, who was to rise quickly
in the new party, and prove to be Cartier's main political opponent in
the years preceding Confederation. But for the moment there were
elections to win, and Cartier threw himself into the organization of the
Reform fight with supreme confidence: the *Rouges* had not yet found
their feet, and the old *Bureaucrats* were in hopeless disarray.

Cartier was finding his way into the main stream of political life.
What he had rebelled for in 1837, and what he was still fighting for, was
soon to be achieved.

Louis-Hippolyte LaFontaine (PAC).

9

"Tell us, gentlement of *L'Avenir*, you who weep so much over the ruins of the past, and over imaginary evils – tell us, at what period in our history has French-Canadian nationality not been more shining, more honoured or respected, occupying a higher position than it holds today?"

La Revue Canadienne, June 1848

The elections of 1847-48 saw a tremendous victory for the Reformers. Upper Canada returned twenty-three Baldwinites to only eighteen Tories; in the lower province, LaFontaine's party – including the "English Liberals" such as Dr. Nelson – managed to take thirty-two seats to only five for their opposition. LaFontaine's personal victory in Montreal City was announced at noon on January 15 to a drenched but delirious crowd of supporters on the Place d'Armes. Cartier and Nelson were there, entertaining the crowd, and leading them, through the rain and sleet, with a rousing "trois *cheers*" for Her Majesty the Queen. The correspondent of *La Minerve*, hinting at the rowdyism of the campaign, reported that Cartier had managed to overcome his "speech defect" and "handled himself with all the ease and self-possession he is becoming known for. His speeches are always interrupted with thunderous applause, not only because he speaks well, but because he has the reputation of being always in the thick of an election, even in dangerous situations."[61]

In 1848, while France and Italy were convulsed with violent partisan strife, the Canadas had their own revolution, in the peaceful achievement of Responsible Government. When the new Reform majority successfully passed a motion of non-confidence in the ministry, and the new Governor General Lord Elgin offered the post of Premier to Louis-Hippolyte LaFontaine, popular sovereignty had at last been accepted. The representatives of the people now were to control the executive of the government, and through it the civil service and the avenues of patronage. On March 11, 1848, a momentous date in Canadian history, LaFontaine and Baldwin accepted their appointments. The revolution was over!

In April, with the way to progress clear, a now financially independent Cartier presented himself in a bye-election in Verchères riding, where his grandfather had sat almost fifty years before. His candidacy was opposed by the *Rouges*, but with the full resources of the party he had helped build behind him, he was a runaway winner. Dr. Nelson spoke by his side. They must have been quite a sight, the descendants of Horatio Nelson and Jacques Cartier, as they stood on the platform, almost a foot of height separating the two, like a great dane and a terrier. The election over, Cartier was escorted from Saint-Antoine to the boundary of the riding in a carriage draped in blue, accompanied by a hundred delirious supporters on horseback.

Three weeks later, his elation at the victory turned to sorrow, for on Easter Day, April 23, Cartier's mother, perhaps overly excited by her son's success, had a heart attack and died in the House of the Seven Chimneys. She was buried beside her husband in the church at Saint-Antoine.

Before taking his seat in the House, Cartier had been active in an incident that shows where some of his first political duties lay: in the battle for control of the clubs and associations that flourished in the 1840s in French Canada. While Cartier had been in the thick of his campaign for Verchères, Father O'Reilly, the Roman Catholic missionary at Sherbrooke, put forward a scheme to prevent the growing exodus of young French Canadians – 20,000 of them in the past four years – to the burgeoning mill towns of New England. Father O'Reilly proposed settling (or "colonizing") them in the still vacant lands of the Eastern Townships. The British American Land Company, burdened by taxes on its unsold holdings, wished to dispose of these lands. Alexander Tilloch Galt, Commissioner of the Company, may have suggested the scheme to Father O'Reilly, and it was quickly taken up with enthusiasm by *L'Avenir* and the *Rouges*.

Galt was one of a brilliant but erratic family who had much to do with the opening up of Canada in the last century. His father John Galt, a Scottish novelist and friend of Lord Byron, had founded the Canada Land Company in the 1830s, and opened up much of Southwestern Ontario to settlers. Betrayed by the Family Compact of Upper Canada, who disliked his methods, the elder Galt languished for a time in debtors' prison in London, England, and died before he could return to Canada. Alexander Galt began his career as a clerk in the British American Land Company, became a railway promoter, an early advocate of Confederation, and then argued for independence from Great Britain. He became spokesman for the English in Lower Canada, and was a close political and business associate of Cartier until after 1867, when the two had a parting of the ways.

Realizing the political blunder he had made in not becoming involved in the colonization scheme, LaFontaine sent his heaviest gun, George-Etienne Cartier, to challenge the *Rouge* domination over "L'Association canadienne-française des townships." Cartier arrived early for the first election meeting, and tried to pack the hall in Sherbrooke with Reformers. Right at the outset he proposed his political ally Augustin-Norbert Morin as President. Morin was narrowly defeated, and the more "neutral" Bishop Ignace Bourget of Montreal elected in his place. After another close fight, Papineau was elected First Vice-President. To rub in the defeat of the Reformers, Dorion nominated Morin as Second Vice-President. Morin was elected, but later arrived at the meeting and refused the seat. Cartier's father-in-law Edouard Fabre, now a con-firmed *Rouge*, was elected Treasurer, at which point Cartier stormed from the meeting vowing to form a rival assocation.[62]

In his early years as a politician, Cartier was involved in many such activities. The year before, he had successfully manipulated Reform control of the influential Saint-Jean-Baptiste Society, and a few years later figured in securing Wolfred Nelson's return as Mayor of Montreal, again against his father-in-law Edouard Fabre.

The 1848 session began with serious battles both within and outside the legislature between Papineau and the Reformers. Cartier was proba-bly the instigator of a newspaper war that opened some of the old wounds of 1837. Three years previously, he had been attacked by Viger's paper, *L'Aurore*, which claimed that he said, regarding the possibility of further rebellion, that "England will be terrified: she spent so much money in '37 and '38 that she won't dare make us resort to the same means as before."[63] Even if he was misquoted, as Cartier claimed he was, it was a pretty perceptive observation. Now the Reformers were deter-mined to play the same game with Papineau. Dr. Wolfred Nelson began the fight with a letter in *La Minerve* criticizing Papineau's conduct at Saint-Denis, suggesting that he had fled from the battle.

The *Rouges* returned the fire with a satirical play in *L'Avenir*, star-ring Cartier and Nelson, and entitled "La Tuque Bleue." The wollen cap with tassel was the emblem of the *habitant*. Cartier appears to have been the prime target of the counter-attack, and Nelson felt obliged to account for Cartier's conduct under fire:

> It is true that Henri Cartier (George Cartier's cousin) remarked that it would be better to retreat owing to the ravages caused by the en-emy, the lack of ammunition and the flight of a number of men in consequence. I strongly opposed this proposal and Henri Cartier vigor-ously supported us during the whole of the day. Georges Cartier never made allusion to retreat and like his cousin valiantly contributed to the success of the fight. Moreover, these gentlemen only left me when I was obliged to leave nine days after this time on the occasion of the second expedition against St. Denis when resistance had become impossible.[64]

L'Avenir attacked again, with an article signed by one Henri Laparre, a brother of Cartier's aunt Perrine,* who said that he had fought at Saint-Denis, and wanted to correct certain erroneous impressions: Papineau did not run away; on the contrary, it was Cartier (called George E.C. to avoid libel) who was the coward:

Imagine, Mr. Editor, the sight of Little George, dressed in an old

* Perrine Cartier drowned in the Richelieu by walking off a dock in her sleep.

homespun jacket big enough for a man, and covered over by an immense blue toque which fell halfway down his back and was as wide as it was long, which if need be could have covered him completely . . .

If you want a true picture of his bravery, imagine him in his real light, relegated for the time remaining in the battle to a little corner of Mme. Saint-Germain's house, in the south-west extremity, that is to say, in the part farthest away from the fight and from his comrades, trembling with all his might and main and demanding, indeed, imploring his cousin Henri C., for the love of God, don't leave me for an instant: and then begging Dr. Nelson to retreat, as we were all going to be massacred if we kept on fighting . . .

At around two o'clock in the afternoon, someone complained that we were out of cartridges, Little George right away heard this and told Dr. Nelson as quick as he could: Doctor, I have at home – I mean at my father's place, at Saint-Antoine – 500-2000 bullets. If you want them I'll go get them and I won't be long. The Doctor, who knew we needed help or were lost, gave him permission, and the little scamp, half-joyful, half-scared, came and told me he was going to Saint-Antoine to get some cartridges. But as it was cold, he would be grateful if I would lend him my gloves, which I did with pleasure. He returned one whole half-hour after he had been told that we were truly victorious, and that the troops had really fled.[65]

Cartier was enraged, and challenged Laparre, who denied writing the piece. He then stormed into the editorial offices of *L'Avenir*, demanding to know who had written the article, so that he could challenge him to a duel. After a quick backroom conference, one of the young editors, Antoine-Aimé Dorion's brother Eric, a diminutive man known as "L'Enfant Terrible," offered to take responsibility for the article, and came out to meet Cartier, who sneered, "I will not fight with a marmoset."[66] The real author of "La Tuque Bleue," twenty-three year old Joseph Doutre, a bright young law student newly graduated from the Collège de Montréal, then emerged and accepted Cartier's challenge. The time and place were arranged without further notice.

The phenomenon of the duel appears to have entered Canada *via* France, but by the nineteenth century, with the ascendancy of the British, pistols replaced the French rapier, and very little blood was shed. Young men, full of European ideals and an exaggerated sense of honour, would utter challenges at the drop of a hat, either to defend their reputation or their lady's virtue, or simply to make a name for themselves. Even before the duel was outlawed in Canada, it came to be well understood that most of them were travesties of the noble originals. Each combatant instinctively knew that he had to aim as close as possible without actually hitting his opponent. When duels began to be fought with gunpowder alone, duelling lost its appeal.

The inhabitants of Montreal had become quite blasé about duelling when, in May of 1838, they had a rude awakening. A lusty young bachelor, Major Henry Warde, had become infatuated with the wife of one Robert Sweeny, Captain of the Montreal Volunteer Cavalry, who had fought against Cartier at Saint-Denis. Sweeny was Her Majesty's Inspector of Potash, and the author of *Odds and Ends*, a slim volume of verse. One day Warde received a bouquet of flowers from another woman, but thinking they came from Mrs. Sweeny, he wrote her a passionate love letter. Sure that Warde was mad, she showed the letter to her husband, who challenged Warde to a duel. At dawn on May 22, at the old Montreal racecourse, Sweeny shot Warde dead with a bullet through the heart. While a coroner's jury tried to whitewash the whole business, Sweeny fled to Burlington, Vermont, then the home of many exiled *Patriotes*, where he remained until the commotion passed. It was not socially acceptable to kill people in duels, and tradition has it that Sweeny, haunted by the spectre of guilt and with the blood of a fellow officer on his hands, suffered horribly until his death two years later. His unfortunate widow, Charlotte Temple, eventually remarried - to Sir John Rose, Bart., Minister of Finance and Canada's business agent in London.

Warde's death greatly dampened the enthusiasm of the British for duelling, but young French Canadians, fresh from a rebellion, frustrated and full of their bravery, carried on the custom for another decade or two.

Duvernay was a veteran of the art – in 1836, he had received a very slight shoulder wound – and coached Cartier in the etiquette of the ritual. At dawn on a bright August day, Cartier and Doutre met up on top of Mount Royal. The terrain was measured, but as the two took their places, the Montreal police, led by Cartier's brother Damien, burst upon the scene and told the two to return to their respective homes and appear in court the following day. The magistrate dropped the charge of disturbing the peace, and let the chastened pair off with a warning.

A week later, the editors of *L'Avenir* let out a rumour that Cartier and his brother had planned the interruption of the duel. When he heard this, Cartier once again went on the warpath. The second duel, much more discreetly arranged, took place across the river on the Chambly road. Cartier and Doutre took their places, walked back twenty paces, turned and fired. Both shots missed, so the two resumed their places and were given fresh pistols by their seconds. This time, Cartier's shot was dangerously close – Doutre's hat was recovered from the ditch with a bullet hole clean through its brim.[67] The two, with their respective honours relatively intact, returned separately to Montreal, where they remained as bitter enemies as before.*

Their duel did not, however, end the problem of who was the coward

---

* Twenty-five years later, however, Joseph Doutre served as a pall-bearer at Cartier's funeral.

at Saint-Denis. Papineau claimed that Nelson had in fact advised him to flee, saying: "Do not expose yourself uselessly; you will be of more service to us after the fight than here."

On September 4, 1848, *La Minerve* countered the accusations of Doutre in "La Tuque Bleue," by declaring that more than fifty signatures from eyewitnesses had been collected to refute the article. Nelson wrote that he had seen Laparre the day of the battle,

> but only at the beginning; I don't remember seeing him later. Whether or not he hid himself in terror in a chimney, as *he himself swore, and afterwards escaped through a window* with the others, as was declared under oath, I can't say. But in any case, and I cannot fail to add it to the many other salient facts I have remarked on, he conducted himself with courage and valour during the battle.

Yet another witness was found to swear that he had seen Laparre so frightened that he could not hold a gun, and so had to hide in a chimney.

By the end of September, *La Minerve* had collected enough evidence to issue a pamphlet, entitled "An Impartial Resume of the Papineau-Nelson Discussion on the Events at Saint-Denis in 1837." In it Papineau was accused of having taken Nelson's horse and galloped away at the first approach of the British troops, and that his desertion led some men to flee the battle in despair. The pamphlet was heavily documented, full of notarized eye-witness statements that proved damaging to Papineau's story.[68] Yet Louis-Joseph Papineau was no military man, and in no way a leader of the armed uprising. Unlike Nelson, he had had no militia experience, and probably would have been useless at Saint-Denis. A month before the battle, he and Nelson had a difference of opinion in public, Nelson insisting that Papineau's doctrine of economic warfare was bankrupt, that the time was ripe to "melt our spoons into bullets."[69] At Saint-Denis, on the home ground of a rabid Dr. Nelson, Papineau's presence would have been extraneous.

The bitterness resulting from this paper battle between the radical and moderate Reformers, between the *Bleus* and the *Rouges*, split their ranks for good, and from then on they developed as separate political parties.

"The history of much of North America might be termed the history of the rivalry of New York and Montreal."   **10**

Arthur Lower

Cartier's early years in Parliament were remarkable for the evidence he gave of a growing interest in railway promotion and financing. He came by it honestly – his father had been a founding shareholder of Canada's first railway, the Champlain and St. Lawrence, a fifteen-mile long portage road, first horse-drawn but later steam-driven, that allowed easy forwarding from the Richelieu Valley to Montreal, and avoided the rapids of the lower Richelieu. Jacques Cartier believed in railways as the key to the future prosperity of Canada, and encouraged his lawyer sons by involving them in his negotiations. For the rest of his life, George-Etienne Cartier's intimate involvement with railways and his understanding of their relation to the economic well-being of the country was his most noteworthy feature. More than any other man, his politics were railways. More than any other, he was the father of the Canadian railway system.

Cartier had spoken at a huge mass meeting on the Champ de Mars in favour of the St. Lawrence and Atlantic Railway back in August of 1846, when he was solicitor for the company. At the same time, he was lawyer for the Sulpicians and had persuaded the Gentlemen of the Order to purchase large blocks of shares in the railway. His family, too, became shareholders. In his 1846 speech, he encouraged the crowd to do the same. "The prosperity of Montreal," he declared, "depends upon her being the entrepot for the trade of the West . . . We cannot keep it unless we secure the best means of transportation from the Western waters to the Atlantic." Montreal's gravest defect as a port was its winter closing. Although almost a thousand miles closer to Europe than New York, Montreal's traffic was hampered by the fog and shoals of the St. Lawrence as well as the ice that bound it for five months of the year. Its natural hinterland, the St. Lawrence basin, was being tapped and its trade siphoned off, through the gap to New York, by railroads and the Erie Canal. "I want to inspire you," he continued, "with the greater zeal for this truly national enterprise." Reviewing the recent commercial history of Europe, Cartier concluded that railways were an absolute necessity for prosperity. He urged his audience to invest in the road by haranguing them with a discussion of the progress of the United States:

> This nation, which formerly had little influence among the nations, is now among the greatest, on account of its political, commercial and industrial might. This is not the time to outline the reasons for its greatness, but we can surely note in passing that one of the main ones is the ease of communication by railway or canal. The Americans have not only enriched their country by activating commerce and industry, but have also peopled the country, by attracting emigrants from all parts of the globe. A man coming from Europe will certainly choose the most comfortable country, where he can easily get about – the emigrant knows that, in three or four days, he can go from one extremity of the United States to the other. I should also point out that every city that has the advantage of being the terminus of a railway sees the value of its property double . . .

There is no doubt that the same future awaits Montreal.[70]

On February 15, 1849, Cartier gave his maiden speech to the legislature, and of course, he spoke on railways, presenting a petition for aid from the public treasury for the completion of the St. Lawrence and Atlantic.[71] He explained his subject well, arguing that the sooner the line was finished the better, so that Canada's expensive canal system, already subsidized to the tune of £ 3,000,000 could be properly utilized. He elaborated for the first time on a subject that was to occupy him for the rest of his political career – the partnership between government and business for the construction of railways. The company, he explained, was not asking for direct financial subsidy, but rather for a guarantee so that it could raise enough working capital. Since many American state legislatures had given direct grants to railways, could not Canada provide at least a loan to help complete the St. Lawrence and Atlantic, to attract a piece of that commerce that all the cities of the south were competing for?

Later in 1849, Hincks was to pass the Guarantee Act, a bill that guaranteed, subject to certain conditions, a 6 per cent interest on half the bonds of railways greater than seventy-five miles in length, once half the line had been built. The St. Lawrence and Atlantic, the Great Western, and the Northern Railway all took advantage of this offer, to the amount of about $7,000,000, but in 1851, when the railway boom threatened to turn into a bubble, the government restricted subsidies to the main St. Lawrence valley trunk line, the Grand Trunk Railway, on the condition that half the railway's board be chosen by the government.

In 1851, Cartier became Chairman of the Standing Committee on Railways. Two years later, he was appointed solicitor of the Grank Trunk Railway, both of which positions he retained until his death. Today such a dual responsibility would be regarded as a flagrant conflict of interest, but it must be remembered that the line was partly a public work, and that the government was well-represented on the Grand Trunk board. Cartier never used his ambivalent position for self-enrichment, as evidenced by the fact that, after his death, his widow found herself almost penniless, and was obliged to petition the Canadian government for a pension. While other legislators made fortunes out of the expansion of railways, Cartier was animated by more complex political aspirations, chief amongst which was the creation and survival of a nation.

The expansion and construction of Canadian railways came at a time not only of threats to the new canal system from American railroads, but also from a depression caused by the Legislation of the free traders and "Little Englanders" in the British Parliament. Sir Robert Peel's budget of 1846, and the repeal of the Corn Laws, had wiped out most of the preferential duties lately imposed to promote imports from Canada.

At one fell swoop, the Canadian wheat and timber trades were crippled, and mills recently built to process grain before shipment were bankrupt. Jacob Keefer, who had built a number of mills along the Welland Canal to take advantage of preferential treatment, wrote to his partner William Hamilton Merritt, M.P.P. and promoter of the canal, "the sooner the connection between Great Britain and Canada is dissolved the better." [72] *La Minerve* echoed Keefer, although not in such strong terms: "If England no longer accords any economic privileges to her colonies," asked the paper, "what can keep the latter attached to the mother country for very long?" [73] Yet *La Minerve* and the Lower Canadian Reformers were prepared to accept Britain's new stance, because, with free trade, the British were also prepared to grant political freedom to British North America. No group could take better advantage of this freedom than the French Canadians. Balanced against this new freedom was the problem of immigration, surfacing as it had before 1837. By the autumn of 1847, more than 100,000 starving, disease-ridden and destitute refugees from the Irish famine had landed at Quebec. The French Canadians again felt that the wretched of the world were being dumped on their doorstep in yet another attempt to drown their way of life in a sea of strangers. Elgin described them as

> a frightful scourge to the province. Thousands upon thousands of poor wretches are coming here incapable of work, and scattering the seeds of disease and death. Already five or six hundred orphans are accumulated at Montreal, for whose sustenance, until they can be put out to service, provision must be made . . . Persons who cherish Republican sympathies ascribe these evils to our dependent condition as colonists. [74]

Canada was eventually reimbursed for its pains by the British Treasury, but the damage had been done, and many Canadians, not just republicans, began to contrast their miserable condition with the happy republic to the south. The Canadas were caught in an economic squeeze, ignored by the mother country and exploited by their neighbours to the south. According to Elgin, with his usual clarity of perception,

> Peel's Bill of 1846 drives the whole produce down the New York channels of communication, destroying the revenue which Canada expected to derive from canal dues, and ruining at once mill-owners, forwarders and merchants. The consequence is that private property is unsaleable in Canada, and not a shilling can be raised on the credit of the Province . . .
> What makes it more serious is that all the prosperity of which Canada is robbed is transplanted to the other side of the line, as if to make Canadians feel more bitterly how much kinder England is to the children who desert her, than to those who remain faithful . . . I believe that the conviction that they would be better off it they were

"annexed" is almost universal among the commercial classes at present, and the peaceful condition of the province under all the circumstances of the time is, I must confess, often a matter of great astonishment to me.[75]

So serious was the economic dislocation of the late 1840s that the population of Montreal actually decreased, from 65,000 in 1842 to 58,000 in 1851. Cartier watched with disgust as his legal business evaporated. Much of the firm's work was in real estate cases in which the brothers had prospered along with the city of Montreal. But during three short years, from 1846 to 1849, property values had dropped fifty per cent. Many citizens, in despair of their government, crossed the border over to the United States, simply abandoning farms, businesses, stock, and a nationality that could have flourished in time. The amazing thing is, as Lord Elgin noted, that the Canadians did not once again take up arms against Great Britain, in a much more serious conflagration than the tempest in a teapot of 1837. For men like Cartier, half-sympathetic to free trade, political liberty was the bait that made the trap worth while.

The man in the middle of this storm, the Daniel in what was treatening to become a den of lions, was the Governor General. Lord Elgin was a direct descendant of Robert Bruce, and son of the British Ambassador to Turkey who had rescued the marble friezes of the Parthenon from destruction in the Greek Revolution. He was well-connected with Lord Durham, having wooed and won Radical Jack's daughter. Lord Grey, the Colonial Secretary, who had offered him the post of Governor General of Canada, was Durham's brother-in-law. In spite of his radical Whig friends, Elgin described himself as "a Conservative, not because I am hostile to progress, not because I refuse to repair what is worn out or to modify what is defective in our political structure, but because I am convinced that in order to remedy effectively one must be determined to preserve religiously."[76]

Soon after his arrival in Canada in 1847, Elgin's sympathies had turned toward the Reformers and especially toward LaFontaine. In a letter to Grey in June of 1848, he had observed with his customary shrewdness that the "sentiment of French-Canadian nationality which Papineau endeavours to pervert to purposes of faction, may yet perhaps if properly improved furnish the best remaining security against annexation to the States . . . Was it, think you, love for England or hatred for these *sacré Bostonais* which stirred the French-Canadian mind in the Revolutionary War and again in 1812?"[77]

With these principles firmly in hand, Elgin went to work, playing for the balance of power he knew the solid bloc of French Canadian Reformers held. He actively supported the colonization movement in the Eastern Townships; and, on his advice, the Imperial Parliament repealed the article of the Union Act that had declared English to be the sole official language of government.

On January 18, 1849, Lord Elgin, smartly turned out in white-plumed hat and blue and silver tunic, strode out from the Château de Ramezay into the bright morning air and stepped into his royal sleigh. He sped down Rue Notre-Dame between rows of scarlet-jacketed troops to the Marché Sainte-Anne, the cavernous old market building that was to be temporary home to the Parliament of United Canada. There, seated under a huge red velvet canopy, he read the Speech-from-the-Throne. Then, breaking all the bounds of tradition, he repeated what he had said in the purest and most elegant French! Some of the Lower Canadian parliamentarians were moved to tears; Cartier, watching from the gallery with Hortense, felt the emotion of the members rising in his own eyes. Here, at last, was a man who knew what they wanted, what they had fought for.

When the 1849 session of Parliament opened, Elgin was expecting the worst, although he was fully aware of the support he would receive from the Lower Canadian Reformers in the conduct of government. He noted, with the satisfaction of a master strategist, that the split between Papineau and LaFontaine was becoming open and ugly. In the debate on the throne speech, Papineau rose and attacked the Reform program point by point, finally directing his fire against the reputation and character of Louis-Hippolyte LaFontaine. LaFontaine drew himself up, and in a rare flash of angry eloquence, gave Papineau a tongue-lashing that, some have said, effectively ended Papineau's political career:

> Here is a man who, obeying his ancient habit of pouring out outrageous insults, dares in the face of facts to accuse me and my colleagues of corruption, of a sordid love of office, of servility to power! To hear him speak, he alone is devoted to his country! I demand no gratitude from him; I demand it from no one; but since he calls himself so virtuous, I ask him to be just, and nothing more. Is he capable of being so? If I had accepted his system of exaggerated opposition where would the honourable member be today? He would still be in Paris, doubtlessly fraternizing with the Red Republicans, or the White Republicans, or the Black Republicans, and approving in turn all the constitutions that follow one after the other so often in France.[78]

The French language had been restored, and the rebels allowed to return home. One of those pardoned had been Papineau himself, and LaFontaine was proposing a general amnesty with reparations. The old Assembly of Upper Canada had passed a bill to pay for damages caused during the Rebellion, and now LaFontaine was, he told Papineau, working on a Rebellion Losses Bill that would give the same benefits to Lower Canada.

LaFontaine's "Act to provide for the Indemnification of Parties in Lower Canada where Property was Destroyed during the Rebellion in the Years 1837 and 1838" was intended to be the bill to test the power of majority rule: it was loaded, and it went off like a bomb. Dr. Wolfred Nelson, the hero of Saint-Denis, put in an outrageous claim for £ 12,000 for property damages and costs arising from his banishment to Bermuda – partly to make a philosophical point about the just causes of the Rebellion, and partly to thumb his nose at the enemies of the French Canadians. This was enough to drive the Tories in the Assembly into paroxysms of rage. To compensate "Dr. Well-Fed Nelson" would be nothing more than to justify treason. LaFontaine backtracked slowly, delighting in the game, but finally amended the bill to exclude payment to those convicted of treason or exiled. The Tories had been pushed to the brink, however, and some, like the gouty old warrior Sir Allan Napier MacNab, saw this "reward to rebels" as the final indignity.

MacNab, son of Governor Simcoe's chief aide, was born at Niagara-on-the-Lake in 1798. At the age of fifteen, he served in the War of 1812 with the British fleet on Lake Ontario. After his admission to the bar, he was elected to the Assembly of Upper Canada, and in 1837, became its Speaker, and commanded the provincial militia during the Rebellion. It was MacNab who cut the rebel steamer *Caroline* adrift above Niagara Falls, and in recognition of his exploits, he received a knighthood. As the wealthy president of the Great Western Railway, MacNab lived in the grand style in his extravagant mansion, Dundurn Castle.*

During the bitter debate on the bill, MacNab furiously gave voice to another frustration acutely felt by the Tories – the weight of a solid and unabashed bloc of Lower Canadians, who knew they could control the Union by exploiting divisions in Upper Canada. MacNab did not mince words:

> The Union has completely failed in its purpose. It was enacted with the sole motive of reducing the French Canadians under English domination. And the contrary effect has resulted! Those in favour of whom the Union was made are the serfs of the others! . . . I warn the ministry of peril, this ministry which treats me like a rebel when all the acts of my life show that I have striven to be loyal: I warn that the course it takes is likely to throw the people of Upper Canada into despair, and to make them feel that if they are to be governed by foreigners, it would be more advantageous to be governed by a neighbouring people of the same race than by those with whom it has nothing in common, neither blood, nor language, nor interests. [79]

MacNab's words were the rallying cry for a whole political generation, and taken up in the years before Confederation by the Clear Grit George Brown, frustrated in turn by the French Canadian solidarity developed by LaFontaine and Cartier.

Cartier took no part in the debate – it would have been foolhardy to

* Dundurn Castle is now an historical museum on the shores of Burlington Bay near Hamilton.

argue with MacNab – and remained calm and cool, savouring this sweet revenge, waiting for the inevitable triumph of responsible government, MacNab's statements were too much for Dr. Wolfred Nelson, however, and the giant rose and accused MacNab of being the kind who "cause revolutions, overturn thrones, drag crowns in the dust, and overthrow dynasties." [80] Nelson's point was taken just one step further by the brilliant Irishman William Hume Blake, perhaps the finest orator in the House. Cartier watched with amazement as two British gladiators fought it out over the honour of the French Canadians, and smiled as Blake's rhetoric hit home: "I am not come here," thundered Blake,

> to learn lessons of loyalty from honourable gentlemen opposite. I have no sympathy with the would-be loyalty of honourable gentlemen opposite, which, while it at all times affects peculiar zeal for the prerogative of the Crown, is ever ready to sacrifice the liberty of the subject. This is not British loyalty – it is the spurious loyalty which at all periods of the world's history has lashed humanity into rebellion . . . The expression "rebel" has been applied by the gallant knight opposite to some gentlemen on this side of the House, but I tell gentlemen on the other side that their public conduct has proved that they are the rebels to their constitution and their country. [81]

This was too much for MacNab. His face went purple with rage. "If the honourable member means to apply the word 'rebel' to me," he bellowed, "I must tell him it is nothing else but a lie!" He demanded an apology from Blake, but Blake refused. Amid shouts and insults, fist fights broke out in the gallery, and the Speaker quickly adjourned the House for the day. MacNab then challenged Blake to a duel, but Blake laughed him off. The young member for Kingston, John A. Macdonald – Elgin had described him as "one of the Tories who is becoming reasonable" – crossed the floor and gallantly issued a similar challenge to Blake. This gesture was wasted, for the Speaker soon re-established order and made the hotheads swear to keep the peace.

In the storm over the Rebellion Losses Bill, Papineau's *Rouges*, feeling a little left out, got into the act, warning the Reformers that their stance was hypocritical and doomed to failure. *L'Avenir* sneered that

> The people will repudiate you, because in America public men must be democrats first of all, because privileges, monopolies, despotism, are venomous plants to which the climate of America is deadly. A third party will form itself, stronger because it will have convictions, purer because it will soak itself in the ideals of liberty, equality and fraternity; and one which will crush you, Tories, and self-styled Liberals, which will grind you like powder, because you have attempted to check its growth. [82]

The bill was passed by a majority of forty-seven to eighteen, however

Elgin delayed Royal Assent as long as possible. On April 25, he felt he could no longer withhold sanction, and in the instant of his announcement, knew he would be better off back in Scotland. An ominous hush fell over the House, then slow murmuring, growing like thunder, then a storm of catcalls and booing erupted in the gallery, which soon was taken up by the crowd outside. The business of the day over, Elgin passed through a line of soldiers, rushed into his carriage and drove rapidly away. A mob on foot and horseback followed the coach, pelting it with stones, horse manure and rotten eggs – one hit him in the face – and chased him halfway up Mount Royal to "Monklands." After his narrow escape, Elgin remained a virtual prisoner in his Viceregal mansion, while down in the city the mood of the populace grew restless. The Montreal *Gazette* declared racial war; *L'Avenir* called on the populace to arm themselves to repel what it saw as a new Iroquois invasion; the atmosphere was charged with tension.

The Tories called for a meeting that night on the Place d'Armes. After dinner, Cartier walked down Rue Notre-Dame, a hat pulled down over his head, a greatcoat wrapped closely about him to ward off the April chill, avoiding the restless crowds loitering in the streets, and the troops of horse that galloped up and down keeping the people moving. The old market building was half-surrounded by a mob of about 1500 people, held back by a few city police. Hardly had he taken his seat in the House for the beginning of debate when there were shouts, the door to the chamber was forced open, guards pushed aside, and part of the mob gained entry, Cartier, with the others, was chased from his seat and led to safety out the back of the building, and into another, where troops guarded the members or escorted them home.

Inside the House, a "gutter Cromwell" lounged in the Speaker's Chair and proclaimed the dissolution of this "French Parliament." The Mace and a painting of Queen Victoria – which later turned up at MacNab's house – were passed to the crowd outside, busy pitching stones at the great windows of the building. The gas pipes were ripped open and the document room of the chamber set on fire. Soon flames roared out of the broken windows into the cold starry night. The mob held off the firefighters, and within a few hours, the old St. Anne market was a heap of smoking ruins, a gutted monument to the fury of the fight between races. The mob ruled for three days, until all its hatred and frustration had spent itself. The houses of Hincks and Nelson were wrecked; every window was broken in Baldwin's house; but for LaFontaine, the mob saved the greater part of its obscene fury; his stables were burned down, his furniture smashed to bits, every piece of china shattered, all his paintings were slashed, and every book in his well-stocked library torn apart and thrown into the street.

During this Tory revolution, Elgin kept a cool head. He felt that the whole nasty business was the work of the Orange Lodge, transferring the religious hatred of Ireland to Canada, and that the mob was backed by "the commercial men who desire annexation and the political leaders who want place." He very wisely refrained from using French Canadian militia to keep order, judging rightly that "all Lower Canada is with us, but the great object is to keep them quiet and prevent collision between the races." [83] Elgin would have little trouble keeping the French quiet; Cartier, whose house was spared the honour of a visit from the mob, was quite content to sit at home waiting for the Tories to cool off, playing with his two infant daughters, until the summer came and they could go on holiday to the banks of the Richelieu River.

MacNab hastened to England, where he was championed by Gladstone. On June 14, the British Parliament approved of Elgin's conduct by a large majority. Apart from a bit of egg on his face, the Governor General had come through unscathed. However, his social position among the British in Montreal suffered immensely: he was expelled from the Thistle Curling Club, and even though he came from one of the oldest and most distinguished families in Scotland, the select St. Andrew's Society in Montreal – whose President was the shipping magnate Hugh (later Sir Hugh) Allan – expelled him as Honourary Patron and returned "the paltry £ 10 he had given them for charity." [84] But as Lord Elgin had decided by this time to remove the seat of Parliament to Toronto and Quebec City, in rotation, the expulsion was probably not too difficult to bear.

The Rebellion Losses Bill had been the policy of his ministers, and he saw no reason to withhold sanction or give in to the wishes of a minority in Parliament, however dangerous their methods. And so it came about that a British Tory peer, despised by the Tories of Upper and Lower Canada, yet aided by former rebels against the Crown, successfully passed the concept of responsible government through its baptism of fire.

11   **"To render annexation by violence impossible, and by any other means as improbable as may be, is, as I have often ventured to repeat, the polar star of my policy."**

Lord Elgin, 1848

After the winning of responsible government, the inhabitants of both the Canadas had to face squarely the sentimental and economic problem, already recognized by the French, of their collective existence as a separate entity on the North American continent. By the mid-point of the nineteenth century, the scattered provinces of British North America stood at the very pivotal point of their survival as anything other than American. The choice offered by destiny to the leaders of these provinces was simple, although it took another ten years to hit home: either make your way together, using your own economic advantages toward gaining control of your future, or join immediately with the prosperous, generous United States of America.

Strange horns of a strange dilemma: either choose to be Canadian, for if you did not you would surely be American; or choose to be American, for if you did not you would starve. But what was a Canadian? For the French, the definition was simple, but for the British, almost impossible: their roots had not yet dug in deeply enough, and the tie with the mother country was still too strong. The British strategists had their own dilemma, as Elgin clearly saw:

> If we refuse to afford all the facilities we can for commercial intercourse between Canada and her powerful neighbour we must certainly create discontent inconsistent with our retention of the Colony – if on the other hand we encourage that intercourse there is every probability that Canada ere long will be Americanized by the influx of Yankees – between the two I have no hesitation in preferring the latter, and if ultimately it should lead to the separation of these provinces from the British Empire, let us hope that this may take place by amicable arrangement instead of by war, and may lead to a division of the Union – British America with some of the Northern States forming one Nation and the Southern States another – This would be no such bad result and in the mean time our trade would prosper and emigration flourish.[85]

But Elgin's speculation went too far – he reckoned without the French Canadians, who feared the American melting pot, whose choice was clear – *survivance* – survival – by whatever means possible. For all his brilliance and perspicacity, Elgin was still a British imperialist, who kept British interests uppermost in his mind. He reckoned without the desires of a people whose roots were too deep, whose families had already dwelt in the new world for eight, nine or ten generations, while their English-speaking neighbours had been largely born in the British Isles, and thought like British natives. Elgin reckoned without the political genius of a man like Cartier, who was to lead his people through Elgin's dilemma like Moses through the desert.

In the summer and fall of 1849, while the Reformers remained silent, other factions went to work through one of those cholera epidemics that swept the Canadas every few years. July saw the formation, in Kingston, of the British American League, whose members were principally Upper Canadian Tories of a more moderate cast than their leader, Sir Allan MacNab. John A. Macdonald, the only prominent member of his party to attend the founding convention, hoped that the League would "put its foot on the idea of annexation."[86] The program passed by the delegates was simple – "Protection to native industry and home manufactures – connection with Great Britain – Reciprocity with the United States in agricultural products – and repeal of the Municipal and Tariff monstrosities of the last session. No French domination, but equal rights for all." [87] The bogey of annexation was scarcely debated at all – only the Montreal delegates wanted the matter aired – and the convention closed by reaffirming its loyalty to the Crown, to the British connection, and to monarchical institutions and the mixed forms of government of the parliamentary system.

At its second session in November, much of the League's discussion and debate centred around the idea of a federative or legislative union of all the British North American colonies. One delegate, J.W. Gamble, stated that "a union of this kind would leave the people nothing to desire from annexation, because, in a few years, this country would be in quite as prosperous a state as the other side of the line." [88]

In Montreal, however, Tories, Liberals and *Rouges* came together in unholy alliance to publish the Annexation Manifesto, urging a "friendly and peaceful separation from the British connection, and a union upon equitable terms with the great North American confederacy of sovereign states." [89] Who was annexing whom? Papineau's band of followers came out strongly behind the idea, *L'Avenir* declaring that

Since the 92 Resolutions, we have not seen a better statement of the principles and a more faithful picture of the needs of the country. It appeals to all classes and parties to forget their former reasons for dissension, to unite, in order to obtain what the country needs most urgently, prosperity with annexation. [90]

The one thousand who signed the Manifesto were united by a strange sort of nationalism gone wrong. They wished for independence and prosperity, yet ignored the other possibility – that of a federal union of the provinces of British North America, a union that might give them everything they asked or needed. The leaders of the movement, tired of being ruined by every whim of British or American legislators, wanted a showdown, wanted action, wanted the British to repent of their free trade heresies and the Americans to stop scalping their industries. Prosperity was the problem, and if prosperity would not come to the Canadas, then the Canadians, orphans of the free trade storm, would go to prosperity, to the bosom of another empire.

At the first meeting of the Annexation Association, on December 12, 1849, the merchant John Redpath – soon to become a sugar tycoon – was elected Chairman, in grotesque combination with the two Dorion brothers, who were Vice-Secretary and Vice-Treasurer. The *Rouges*, thrilled by the European revolutions of 1848, were perhaps attracted to the movement more by a love of Republicanism than by any overwhelming desire for prosperity.

Most of the Annexationists were members of the mercantile elite of Montreal – Redpaths, Molsons, Workmans, Torrances – not all Tory but certainly well-off. In addition, a future Prime Minister, J.J.C. Abbott, and four future Cabinet Ministers, John Rose, D.L. Macpherson, Luther Holton and A.T. Galt also signed the Manifesto. There were a significant number of Americans in Montreal who provided further support. Underlying the whole affair, from the English point of view, was their desire to rid themselves of French domination by joining the United States. Militia officers who signed the Manifesto or who were members of the movement soon found that their annexation sympathies were considered treasonable, but Elgin's only action against the movement was to deprive these officers of their commissions.

For those who signed the Manifesto, annexation was more than a slap to the wrist of the mother country; it was a desperate political ploy designed to cause outrage and action. Some did not believe the Manifesto would have any result, but signed it anyway. Even in their first generation as Canadians, many immigrants felt the stirrings of a new sense of nationhood. In the beginning it took the nature of either pro- or anti-Americanism, the latter based on simple hurt pride. An English traveller, James Silk Buckingham, who visited Canada for two months in 1839, noted this particularly. In fact, in the town of Toronto, "every opportunity is seized of disparaging America and Americans, and speaking of them with unmeasured contempt." Travelling on to Montreal, he found that "there is one point on which nearly all the British Canadians appear to agree, and that is, in abuse of the Americans, toward whom the feeling of hatred and contempt seems to be universal, and to be expressed on all occasions."

Buckingham pointed out to Canadians that travellers were constantly comparing Canada with the United States, and downgrading the economic progress of the former. The Canadians invariably replied that any differences between the two countries were caused not by the enterprise of the Yankees, but by "English liberality in lending a large amount of capital to carry forward their great public works, which capital, if it had been invested in Canada instead of the United States, would have produced results equally advantageous to this country." [91]

Perhaps the Annexation Manifesto had its desired result, for English capital, which had financed so many American canals and railroads, at last began to flow into Canada in the years after 1849.

There was opposition to the Manifesto in Lower Canada, but little in the upper province, where it was largely ignored. On October 15, *La Minerve* published a counter-manifesto protesting the activities of the Association. Cartier helped to draw up the document, and with Nelson, Morin and nine others, attached his signature to it, appealing to

the wisdom, the love of order, and the honour of the inhabitants of this country . . . to oppose by every means in their power an agitation tending to subvert a constitution which, after having been long and earnestly sought for, was received with feelings of deep gratitude toward the Imperial Government – an agitation, moreover, which can result in nothing beyond a continuation of the scenes which this city has already so severely suffered.

Cartier and his friends were warning that annexation would lead to civil war, and seriously threatening that if it ever came about, they were prepared to fight and die in defense of their hard-won constitution. They were supported in their views by none other than Queen Victoria, who, according to Lord Elgin in his 1850 throne speech, was prepared "to assert all the authority which belongs to her for the purpose of maintaining the connection of Canada." [92]

12   "A reformer with a completed program is a Conservative."

Arthur Lower

In the decade of the 1850s, prosperity returned to the Canadas from three directions: from increased American and British demand due to the Reciprocity Treaty and the Crimean War; from Britain's repeal of the Navigation Acts, which lowered transportation costs and opened the St. Lawrence to world shipping; and above all, from the avalanche of capital that poured into British North America in an orgy of railway building. This was largely British money, primed and prodded loose by a more enlightened Colonial Office. It was to revolutionize the Canadas.

With renewed growth and the successful attainment of responsible government, Baldwin and LaFontaine realized that they had outlived their usefulness – indeed, that the Reform Party had lost its *raison d'être* – and so they made the decision to retire, Cartier spoke at a dinner in honour of his chief, and praised LaFontaine for having "eliminated the system of arbitrary government, and replaced it with the one we have today, pure representative government." In Upper Canada, the Reform Party lost no time in splitting into two groups led by Francis Hincks and George Brown. Hincks was a lean, sharp-featured Toronto financier, born in Ireland, and the only one of a family of five boys who did not enter the church. He made his mark early, not only by his head for figures, but from his ferocious oratory in the legislature, where he was known as "The Hyena." Where Hincks was stoop-shouldered and small, George Brown was a six foot four giant whose moral rectitude was only matched by his physical stature. Born in Alloa, Clackmannan, Scotland, he came to Canada with his brother Gordon, and in 1844, established the Toronto *Globe*. A dogmatic Free-Kirker who abhorred any connection between Church and State, he soon clashed with the moderate Reformers and made himself head of the Clear Grit group, allied tenuously with the Lower Canadian *Rouges*, and in opposition to Hincks and most of the rest of the politicians of Canada.

The members of MacNab's Tory party eventually followed the example of their brothers in Britain, and, under the leadership of John A. Macdonald, painfully adjusted themselves into more moderate Conservatives.

In Lower Canada, Antoine-Aimé Dorion rose to the leadership of the *Rouges*, and the Reformers, known increasingly as *Bleus*, selected Augustin-Norbert Morin, who had followed Duvernay as editor of *La Minerve*, to step into the large shoes of Louis-Hippolyte LaFontaine. The gentle, tireless Morin was an old friend of Cartier, had witnessed his marriage, and was married to Cartier's cousin Adèle.*

Strangely enough, the prospect of having Canada fall into their laps by annexation alarmed many Americans, by this time the proud new proprietors of Oregon, Texas, and gold-rich California. The westward expansion of the United States had occupied much of its people's collective energy, however as the steamroller of expansion stopped at the Pacific, some of that energy turned, in its momentum, south to Mexico and north to Canada. According to some warhawks ranged under the banner of "Manifest Destiny," America would soon stretch from the North Pole to the Isthmus of Panama. But other, more sinister forces began to rise within the American Union, and for the next ten years, a succession of governments tottered in delicate balance between North and South. If ever admitted into the Union, non-slave holding states such as the Canadas would disturb this balance in favour of the North. President Zachary Taylor saw this clearly, and during the annexation crisis, kept the United States scrupulously aloof from the dispute. Perhaps the main reason, then, for the American decision to enter into a reciprocal trade agreement with Canada was this desire to keep Canada happy and prosperous and unamerican, at least for the time being.

When the annexation squall had blown itself out, most Canadian commercial men vowed that they would never again be caught in a leaky boat on the open seas.This was the essence of their nationalism, financial at first, but as they came to forget the fog and grime, the mists and moors of old Britain, and began to know and love the crisp snow under their sleigh's runners, the ferocious heat of summer, and the great rivers and forests, as they came to forge their own lives and cement their own social relationships, they forgot the old order, the old land, and only half-remembered why they had ever left at all. Now they were discovering themselves, defining their new limits, and annexation was only a foray into the possible. The horrors of the American Civil War, reported

* the Laurentian town of Ste. Adèle is named after her.

in lurid detail ten years later in the Canadian press, killed off any remnants of annexationist sentiment in Canada, and by the time the depression which followed that war made itself felt, the majority of them were ready with an answer – Confederation.

As the new half-century began, natural demand from such burgeoning cities as Chicago for Canadian wheat and timber led to economic recovery and an unprecedented boom. To take advantage of American demand, the British Colonial Office enforced the old Fisheries Convention and forced the Americans to the bargaining table. In 1854, Lord Elgin visited Washington, and by liberally oiling Southern senators with champagne and dazzling their wives and daughters with gala balls, convinced them that reciprocal trade would not mean annexation, but rather would keep the provinces of British North America prosperous, and out of the Union. The Northerners got their fish, and British North Americans their treaty.

Re-elected to Verchères in 1851, Cartier continued to throw his weight behind the Reform Ministry, now led by the co-Premiers* Hincks and Morin. The following year, he was offered the cabinet post of Commissioner of Public Works, but declined, as he explained to the House, "for personal reasons. The meagre stipend attached to this post is one. Small salaries have always resulted in the advancement of the rich, or those without much influence in society. I have the good and perhaps ill fortune to be neither rich nor poor, and to accept this trust would impose sacrifices not only on myself, but on those who have entrusted the conduct of their affairs to me." [93] Perhaps the real reason he declined was that the position of Chairman of the Railway Committee was a more challenging one, and work involved in the establishment of the Grand Trunk Railway much more fruitful toward building up a base of political support for himself, and a strong economy for his country. A year later he again rejected the offer of a cabinet post held out by Morin, just as he had twice refused to run for Parliament in the 1840s, until his financial position was secure. He wished to see a more professional government, paying realistic salaries, and waited until 1855 before accepting the post of Provincial Secretary, at what he then thought was adequate remuneration.

Cartier had enough on his platter as it was. Besides being solicitor for the Sulpicians, the St. Lawrence and Atlantic Railway, and the municipal council of the town of Longueuil, he was a trustee of the Montreal City and District Savings Bank, a Director of the Canada Life Assurance Company and a Commissioner of the Port of Montreal, as well as being involved in a firm called the British American Mining Association, with properties in the Eastern Townships. And so, realizing the transitory

* Governments of the day were expected to be led by the leaders of the majority in each section of the Canadas. The leader chosen to form this two-headed monster was described as "Prime Minister."

nature of the Hincks-Morin Ministry, he was content to wait his turn for power, building up a financial base, all the time watching the shifting political fortunes in the two Canadas, getting the feel and the measure of the younger English-speaking politicians he knew he would have to work with.

"Far away to the South is heard the daily scream of the steam-whistle – but from Canada there is no escape: blockaded and imprisoned by Ice and Apathy, we have at least ample time for reflection – and if there be comfort in Philosophy, may we not profitably consider the PHILOSOPHY OF RAILROADS?" **13**

T.C. Keefer

The idea of the Grand Trunk Railway arose from four directions: the desire of the Port of Montreal to capture more western trade; the feeling that Montreal's winter outlet, Portland, Maine, could divert more trade away from New York and Boston; the willingness of the Barings and Glyns, London financial agents of the Union, to finance the line; and, at the propitious moment, the readiness of the British engineering firm of Peto, Brassey, Jackson and Betts – builders of theatres, dockyards, Nelson's Column in Trafalgar Square, the British Houses of Parliament and railways all over the world – to build the Grand Trunk without further delay. The firm's equipment was idle, and when they saw the opportunity in Canada, they moved to exploit it. One of their first steps was to engage George-Etienne Cartier as their legal counsellor.

The Grand Trunk project was first suggested to Hincks, who threw his energies behind it. Because of his experience with the St. Lawrence and Atlantic, Cartier had been approached to serve as solicitor for the railway, and in the 1852 session, he drew up and presented the first of his many railway acts to Parliament – his "Act to incorporate the Grand Trunk Railway of Canada." The firm was capitalized at £ 1,000,000 and was given a government subsidy of £ 1,000 a mile, to build a railway from Hamilton in Upper Canada to just opposite Montreal. Further of Cartier's acts provided for the amalgamation of other lines with the Grand Trunk, and the construction of the mammoth Victoria Bridge, which brought the railway into Montreal proper. Canadians were to hold the majority of seats on the board of directors, although only about 2 per cent of the stock was eventually sold in Canada.

After further negotiation, the Company was recapitalized to the tune of £ 9,500,000 and a prospectus issued for the London money market. Its preamble was the quintessence of Victorian optimism:

This great and comprehensive scheme of railway communication throughout the most wealthy, populous and important colonial dependency of Great Britain is not now offered as a new project to the public. It comes with the guarantee of the province of Canada, which has embarked upwards of £ 2,000,000 sterling on the project; it is supported by the most intelligent, far-sighted men in the colony; and it has the security of nearly half a million sterling of private Canadian capital invested therein.[94]

Unfortunately, the prospectus did not fully take into account the expenditures of the line, and the estimated profits later proved over-inflated. Cartier wisely bought only a few shares, which he soon sold.

Of the nine men present at the first meeting of the Grand Trunk board of directors in Quebec on July 11, 1853, seven were or had been cabinet ministers, including the Premier, Hincks, and Cartier's life-long friend and intimate colleague, Etienne-Pascal Taché.

Much of the burden of the line's later difficulties was borne by the London banking firms of Baring Brothers, and Glyn, Mills. The Barings, in particular, had bankrolled much of the railway construction south of the border, and many states of the union were held tightly on the Baring financial leash. They intermarried with Americans, and became, through members of the family such as the Lords Ashburton, Cromer and Revelstoke, the real power behind Imperial policy in North America. Their prosperity was bound up with the peace and stability of the continent, and when the need arose, they could wield their awesome power like warlords. When they decided, through the British Colonial Office, that Canada should eventually be a prosperous transcontinental nation, that this was in their financial interests, then Canada would quite probably be so. As Cartier was beginning to see, the aspirations of the French Canadian people could be served by the same ends that the Barings had in view. From that time forth, he was the chief agent of their grand imperial design.

The Barings could mount a fine lobby, as their flamboyant advocate Sir Edmund Hornby described on one visit to the Canadas in the 1850s:

Barings asked me to go out to Canada to argue a case before the House of Representatives at Quebec – gave me a thousand guineas on my brief and paid all expenses. This work occupied about ten weeks. I won my case and returned. Among the ministers I made many friends – John (usually called Jack) Macdonald, Sir Francis Hincks, Sir Allan MacNab, Cartier, Brown a journalist – all able men with unlimited powers of consuming champagne.[95]

"Upon my word," declared Hornby, after warming up the colonials further, "I do not think there was much to be said in favour of the Canadians over the Turks when contracts, places, free tickets on railways, or even cash was in question." [96]

As insiders, the Barings were able to make themselves and their important associates wealthy through stock options and the awarding of fat construction contracts. It is no coincidence that the Webster-Ashburton Treaty, which gave the United States the border they wanted with New Brunswick, was their work, and in their interests; no coindence that Francis Baring, Chancellor of the British Exchequer in the 1840s, ensured that the family bank would become loaners-in-chief to the provincial government of Canada. In fact, the Union Act of 1840 was partly their work. Upper Canada, whose securities they had largely underwritten, was practically bankrupt before the Union, and it suited the Barings to shift the burden of payment onto the exchequer of the more prosperous lower province.

Although George Brown's newspaper felt that "whoever may get the milk, the Barings and Glyns will have the cream," [97] these merchant bankers had much worse luck in the Canadas than in the United States. They sustained many of the early losses of the Grand Trunk out of their own pockets, particularly in the panic of 1857, but through the efforts of Cartier and others, who saw that the road was essential for Canada's survival and prosperity, better management was obtained.

One obstacle to the British dominance in railway building came from such native capitalists as Alexander Galt, David Macpherson, Luther Holton, and Casimir Gzowski, who, by some clever incorporations, threatened at one time to duplicate the Grand Trunk route. The smart colonials were neatly and happily absorbed, however, to the financial well-being of all concerned – it cost the Company £ 2,250,000 to buy out Alexander Galt – and construction proceeded rapidly with their help. By the end of 1853, 250 miles of track had been laid; by 1860, 1,894 miles – the longest single railway in the world – from Sarnia on the west to Rivière-du-Loup on the east. It was a difficult road to build: the Brassey engineering firm lost £ 1 million on the job. But the colonials had proven their worth, and a shotgun wedding between railways and governments, politicians and promoters consummated, largely through the mediating efforts of Cartier's Standing Committee on Railways.

The first casualty of this marriage was the politician Francis Hincks. The wedding went off well, but by 1854, opposition politicians began to criticize the fiscal conduct of the Hincks-Morin ministry, and Cartier himself was criticized by William Lyon Mackenzie as being a paid agent of the Grand Trunk, which, of course, he was. In 1854, the ministry decided to seek a new mandate and called an election.

Animated by his hatred of Hincks and the new railway moguls, the up-and-coming Clear Grit George Brown went so far as to throw his weight behind Conservative candidates in some ridings. In particular, Brown was furious at the French Canadian control of the conduct of government. "Can anyone fail to see," he pleaded in the *Globe*, "that so long as Lower Canada has one-half of the representatives, and four-fifths of the Lower Canadian members vote as one man – that by political divisions of Upper Canada the views of a compact body will control the progressive opinions of the majority of the legislature?"[98] Historians have criticized Hincks for not offering Brown a cabinet post, but the truth was, no French Canadian Reformer would sit in the same cabinet with a man of such fiery opinions as the following, expressed in the *Globe* of June 18, 1853:

> Rome is blindness, Rome is intolerance, Rome is despotism, and we will permit none of them to exist in Canada by force of law. Let Papists preach and pray, build churches and print, if they please, it is free to all to do so, but no giving of Protestant money to aid their work, lending the influence of government to help it on, no granting of more power over the misguided people, save what is yielded by their superstitious reverence for the priest.

Yet Brown's opinions were gaining ground over those of Francis Hincks, who waited for the elections with some sense of trepidation.

The elections, held in July and August, 1854, gave no party a clear mandate. Cartier had entered the campaign with a heavy heart. On July 9, his new baby daughter, Reine-Victoria,* had died, possibly a victim of the cholera epidemic of that year. Another victim was his father-in-law, the gentle *Patriote*, Edouard Fabre. Yet in spite of his family tragedies, he fought hard, and was an easy winner in Verchères.

At opening division, the House sat as follows:

Government: 25 Hincksite Reformers – Upper Canada
　　　　　　　35 Morin Ministerialists (including 9 English) –
　　　　　　　Lower Canada
　　　　　　　3 Independent Liberals led by Alexander Galt

Left Opposition: 14 Clear Grits (Brown) – Upper Canada
　　　　　　　　　16 Rouges and Liberals (Dorion) – Lower Canada

Right Opposition: 25 Conservatives (MacNab) – Upper Canada
　　　　　　　　　　9 Moderate Reformers (Cauchon) – Lower
　　　　　　　　　　Canada[99]

Hincks and Morin decided, as a first trial of strength, to put the name of George-Etienne Cartier forward as their candidate for Speaker. In the debate over Cartier's candidacy, William Lyon Mackenzie rose to the attack, arguing that they should "leave Mr. Cartier on the floor of the House to draw his salary of £ 1,000 as the creature of the Grand Trunk

* "Queen Victoria"

Company, instead of controlling the influence of Parliament in its favour."[100] Cartier was defeated by a close margin, sixty-two to fifty-nine, and Hincks, who had no love for the candidate proposed by a rare alliance of Conservatives and Grits, put his vote and those of his supporters behind Louis Sicotte, once a Reformer and now the candidate of the *Rouges*. The Hincks-Morin ministry was able to carry on with Dorion's lukewarm support until September 7, when it was defeated on a question of privilege.

The election had solved nothing, and a new one was now possible, to recapture or shake out the so-called "loose fish" (independents) who plagued the formation of government and weakened Parliament. Elections in this period were not all held on the same day, and not until 1874 was the secret ballot used. Safe constituencies usually voted a week or two before the others, to give the illusion of a victory sweep for the party in power, to give those who feared a return to economic chaos a chance to vote for the party most likely to succeed. In the 1850s, the electorate generally disliked partisanship, and voted for winners, yet sectionalism and group government were the order of the day. While putting on the aspect of a united front, the ministerialists were constantly, desperately trying to keep hold of the "loose fish," members whose votes could not be completely relied upon, who had to be caught in the net of patronage. Parties at this time were simply loosely-bound interest groups, rather than the relatively well-oiled machines of today.

There were certainly favours to be had from government in the 1850s. In an orgy of development and speculation, perhaps as much as $100,000,000 was dumped into the Canadas for the construction of railroads. By late 1854, the Grand Trunk was paying out £ 15,000 a day in wages alone. Because he was so close to the reins of railway patronage, Cartier was able to marshal the solid political support and accumulate the basic political capital that was to last him for the next twenty years, until the capital and the man were both spent and exhausted, before a new and greater railway finally put an end to his life and career.

Over the summer, Hincks had lost six supporters to George Brown. Now, to head off an election, he was forced to bargain for a coalition with the Conservatives, to prevent them from joining with the Grits and *Rouges*, either to rule – an unlikely prospect – or to force the election he so desperately feared. And so the props of politics began to be shuffled about backstage, just as Elgin had predicted four years earlier:

> If Clear Grittism absorbs all the hues of Upper Canadian liberalism, the French, unless some interference from without checks the natural course of events, will fall off from them and form an alliance with the Upper Canadian Tories.[101]

On June 20, Cartier warned the Conservatives on the floor of the House that they had not yet "shown that they are ready to form such a coalition. If so," he threatened, "they would have to renounce many of their principles." But Cartier clearly saw that there was no other way out, since Lower Canada would never stand for an alliance with the Grit George Brown, "a man who daily insults in such outrageous manner our beliefs and our ideals." [102]

On September 11, 1854, an alliance was formed, led by MacNab and Morin, eventually to be christened the Liberal-Conservative Party, Cartier, still reeling slightly from finding himself in bed with Tories, argued for the record that it was not really a coalition. On September 20, he took to the floor of the House and warned the Conservatives that French Canada did not recognize the existence of such a thing:

> There has not been for us any coalition. We still support the same ministers. The Lower Canadian section of the Cabinet was not affected by the vote of non-confidence last June. That section of the Cabinet was then sustained by a majority of the Reformers of Lower Canada, it still counts a majority in the House, and it has never been condemned by them. For these reasons I believe that it is wrong to say that the Government is a coalition Government: as far as concerns Lower Canada to call it so is a false designation. It is true that a coalition has taken place in Upper Canada and that the Hon. Mr. Morin has accepted it, I do not like coalitions. I am a party man. I like a government which represents my sentiments and my principles. At the same time I admit that a coalition in Upper Canada has become necessary, and I will support it. [103]

Cartier still hoped that the old Reform Party could be kept solvent, but the writing was on the wall, even for the old-fashioned Tories across the House.

In October, newspapers reported that Francis Hincks had received a subscription of more than a thousand shares in the Grand Trunk before the shares had been offered to the public. Hincks replied that he did not know of the existence of the shares, but Sir Morton Peto of the Brassey engineering firm explained that he had personally alloted the shares to Hincks without his knowledge, and had paid for them out of his own pocket. Fair enough, but when it was later alleged that Hincks had purchased land near the Quebec City terminus, and had profited by the sale of some £ 10,000 worth of City of Toronto bonds, bought earlier at a 20 per cent discount, his reputation was severely damaged. A committee of the House whitewashed the case. John Ross, president of the Grand Trunk, said that the rumours concerning Hincks were broadcast by local contractors whose pride had been hurt by the employment of English engineers. However, even though Hincks had given a great deal of himself toward the financing and construction of railways, his political career now seemed finished. Only after a long fifteen-year exile as

Governor of the Barbados and British Guiana did he return to Canadian politics, at Cartier's invitation and insistence, as Finance Minister of the Dominion of Canada.

With the exception of an interval or two, the Liberal-Conservative Party "coalition" was to hold power until 1896 and the death of John A. Macdonald. For the first twenty years of its existence, it survived largely through Cartier's skilfully managed bloc of support in Lower Canada and then Quebec. Like the Hincks-Morin government before it, the MacNab-Morin ministry that took office in 1854 was also of a transitory nature. The real hopes of the alliance were pinned on the persons of two forty-one year old members of the legislature – John Alexander Macdonald and George-Etienne Cartier.

ditto.   ns J....,
ditto.   10 February.   ~...
The Inland postage to Halifax, on letters for Europe must be paid, else they cannot be forwarded.

Post Office, Quebec, 6th. November 1807.

TO BE LET for two or more years—The manufacturing MILL of JACQUES CARTIER having 5 pair of Stones capable of grinding 40 to 50 thousand bushels of grain.   Also another Mill with two pair of Stones capable of grinding 15 to 20 thousand bushels of grain, with bakehouse, kilns and stores.——TO BE SOLD on easy terms : A STONE HOUSE neatly fitted up containing 4 stories and two Cellars with every conveniency for a large family well calculated for a whole sale or retail merchant situated in Fort Street No. 23. Also a STONE HOUSE in same Street having 3 stories and Cellar with a WHARF in front towards the River adjoining the old Custom house: enquire on the premises No. 23, Fort Street
Quebec 21st January, 1808.

Quebec *Gazette*.

Cartier in 1855 (PAC).

PART TWO

SIAMESE TWINS
(1854-1868)

"The truth is that you British Lower Canadians never can forget that you were once supreme - that Jean Baptiste was your hewer of wood and drawer of water. You struggle, like the Protestant Irish in Ireland, like the Norman invaders in England, not for equality, but *ascendancy* - the difference between you and those interesting and amiable people being that you have not the honesty to admit it . . . . Treat them as a nation and they will act as a free people do - generously."

John A. Macdonald to
Brown Chamberlin of
the Montreal *Gazette*,
January 21, 1856

"I liked Cartier very much. Whenever I met him socially, he was very nice to me, but he had an insufferable mania. Because he knew I was quite a good musician, he would always ask me to play the piano at his gatherings. There was no question about it – 'Come now, do it as a favour to me. I want to show the English, who know how to make money better than we do, that we are finer artists than they are.'"

The wife of Senator B____
to Alfred de Celles

At the halfway point in the century, Cartier's Montreal was booming. One traveller described it as "presenting one mass of glittering steeples, domes and massive stone wharves, fully a mile in extent, and the most costly and substantial in North America. Shipping of every size and nation, crowds of steamers, American and English, bateaus, canoes, timber rafts, schooners in full sail, all covered the surface of the river; and the city, with its dark stone buildings and iron shutters, gave an impression of ancient grandeur." [1] Cartier was determined to preserve and increase its prosperity, in the face of new dangers and new challenges.

One of Lord Elgin's last acts in 1854 had been to summon Sir Allan MacNab to form a ministry. Seven years before, Elgin had predicted, with his customary foresight, that the English and French moderate conservatives would inevitably unite. MacNab easily succeeded in forming an alliance between his followers and the Lower Canadian Reformers under Morin. It was as significant a union as one today between the Liberals and Conservatives.

There remained two basic reforms necessary to put the Canadas on the road to independence: secularization of the clergy reserves and the abolition of seigneurial tenure. Both questions were settled without too much difficulty. The reserves, granted by Pitt after the Conquest to provide support for the established Church of England, were an unpopular drag on land settlement, but they were restored eventually to the Crown by making provision for clergymen who depended on their revenue for a living.

Seigneurial tenure in Lower Canada was a much more difficult proposition, but Cartier, eager for the task, managed to hammer out a settlement where the seigneurs were eventually paid off through a brain-child of Hincks, the Municipal Loan Fund. The fund had been established to allow towns and cities to make improvements in their public works or to subscribe to railways that would benefit their particular locality. To balance the account between the two sections, an amount equal to what it cost to buy out the *seigneurs* was deposited in the Upper Canada Loan Fund.

Although the seigneurial system had contributed to the colonization and stability of Lower Canada, it had outlived its usefulness. The demands of most *seigneurs* on the *habitants* had come to be if not oppressive, then at least annoying. The *habitant, censitaire,* or tenant was free to sell his farm, but the *seigneur* was entitled to the *droit de lods et ventes,* one-twelfth of the selling price, a fee which did not encourage the *habitant* to make improvements before sale, nor allow easy land transfer. In addition, the *seigneur* had the right to all running water and the erection of mills. Tenants were obliged to have their grain ground at the *seigneur's* mill, and owed him any stone or wood demanded from their holdings. Although rental and service obligations to the *seigneur* were minimal, and generally did not leave the *habitant* in a servile position, these "feudal" holdovers, once so necessary for the survival of the colony, were severely hampering agricultural and social development.

LaFontaine was invited to preside over the court of indemnification, and when the court finished its great work seven years later, it had cost the province more than $10,000,000 to bring French Canada into the modern world. To Cartier, fearful of the consequences of maintaining the system any longer, it was money well spent. "We have the satisfaction," he declared, "of being able to suppress the system with the least amount of trouble and bloodshed."[2] He had always believed in the broadest possible ownership of land as the foundation of prosperity and stability. Already, with the prospect of Confederation forming in his mind, he began to push the Lower Canadian caucus to work toward putting the province on an even footing with her more enterprising brother to the west.

At the close of 1854, Lord Elgin announced his retirement as Governor General. He was to round out his brilliant career in missions to China, Japan and India, where he was Viceroy until his death in 1863. To succeed him, Elgin recommended his friend and old Oxford examiner, the scholarly, donnish Sir Edmund Walker Head, who was moved up from the Lieutenant-Governorship of New Brunswick.

Although he was to involve himself deeply in politics, perhaps too much so for a man in his position, the tall, stately Head was the right choice for the post. As the American fact loomed larger before British

North America, as skilful diplomacy and defensive precautions assumed greater importance, Head worked hand in hand with the colonial politicians, and especially Cartier, toward putting the provinces on a sound military and economic footing.

Head was cautious toward the United States, but he came by his caution honestly. His grandfather had emigrated to Charleston, South Carolina in the 1760s, and in 1775 was elected a delegate to the Second Continental Congress. But he was a loyalist, and refused to take his seat. The rebels eventually confiscated his property and clapped him into jail. A year later, he was back in England, having barely escaped with his life. With such a family history, it is hardly surprising that the new Governor General had a profound distrust of American motives with regard to British North America. In a letter to a friend shortly after his appointment, he said that it was the policy of the Americans "always to smooth down difficulties in private communications with foreign ministers and then, if popularity requires it, to burst out in an entirely different sense with some bombastic assertion of American rights." Head held a healthy respect for their brand of diplomacy, and worried that "they may commit some desperate act in the hope of reviving popularity by an anti-British cry." [3] In short, he felt they could not be trusted.

In his days at Oxford, Head had been known as a "mirthful" and brilliant young liberal, but attacks of epilepsy and a bad heart had transformed him into a rather shy, retiring, irritable intellectual. He had written a *Handbook of Spanish Painting* and a volume of poetry, and during his stay in Canada, managed to find time to write a treatise explaining the different uses of "shall" and "will." Yet in spite of such seeming preciosity, Head was a man of deep emotions, of heart and soul, and the challenge of Canada's predicament gave him new life.

Head was to become an intimate friend of Cartier and Macdonald, and together they set the scattered provinces of British North America on the road to nationhood. At this early date the road was not a smooth steel track carving through the countryside and leaping across rivers. Cartier was to discover that it led through a political jungle, and would have to be hacked out every inch of the way. It was a path away from the south and its border, a way that had to be built for his people to survive. Above all, it was a journey of slowly enlightening purpose, and Head provided much of the inspiration.

For the next seven years, half of them with Cartier as his Prime Minister, Head played a cool, calculating game of chess with the Americans. His main responsibility as Governor General was the defence of British North America; and the militia were entirely under his jurisdiction. He so influenced Cartier along these lines that Cartier chose, as his first cabinet post in the 1867 government, the Militia portfolio.

The first of a long line of crises for Head came early in 1855, when the Nova Scotian Joseph Howe, carried away by patriotic zeal, attempted to recruit Americans for service with the British Army in the Crimean War. U.S. Secretary of State William Seward knew that most of the British regulars in North America had been withdrawn to the Russian front, and rattled his sabres against Howe's "un-American" activity. While Seward's followers whipped up a campaign of annexation, Head feverishly set to work furnishing the tiny Canadian militia with old flint muskets and swords. By the spring of 1856, the crisis had eased, but the danger remained. Head gallantly wrote to a friend that "if we have a war I suppose we shall have to stand the first blow. There is nothing as yet to hinder my being taken prisoner any day, for as things now stand, the Yankees would have command of the Lakes. If I am carried off to Boston or New York I will apprise you of the change in my address, but I think we should have a fight of it first."[4]

As the extent of the danger from south of the border grew clearer in Head's mind, so too did schemes for the ultimate defence of Canada. The winter of 1855-56 had taught him one paramount and appalling fact – in the event of a winter attack, Canada was helpless, her only access to the sea by Portland, Maine. Only the winter's bitter cold would hold off the enemy, and only the growing North-South split in the U.S. Congress prevented a unified American effort against Canada. Two things had to be done immediately. The seat of Canada's government had to be moved away from the frontier, and a railway built to link Canada and the Maritimes.

But this was all of momentary significance. Like sleepwalkers only half-conscious of what they were doing, the politicians of British North America were slowly groping toward the one final answer to the threat – the creation of a viable nation state – Confederation. Cartier was to be the man who would lead them to that goal.

On October 21, 1855, the remains of Ludger Duvernay, founder of the Saint-Jean-Baptiste Society, were transferred to the new Côte des Neiges Cemetery on the slope of Mount Royal. At the grave side, close to the spot where he himself would be buried, Cartier urged his compatriots to remember Duvernay's work, to ensure the permanence of French Canadian nationality. "Population," he declared, "does not make a nation. Territory is also necessary. Race, language, education and customs form what I would call the personal element of nationality. But this element would perish if were not accompanied by the territorial element . . . The giant Anteus found new vigour every time he touched the earth. So it will be with us. A century ago we numbered barely sixty thousand, scattered along the banks of the beautiful St. Lawrence. Today, we French-Canadians are six hundred thousand strong, and proprietors of at least three-quarters of our arable land." He urged them to engage in friendly rivalry with the English, to be enterprising but not envious. "In this peaceful struggle, remember that the majestic maple is the first tree of the forest and grows always on the best soil. French

-P. Taché (Metro.Toronto Library Board).

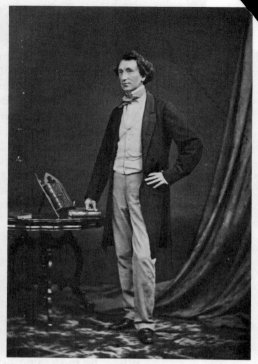

John A. Macdonald, c. 1863 (Notman).

ctor Langevin (PAC).

A.-A. Dorion (PAC).

Canadians should, like it, take root on the best and most fertile ground. The maple, whose leaves we wear on our national feast day, as it shades the tombs of our departed, should grow on a soil which is our own. Heaven grant that the day may never come when the French Canadians will cease being owners of it, for on that day our nationality will die." [5]

As Cartier stood before Duvernay's grave extolling his people's nationality, a new threat to that nationality was quickly taking shape, not from the British in Lower Canada, nor even yet from the American colossus, but from the rapidly developing area of Toronto and Canada West.* In the ten years from 1854 to 1864, Cartier would have to summon all of his energy and all of the political talents he had sharpened in the 1840s to meet the threat and turn it into an advantage.

2   "Our French rulers are not over particular, we are sorry to say, and we are powerless. Upper Canadian sentiment matters nothing even in purely Upper Canadian matters. We are slaves. The French may sell offices, spend our money, do with us as they please. J.A. Macdonald may allow his friend to buy an office, he may even take a thousand pounds of the plunder, if he likes; so long as he pleases Lower Canada he may rule over us."

The Globe, 1858

In 1855, with a strong coalition secure under MacNab, Morin retired to the Bench, and Étienne-Pascal Taché, senior member of the cabinet from Lower Canada, stepped up to take his place as co-Premier. Taché was a small-town doctor from Kamouraska who had been a *Patriote* in 1837. A generation older than Cartier, he had served in the War of 1812 against the Americans, and was present at the great victory of Chateauguay. He had been in LaFontaine's house when it was attacked by the Tory mob in 1849, and was accused by the English of having fired a shot that killed one of the rioters. Whether or not this was true, Taché was a likeable gentleman, who came to be admired by all who knew him. He was affectionately known throughout the Union as the "Colonel."

With the retirement of his friend Morin, Cartier was persuaded to accept a cabinet post, becoming Provincial Secretary, Canada East. His appointment obliged him to seek a new mandate from the electors of Verchères. The *Rouges* correctly saw Cartier as the rising star of the

---

* Upper Canada. With the Act of Union, Upper and Lower Canada officially became "Canada West" and "Canada East." The name "Canada East" was rarely used in the lower province; Cartier preferred to continue the old name.

Bleus, and brought out their troops in force, portraying him as "the partisan of monopoly, defender of lucrative posts, upholder of privileges, supporter of corruption, ally of the *seigneurs* and enemy of the *censitaires*,* the adversary of justice, champion of illegality, apostle of slavery, preacher of passive submission, a trafficker in human consciences, a Tory agitator, jobber," [6] and so on. Cartier fought back, accusing Dorion of being linked with annexationist merchants such as Redpath. He denied he was a Tory: "The old Tories have watered down their wine, and renounced the obsolete ideas that were their characteristics. In the alliance we have made, it is Sir Allan MacNab who has come to the Lower Canadian majority. We have never abandoned our old position." [7]

Despite ferocious opposition – and the usual election gang warfare – Cartier was re-elected with a majority of 186 votes, and escorted in triumph back to Montreal, surrounded by more than a hundred carriages draped in blue.

The MacNab-Taché ministry did not last long. MacNab's ill health forced him to retire. Some behind-the-scenes manoeuvrings by Macdonald led to the May 24, 1856 formation of the Taché-Macdonald government. In their year together in cabinet, Macdonald and Cartier had to come to know and appreciate each other's talents and potential, although in February of 1855, Macdonald was still of the opinion that Joseph Cauchon from Quebec City was a more impressive politician. He called Cartier "a Montrealer body & soul" and thought him "well qualified for the duties of his secretariat, which only requires industry and method, both of which he has in a remarkable degree." [8] Macdonald soon came to an understanding of the power structure of Lower Canada, and his respect for George-Etienne Cartier increased, mellowed and turned into real friendship. It is quite possible that they put their heads together in the formation of this ministry. Louis Drummond, who had been Attorney-General of Lower Canada, wished to be recognized as Premier instead of Taché. John A. Macdonald refused to serve if Drummond were chosen, on the grounds that Drummond was English, and had only a small following in his province. Head, who may have been a party to the intrigue, was thereby forced to choose Taché as Premier. Drummond of course resigned, and Cartier stepped up to be Attorney-General. A neat political coup, likely well-orchestrated from start to finish.

Old William Lyon Mackenzie, still hammering away at corruption, welcomed Cartier to his new post, hailing him one day in Parliament and bragging: "There's the attorney-general for Lower Canada – when the British Government placed an estimate upon our heads, they valued mine at four thousand and his at only two thousand." [9]

The political power of Cartier and Macdonald, conceived at this time, was based on the simple principle that in unity there is strength. They

---

* indentured farmers.

realized that if they held together and stayed together, they would be practically unbeatable. Their private, almost secret formula for rule was to play off the differences between Upper and Lower Canada, and even, play on their respective prejudices; if there was a storm in one province, they could successfully ride it out in the other. It was a formula ruthlessly based in political reality, yet while they were to be ruthless, they were never cruel. They shared the same good humour, the same almost pessimistic objectivity, the same organic view of society, and almost identical political principles. What was more important, they perfectly complemented each other in their management of men and the ship of state. They were men with one long term purpose, to create a viable nation state, and they were very careful not to damage their unity by stabbing each other in the back. Their grasp of political reality is well illustrated by a statement of John A. Macdonald: "The great reason why I have always been able to beat Brown is that I have been able to look a little ahead, while he could on no occasion forego the temptation of a temporary triumph." [10]

Macdonald and Cartier enjoyed the game immensely, and enjoyed each other. Cartier, a driving restless dynamo who commonly put in a fourteen hour day, admired Macdonald's easy personality and his way of dealing with others, by a ribald story, a wink, or by outrageous flattery. Macdonald marvelled at Cartier's superhuman energy, his relentless logic, his ability to get to the heart of the matter, to make laws and drive them through Parliament. As an immigrant Scot, he admired the established and vital society of the French Canadians, and was amazed by the fact of their survival. More than anyone else, Cartier inspired him with the spirit of nationhood, a spirit Macdonald carried on long after his friend's death. The two, if we can believe Macdonald, never had a serious political difference in their two decades of friendship. Their unanimity was nothing short of incredible. Cartier's assistant Sulte relates an amusing and enlightening story:

> Sir John A. Macdonald, who was fond of reading French novels – he always kept them close at hand and even in his desk – one day strode into our office and emptied his briefcase. In the middle of his papers, I spied *Le Diable Boiteux* [The Devil on Two Sticks] by Lesage. He noticed me looking at him and said in French, "N'allez pas me trahir!" ["You won't betray me, will you?"] Cartier stretched a hand out toward his own table and showed us *Les Aventures de Capitaine Beauchêne*,* by the same author. Here, in a nutshell, is the history of Canada. [11]

---

* Alain-René Lesage (1668-1747) was a Breton author of picaresque novels, and is known primarily for his masterpiece, *Gil Blas*. It is easy to see why *The Adventures of the Chevalier de Beauchêne, a French-Canadian who was brought up by the Iroquois and became a Captain of Fusiliers* (1732) was

Put side by side, the two men appear as different as night and day. Cartier, on the surface elegantly and fastidiously turned out, a self-contained dynamo with clear-cut principles, who let nothing get in his way for very long, seems to pale before the more colourful *persona* of Macdonald.

A man whose illnesses and drinking bouts often rendered him incapable of dealing with government for months on end, Macdonald came by his colour honestly. In his early political years, the jaunty dress, the mop of curls, the bulbous whisky nose and the off-colour jokes, in short, the get-up of a clown, all hid the anguish of a man who had experienced the worst life had to offer. At the age of seven, he had seen his brother beaten to death by a drunken servant. His father died while he was still a boy, and he became the sole support of his family. Macdonald's marriages were marred by misfortune. His first son died from a fall at the age of two, and up to the end of his life, he kept in his room a box filled with the child's toys. For years he neglected his career and sat by his wife Isabella's bed watching her slowly die, probably addicted to the opium she took for her condition. A daughter of his second marriage was retarded with water-on-the-brain.

To the citizens of Upper Canada, John A. Macdonald was regarded as either one of the boys, or the devil incarnate. Brown attacked him often for intemperance, but Macdonald knew that his weakness had certain political advantages. After retching right on stage at a political meeting, Macdonald straightened himself out long enough to utter the classic remark: "I know the electors of Canada would rather any day have John A. drunk than George Brown sober."

He could be a hot-tongued orator. At age sixty, he had a fist fight with an opponent on the platform. He often threatened to do the same in

one of Cartier's favourites. It is about a rebellious scamp whose favourite occupation is shooting all the dogs and cats in the neighbourhood. He is such a terror that he even scorns his parents as too peace-loving, and offers his services to an Iroquois chief. For six years, he delights in going on the war-path, pillaging and collecting scalps. Then he joins the Algonquins, helps them attack Montreal, and is captured. His Indian friends are upset when he discovers that trading in brandy and furs is a much more challenging and blood-thirsty profession. He becomes Captain of a troop of fusiliers, and rejects his old warrior friends, who slip sadly back into the woods.

Macdonald's favourite book is a witty reflection on his personality as well. *The Devil on Two Sticks* is, generally speaking, about the tyrannies of fashion and the folly of amorous adventures. The particular devil of the story describes himself as a very considerable one: "I make ridiculous matches, and marry old greybeards to raw girls under age, masters to their maids, ladies of slender fortunes to lovers who have none. It is I that has introduced to the world luxury, debauchery, games of chance and chemistry. I am the inventor of carousels, dancing, music, plays and all new French fashions." A good devil for politicans and makers of constitutions, no doubt.

Parliament, and was once arrested by the Sergeant-at-Arms to prevent him from challenging a Liberal to a duel. He provided a good show; he was an entertainer. But he was also a consummate politician who knew every trick in the book. Once, when Governor General Dufferin gave an address to a university in Greek, Macdonald told the press that "His Lordship spoke in the purest ancient Greek, without mispronouncing a word or making the slightest grammatical solecism." Langevin asked him the next day whether he knew any Greek, "No," he replied, "but I know a little about politics."

Known as "Old Tomorrow" for his habit of deliberate political delay, to let problems settle themselves, if possible, Macdonald supplied the gentle subtlety, the real day-to-day political management missing from Cartier's tough and autocratic brand of politics. In terms of law-making, and the handling of the House of Commons, Cartier involved himself in the hard slogging, in burning the midnight oil, in the facts; Macdonald was the front man, the fencer, the actor, the clown. Macdonald wooed the electorate like a passionate lover, and supplied his candidates with the "good bunkum arguments" indispensable to any campaign. Cartier was like a priest, carrying the survival of his people on his shoulders, educating them with the facts of life, and reciting to them the dogma they already knew deep within their souls. In Parliament, they complemented each other – where Macdonald was forced to bluff, inspire or cajole, Cartier preferred logical persuasion and brute force. When he had finished a speech, there was very little anyone else could add. Cartier was nicknamed "The Lightning Striker" for very good reasons. When he grew tired and exasperated by opposition niggling, his solution was simple – "Call in the Members" – get the matter over with by a vote.

Macdonald's alliance with Cartier gave the Liberal-Conservative Party an unbeatable combination of brute force and deadly persuasion, of drive and intrigue, of British heart and French soul. Opposition politicians fought against this two-headed dragon with little success, for each head would take the other's part, and while the one in danger hid, the other would pretend to fight. Together they drove, intrigued and whipped the British North Americans into Confederation, and with the last breath of one of the heads, cast their mutual spirit, their new-born nationality, across bush and prairie and mountain as far as the Pacific sea.

The political and personal friendship of "the Siamese Twins" is the most significant relationship in Canadian history, and a microcosm of our greater nationality. Macdonald needed Cartier because of the power of French Canada's unified political front. He wisely saw that he had no hope of power without it. Cartier needed Macdonald because John A. was one of the few *anglais* who appreciated the justice along with the political advantages to be found in Cartier's demands for the French

Canadians. They needed each other to survive.

By the middle of the 1850s, Cartier had built up a strong backing in his own province, and was emerging as its real leader. He and Colonel Taché developed a fine working relationship. A silver-tongued and elegant orator, Taché served at intervals as front-man for the Lower Canadian section of the party, and he did his job well. He had not the political or legal acumen of a LaFontaine or Cartier, and was no great leader of men, but he was a kind of diplomatic bishop who could smooth troubled waters with a visit to the parish and a few well-chosen words. Taché was the soul of political sanity. Whenever Cartier menaced his own political safety by his authoritarian acts or arrogantly refused to patch up party quarrels, Taché was there to calm the troops. He was the pleasant, respected, beloved third man, acceptable to almost everybody, including, at times, the opposition, who preferred him to Cartier. As we shall see, Taché was to throw his wet blanket over many of Cartier's brush fires.

Joseph Cauchon, Hector-Louis Langevin and Jean-Charles Chapais were Cartier's other party colleagues in Lower Canada. The bearded, bespectacled Cauchon, tough-minded editor of *Le Journal de Québec*, was a power in the Quebec City area, where he had a personal following of about eighteen members. Although he eventually went over the the *Rouges*, Cartier was able to hold him on the leash of patronage, and by promoting Cauchon's Quebec North Shore Railway extravagance, long enough for Confederation to be achieved. Cauchon was jealous of Cartier, but could bear Taché, and although opposed to Confederation at the outset, he came around at the older man's urging. Cauchon's argument for his own following was that Confederation was infinitely better than annexation to the United States, to becoming another Louisiana, that it was preferable for the French Canadians to be in a country where the ratio to English was one in three, rather than only one in thirty. He was well known to the parliamentarians of the Union as a man who did not suffer fools gladly. Whenever debate dragged on or became inconsequential, Joseph Cauchon would pull out his comb and a piece of paper, and buzz his favourite voyageur song on it until the Speaker roused himself and called for order.*

Hector Langevin came from a prominent Quebec City family. He had articled under Cartier, and like Cauchon, served for a time as Mayor of Quebec, but on entering Parliament, Langevin soon chafed under the awesome weight of his leader Cartier. He was tempted by his friend Louis Sicotte to go over to the *Rouges*, but was eventually convinced of the absolute necessity of Cartier's course of action. A deeply religious man from a family of bishops and priests, Langevin ended up defending Cartier against the Church, and succeeded him as leader of the Quebec wing of the national party.

* Cauchon was quite good at bird imitations as well, and later took up the Jew's Harp.

Jean-Charles Chapais, a merchant who had drifted into politics, similarly rebelled against the stifling atmosphere for young politicians in the Lower Canada of Cartier and Taché. He was a good man of high principles; in fact, "honest as Chapais" was even then a proverb in his home county. He eventually reconciled himself to Cartier's rule, but in 1858, he needed convincing that the party plan for French survival would work, as this extraordinary and revealing letter from the avuncular Taché shows:

Should John A. Macdonald succeed in drawing up his administration for Upper Canada, with or without the different elements of that Province, it matters little to us; the important point for us is the unity of a Lower Canadian phalanx, formidable, and steadfast in its cohesion. We have that unity . . . But if Macdonald's next attempt to recruit support in Upper Canada proves to be abortive, it may well be that he will retire entirely, at which point the Governor-General will have to call upon Cartier to help him reconstruct his Cabinet, since Cartier is the leader of the strongest party in the House. Then Cartier will have his great role to play, and, casting Brown aside, can approach Sandfield Macdonald or any other "Clear Grit" with confidence, and make his demands, which will be accepted, whatever the cost, as the bait of power . . . Again, the important thing to remember is that the unity we have just consolidated in Lower Canada, whoever are our Upper-Canadian colleagues, ensures that *we are the* de facto *rulers of the entire province.* We must not forget that Upper Canadian *division* can only increase the strength that has resulted from our unanimity, and finally give us the security we are looking for. It is true that envy, jealously and small-mindedness reign in our camp, but to a lesser degree than in Upper Canada, among our anglo-saxon fellow subjects . . .

It may come about that, in their impotent rage, we will soon hear weeping and gnashing of teeth from the Upper Canadians, and incessant demands for the repeal of the Union. Fine, it is at that precise point that we must wait for them . . . In the name of God, do not take the initiative for the repeal of the Union; in your speeches, do not even reveal what you really desire, for it seems to me perfectly clear that it is wise for us to act in this way. Lower Canada, although compact, is unbreakable. All the cursing and blustering of our enemies will vanish into thin air, while we go forward, *govern*, progress, in spite of the madmen who only have impotent threats to throw in our faces. And we will do more; we will safeguard our institutions and preserve them from impure contact with Cleargrittism, with the very same Constitution that was bestowed upon us with the avowed intention of destroying us.[12]

At the heart of French Canada's conspiracy for survival was George-Etienne Cartier, but he could not play his "great role" without the support of the young turks of the party such as Langevin or Chapais. As well as being a political front man, Taché was responsible for much of the diplomatic leg-work behind Cartier's political successes. He whipped the troops into line.

The power of the *Bleus* was now secure, and their *Rouge* opposition in disarray, but now a new gladiator came riding out of the west. As Taché's letter to Chapais underlined, the second great preoccupation, besides defence, in the decade up to Confederation, was the doctrine of "Representation by Population," the cornerstone of George Brown's Clear Grit radicalism, and the foundation of Brown's political career.

"What was at work was a clash of the radical democracy of the Clear Grits, with its belief in popular rule exercised by the majority vote of individuals, and the conservatism of Catholic and Orange Canada. This latter strange pair were united by their common belief in the corporate personality of church and nation, and in the development of society not so much by the rational decisions of legislation and administration, as by the organic growth of tradition and custom." **3**

W.L. Morton

The Union of Upper and Lower Canada had been conceived in sin. Its aim, as outlined by Lord Durham, was nothing more than the destruction of the French Canadian nation and its assimilation into the orbit of the English-speaking Empire. In this respect, the Union was a dismal failure. Thanks as much to the enlightened policies of Baldwin and LaFontaine as to political necessity – one French vote happened to equal one English vote – the Union began to work in different directions. Its Parliament was first and foremost the natural political forum of the commercial empire of the St. Lawrence basin. In good times, its canals, railways and rapids were a cornucopia pouring out fur, timber, wheat and potash, through Montreal and down to Chicago and New York.

The period of Union government coincided with the rise of talented and loyal French Canadian politicians willing to work within the framework that had been hammered out. The British government had to forget its plan to assimilate the French. The Crown eagerly accepted the contributions of a man like Cartier, chief protagonist of the St. Lawrence empire, who came to have better relations with British governments than the vast majority of his English-speaking counterparts.

For a time, it seemed that the bastard quasi-federal Union might survive. However, the years up to 1864 saw the ascendancy of two racial gladiators who were determined to wrestle it to the ground – George Cartier of Montreal and George Brown of Toronto. The area Brown came to represent was the expansive, burgeoning region of western Ontario, and there he was king.

An examination of the shift in population balance reveals the major reason for the failure of the Union. At the time of the Union in 1841, the inhabitants of Lower Canada numbered 600,000, 200,000 more than Upper Canada. The census of 1851 revealed that Upper Canada had passed Lower Canada by 60,000 people. Ten years later, the lead of the western province had increased by several hundred thousand, out of the total 1861 population of 2,507,677. What was worse, the wealthier province of Upper Canada by that time contributed four or five times more tax revenue to the public purse than Lower Canada.

The situation that developed was clearly inequitable to the English, but no more so than it had been to the French in the 1840s, when they were represented inadequately. In the parliamentary session of 1856, William Lyon Mackenzie had proposed repeal of the Union as being in the best interests of both sections. The *Rouge* chief Dorion disagreed, saying that he preferred representation by population in a federal union of the two provinces, each with its own legislature. George Brown came out purely and simply for what was soon called "Rep by Pop" as the immediate Reform principle.

What particularly rankled Brown, a firm believer in the separation of Church and State, was the fact that, in 1855, separate schools' legislation had been expanded into Upper Canada, even against the votes of the majority of the Upper Canadian members. Brown got no sympathy from John A. Macdonald, a self-confessed "Central Canadian," firmly aware of where his own best interests lay – unwilling to allow Brown the unanimity he required to make any dent in the French armour.

In 1859, in Toronto, the Grits held a great Reform Convention to air their grievances and formulate a policy and plan of attack. Attended by 600 delegates, the Convention was George Brown's first move in a campaign to change the basis of union. The delegates unanimously adopted a resolution in favour of Rep by Pop, and proposed annexation of the North-West, as well as a federal system of government which would, in the words of the *Globe*, "draw the teeth and cut the claws of Lower Canada."

But Cartier would hold out and hold on – George Brown would have to learn by bitter experience how much and how long. Cartier knew that the Grit Reformers were helpless, caught in a constitutional trap. Any way out could only rebound to the everlasting advantage of French Canada, so as George Brown, Malcolm Cameron, and William McDougall fretted and fumed, Cartier enquired mockingly from behind his forty-odd-vote fortress:

Has Upper Canada conquered Lower Canada? If not, by what right does it now demand representation based on population? With the object of governing us? Everyone knows that the union of the two provinces was imposed on Lower Canada, who did not desire it at any price. But Lower Canada has worked in the Union loyally and sincerely, with the determination to maintain it on its present basis.[13]

When he became Prime Minister, Cartier did not change his tune. In 1861, he gave his considered opinion that the Union rested "on the principle that the two provinces co-exist with equal powers, and that neither should dominate the other in Parliament."[14] As George Brown's blood boiled on the opposition benches, Cartier mildly suggested that the Union be given more opportunity to prove its worth: "Lower Canada and Upper Canada are united by the St. Lawrence, by railways and canals, and each of the two is absolutely necessary to the prosperity of the other. I approve of no hostile sentiment towards any. I am ready to render justice to Upper Canada as well as to Lower Canada in maintaining the Union."[15]

But true justice would have to wait until 1864, when a rapid succession of group governments, of thrown-together, rag-tag ministries of racial or religious cliques, of little political empires, proved too much for the fabric of Union. The participants of this ten-year political debauch were worn out. By 1864, everyone had had their opportunity to rule, to try their hand at ministry-making, and the parliamentarians of the Union were exhausted.

The decade from 1854 to 1864 saw the rise and fall of no less than ten ministries:

1854-55 – MacNab-Morin coalition (Liberal-Conservative)
1855-56 – MacNab-Taché – Cartier Provincial Secretary
1856-57 – Taché-J.A. Macdonald – Cartier Attorney-General East
1857-58 – J.A. Macdonald-Cartier
1858 – Brown-Dorion "Short Ministry"
1858-62 – Cartier-J.A. Macdonald
1862-63 – J.S. Macdonald-Sicotte
1863-64 – J.S. Macdonald-Dorion
1864 – Taché-J.A. Macdonald
1864-67 – Coalition

George Brown had his moment of glory in 1858 when he was able to make his ministry with Dorion last for two days. John Sandfield Macdonald, a Centre-Liberal who at the outset was opposed to Rep by Pop, managed to survive for less than two years in coalition with Sicotte and then Dorion, and partly under Cartier's sufferance. Apart from these two intervals, the years 1854-64 saw Cartier's *Bleus* hold the balance, and therefore the reins of power. By 1864, Cartier was easily able to persuade Brown that the Union had come to the end of its tether, that a truce must be called to work for the final solution – Confederation.

Brown had the good grace and intelligence to realize that the game was up, that he could never achieve power without any real following in Lower Canada, where his name was anathema to the broad mass of Catholics. Dorion had committed political suicide by agreeing to be his Lower Canadian counterpart. In 1856, Cartier correctly warned Holton and Dorion that they would be hounded out of Montreal for supporting "the nauseous political banner of the member for Lambton." [16] In addition, John A. Macdonald controlled just enough of the upper province to limit the English unanimity Brown required to force a showdown.

Goldwin Smith's sneer that "the Father of Confederation was said to be Mr. So-and-so, or Mr. So-and-so, but the real father was Deadlock," has to be taken with a grain of salt. If anything, deadlock was Cartier's creation. It perfectly suited his aspirations for the French Canadians. Confederation was his creation, his more than any other's. While he used deadlock as a means to an end, he already had the end firmly in sight, and six years before the ridiculous two-headed Union of the Canadas gave up the ghost with Brown's entry into coalition, Cartier had already set in motion the chain of events that led eventually to Confederation.

4   **"It would be hard to say whether the Grand Trunk corrupted Canadian politics or Canadian politics corrupted the Grand Trunk."**

Chester Martin

French Canada had to be prepared for the great event, and carefully eased into the broader form of union with the English that she so justly feared and distrusted. A number of fortunate events helped pave the way. In 1855, the Universal Exposition opened in Paris. One of the more successful exhibits on display was one set up by the government of the Canadas, depicting the natural resources of the country. The Commissioner of the exhibit was J.C. Taché, a nephew of E.P. Taché and later Cartier's Minister of Agriculture. The younger Taché had several meetings with French officials, which happily led the forgetful mother of the French Canadians to re-establish commercial relations with her old colony for the first time since the Conquest.

The British and French were about to go to war with Russia in the

Crimea, and the entry of a French warship into Canadian waters on a good-will tour proved to be a national event for the *Canadien.* Long-dormant memories were awakened from one end of Lower Canada to the other. *La Capricieuse* was welcomed with cannon salutes, bonfires and festivals all up and down the St. Lawrence. Commander de Belvèze, his officers and crew were tearfully embraced like long-lost brothers and subjected to an endless round of banquets and receptions. Poets, journalists and orators outdid each other proclaiming the past glories of New France. A French Consulate was established and a monument to Wolfe and Montcalm unveiled in the presence of the French Commander on the Plains of Abraham.

The Crimean War, which saw the blood of French and English spilled together, did much to ensure the success of the French mission. It seemed that post-revolutionary France was coming to its senses – the Emporor was a good Catholic. The French Canadians began now to sense a certain feeling of kinship and brotherhood with their former British enemies, and with it an awareness and pride in the dual nationality of the Canadas. At a banquet in Toronto, Cartier proclaimed "the glorious privilege of seeing these two nations united at last, fighting beside each other against the enemy of civilization and progress with the same courage and valour they formerly displayed against each other. My most passionate desire is to see this union strengthened – it can be most fruitful for France, for the whole British Empire, and particularly for Canada." [17]

The country that had defeated Napoleon forty years before was now fighting alongside France, yet there remained a great deal of hard and concrete work to be done before the union of the races could be strengthened. Here Cartier was in his element. As usual, the more urgent problems of the Union were financial. The Grand Trunk project was running into rough weather. A tight-money market in England due to the war had left the Grand Trunk without working capital; moreover, the Railway's problems of poor management, land speculation, and high salaries were beginning to take their toll. At Cartier's urging, Inspector-General William Cayley put forward a bill granting the line a guarantee of £ 2,-000,000 in government bonds, followed the next year by a further £ 750,000 grant. George Brown was furious, and the *Globe* raged that "the big Grand Trunk pig has had its fill from the trough, and now the smaller unclean animals may come in. Look out for rapid legislation and a general saturnalia among jobbers. Oh, for a Cromwell or a general election to cleanse the Augean stable of this Parliament!" But Brown was politicking, as Cartier pointed out on the floor of that very same Parliament: "He possesses lands which will be crossed by the railroad, a fact that will enhance their value. In his dreams for the future, the Honourable Member has perhaps glimpsed Brown City rising out of the ground." [18]

Dorion voted for the Grand Trunk Aid Bill, seeing that it would allow the railway to open new areas of Lower Canada for colonization, but Joseph Cauchon, fearful that the expansion of the Grank Trunk along the south shore would leave Quebec City in a backwater, resigned as Commissioner of Crown Lands. The finances of his city were in a mess; business was suffering from the ascendancy of Cartier's Montreal. Cauchon, Langevin and the Quebeckers were in favour of a north shore line from Montreal through Trois-Rivières and Saint-Maurice, with a bridge at Quebec. Cartier was able to appease Cauchon with a grant for his north shore railway scheme of 1,500,000 acres of land, but Langevin was unable to raise any capital in London; the line was too obviously a competitor for the Grank Trunk. When Langevin returned, he approached Cartier for government grants in cash, but he was turned down flatly – the Grand Trunk had first priority. The enraged Langevin wrote to his father that Cartier wanted to "slow the matter down, on the pretext that there were many other important matters before the Council . . . I had to summon all my cold-blooded determination to prevent myself from smashing something, or to stop myself from telling him the cold facts. I pretended to take all this into account, thanked him for his good will, etc etc. He seemed to think I was mocking him, but in the interests of the enterprise, I could do nothing else." [19]

Langevin hurried to Toronto to put the matter before the British merchant banker, Charles Baring, then in Upper Canada inspecting the progress of the Grank Trunk. Baring probably suggested to Cartier a way of rescuing the city of Quebec from bankruptcy, and in a neat form of cash subsidy. Cartier arranged for the government to buy back the land grant. Although the Quebeckers were once more appeased, the north shore line still languished. It was only later, when he left the mayoralty and entered provincial politics, that Langevin came to see that delaying the line was the only way to hold Joseph Cauchon in the party, and therefore an unfortunate political necessity.

Although railway matters were pressing, Cartier poured most of his energies as Attorney-General into a project to codify the civil laws and civil procedures in Lower Canada. His timing was opportune – seigneurial tenure had just been abolished, and as he felt that the Union's days were numbered, a project of such magnitude should be undertaken without delay. In fact, the task took five years to complete. The old *Coutume de Paris* and French commercial law were a maze of obsolete old rules that had no place in a country whose commerce was growing as quickly as Canada's. Transactions with other legal systems were a legal nightmare, and, in fact, Cartier's law firm of Cartier, Pominville and Bétournay specialized in guiding English businessmen through the unfamiliar shoals of French commercial law. One particular horror was the different systems of property law prevailing in the Eastern Townships, depending on whether the deed was French or English.

Cartier's bill set up a Commission which began its work in 1859. The new system of law was modelled on the *Code Napoléon*, basis for much of the legal system of Europe. On June 26, 1866, Cartier-a new Napoleon-presented the completed work to Parliament: "In the twilight of the Union government, as we prepare to change our political system, we can now say, in retrospect, that in the last ten years, more has been done to improve and simplify our system of laws than in our whole history. In a few months we will enter a Confederation, possessing a total legal system, classified and codified in the two languages." [20] Cartier's massive reform was one of the cornerstones of the Dominion.

On February 8, 1866, Osgoode Hall was packed for a banquet honouring John A. Macdonald. As dinner drew to a close, and the speeches and toasts began to erupt, Macdonald remarked that Cartier should share the honour of the evening, "because I have never appealed to him or the Lower Canadians in vain. There is no one in Canada whose heart is more devoted to his friends." After warm applause, the President of the Bar of Toronto proposed a toast to Cartier, noting that "today the Attorney-General of Lower Canada has been made a member of the Bar of Upper Canada. We made him sit for an oral examination; and among the questions we asked was this: 'Which is better, the English system or the French system?' He replied that the best system was a combination of the most perfect between the two. Needless to say, we admitted him without further questioning." [21] In reply, Cartier spoke of the work of codification:

> I wished to serve by it, not only the interests of my people, but also those of the other inhabitants of Lower Canada, English, Scots and Irish. When I submitted the project, they predicted it would be a fiasco; but as I am a bit opinionated, I spared nothing to have it adopted. The project became law. When you examine this sytem you will discover many laws which govern both provinces. It will be almost as useful to Upper Canada as to Lower. [22]

It was indeed useful to both, for Cartier's codification provided a unified system which benefited the trade and commerce of the whole St. Lawrence basin, as well as putting the French Canadians on a more competitive basis with their aggressive neighbours to the west.

In November of 1857, E.P. Taché announced that he would retire. Head called on Macdonald, as the senior member of the cabinet, to reconstruct the ministry, and on November 26, the first nominal ministry of the Siamese Twins took office. Cartier's first act on becoming Lower Canadian leader was to attempt to draw support away from the *Rouge* party. The moderate liberals Narcisse Belleau and Louis Sicotte agreed to enter the ministry, but Dorion refused the post of Provincial Secretary on the grounds that his supporters would regard him as a traitor to his principles. John Rose, looked on by the Grits as a thinly-disguised Hudson's Bay Company agent, was brought into the cabinet as Solicitor-General, Canada East.

The government was immediately dissolved, and an election called for December and January. Cartier, following the law of the day, presented himself as a candidate in two ridings, Verchères and the triple riding of Montreal, which gave seats in Parliament to the three candidates with the highest number of votes. He was returned in his home riding, but lost in Montreal, which returned Dorion, John Rose, and another "former rebel," the Independent Liberal Thomas D'Arcy McGee. In response to Cartier's gibe that he was "an Irish adventurer," McGee referred to him mockingly as "the member from some country constituency."

Overall, Dorion and the *Rouges*, damaged by their alliance with Brown, slipped from nineteen to six or seven seats, measured against Cartier's forty-nine, but in Upper Canada, Macdonald lost a lot of ground. Three cabinet ministers, William Cayley, Robert Spence and Joseph Morrison were defeated, and George Brown found himself in a majority, with thirty-three seats to Macdonald's twenty-eight. Cartier had beaten Dorion by 502 votes in the French section of Montreal riding, but lost by 723 votes in Griffintown, the Irish district. If the riding had been split in three, as he arranged that it be in the next election, Cartier would have won handily.

The sixth Parliament of United Canada met at Toronto on February 25, 1858; the era of Cartier and Macdonald had begun.

5   **"Whatever may be the personal convictions, and whatever may be the religious beliefs of a Canadian politician, he must school his mind to principles of tolerance and he must learn to respect the feelings and even the prejudices of others who differ widely from himself."**

Head to Labouchère

The Macdonald-Cartier ministry ruled for five months, until July 29, 1858. It was doomed from the outset, and subject to serious attacks from George Brown and the Upper Canadian Grits. Macdonald, in a minority in his own province, was hard-pressed to defend the Union Constitution, even among his own followers, and often took solace in the bottle. But Cartier easily carried the weight of government. This came to be a common characteristic of the twins: in times of stress, it could be said that Cartier worked like a dog and Macdonald drank like a fish.

They were in a dangerous position, and they knew it – the increasing polarization of the two Canadas must be avoided at all costs, and something had to be done to regain seats in Upper Canada, even at the expense of Cartier's embarrassingly large Lower Canadian majority.

The session was significant for two reasons: Cayley's introduction of the first tariff expressly designed to protect fledgling Canadian industries, and the federation resolutions introduced by Alexander Galt on July 5. Galt suggested a division of Canada into two or three provinces under a federal union, local government for the Northwest and the Red River Settlement as a prelude to their entering the federation, and a union of all British North America. The House listened skeptically – they had heard it all before – and although the majority of speakers approved of the project in principle, the consensus was that the time was not ripe. The Toronto *British Colonist* cast a jaundiced eye on the whole proceedings:

> Mr. Cartier alone mustered pluck to speak; and certainly he shrieked to perfection. It was a pitiful hit, most appropriate manifestation of Ministerial weakness to see the Attorney General East, – the only spokesman of the Government on the occasion – dodging the questions before the House; dodging the question of Representation by Population, and the question of Federation; and rendering himself ridiculous by uttering oracular and most ignorant statements in reference to the workings of the American system of Government. The significance of Federation, as a method of relief amidst the difficulties that now beset the politics of Canada, was felt by every unofficial member; the Government alone, lacking courage or principle to meet matters on their merits, struggled to preserve a silence.[23]

Although Galt's resolutions were a way of testing the waters, they were introduced at a bad time politically. Macdonald and Cartier were failing to keep the independents in line, and their dual ministry was in real danger of falling at any moment.

They began casting around for a more immediate solution, and as master strategists, had to consider the most advantageous means to lose power.

They found their issue in the need to choose a permanent capital city for Canada. Bytown, now Ottawa, was the obvious choice, both strategically, culturally and, of course, politically. This bustling shanty town, where timber was king, sat at the head of the Rideau Canal and away from invasion routes. It was situated on the border of the two provinces, so its choice could be a compromise. Montreal, Quebec, Kingston and Toronto M.P.s, with ears cocked to their own ridings, would of course argue in their own interests – there was a great deal of money and pride involved – but in the end they would have to choose a wholly new location. So the great Capital City Sweepstakes, a fixed race engineered by Cartier and Macdonald, and possibly with the connivance of Governor General Head, started in earnest.

When the idea of Ottawa was first brought forward, the London *Times* disapproved, announcing that it preferred Montreal because it was located in Upper Canada. This gaffe set the tone for much of the discussion. Cartier naturally came out for Montreal, but in the face of protests from Quebec City, publicly resigned himself to the choice of Ottawa.

It was decided to put the choice to Queen Victoria, to whom petitions were sent. Advised by the strategy-minded Head, she of course chose Ottawa. On July 28, a *Rouge* member, E.-U. Piché, moved an amendment asking the House flatly to reject the Queen's choice. In what was considered a free vote, his question passed by a margin of sixty-four to fifty. George Brown followed with a motion to adjourn – in effect, a non-confidence motion – but he was defeated. The next day, however, Macdonald and Cartier surprised the House by proclaiming Piché's amendment a motion of non-confidence, as a parliamentary disgrace and as an insult to Her Majesty, and promptly resigned.

Brown could not hope to govern without Lower Canadian support. He approached Dorion and suggested that they induce Joseph Cauchon, waiting in the wings with his Quebec City followers, into a new ministry. Impatient with Cartier, and a critic of the Liberal-Conservative coalition, Cauchon would almost certainly have agreed to become part of the ministry, but Dorion was fearful of Cauchon's influence and power, and threatened to withdraw support if Cauchon were approached. Brown gave in to Dorion, and did not approach Cauchon. This was fatal to Brown, for with Cauchon he might have gained a strong enough inroad into Lower Canada to draw support away from Cartier. As it turned out, he became saddled with Dorion, a politician too radical for the mainstream of French Canadian voters.

When the Governor General approached Brown and asked him to form a government, he warned him at that the same time that, if Brown's ministry were defeated in the House, he could not guarantee to dissolve Parliament, because an election had recently taken place. As Head later wrote, "Brown knew & I knew that he could not get a majority of the present house. I told him plainly I would not promise to dissolve for the reasons (among others) in my printed paper. He took office notwithstanding on the speculation that he could bully me into dissolving and he was mistaken." [24] Brown's biographer suggests that his simple, direct, essentially unpolitical mind could not grasp Head's warning. This is unlikely, since Brown's potential defeat could only strengthen his hand in Upper Canada, and reinforce his argument that the French Canadians ruled the Union. He would lose, but he would keep his honour intact, and have one more platform argument for his constituents, one more reason for them not to vote for Macdonald, that is, the connivance of Head, Macdonald and Cartier in keeping him out of power.

So Brown wrestled with his conscience, and won, but his ministry with Dorion, the "Short Ministry," was defeated August 3, on Langevin's motion of no confidence, by a vote of seventy-one to thirty-one. Head refused him dissolution on the grounds he had previously stated, that an election had taken place just seven months before, that there was unfinished business before the House, and that it was harvest time.

Brown was enraged, and his *Globe* erupted with scorn and vituperation. The Governor General was, with some justice, called "an embryo dictator" surrounded by "closet counsellors." His principles "once cost an English King his head, and should now cost this Head his office." [25] But Head was within his constitutional rights; and Brown was not his idea of a man capable of running the country, promoting its defence, and building its capital city at Ottawa. Head had first of all to explore the possibility of forming a neutral government, and in what was probably one more strategy, approached Alexander Galt. Galt was at that time in close contact with Cartier, and may have been a party to some of the intrigue. He was the acknowledged leader of a small group of Independent Liberals in Lower Canada, as well as spokesman for the English of the province. Cartier and Macdonald now needed his support, because if he were brought into the ministry, he could help prevent a parliamentary split along language lines. In addition, they feared that if Galt could ever moderate his hatred of George Brown, he might eventually link up with the Upper Canadian Grits. Macdonald had been courting him for over a year:

Toronto, 2nd November, 1857

My Dear Galt:

. . . You call yourself a Rouge. There may have been at one time a reddish tinge about you, but I could observe it becoming by degrees fainter. In fact you are like Byron's Dying Dolphin, exhibiting a series of colours – "the last still loveliest" – and that last is "true blue", being the colour I affect.

Seriously, you would make a decent Conservative, if you gave your own judgment a fair chance and cut loose from Holton and Dorion and those other beggars. So pray do become true blue at once; it is a good standing colour and bears washing.

Yours always,
John A. Macdonald [26]

A brilliantly persuasive letter, right down to the choice of metaphor – Galt's father had been a personal friend of Lord Byron!

It was obvious that Galt would have no chance to form a ministry without Cartier or George Brown, and Brown would of course refuse to have anything to do with Galt, yet by bringing Galt's name forward,

Head was doubtless trying to force the idea of Confederation on the parliamentarians of Canada.

Cartier was well prepared. In the year previous to this crisis, his lieutenant J.-C. Taché, Colonel Taché's nephew, had written a series of thirty-three articles advocating and showing the inevitability of federation. The articles were worked over probably with Cartier's assistance, and published in Langevin's newly-founded *Courrier du Canada*. They proposed a central government limited to criminal justice, commerce, customs, public works, navigation and militia; the provinces would have the residual power and control over "l'ordre moral." The articles had much to do with convincing the French Canadians that a change in union was certain, that they had better prepare themselves, practically and psychologically, for the inevitable.

Galt, too, was well prepared. He refused Head's invitation, and suggested his personal friend and Grand Trunk colleague, George-Etienne Cartier, as Prime Minister. The Cartier-Macdonald Government was a wonder ministry, at least for that period. It took office on August 6, 1858, and was in power for almost four years.

Galt's proposal for federation, defeated the month before, differed significantly from Taché's and Langevin's in that it gave the central government residual powers, and in addition recommended the new step of approaching the Maritime Provinces to join with the Canadas. It was no coincidence that negotiations for a railway linking the two sections of British North America were being actively promoted at this time, and that Sir Edmund Walker Head was a prominent mover behind the scenes.

Cayley was induced to step down as Finance Minister (as the position of Inspector-General was now called), and the portfolio offered by Cartier to Galt. At first, Galt ostentatiously refused to serve unless his federation project was made a policy plank of the Cartier-Macdonald government. Cartier needed to have an excuse to pursue Confederation; Galt's demand provided that excuse, and Cartier was able to satisfy the "loose fish" of his party by making a show of accepting the inevitable, as the price of power. But many members of his party were not yet convinced that federal union was a safe course of action for the French Canadians to take. The new French Consul, Abel Gauthier, wrote that "Mr. Georges Cartier appears to be committed to defend that undertaking; the obstacles it meets are however imposing, and the French Canadian party in Montreal is not inclined to support him."[27] They could, however, support his choice of Alexander Galt as Finance Minister, since Galt's talents were unquestionable, and it may have been that they accepted Galt, even as they were cold to the idea of federation, hoping that Cartier would take advantage of Galt's financial expertise and not his other policies.

Head had already discussed the matter fully with his chief advisors.

Cartier realized the dangers the Union faced, along with the opposition a larger federation would meet with in his own province, but it is certain that he fully supported Head's understanding with the Colonial Office, that if a stable parliamentary majority could not be had from a dual community, it should be replaced with a wider federation of all the provinces of British North America.

Cartier's assumption of power was certainly well-planned, and doubtless with the connivance of the Governor General, but there remained one further matter to dispose of. An 1857 act designed to ease the transfer of cabinet posts allowed ministers to shift office without having to seek re-election, if they resigned and accepted another post within a month. But this was a new ministry, and elections should have been called for new ministers. Cartier got around this by announcing his cabinet on August 6 with all the members in new portfolios. The following day, the ministers reverted to the positions they had been in under the Macdonald-Cartier government. This "Double Shuffle" enraged the Grits and *Rouges*, but Cartier, desiring "to prevent any unnecessary elections,"[28] and mindful of the probability that he would have won a vote of confidence by about seventy-eight to forty-eight, had followed the letter of the loophole in the law. His government was secure with a large working majority, and ready to begin working toward its great goal – a federation of the provinces of British North America.

"We can accept a federal union of all the colonies, without by this accepting union with Upper Canada, because, with the former we will conserve our local legislature for our own law-making, with the latter we will lose it."

6

Etienne Parent,
Le Canadien, July 18, 1838

The Cartier-Macdonald ministry was the first to concern itself actively with the practical accomplishment of Confederation. The great idea had a long and honourable history. It originated with no one in particular, but was an obvious possibility in the minds of most British North Americans who cared to glance over their shoulder south of the border, or gaze west into the future. It was a vagrant idea that would settle when its time came, but Cartier was determined to see it settle soon, and encouraged his colleagues to begin preparations for the inevitable. Taché's scheme and Galt's proposals, both promoted one way or the other by Cartier, were merely clarifications of earlier proposals.

The success of the American Revolution had still left room on the continent for experiment in free colonial self-government, and in a different type of federal system. In 1778, Colonel Robert Morse, the British Army's chief engineer in North America, had written to Sir Guy Carleton on the subject of fortifications in Nova Scotia and New Brunswick, adding that his mind was 'strongly impressed with the idea of uniting these Provinces with Canada, to the advantage of both countries, and that by establishing the same laws, inducing a constant intercourse and mutual interest, a great country may yet be raised up in North America.'' [29]

Morse's remedy was recommended again and again up until the late 1850s and elaborated upon each time. The chief argument was defence – such a union would provide a workable political alternative to the American fact on the continent, and could bear a larger proportion of the expense of defending itself. We know virtually nothing of the leverage the Barings and the British Foreign Office put on Lincoln, Jackson and the Canadian politicans to prevent war, but we can be sure it was extensive. The annexation of Canada would surely mean war. The alternative would surely have to be peaceful coexistence and a unified transcontinental Canada. Political federation would be merely the icing on the cake; the widely scattered provinces of British North America would have to be tied together economically, and the old east-west patterns of the fur trade reconstituted by new means, by the steel rivers and iron canoes of the Intercolonial and Canadian Pacific Railways.

Until his death in 1873, Cartier was the chief servant of Britain's imperial design in North America, at the same time as he was the personification of the growing desires of his own people. He saw that the forging of a Canadian nation was totally in the interests of the French Canadians, however much they might protest against the fact.

An established federation would give the French Canadians back their birthright; it would return to them their own legislature, make their chief metropolis Montreal the terminus of east and west rail lines, remove the danger of American absorption, hopefully forever, and put them in a federal union where they would be quite likely again to hold the balance of power.

The central fact of Canadian politics – the French Canadian fact – emerged in the Union years. Since 1867, it has become apparent that Quebec's influence in Confederation is not much less that Lower Canada's was in the Union. Any political party that can control Quebec and more than half of Ontario can, in the great majority of cases, form the federal government. Although this fact has led to stresses and strains within the fabric of our federation, the benefits it bestows on Canadian nationality far outweigh the disadvantages. The fact of a nation within a nation makes it impossible for Canada to develop a melting-pot philosophy, and more difficult for us to render a single national myth recogniz-

able to all. Unlike the United States, we have no tailor-made my
Wild West, no "Log Cabin to White House" spurs to drive us.

Until the 1850s, Confederation was never the absolute necessit
the English-speaking Canadians that it was to the French. The son
England, Scotland and Ireland could have painlessly and profitably joined the United States at any time, either by choice or by slow drift. In
fact, many did just that, voting against the poorer opportunities in the
Canadas by pulling up stakes and migrating south. But as the century
passed the halfway mark, as colonial communications improved and
intermingling politicians discovered a common pride in their institutions, as pioneers and railway-builders and merchants and factorymen
stepped back from their handiwork and were amazed at what they had
accomplished, the great idea took root.

French-speaking North Americans, with a much broader historical
and cultural perspective, had desired and worked for their own independence since that day on the Plains of Abraham when Wolfe's last act set
in motion their nationality. By the middle of the nineteenth century,
they had overcome Durham's threat to their nationality, and ruled the
Union. But their control, as Cartier clearly saw, rested on the letter of
the Union Act, which could be overturned at any time, by a whim of the
British. So the French Canadians played for time, and Cartier played
out his magnificent role, waiting for the great change, the great idea. If
Confederation could ensure the national survival of the French Canadians, as Cartier was determined that it would, then and only then would
they accept it.

On August 7, 1858, Cartier announced through the Throne Speech
that the federation of the provinces of British North America would be
an object of his government. On August 16, in proroguing parliament,
the Governor General announced that he planned "to communicate
with Her Majesty's Government, and the Governments of the sister
Colonies, on a matter of very great importance. I am desirous of inviting
them to discuss with us the principles on which a bond of a federal
character, uniting the Provinces of British North America, may perhaps
hereafter be practicable." [30]

Early in October Prime Minister Cartier, along with John Ross and
Alexander Galt, sailed to England to take the matter up with the new
government of Derby and Disraeli, and in particular with its Colonial
Secretary, author of *The Last Days of Pompeii*, the versatile Sir Edward Bulwer Lytton. Unfortunately, Lytton had convinced himself that
Head's conduct during the "Double Shuffle" was of doubtful merit, and
felt that he should not have taken the initiative for Confederation by
speaking to it in the Canadian legislature. In addition, Lytton suspected,
with some justice, that the scheme was being promoted as a way of

solving the peculiar difficulties of Canada without regard to the interests of the Maritime provinces. And not even the Canadians were unanimous in agreeing to the prospect.

This was the man Cartier had to deal with as he made his first pilgrimage to Westminster, but there were compensations. He and his two colleagues were warmly received and entertained by the wealthy and great, and treated like oriental potentates at every opportunity. Cartier spent three days as a guest of Queen Victoria at Windsor Castle, where it is possible that, as well as inviting her to visit Canada, he may have entertained her with his singing. But the Empire knew how to dazzle her sons into submission, and the three returned empty-handed to Canada.

They came home without any aid for the Intercolonial Railway, and a warning that Her Majesty's Government would not sanction any conference on federation without the agreement of all parties, that is, without the assent of the Maritimes, who were proving to be quite cool about the whole idea. The first step had failed, but not utterly. Cartier's enthusiasm for the project had not diminished, and for the remainder of his tenure as Prime Minister, he applied himself diligently to the slow, careful preparation he now realized was essential. Time was needed for the seed to germinate, and time he gave to it.

He returned to a Canada still divided on the question of the site for the capital city. Louis Sicotte, his Minister of Public Works, was threatening to resign if the Queen's choice of Ottawa were ratified; Macdonald declared that he would resign if it were not. The maverick from Ste. Hyacinthe was expendable; in a speech interesting for the depth of Cartier's constitutional *savoir-faire*, he criticized Sicotte's political principles as well as outlining his own. Sicotte, he said,

> has concluded that the government always follow the wishes of the House. It is true that a government cannot remain in power if it does not have that confidence, but it sometimes happens that majorities are not always right, and then the ministry is within its rights to resist them, especially if their will is contrary to the law of the country. The Brown-Dorion ministry that [Sicotte] has praised because of the noble conduct it followed in resigning, did not resign because it had the majority of the House against it, but because the Governor-General refused to allow it to dissolve Parliament on the grounds that its own followers were in a minority. In other words, this ministry believed that the majority were wrong in not giving them their confidence – so it was not respect for the wishes of the majority that made them hand in their resignations.

For a final time, Cartier argued for the Queen's decision in favour of Ottawa, this time in the context of advantages to the French Canadians:

> It is true that Ottawa is in Upper Canada, but in terms of business, it is

a Lower Canadian city, linked to Quebec by the timber trade, and to Montreal by its demand for imports. There, the French Canadians will feel themselves in a sympathetic environment, because they number 5,000 out of a total population of 12,000, the majority of whom are Catholics. They will find colleges, convents, churches and all that is especially dear to them in Lower Canada. For all these reasons, Ottawa is an excellent choice, not only as our capital city, but as a means of increasing prosperity and attracting colonization to the region. It is a fortunate choice, a disinterested one, one that must satisfy all reasonable men.[31]

On February 2, 1859, in a tight vote, the Queen's choice was ratified, and one more weight taken from the shoulders of Cartier.

Sicotte had used the seat-of-government question as a means of drawing support away from Cartier. One special target was their mutual friend Hector Langevin, for Sicotte knew that Langevin was not at all pleased with Cartier's handling of the North Shore Railway project. Sicotte's correspondence with Langevin is full of gibes and cracks at Cartier. Langevin, with his Quebec City support and strong Church connections, would have been a powerful ally for the Moderate Liberal Sicotte. "Friend Georges," wrote Sicotte, "has a talent for making everything tempestuous, and it is for that reason he has had to form three or four governments since 1855." He criticized the methods of the Siamese Twins, saying that "it is in the political nature of Mr. Cartier and Mr. Macdonald to keep the ambitions of others constantly on the boil," [32] and further, that their conduct was "dictated by a machiavellian egoism." [33] But Langevin, already warned by Taché of the dangers of disunity, did not jump at the bait, and Cartier's movement for Confederation was for the time being secure.

"The union of British North America would have been a farce till the success of railways was an economic fact."

7

W.L. Grant

A return to financial depression in Britain and America in the late 1850s slowed the projects of the early years of the Cartier-Macdonald ministry. Along with the federation proposals, the Intercolonial Railway scheme was temporarily shelved. The railway bonds the Province of Canada had guaranteed in the heady, optimistic days of the early 1850s now had to be shouldered by the taxpayers. As rail traffic fell off, the Grand Trunk, Great Western, and Northern railways were unable to pay the interest on their capital, and in 1858, Cartier's government doled out over a million dollars to keep the lines solvent.

Galt diligently applied himself to the problem, and increased the tariff system Cayley had established for protection of home industries. By Confederation, the books of the Union nearly balanced, although the Grand Trunk continued to gobble up enormous subsidies. History has shown us that Cartier's policy of railways was well worth the price. Without rail lines to Montreal and the sea, the agricultural produce of the Canadas would not have been competitive in the world market. Montreal would have lost its trade to New York and languished in a backwater. In 1845 it had cost three shillings to forward a barrel of flour from Lake Ontario to Montreal. By 1858, the cost had dropped to six-pence, and the whole St. Lawrence system was flourishing. By 1860, with the opening of the Victoria Bridge, the Grand Trunk had become the longest single railway in the world.

As Chairman of the Railway Committees of both the Union and the Dominion, from 1851 to 1873, Cartier laid down the skeletal founda-tion of this country. It is an indication of his amazing energy and ability that he was able to carry this load while Prime Minister and Attorney-General East, in addition to keeping the howling curs of his own party and those of the opposition at bay. His political success was due largely to the immense power he wielded through his railway committee; there was rarely a politician who did not dabble in railways, who did not depend on Cartier's largesse. Small wonder that he was regarded as a tyrant and autocrat by those he offended. He had little time for diplo-matic niceties, driven as he was by his sense of the emergency of the time – Taché was the mender of fences; Cartier was the Lightning Striker. His ideas were now crystallizing and his energies were at their peak, propelling him and his party and country across the gulf between dream and actuality, into the heaven of politicians, where plans begin to bear fruit.

Late in the 1859 session, Cartier's invitation to the Queen to visit Canada was formalized by the Canadian Parliament. Unfortunately, ocean voyages did not suit the mother of the greatest maritime nation on earth. Her eldest son was chosen to make the first royal tour overseas. On August 12, 1860, Albert Edward, the Prince of Wales and the future King Edward VII, entered Gaspé Bay, along with the Duke of Newcas-tle, the new Colonial Secretary, on board the *H.M.S. Hero*. He was met there by Head, Cartier and a government party, and escorted upriver to Quebec. The journey was a merry one, as one participant noted:

> The scene towards nine o'clock was utterly void of stately or ceremo-nious conditions. Grouped together on the main deck, the Prince and his party, officers from other ships and visitors from the halls of Cana-dian governments smoked and sang and frolicked in a manner calcu-lated to quite dispel the doubts as to the capacity of gentlemen with large titles and severe responsibilities to participate in humour and natural enjoyment. At the close a minister high in provincial fame,

impelled solely by melodious instinct, stepped to the centre and broke out in a very earnest Canadian song of emphatic intent and tender purport. A circle encompassed Mr. Cartier and listened approvingly. The chorus was found to be attainable with little effort. Now a few voices chimed in, the Prince leading, then others, maturer, the Duke's beyond a doubt among them. Afterwards others not less distinct, then finally everybody's. As each verse ended the refrain came clearly out, all that could tune a tune, and some perhaps that could not, uniting with determined ardour and sending forth to the waves, which sang their own gentle song, the refrain, "Jamais je ne l'oublierai." [34]

Cartier's song was his favourite, the old French air, "A la Claire Fontaine."

Canadians who were later presented to King Edward VII have mentioned that he often spoke of Cartier in the warmest of terms. As an eighteen-year old Prince, just assuming his duties, Albert Edward must have been deeply moved by the spontaneous welcome of the Canadians, and impressed by the breathtaking scenery of their Saguenay, viewed from on board ship on a warm summer's evening.

The royal visitor was escorted by Cartier and Taché up the St. Lawrence to open one of Cartier's great projects, the Victoria Bridge, the longest in the world. Next day, the party attended a luncheon at Sir George Simpson's country estate on Dorval Island, three miles west of Lachine. Cartier enjoyed the trip greatly, travelling there and back with the Prince in a huge Hudson's Bay Company trading canoe, paddled by painted and feathered Iroquois. Governor Simpson was seventy-three at the time, and the excitement was probably too much for him – three days later he died of a stroke. A few days later, the party travelled up to Ottawa, and on September 1, 1860, the Prince laid the cornerstone of Canada's Parliament Buildings in that shanty town the Queen had wisely chosen to be the capital. Led now by Macdonald, the Prince continued on through Upper Canada, carefully avoiding the banners and expressions of loyalty of the Orange Lodge, at that time illegal in Britain. Then travelling incognito as "Baron Renfrew," he and his party said farewell to Canada and travelled down through the United States. In the company of President Buchanan, he laid a wreath on Washington's tomb at Mount Vernon. The Prince's anonymity did not survive for long in the melting-pot of the Republic. Just before sailing home from New York, his identity was discovered, and he was mobbed by politicians and reporters.

Back in Parliament, Cartier was teased by Thomas D'Arcy McGee for his part in the royal tour:

He has told us himself of one of the functions he discharged during that historical period – his dancing – but he modestly suppressed all reference to the other constitutional duty he discharged, namely, his singing. Yet we have it set down in sundry places in a history of the visit dedicated to the Commissioner of Crown Lands, how the honourable gentleman transformed himself both on the St. Lawrence and on the Ottawa from a severe Prime Minister into an amusing Primo Boffo. At one place – I quote the page of history – Mr. Cartier is represented as volunteering a very earnest Canadian song of emphatic accent and tender purport. Oh, Mr. Speaker, if he would only have his speeches set to music and sing them from the Treasury Bench in the manner of an operatic hero, what a saving it would be to our ears, and who can tell but such siren arts might win over some of the stubborn Opposition.[35]

"Baboon," muttered Cartier.

A former rebel like Cartier, McGee had fought against the British Crown in Ireland, but made his separate peace. The dark, tousle-haired orator was now a power among the Irish in Montreal, and Cartier was determined to win him over away from the Moderate Liberals. McGee was a quick-witted orator and a superb parliamentarian whose gifts were wasted in opposition. Where Cartier was a hard-driving, logical debater, who came out with all guns blazing, and could speak seven hours in English and then seven hours in French, McGee could make his points rapidly and effectively. Cartier was often stung by his remarks, and swatted back at this Irish gadfly. After one particular torrent of criticism from Cartier, McGee concluded,

I must be permitted to remark on the characteristic exhibition of the Hon. Attorney-General East. The honourable gentleman has been in rather an amiable mood during four or five days, and some of us began to have hopes of his having abandoned the personalities of previous sessions . . . But tonight he returns to his old confirmed habit of abuse and recrimination. He made what I may call an extra-human exhibition of merely animal spleen and venom in his attack upon myself, and I can never look at him, Mr. Speaker, in one of these paroxysms, without having my doubts excited as to what Mr. Hugh Fraser Murray states in his history of this country. The very singular statement he makes is that monkeys are not indigenous to British North America.[36]

Whenever the opposition particularly annoyed Cartier with their incessant debate, he would usually "call in the members" for a vote, but on more important occasions when the mosquitoes of opposition buzzed him too closely, he would all of a sudden blow his stack, marshal his facts, and then roar down the track at full throttle, his whistle screaming angrily. An amazed and aghast George Brown wrote to his wife, asking

Would you believe it? Cartier commenced on Thursday at 4 o'clock and spoke till 6; he resumed at 8:30 and spoke till 11:15; resumed yesterday at 3 o'clock and spoke till 6; resumed at 7:15 and spoke till 1:15 . . . The little wretch screetched – is that the way to spell it? – thirteen hours in one speech. They used to charge me with being long-winded, but Cartier outdoes all the world, past, present, and to come.[37]

When the crusty Nova Scotian Joseph Howe came to Ottawa in 1867, his impressions were much the same: Macdonald's style, he wrote his wife, was "trenchant, animated and effective, but Cartier is the most overrated man in the House. He screams like a seagull in a gale of wind, has a harsh, bad, dictatorial manner and an illogical mind."[38] Howe later changed his tune, and most opposition members took Cartier more seriously when he was roused to such a display. His speeches were massive, total arguments, full of history, economics, constitutional law and precedent, ethics and common sense, all boiling within a cauldron of emotion. When his single-minded purpose was checked, he became a seething mass of frustration, and poured this out on the poor parliamentarians. And now Confederation was in sight. The railways, the seat of government, the Lower Canadian law and land reforms were all secure; but now a new hill, a heavier gradient loomed before him, and as he poured on coal and built up a head of steam, his wheels spun uselessly under him, screeching and throwing off sparks.

His timing was off. The Colonial Office had adopted a policy of delay. And new dangers were threatening: the independents of his party were becoming restless, a conflagration south of the border was becoming more inevitable with each passing day, and worst of all, his friend and mentor, the Governor General, Sir Edmund Walker Head, was to be recalled to London.

Cartier was worn out. His thunderbolts needed recharging. He went on a binge, something he rarely did at all, prompting a solicitous yet teasing John A. Macdonald to write to Sidney Smith, "Cartier was drunk on Monday – He denies it – write him a serious letter about the certainty of his going to the devil if he goes on so."[39] Of course, Macdonald knew perfectly well that the government could not afford *two* drunkards.

At this frustrating point in Cartier's career, one of the unsung heroes of Canadian history arrived in British North America. The charming, ebullient Edward Watkin, a successful British railway administrator and confidant of the Duke of Newcastle and the Barings and Glyns was one of those behind-the-scenes Victorian visionaries who were the mainstay of Empire. He was a catalyst of progress, a financial genius who could cut to the heart of the matter, who could take an ailing business and make it profitable.

Ostensibly Watkin's task was to find ways of making the Grand Trunk pay, and this he easily did, re-equipping the line, suspending interest payments, and removing the head office to London. In fact, his true mission, his real objective, inspired by Newcastle, was nothing less than to ensure permanent British rule across the northern part of North America.

From 1851 to 1886, Watkin crossed the Atlantic thirty times, and travelled on most American railroads. In 1861, he made a vow with Sir Leonard Tilley, then Premier of New Brunswick, that neither of them "would die, if we could help it, until we had looked upon the waters of the Pacific from the windows of a British railway carriage." [40] In a letter to a friend, Watkin seemed almost embarrassed to find that the solution to the problems of British America and the Grand Trunk Railway should be so simple:

> I may be looked upon as somewhat visionary for even suggesting it, but that way to my mind lies through the extension of railway communications to the Pacific. Try for one moment to realize China opened to British commerce; Japan also opened; the new gold fields in the territories in the extreme west, and California also within reach. Try to realize again, assuming physical obstacles overcome, a main through railway of which the first thousand miles belong to the Grand Trunk Company, from the shores of the Atlantic to those of the Pacific, made just within – as regards the north-western and unexplored district – the wheat-growing latitude. The result to the Empire would be beyond calculation – it would be something in fact to distinguish the age itself; and the doing of it would make the fortunes of the Grand Trunk. [41]

Cartier, Brown and the more visionary colonial politicians had already made the same conclusions, but Watkin came to Canada with the significant news that the Colonial Minister, the Duke of Newcastle, had now come around to the same opinion. Watkin described his last interview with the Duke before sailing for Canada:

> The Intercolonial Railway, to connect Halifax on the Atlantic with the Grand Trunk Railway at Rivière du Loup, 106 miles below Quebec, he described as "the preliminary necessity". The completion of an iron road, onwards to the Pacific, was, "to his mind, a grand conception." The union of all the provinces and territories into "one great British America" was the necessary, the logical result of completing the Intercolonial Railway and laying broad foundations for the completion, as a condition of such a union, of a railway to the Pacific . . . In bidding me goodbye, and with the greatest kindness of manner, he added: "Well, my dear Watkin, go out and inquire. Master these questions, and, as soon as you return, come to me, and impart the information you have gained for me." Just as I was leaving, he added, "By the way, I have heard that the State of Maine wants to be annexed to our territory." I made no reply, but I doubted the correctness of the Duke's information. Still, with a civil war just commencing,

who could tell? . . . from that 17th July, 1861, I regarded myself as the Duke's unofficial, unpaid, never tiring agent in these great enterprises.[42]

Travelling with the Prince of Wales through Albany, New York, a year earlier, the Duke was quite stricken with the contrast between the warm welcome the royal party had received in the colonies, and the hostility rampant towards anything British in the United States. In fact, the American Secretary of State, William Seward, had buttonholed Newcastle as the two were walking together after the welcoming ceremony, and said, "we really do not want to go to war with you; and we know you dare not go to war with us." The Duke drew up his proud and fusty old frame and replied, "Do not remain under such an error. There is no people under Heaven from whom we should endure so much as from yours; to whom we shall make such concessions. You may, while we cannot, forget that we are largely of the same blood. But once touch us in our honour and you will very soon find the bricks of New York and Boston falling about your heads."[43]

The British Navy was still a power to be feared.

The prize from such a war would be the northern half of the North American continent. Newcastle was determined that its north-west would be won by means other than a war, but events in the American Union now seriously threatened to make forcible annexation by the United States a distinct possibility.

'That shot fired at Fort Sumter was the signal gun of a new epoch for North America, which told the people of Canada, more plainly than human speech can express it, to sleep no more except on their arms."

8

Thomas D'Arcy McGee, 1861

The Confederate guns began firing on Fort Sumter on April 12, 1861. The first cannon shot heralded the beginning of one of the bloodiest wars in history, one that not only tore the American states apart and welded them back together again with the largest army in the world and a navy rivalling Britain's, but a war that forced a common identity on British North America, that breathed this country into life. The ultimate plans of the North were laid out in a new verse for *Yankee Doodle* often heard sung by the armies as they marched to victory:

Secession first he would put down
    Wholly and forever,
And afterwards from Britain's crown

He Canada would sever;
Yankee Doodle . . . etc.

In one great explosion, the balance between North and South, the safety lock that Lord Elgin had banked on when dealing for reciprocity, had been shattered. But the anarchy of the Civil War gave the British Americans breathing space, an interval in which to build up their defenses, to turn the Canadas and the Maritimes into an armed camp prepared for the battle they suspected would follow the victory of the North.

For the now disunited states, a foreign war could no longer extinguish a civil war. Fortunately for Canada, the United States had missed the opportunity to invade Canada as a panacea for their own internal dissension. However, the politicians of British North America and the Foreign Ministers of Great Britain would have to exercise the utmost caution in dealing with the belligerents, so as not to give the North the excuse she needed to invade Canada. Even though British mills were suffering from a lack of cotton from the South, the United Kingdom steadfastly refused to join France in recognition of the Southern Confederacy. Canada was worth at least that much.

Watkin arrived in Canada at a time when great changes were over the horizon, and great dangers over the border. In his memoirs, he described his first meeting with Cartier:

Leaving Montreal by the night boat, I arrived at the wharf at Quebec; and, after a visit to the hotel and a walk round the city, called on Mr. Cartier, the Chief Minister of Canada, at the small house he then inhabited . . . After I had waited in his salon for a few minutes, he entered: A man under middle height, hair turning a little grey, eyes grey blue, sparkling and kindly; face almost Grecian; figure spare but muscular; well-proportioned; manner full of almost southern fire, and restlessness. We discussed our Grand Trunk affairs . . . Mr. Cartier knew, of course, all the ins and outs of the Grand Trunk . . . [his] sole query was, "Have you arranged with the Government at home as to the Military Revenue?" – to which I replied, that there was no occasion: the Government made no objection, and regularly paid the moderate charges made for the conveyance of men and material over the Railway* . . . I told Mr. Cartier that I had been in Canada in 1851, and had at that time seen Papineau, Mackenzie, and others, whose resistance had led to peace and union, and greater liberty for all. This remark fired his eye; and he said, "Ah! it is eight years that I am Prime Minister of Canada; when I was a rebel the country was different, very different."

* referring to the cost of arms and troops transported on the Grand Trunk during the alarm over the *Trent* affair.

Mr. Cartier often preceded his observations, I believe, by the words "When I was a rebel"; and old George Crawford, of the Upper Province, a magnificent specimen of a Scotch Upper Canadian, once said, "Cartier, my friend, ye'll be awa to England and see the Queen, and when ye come back, aw that aboot ye're being a robbell, as no doubt ye were, will never be hard again. Ye'll begin, mon, 'When I was at Windsor Castle talking to the Queen.'" [44]

In 1858, when Cartier was presented to the Queen by Bulwer Lytton, he told Her Majesty that a Lower Canadian was "an Englishman who speaks French." Cartier had another version of this same theme, that he would use when questioned about his people: "The French Canadians are descendants of the Normans who conquered England."

In the autumn of 1861, Cartier gave a small farewell dinner at his house in Quebec for Sir Edmund Walker Head. Head's parting words to his friends saddened them all. As Watkin witnessed it, he told them how much his health had been bothering him, "admitted his suffering – before concealed from outside people – and expressed his apologies in a manner so feeling and so gentle that the tears came into everybody's eyes. I heard more than one sob from men whose rough exterior disguised the real tenderness of their hearts." [45] Head was to leave behind more than friends in Canada: in 1859, his only son John, heir to the baronetcy, was drowned in Shawinigan Falls.

A week after the arrival of the new Governor General, Charles Stanley, the Fourth Viscount Monck, Cartier and Ross accompanied Head to Boston, and on October 30, bade farewell to a faithful servant and defender of their country. Yet Head's contribution to Canada was not finished, and Cartier would meet him again. A year and a half later, Head was elected, largely at Watkin's insistence, to the Governorship of the Hudson's Bay Company.

Viscount Monck had arrived at Quebec early on one of those funereal October mornings when life seems at its lowest ebb, when the colour and glory of autumn have passed, and driving rain rips the leaves from the trees, laying them down in a sodden slippery carpet on doorstep and pavement. Cartier roused himself well before dawn, and negotiated the steep Côte de la Montagne on foot, to wait with his colleagues for the Allan Line Steamship *North Briton*, now visible through the mist. Monck, his wife and four children, his vivacious sister-in-law Frances and his civil secretary Denis Godley (later known to Canadian politicians as "Almightly Godley"), together with all their belongings, came ashore to the applause of a drenched and miserable populace and a muffled "God Save the Queen" from the band of the 17th Regiment. The *North Briton*, wrecked on the return voyage, banged out what was to be its last salute, as the vice-regal party made some hasty handshakes and bows and then was bustled off to a warm fire in the Citadel.

It was not an auspicious beginning for a man who, as formal head of the government and nominal Commander-in-Chief of the British forces in North America, was expected to convince the colonials of the need for self-defence and federation, before events forced them into a shotgun wedding.

Britain would eventually deliver 14,000 more troops to North America to meet the American challenge, but for the interim, Canadians would have to be satisfied with one of Britain's better quiet diplomats and administrators, a man who would not appear to favour any one party over the other, but a gentle and firm persuader, the eventual pacifier of Upper and Lower Canada.

A heavily-bearded, square-shouldered man of regal bearing and friendly, open countenance, Monck was a prominent member of the notorious Anglo-Irish landowning class, but he was so considerate of his tenants, and such a good manager of his beautiful estates south of Dublin, that his lands were not disturbed even during the worst of the Irish troubles.

Head had been judged a poor diplomat, too precipitate, too headstrong, and too much the crony of Cartier and Macdonald. The Duke of Newcastle, of the opinion that "the necessary preliminary to a Legislative Union of the Lower Province is an Intercolonial Railway, and the completion of *both* these schemes must proceed a Union with Canada,"[46] wisely sent two individuals to Canada to replace Head: the Grand Trunk wizard Watkin, who could work hand in glove with that company's solicitor Cartier, and the gentle and impartial Monck, who could and did inspire the politicians of the provinces to abandon their childish sectional differences. Because of the American Civil War, railways and defence now had to assume the preponderant role in colonial politics. Rep by Pop could be achieved and Confederation assured, but by first emphasizing mutual cooperation in the more important matters at hand. The grand immediate project of the Cartier-Macdonald ministry would have to be delayed, and federation obtained step by careful step.

From 1858 to 1861, Cartier had kept up a good momentum, but now there was a new Governor General who preferred, who in fact had been advised, to remain aloof from party politics. The opposition members were pressing hard for an explanation of Grand Trunk difficulties, and a Royal Commission could only hold them off for so long. But Cartier was delivered from his troubles when Brown's lieutenant William McDougall foolishly argued on the floor of Parliament that Upper Canada was oppressed by a "foreign race," and that if the Anglo-Saxon race were not given relief from the injustices of the Union, they would resort to some other plan. "Suppose," he suggested, "that in addition to our political grievances and present commercial difficulties, there were a bad harvest and consequently great distress, they would have no alternative but to look to Washington."[47]

The Siamese Twins had been handed a sure-fire election plank, and the Toronto *Leader* thundered out that McDougall's speech revealed the "undercurrent of the clear Grit party."[48] McDougall had indeed made a political blunder, one that could be capitalized on quickly. With a dangerous census in the works, one that was expected to prove Upper Canada's population ascendancy, and with a proper kettle of nationalism on the boil, Cartier made his move and dissolved the House.

The election of 1861 was the turning point for the Cartier-Macdonald ministry. Macdonald had written to a friend that it would "determine the future of Canada – whether it will be a limited Constitutional Monarchy or a Yankee democracy."[49] The argument worked well in Upper Canada, but not so for Cartier: when the votes were tallied, he found that he had personally defeated Dorion in Montreal, but lost thirteen seats over all, retaining a total of thirty-three. Some of these losses had been defections during the last session, and some due to Church dissatisfaction, but the majority of them stemmed from a partly-justified fear that the Upper Canadian wing of the Liberal-Conservative coalition was being forced by political expediency to come out also in favour of Rep by Pop. This state of affairs had certainly led to the electoral strategy developed by Cartier and Macdonald – a mild support for the principle in Canada West and total opposition in Canada East – and overall it worked. But it was a trade-off; Cartier was consoled for his loss of seats by the fact that George Brown went down to defeat in Toronto. Although Brown soon found another seat, he felt it best to retreat, and accordingly resigned as head of the Grits. Macdonald had gained five seats overall, for a total of thirty-two, some of whom were very loose fish indeed.

Upper Canadian sectionalism had once again worked in Cartier's interests, to preserve the Union and his own government. The Grits were not only beaten by McDougall's political blunder, but from opposition to Rep by Pop by Catholic Reformers led by the moderate from Cornwall, John Sandfield Macdonald.

While Canada voted with ballots, the American states resorted to bullets. By the fall of 1861, the newly formed Confederate States had gained their first victory, at the bloody slaughter of Bull Run. Although the British recognized the Confederates as belligerents only, even more British regular troops were committed to North America. Seward considered this war-mongering, and sent a circular to governors of Northern States advising them to prepare fortifications to resist a British invasion. Although President Lincoln held Seward on a short leash, the New York-born Secretary of State, through newspapers in New York City and Boston, continued to threaten British North America with reprisals. Jealous of the rising prosperity of Montreal, Seward and his friends jumped at any opportunity to aggravate feelings between the United States and Britain, with the eventual aim of seizing not only the trade of the St. Lawrence basin, but the whole of British North America.

The horror most Canadians felt at the news of Bull Run, and their rising bitterness against Seward and Lincoln, were aggravated when, on November 8, 1861, an American naval officer, Captain Charles Wilkes, stopped the Royal Mail steamship *Trent* in the Bahamas Channel and removed two Southern diplomats bound for England and France. Her Majesty's Government demanded that the pair be released, and immediately sent out eleven more batallions – 14,000 troops – to Canada. Macdonald ordered out 38,000 of the Sedentary Militia, and Cartier was pleased to find the French Canadians as enthusiastic as the English.

Seward backed down, and the crisis passed on Christmas Day, with the release of the Confederates, but by that time all of Canada and the Maritimes were convinced that war with the United States was entirely possible. There was no time to lose, and Cartier immediately established a new Cabinet portfolio, the Ministry of Militia Affairs, headed by John A. MacDonald. In January, 1862, a commission composed of Cartier, Galt, MacNab, Taché and three colonels, with Macdonald as Chairman, met to discuss the reorganization of the militia and prepare a bill for Parliament. It was this bill which was to bring down the Cartier-Macdonald Government.

9   **"There seems little reason to doubt that Mr. Cartier and his colleagues have known for some time that they could not get through the session and that they elected to fall on the Militia Bill."**

The Globe, May 21, 1862

The Census of 1861, published shortly after the 1861 election, revealed that Canada West outnumbered Canada East by 285,000, and many in Macdonald's wing of the party, including the cabinet member Sidney Smith, now began to argue seriously for representation by population. This demand, combined with discontent in the Orange Order over the Prince of Wales' avoidance of their expressions of loyalty during his royal visit, forced Macdonald to go on a speaking tour to justify his position. But the writing was on the wall, and party loyalties began to fly apart. Amazing to behold, George Brown was now a champion of the Orange Order, and some Orange bands had played election marches for Grit candidates.

To keep their partnership alive, the twins now found that Macdonald would have to soften his opposition to Rep by Pop. Faced by six cabinet members who favoured the principle, ministers who had been told by their constituents, in no uncertain terms, that they would be voted out unless they changed their stand, Macdonald had to declare "sectional equality" an open question for the western Liberal-Conservatives. Among Cartier's Lower Canadian *Bleus*, there was no question that Rep by Pop had to be opposed at all costs, yet most of them realized Cartier's dilemma. We have no record of what went on in the pragmatic minds of Old Tomorrow and the Lightning Striker as they met to plan their strategy, fearful of the dangers their formula for rule faced. As usual, they were realistic about their mutual future. Their plan seems to have been to move into the centre, where the moderate Reformers (Baldwinites) and *Mauves* (or *Violettes*, halfway between *Rouge* and *Bleu*) dwelt.

Brown's chief Reform rival, the lean, semi-invalid Scots Catholic John Sandfield Macdonald, whose brother-in-law was a Confederate colonel from Louisiana, was an upholder of the duality of Canada and cooperation between English and French. He was not yet convinced that Rep by Pop was a feasible solution to the problems of the Union.

Before the Grits introduced their annual resolution on the subject, John A. Macdonald reluctantly declared in Parliament that Rep by Pop was an open question for his followers. Brown's motion was defeated seventy-six to forty-two by the combined forces of Cartier, Sicotte and Sandfield Macdonald, with a smattering of John A.'s Conservatives. In Canada West, Rep by Pop was supported overwhelmingly, with only Sandfield Macdonald's followers limiting that province's unanimity. Once again the fabric of the Union was threatened by the increasing polarization of the Canadas. Even though he had been forced to declare an open vote, almost half of John A.'s followers could not see the rocks ahead, and voted against their leader. Cartier's great bloc of votes, the basis of their formula for rule, could not hold out in another election if it appeared that Cartier was allying himself with a party – Macdonald's Conservatives – that was veering towards Rep by Pop.

Macdonald's failure to hold off Rep by Pop in his ranks meant that the time was ripe for a good old ministerial blow-up. In the face of almost certain defeat, he and Cartier would force the issue, manufacture an explosion, go down fighting, and later pick up the pieces as they had done in 1858 with Brown and Dorion. As they considered the long-term advantages of their inevitable defeat, their political instincts told them that they would perhaps be better off regrouping in opposition, blowing off steam, and letting the Reformers defeat themselves.

To some extent, they had both been hurt and insulted by Britain's delay of the federation proposals, so obviously the right path to follow. They still had not recovered from that grievance when, to add insult to injury, some members of the British Commons, the so-called "Little Englanders," led by the President of the Board of Trade, John Bright, voted to reaffirm the doctrine that self-defence was the main corollary of colonial self-government. In other words, if they wanted Confederation *now*, they would have to pay for it. With a dangerous war raging south of the border, arguments like these could be disastrous, not only to Canada and the Maritimes, but to such British interests as the Grand Trunk Railway and the Hudson's Bay Company. This was also an imperial quarrel – the stakes were nothing less than the whole northern half of the continent – and the Imperial Government should be prepared to back up British North America with all its might.

When they were defeated in Parliament, as Cartier and Macdonald expected to be, who would Monck call upon to form a government? George Brown, at that point quite ill, was a "governmental impossibility," his Reform rival Michael Foley had a worse drinking problem than Macdonald, and there was no Lower Canadian of Cartier's stature, although Sicotte was hungry for power. That left John Sandfield Macdonald, the man in the middle, the man of the hour. They could eventually absorb his followers. He would surely not court political suicide by choosing Dorion as his running mate, but would try and cut into Cartier's bloc by governing with Louis Sicotte, the dissident *Bleu-Violette* who had broken with Cartier over the seat-of-government question. But he would fall as surely as the leaves from the trees. The British government would not find him easy to deal with, and Rep by Pop would eventually split his government in two.

Exactly. Cartier and Macdonald had always done well by appealing to the loyalties of Canadians, and now was the occasion for some absurd heroics – a mock pat on the back for the Little Englanders and a melodramatic suicide for the benefit of George Brown.

In March, the militia commission presented its report, which was accepted as a matter of course by Cartier's government. On May 2, Macdonald rose to present his bill. It was a comedy of errors – rather than impressing the House with the need for the measure, a well-fortified Macdonald rambled through the report, getting lost in its details, while Prime Minister Cartier sat beside him without a word throughout the whole sham. Galt, too, appeared to be confused – rising to defend the government, he said that he was uncertain as to the real cost of the measure since he did not know what the Imperial Government planned to do about supplying arms. The plan would, however, cost over $1,000,-000 a year, for the training and equipping of 50,000 men. When the time came for the second reading of the Bill, Macdonald did not even show up. His friends said he was indisposed. "He has one of his old attacks," reported the *Globe*. "It must be confessed that Mr. Macdonald's 'illnesses' occur at very inconvenient times."[50] In the absence of John A., Galt decided that he might as well present his budget, another real shock to the members. The total expenditure would be $12,527,-000. Galt suggested that he could raise $7,375,000 of this amount, leaving a potential deficit of $5,152,000. $1,341,000 could be raised by new taxes, the remainder by borrowing. $700,000 would be required to pay the extra bills incurred in building Canada's new Parliament Buildings.

It was a bill and a budget which would infuriate the opposition, as well as some, if not most of the French Canadian *Bleus*, not fond of taxes in any form. Like a red flag to a bull, the militia bill was seen by the opposition as offering the government tremendous scope for patronage.

On May 20, Macdonald roused himself long enough to present the bill for third reading. Wondrous to behold, not one member rose to speak to the bill. A heavy silence, a few nervous coughs, and a slight rustling of papers were all that could be heard in that cavernous room at Quebec. Prime Minister Cartier sat glaring at the opposition, tight-lipped and impatient. Members glanced around; the Speaker looked, but saw no hands; no member wished to be recognized, and Macdonald slumped in his desk, looking haggard and hung-over.

The Speaker broke the silence and called the members to vote. At division, the Militia Bill of the Cartier-Macdonald government was defeated sixty-one to fifty-four. "We fall," said Cartier, finally deigning to speak, "on a measure designed for the protection and defense of our country, a measure which we believe necessary to put Canadians in a state to enjoy freely their political institutions beneath the glorious flag of Old England." [51] Although "loyal" Upper Canada gave the bill a majority of seven, sixteen *Bleus* voted with Sicotte. The Cartier-Macdonald ministry resigned with an almost perverse sense of relief. "Well," said Cartier to Watkin, "I have saved the honour of my country against those Grits and *Rouges* – traîtres, traîtres."*[52] John A. Macdonald "took the matter very quietly, merely remarking that the slightest tact might have prevented the occurence."

Monck had no choice but to ask Sandfield Macdonald to form a ministry. A cautious but mediocre political animal, J.S. Macdonald had much to recommend himself in the eyes of Cartier and Macdonald, and for the time being, at least, they decided to support his ministry. His opposition to Rep by Pop would prolong the life of the Union and give the federation movement a much-needed breathing space. And he was prepared to spend at least $250,000 on building up the militia; not quite the million Galt had suggested, but little enough to give the Colonial Office cause for concern!

The Macdonald-Sicotte ministry drew support from a wide spectrum of Canadian politicians, from *Bleus* impatient with Cartier, to a seatless Dorion, to Thomas D'Arcy McGee, to compromising Reformers like Brown's old ally McDougall. The *Globe* was outraged by this drift into the centre, and bitterly denounced McDougall's abandonment of Grit principles. Brown wrote to Holton that "a greater set of jackasses- . . . was never got by accident into the government of any country." [53] In this opinion he was seconded by none other than the Governor General

* "traitors."

himself, who, in a letter to Newcastle, called them "a wretched lot," none capable of "rising above the level of a parish politician." [54] Newcastle decided to get tough with the new ministry, and on August 21, sent the cabinet a demand that Canada raise a 50,000-man militia. The demand was accompanied by a sweetener, offered through Watkin, who had been assiduously cultivating the new Prime Minister: Britain was prepared to guarantee a loan of £ 3 million to build the Intercolonial Railway linking the Canadas and the Maritimes, on the condition that the line was built well back from the United States border.

Ignoring for the moment Newcastle's militia demands, Sandfield Macdonald jumped at the Intercolonial offer. In the process, he alienated Dorion, who loathed Grand Trunk politics. In September, Joseph Howe of Nova Scotia and Leonard Tilley of New Brunswick, together with a retinue of ministers, travelled to Quebec to meet with Sandfield Macdonald. They of course decided to accept Newcastle's offer, and communicated this to him through Monck. Newcastle shot back that they would not get their railway until militia funds were increased. This Sandfield Macdonald could not do – it was not the policy of his government – and the Intercolonial Railway project was dropped for the present time.

Much to Sicotte's chagrin, Dorion could be kept in the ministry only by being given *carte blanche* in Lower Canada, and Cartier's lost sheep, terrified by the *Rouge* wolf, began to wander back to the fold. Yet Sandfield Macdonald held on for another year. Slowly, just perceptibly, the pieces began to fall back into place. And new pieces, old Reformers, left the ministry's side and found refuge in the Cartier-Macdonald camp. George Brown's successor Foley was one. Thomas D'Arcy McGee could not be held, and finally drifted over to the Liberal-Conservatives, where he was welcomed like the Prodigal Son and taken on the political warpath by John A. Macdonald. McGee was replaced in cabinet by L.T. Drummond, who began arguing, with some truth, that Canada's best defence was no defence. War with the United States would be Britain's war, and only Britain could decide how worthy was Canada of real financial commitment.

The Macdonald-Sicotte ministry became the Macdonald-Dorion ministry when Sicotte, angered by the drift to the left and Dorion's ascendancy, left the government. But Dorion was no LaFontaine, and the new ministry tottered on the shakiest of foundations, kept in power only by the votes of Cartier's increasingly loyal *Bleus*.

Cartier knew the government was ready to fall, but what would replace it? As always, the great problem in forming a ministry was Upper Canadian sectionalism, and the crux of the matter was George Brown's adamancy for a change in the Union. Although prominent Clear Grits such as Foley and John Hillyard Cameron had come around to the Cartier-Macdonald way of thinking, Brown nobly stuck to his principles; Macdonald had failed utterly to shatter Brown's rock-hard shell.

By the summer of 1863, Cartier was seriously committed to bringing Brown around. When Brown put himself up for election in the vacant constituency of North Oxford, the local Conservatives gave him their enthusiastic support. As a letter from Cameron to John A. shows, Cartier was sending out feelers to Brown, offering him a share in any new ministry:

> I saw Brown, and nothing is nearer to his heart than to upset the ship, but it is to him impossible unless Rep by Pop is in some way got over, and he says he understands the Cartier party was prepared to give two or three members to the West.[55]

Six months earlier, Macdonald had tried the same tack and failed. Brown knew the key to power, and was much more interested in uniting himself alone with Cartier, in supplanting Macdonald as one of the Siamese Twins. But with an election in the works on July 1, Cartier was holding his cards close to his chest and blustering at the ministry. On March 3, the banker and politician John Rose had written to "Old Bear" Ellice of the Hudson's Bay Company that

> Your old friend Cartier is unbecomingly eager to get back to power, but there are very great objections to him, and yet there is hardly a Frenchman to take his place. If he would but show himself superior to office, and agree to support some friendly government for a time, he would do himself lasting credit and the country a service. Macdonald – the late Attorney-General – is all for taking this course and anxious that Cartier should.[56]

Unknown to Rose, Cartier was now beginning to deal in earnest with Brown. The July elections had left them both in slightly better positions: in Montreal, Cartier, Rose and McGee defeated Dorion, Holton and Young, but in Canada West, John A. Macdonald's group was cut to about twenty members. It was a repeat of 1861, where an Upper Canadian action led to a Lower Canadian reaction. It was another trade-off, and as the politicians of the Canadas searched desperately for another way out, the Macdonald-Dorion ministry teetered over the brink.

On July 3, 1863, the troops of the Southern Confederacy went down to defeat at Gettysburg. The danger was becoming real, and a successful South was no longer Canada's best defence. The writing on the wall was becoming discernible: Confederation or Annexation.

Surely George Brown would come to his senses and accept Cartier's hints, at least until the dangers of war with the United States were over. We have no record of their dealings in this period, but from strong circumstantial evidence, it is reasonable to conclude that the two met privately in the recess, possibly with the Governor General, and argued out some form of cooperation, some bold new stroke to extricate the Union from its difficulties.

The way out came in the new year, as the winter ice at the mouth of the St. Lawrence began to soften and break, and move down the River of Canada in great crunching floes. On March 14, 1864, George Brown stood up in Parliament and moved for the establishment of a select committee of nineteen to examine the problems of the Union constitution, to consider Cartier's federation memorandum of 1858, and to make its recommendations to the House.

10   **"Sandfield Macdonald didn't possess even a drinking majority; a man daren't go out to drink for fear the Ministry would be defeated before he got back."**

Anon.

Although somewhat taken aback by the refusal of the Canadians to bear a greater burden of defence, the Duke of Newcastle, supported by the Grand Trunk interests and with Watkin on the scene, continued to press for railway expansion, and ultimately, federation. Cartier was their chief political agent. In order to demonstrate Britain's resolve to keep sovereignty over the whole northern portion of the continent, the Duke backed Watkin's organization of the Atlantic and Pacific Transit and Telegraph Company, which proposed to build nothing less than a road and telegraph line from Canada to distant British Columbia. It was as if the British government had just discovered that the world was round – that the most direct route to the Far East from Britain was through lands that had been controlled by the Hudson's Bay Company for the last two hundred years. Behind Watkin's dirt road was nothing less than a transcontinental railway and a new continental nation.

In 1863, the International Financial Society, newly composed of Grand Trunk interests and merchant bankers acting for clients,* purchased control of the Hudson's Bay Company, and on July 3, Newcastle arranged for the election of Sir Edmund Walker Head, former Governor General of Canada, as Governor. With this bold stroke, largely the inside work of Watkin, the capitalists of the Grand Trunk succeeded in putting themselves and their political friends in Canada – chief amongst whom was Cartier – into a much better bargaining position with the Maritime Provinces for federation and the Intercolonial Railway. Interests

---

* The London branch of J.S. Morgan purchased a 10 per cent interest, the only Americans to do so.

friendly to Central Canada now owned an enormous portion of the continent outright, an area that would be surely sold or granted in some way or other to the future federation in return for Grand Trunk considerations.

Again, we have no documentation of Cartier's role in the proceedings, but we can be sure that, as Grand Trunk solicitor and Chairman of the Railway Committee, he was intimately involved. In 1862, he had been feeling out the attitude of the Hudson's Bay Company with regard to stage or even steam communication with British Columbia, although Alexander Dallas, Overseas Governor of the Company, was quick to see Cartier's political motives. In a letter to a fellow governor, Dallas explained that he knew "Mr. Cartier cared little for us, and that his object was to show to the people of Canada, that he was not inimical to the political and geographical extension of Upper Canada."[57] But Cartier had much more on his mind than this, and his special role all along had been to reconcile George Brown to the needs of the Grand Trunk and Intercolonial (now being planned by Watkin), and to demonstrate to Brown that the success of the railway was essential to the prosperity of the Canadas and to the creation of a new nation. Brown had been a constant critic of the hegemony of the Hudson's Bay Company in the west, and continually pressed for its annexation to the Canadas, and to Upper Canada in particular, with great political success. Cartier was dangling a bait before Brown, and playing a little hard to get. In 1858, he had told Sir Edward Bulwer Lytton that

> as the head of the Lower Canadian party, any proposal of the kind would meet with his determined opposition as it would be putting a political extinguisher upon the party and the Province he represented; and, if carried out, would lead to a dissolution of the Union. He admitted the desirability of throwing open the trade of the Hudson's Bay Territory to Canadian capital and enterprise, and would willingly agree to Canada's contesting the validity of the Company's charter before a court of law, and bearing the expense – provided that the territory taken from the Company should not be annexed to Upper Canada, but should be a separate colony, to form part of a general federation of the British Provinces.[58]

Cartier feared that Canada West would look upon the North-West as its own private preserve. It was certainly in the minds of Brown's readers: "The North West territory lies open before us," the *Globe* assured them, " – a field white for the harvest. We must not enter upon it; Lower Canadian interests forbid it."[59]

Early in 1864, Watkin, through his chief administrator C.J. Brydges, tried to bring Brown around by offering him the chairmanship of the Canada Board of the Hudson's Bay Company. According to Brydges, "he was a good deal impressed, but would not say positively . . . I showed him that nothing could be done about the Northwest without the Inter-colonial [Railway]. On the latter point he is much mollified." [60] Brown did not take the bait, but nevertheless began to let it be known that he was becoming more reconciled to Cartier and Macdonald, as they were to him. He proposed to Brydges that an omnibus arrangement, including the Intercolonial, the North West, Rep by Pop and a low tariff could be cooperated on and carried within the context of federation. This new breakthrough – the fact that George Brown was now in the game in earnest – was soon communicated to Cartier, who knew all along that Brown's support was the key to his plans. Although it was extremely unlikely that Brown would allow his individuality to be smothered in coalition with Cartier and Macdonald, his involvement, even if tempo-rary, would at least ensure that progress could be made.

Cartier had made good use of his year in opposition, particularly in sizing up the potential new nation's future relationships with the United States. On New Year's Day, 1863, he left Montreal for Washington to examine the effects of the Civil War first hand. Lincoln had just freed the slaves, and after a cool meeting with William Seward, the new Sec-retary of State, Cartier met the Great Emancipator himself. Lincoln and his government went out of their way to express friendship and goodwill toward the Leader of the Opposition of United Canada. They knew very well of the influence of the man they welcomed, and of his loyalty to Britain, and realized that a key to their future victory would be to keep Canada and Great Britain as neutral as possible, at least for the time being. They treated Cartier like a visiting head of state, and 10,000 citizens of Washington turned up to hear Cartier speak at a banquet in his honour arranged by the British Minister, Lord Lyons.

One of Cartier's chief concerns in Washington was to ascertain whether the Americans would continue to support reciprocity. Canada was doing very well supplying a Civil War economy, and could not afford to lose the benefits bestowed by reciprocity. The treaty was for the time being secure, and it was not until late in 1864 that the victorious North decided it would be better off protecting its inflated industries by cancel-ling reciprocity. What alarmed George Brown and forced him to con-sider joining forces with Cartier was his increasing awareness of the isolationist potential of the Northerners, and the desperation of the Confederacy, as they hacked their bloody way to Appomattox.

The old was giving way to the new. On February 26, while seated at his desk in the Assembly at Quebec, Cartier learned to his great sorrow that his old friend, and mentor, the great statesman Sir Louis-Hippolyte LaFontaine, had died in Montreal at the age of fifty-six. A great pall of mourning passed over the country, and a grief-stricken Cartier could not bring himself to attend the funeral.

Brown's proposal for a select committee to examine problems of the Union passed by a close vote, but in the debate on the motion, John A.

Macdonald made a curious statement on the broad topic of federation that deserves our analysis. He declared that British North American union, unlike American union, must be "not merely a federal one; that instead of having a federal one, we should have a legislative union in fact, in principle and in practice."[61] Brown wryly enquired whether Macdonald's new policy tallied with the previously announced Liberal-Conservative program. "That is not my policy," Cartier said grimly, to the delight of the opposition.

Was Macdonald's curious declaration evidence of a chink in the armour of the Siamese Twins? Was he muddled with drink? According to some eye-witnesses of the Confederation period, this difference of opinion between Cartier and Macdonald persisted right up to Cartier's death and was responsible for a great deal of bad feeling between the two.

As late as 1887, Louis Archambault, a member of the Quebec cabinet, published a signed affidavit in *La Patrie* swearing that Cartier had complained to him that Macdonald's conduct up to and after Confederation left much to be desired. Archambault, a junior M.P. at the time of Confederation, quotes Cartier as saying that Macdonald's real aim was to

'annihilate the Province of Quebec and turn it into an English Province instead of the French one it now is . . . ' He [Cartier] begged me to remember what he had told me during the last session concerning Sir John A. Macdonald, and added: 'Beware of him. He has no love for the French Canadians; in fact, he detests them.'[62]

This statement, concocted in the aftermath of Riel's trial and execution, when racial feelings ran so high, is doubtless nothing more than an elaborate political fabrication designed to play on the mood of the time. It was certainly not characteristic of Cartier to criticize Macdonald for political ends, to tell his young turks what they wanted to hear. It is a cruel joke and an insult to his memory. It is also uncharacteristic of Macdonald, who always prided himself on his ability to work with French Canadians, at least during the Confederation years. Sometimes his mouth ran away with his reason, but this is a common enough failing in politicians. Adolphe Chapleau recalled an occasion where Macdonald told the Cabinet, "I have always stood by the French," to which Chapleau retorted, "Don't you think, Sir John, it would be more correct to reverse the proposition, and say: 'the French have always supported me'?"[63]

The problem facing Cartier was this: what he had to do was join forces with Brown to carry Confederation. However, Brown was despised in Lower Canada, and Cartier would seriously damage his political credibility by dealing with the man. But it had to be done, and done as painlessly as possible. What complicated matters for Cartier was the fact that John A. Macdonald was now becoming almost as much of a political liability as Brown. His wing of the party was now almost solidly in favour of Rep by Pop.

Faced by dissension in Macdonald's ranks, and a serious challenge to their continuing partnership, it is likely the Siamese Twins agreed that it was time for a little sustained play-acting. When Brown's committee presented its final report, merely recommending further active study of the federation question, Macdonald joined with Sandfield Macdonald in opposing the adoption of the report. Then, to alienate himself further from Cartier in the eyes of the Commons, he took an outrageous position – for one single legislative union – a stand he knew would damage his reputation in Lower Canada, where the French Canadians would settle for nothing less than a strong provincial government in a wider federation. Macdonald was not only playing the Devil's Advocate, but easing the path to coalition. By deliberately making himself less attractive to the French, Macdonald's strategy was doubtless intended to make Brown more attractive, so that Brown, setting aside Rep by Pop, could approach a French Canada more reconciled to a federal system than Macdonald's legislative union.

Macdonald's outrageous proposal was for nothing less than one strong central government, in the British model, a government in which the French Canadians would be lost. Macdonald had nothing to lose, but much to gain in the long term. He had only half the strength of George Brown, but if Cartier could safely get Brown into coalition, the foundering Union could be dissolved with honour on all sides, and then the grand design accomplished. After Confederation, their partnership restored, Cartier and Macdonald could pick up the pieces, aided by new blood from the Maritimes.

The great triumvirate, Cartier, Brown and Macdonald, began to play their hands. Sandfield Macdonald was in trouble: the confidence of the independent members in his ministry had been severely shaken by a scandal in the autumn of 1863, when it was charged that he had tried to bribe the Grand Trunk into supporting his party by increasing the government's mail subsidy to the line. Brown made the first move, and withdrew his support from the ministry. Sandfield cast desperately around for support, but he was failing fast. On March 17, 1864, he approached the venerable and respected Sir Etienne Taché to suggest a coalition of Moderate Reformers and Conservatives, including John A., but, excluding Cartier, on account of Dorion. It was not good enough for Colonel Taché, and he refused to be drawn in with Dorion, or without Cartier. Sandfield did not even have the opportunity to suggest a compromise before Dorion got wind of the bargaining and the entire *Rouge* wing of the ministry resigned. The government followed suit, and on March 23, Monck approached Cartier to form a government.

Cartier delayed giving the Governor General a definite answer until he could meet his friends. That afternoon he called on Monck and an- nounced his acceptance. Later in the day, he thought better of it and changed his mind. He decided to keep a low profile. Taché agreed that Cartier could do more behind the scenes, and that it would be better for Cartier's political career if Taché were seen to unite with Brown, and not Cartier. Taché had less to lose. The two then called on Monck and Cartier asked that Taché be made Prime Minister. The Governor General accepted his recommendation.

A weary Taché, now with little more than a year left to live, had once again agreed to front for Cartier, and while Cartier and Brown waited in the wings for their *pas de deux*, the Taché-Macdonald ministry took power. Apart from the Irish Catholics McGee and Foley, there were few new faces. It was the same Cartier-Macdonald union of minds, once again in office. But the ministry would not last. No one, least of all Cartier and Macdonald, intended it to, and while Canada paused for a deep breath and the ministerial bye-elections, McGee wrote to Tilley, the Premier of New Brunswick: "Hold on to the Intercolonial. You have now men in power in Canada who will resume the project with perfect sincerity." [64]

On June 14, the Brown Committee presented its final report, Brown calling on his "honourable friends opposite to take that course now which they considered it desirable to take five years ago." The House gave its verdict, and the report was accepted. But rumours were flying fast. The day-to-day business of government suddenly seemed strangely irrelevant to the back-benchers on both sides of the House, and later in the day they voted the Taché-Macdonald ministry out of office. As the curtain again lowered between acts, George Brown suggested to the House that "in the position of great gravity in which the honourable gentlemen opposite were now placed, they should be allowed every fair opportunity to consider what course they should pursue." [65]

There was much shuffling of scenery and stage sets behind the curtain as the Canadas waited and watched. "The time for party Governments has passed away," remarked the Conservative Hamilton *Spectator*, "and we do not think the old landmarks can ever be restored." [66]

Brown's party faithful were almost unanimous in urging him to enter into a coalition. Governor General Monck and Thomas D'Arcy McGee sent him appeals to do likewise, and on Friday June 17, he agreed to meet with Galt and Macdonald in the Hotel St. Louis. The three sparred and parried, finally agreeing that the recommendation of Brown's committee, that changes should be made "in the direction of a federative system, applied either to Canada alone, or to the whole British North American provinces," could be the basis of a coalition. Their discussion was severely limited without Cartier, who was enjoying the whole proceedings immensely, while he waited in the wings. That night he attended a dinner at Spencer Wood, and as the Governor General's sister-in-law Frances Monck recorded it, "when everyone was gone but our own party – Cartier and Colonel Gordon – I sang "The Cure," and most of the gentlemen danced it. Cartier jumped higher than anyone." [67]

The next day Cartier joined them. Entering the hotel room, he strode up to a smiling George Brown, past his outstretched hand, put his arms around Brown's shoulders and embraced him warmly. This was the great moment, the symbol of union. The rest was anticlimax. All the plans and meetings and arguments and resolutions of the next three years were merely postscripts to this moment, this wordless understanding between the two founding races of Canada.

11   **"No man, perhaps, is in so good a position as myself to say who contributed most towards the success of the great Constitutional changes that have just been accomplished, and I have always said and am ready to maintain, that without your aid, they could not have been accomplished. Lower Canada was the difficulty in the way ... You ran the risk of political death by the bold course you took, Mr. Macdonald ran no risk whatever."**

**George Brown to Cartier,
February 17, 1868**

While it is tempting to regard Brown's decision to enter a coalition as the "papist hater" burying the hatchet with the "screetching little wretch," this is unfair to both men. Their union was indicative of the change of heart and mind among most British North American politicians, as they became converts to the "Great Idea" and went out into the world to preach the gospel of a new nationality.

On June 22, 1864, before a packed and eager House, the coalition announcement was made. Macdonald spoke first, following which Cartier made the same announcement in French. After a number of congratulatory speeches, George Brown, shaking with nervous excitement, rose from his bench. He began haltingly, urging the politicians of the Canadas to work for federation, and unite "to consider and settle this question as a great national issue." Most important of all, Brown downgraded his own sacrifices and praised Cartier and Taché for their political bravery in agreeing to unite with him in coalition. It was they who ran the risks, not he.

When Brown took his seat, there was silence as the Speaker moved from his place. Then, as one man, the House erupted in a great roar of applause. The weight of ten years of frustration and bitterness and faction had been suddenly lifted from their shoulders, and they were delirious with joy. Cartier, Brown, Taché, Macdonald and all the front benchers shook hands and clapped shoulders. One diminutive *Bleu* member sprang across the floor, kissed a bemused Brown on both cheeks, and hung from the giant's neck like a terrier on a bull.

Only Dorion and the *Rouges* sat back aghast at the whole performance, feeling betrayed, scandalized by Brown's bold leap into the centre of the stage.

On June 30, Parliament was prorogued and the coalition government formed. Two cabinet seats were taken away from Macdonald's wing and given to the Reformers William McDougall and Oliver Mowat, Macdonald's former law clerk. Taché remained as Premier and Brown entered the government as Chairman of the Legislative Council.

Cartier and the *Bleus* were generally pleased with the settlement, but remained cautious optimists. *La Minerve* considered it "a truly great and admirable deed," praised Brown's "talent, business experience, knowledge of the country's resources, his love of work and his boundless energy," and above all marvelled at "the sincerity of Mr. Brown's repentance." [68] "It is a great advantage to hold the key to the shop," wrote Taché, "I can always shut it again if things do not work out for the best." [69]

On hearing the news, some Conservative supporters in Canada West felt oddly betrayed, although not as badly as the *Rouges*. They had made the sacrifices, they had given up the Cabinet seats to Brown's Reformers. This was not quite their victory – this union of Cartier and Brown – but their day would come – Macdonald would see to it.

On that same day, Monck wrote to the Governors of Nova Scotia, New Brunswick and Prince Edward Island requesting that a delegation from the new Canadian coalition be permitted to attend the proposed conference on Maritime Union, initiated earlier that year by the new Nova Scotia Premier, Dr. Charles Tupper. The Maritimers showed their readiness to welcome the Canadians, and a formal invitation was sent to Taché and all the important newspapers in the Canadas.

A party of about a hundred Canadian reporters was the first to make the trip east. A man from the Saint John *Morning Telegraph* was one of those who met the Canadians at Portland in early August. He sailed with them back up the Bay of Fundy and wryly observed, as they slept in open spaces below the decks, that "sleep is the great leveller. There lay the Toronto *Globe* with the *Leader* stretched lovingly beside him. The Montreal *Witness* and *Telegraph* snoozed peaceably together, while the *Gazette* clung affectionately to the neck of the *Herald*." [70]

Landing at Reeds Point wharf at eight in the evening, the Canadian reporters were enthusiastically greeted by a vast crowd of about 10,000 people, and a salute from the *Morning Telegraph*:

You come, proud sons of a noble state.
Too long estrang'd and too long unknown. [71]

The welcome and the weather augured well, and after wining and dining the newcomers, the Maritimers were treated to some voyageur songs by the French Canadians. They watched with amazement as the *Canadiens* whooped and swept from verse to verse, swinging their imaginary paddles in unison.

Back in Quebec, the cabinet met almost constantly during the months of July and August, researching, arguing, clarifying and finally formulating the proposals they would present to the Maritimers. McGee was sent on ahead to prepare strategy with Tilley, already a strong convert to the movement. On July 21, Cartier was again dining at Spencer Wood, and Frances Monck again reported his good spirits: "Mr. Cartier is an oddity; his laugh is so funny, it goes rattling on so long and loud. He screams and whoops at the end of some of his Canadian songs. Mr. Cartier and Mr. Stanley danced "The Cure," Cartier shouting it at the top of his voice all the time." [72] On Monday evening, August 29, Cartier bid adieu to his wife and daughters and boarded the Canadian government steamer, *Queen Victoria*, moored at the Port of Quebec. Brown, Macdonald, Galt, Langevin, McDougall, Campbell and three government secretaries made up the party for Charlottetown.

A clear, beautiful summer's day greeted them as they came up on deck the next morning. The *Queen Victoria* hugged the south shore of the St. Lawrence, and the politicians of the Canadas, freed at last from the stuffy meeting rooms of Quebec, lounged in the deck chairs, watching the little villages and long farms of French Canada thin out and disappear.

Early Thursday morning, Prince Edward Island was visible, a green jewel sparkling with white cottages, framed by white sand beaches and red ochre bluffs. Normally a peaceful little town of 7,000 souls, Charlottetown was bursting at the seams by the sudden influx of visitors. The Nova Scotians and New Brunswickers had already arrived, and Slaymaker and Nichol's Olympic Circus, in town for a three-day run, had brought in many country people as well as attracting most of the members of Colonel J.H. Gray's Island government. Provincial Secretary Pope was the only one present to meet the distinguished Canadian visitors. He was rowed out in a little oyster boat, and seeing so many Canadians (he had expected only four), he informed them that there were not enough hotel rooms to go around. Most of the party agreed to stay on board the well victualled *Queen Victoria*, probably the largest floating bar ever seen in the Gulf.

The perceptive correspondent of the Saint John *Morning Telegraph*, noticing the crowds in the street, asked some of them, "What is the cause of this 'wonderful migration'?" "The circus, Sir, the circus," a dozen passersby replied.[73]

The Maritimers met the same day, and voted to defer their own discussion on Union, and to open the proceedings to the Canadians. At ten o'clock the following morning, in closed session, George-Etienne Cartier rose to present the Canadian case for union. A long and detailed summation of Canada's proposal, Cartier's speech mesmerized the delegates with the force of its argument. The Maritime Provinces were particularly impressed with Cartier's passionate plea for a federal system. French Canadian nationality, he argued, would be preserved by means of a provincial legislature. This was what the Maritimers wanted to hear – any thought of a single legislative union was anathema to them. Their local autonomy, as Cartier explained it, could be preserved in a federal system.

Questioning followed that afternoon, and both Cartier and Galt attempted to explain the desperate need for a common defence against the United States, the proposed financial settlement, and the future progress of the Intercolonial Railway. But details bored the delegates – of course they could be ironed out! – the Maritimers wanted more philosophy, more good rousing national sentiment. Macdonald supplied it the next morning with his usual wit and persuasion, and at three o'clock that afternoon, the thirty-three delegates adjourned to the *Queen Victoria*, now called "the Confederate Cruiser," for a lavish luncheon. As the champagne corks popped and the toasts began, the Maritimers needed no more convincing, but Cartier and Brown gave it to them again, aided this time by the breathtaking oratory of McGee. The flushed and warmed-up politicians followed their words, travelling up the great St. Lawrence, over the inland seas, across rolling plains and through mountains like cathedrals, as far as the other ocean, the great Pacific. As evening fell, the singing began, and Cartier's song, "O Canada, Mon Pays, Mes Amours," could be heard drifting across the peaceful waters of Charlottetown Bay.

The delegates moved on to Halifax, and then through Saint John and Fredericton, banqueting as they went. Their ardour had begun to cool as the enormity of their decision and the work they had pledged to continue struck home. At a dinner in Halifax on September 12, Cartier assured the faint-hearted that "you needn't be frightened of us because we come from Canada, and because that country is larger and more populous than yours. Do not fear us – do not reject our proposals – do not answer us in the words of the Latin poet: Timeo Danaos et dona ferentes.* The promises we have made you are sincere and loyal, and in the union we ask for, we wish your happiness as much as our own."[74]

The well prepared Canadians had taken the Maritimers by storm, yet

---

* "I fear the Greeks bearing gifts": a reference to the Trojan Horse.

they themselves were amazed by the speed of the conversion and the evangelical fervour of all those who left Charlottetown for the rock of Quebec.

To father a nation!

It had already been done in those six heady days of Charlottetown. It had passed into their minds as a *fait accompli*. In the rain-sodden three weeks of Quebec that October, the red baize table in the Assembly room would see them argue and cajole as they bargained over the details of their undertaking, but they were now blood-brothers, liberated from their narrow provincial towns and parliaments, freed from the sickening feeling of sliding slowly and inexorably into the maw of the neighbouring Republic.

It was a politician's seventh heaven, full of laws and principles and instant immortality, and in the evenings as they left their room with the high round-arched Georgian windows and their sweeping view down the St. Lawrence, and scurried up the street through the never-ending drizzle to the Hotel St. Louis, to emerge, squiring wives and sons and daughters to the glittering balls and gatherings, it seemed to them as if they were witnessing the birth of a new and glorious phoenix.

Macdonald assured Lord Monck's sister-in-law Frances that she had "come out here in time to found a new empire." [75]

12   **"I need not tell you that nations drift into wars."**

Bright to Sumner

The Seventy-Two Resolutions hammered out at Quebec were to be the foundation of a new nationality. After two and a half weeks of hard negotiation and compromise, the delegates came away drained but elated. As George Brown put it to his wife,

> We got through our work at Quebec very well. The constitution is not exactly to my mind in all its details; but as a whole, it is wonderful – really wonderful. When one thinks of all the fighting we have had for fifteen years, and finds the very men who fought us every inch now going far beyond what we asked, I am amazed, and sometimes alarmed lest it all goes to pieces yet. We have yet to pass the ordeal of public opinion in the several provinces, and sad indeed will it be if the measure is not adopted by acclamation in them all. For Upper Canada, we may well rejoice the day it becomes law. Nearly all our past difficulties are ended by it, whatever new ones may arise. [76]

On October 27, the delegates, courtesy of the Grand Trunk, took a special train to Montreal, where at a great banquet in the St. Lawrence Hall, the final report of the Quebec Conference was adopted.

It fell to Cartier to make the first public statement on the results of the conference, and he lost no opportunity to blunt the attacks of the *Rouge* press, who were suggesting that French Canada was to be sold down the river. In a speech soon after adjournment, he was able to announce the great concession, the first principle he had demanded all along from the English, that "Lower Canada will have her own local government, and as much legislative power as she now holds." He was very careful to distinguish between cultural and political nationality, and argued that "the establishment of a federal government will strengthen the culture that is so dear to us. A federal government is the only system in which the survival of French Canada will be secure." [77]

While the other delegates travelled on in triumphal procession through Ontario, Cartier remained in Montreal to deal with a matter of extreme urgency. The armies of the North were closing in for the kill, and a desperate Southern Confederacy had decided to concentrate on incidents that would draw some of the North's strength away from the battlefields, and if possible, force them into a war with Great Britain, a war that would be fought on the soil of British North America.

The British were terrified by any prospect of war with the United States. Some felt that the abandonment of the North American colonies would be a small price to pay for peace, and the *Times* whined that "Our colonies are rather too fond of us, and embrace us, if anything, too closely." [78] With the balance of power in Europe shifting toward the Germans, too great a commitment in North America was felt to be foolhardy. The British garrison in North America was already stronger than it had been at the end of the War of 1812. Early in the Civil War, the idea of "compensation" had been considered on both sides of the Atlantic; even the British statesman Gladstone had entertained it. This idea, as promulgated in Seward's organ, the New York *Herald*, was that the Confederate States could be abandoned, that British North America, except for French Canada, was more compatible with "the Northern way of life," and should be annexed. According to the *Herald*,

> The contracted views of the people of Lower Canada will be enlarged and expanded by an infusion of the Anglo-Saxon element and the energy of the people of the free States, who being cut off from a southern field of enterprize, must, by the law of their nature, expand northward and westward. Such is the decree of manifest destiny, and such is the program of William H. Seward, Premier.* [79]

This sort of thinking, widely entertained and at least partly sensible to

* Seward regarded himself as Lincoln's Premier, or "first" in the Cabinet.

Edward Watkin (Notman).

some English-speaking Canadians, angered Cartier, making him redouble his efforts to keep his people independent through Confederation.

Although the bogey of annexation had been successfully used as a vote-getter by both Seward and Senator Charles Sumner in the United States and by Cartier and Macdonald in the Canadas, it was now becoming a real possibility, especially with the presence of the powerful but erratic William Seward in a position of power, and quite probably Lincoln's heir apparent. Governor General Monck realized only too well the nature of the danger, and when his brother Richard gave him a horse for his coach that proved to be high-strung and rather difficult to handle, the family called it "Bill Seward." After a time his daughters had it so well-tamed that it would eat sugar out of their hands.

The real Bill Seward often had to be pacified with British sugar during and after the Civil War years. The North's seizure of two Confederate agents off the British steamship *Trent*, and their subsequent release by Seward in the face of British diplomatic pressure, fanned the flames of hatred still higher. "Out of this Trent affair," said the Buffalo *Express*, "has come one permanent good. The old, natural, instinctive and wise distrust and dislike for England is revived once again in the American heart, and will outlive all the soft words and snivelling cant about international brotherhood and reciprocity. These are 'our Canadian brethren,' these suckling Britons to whom, like fools, we have opened our ports."[80]

The *Trent* affair occurred early in the war when international tempers ran high, but soon the great American fratricidal war was being fought in earnest, and the quarrel with Britain largely forgotten. 1862 and 1863 were years of peace for British North Americans, who profited considerably from the demands of war. Yet Seward never forgot the prize to the north, and turned some of his attention to building up a consular force in the Canadas and Maritimes. These "intelligencers," sent ostensibly to watch over Confederate activity, were viewed by Watkin and others as mere spies sent to watch over British troop movements and the work of fortification and defense.

As the horror of the war began to manifest itself, the political leaders of British North America were exposed to a lesson in constitution-making. In the union they were considering, a powerful central government was essential, to prevent such a civil war from ever happening. To combine this government in a federal system such as that demanded by Cartier was the chief constitutional problem they faced. Cartier had studied and discussed the debates of the Philadelphia Convention of 1787, and Hamilton's *Federalist Papers*. He and Macdonald were determined not to make the same mistakes as the American Founding Fathers, and throughout the American Civil War, they continually urged strict but friendly neutrality and intensive defensive preparations against the threat to this constitution they were now developing. Like Monck, they would tame this horse called Seward who menaced their very survival.

Early in 1864, Cartier again travelled to Washington, this time with one purpose in mind – to discuss the renewal of the Reciprocity Treaty, which was due to expire in two years. After amiable discussions with Charles Sumner, Chairman of the Senate Foreign Relations Committee, a lanky, upright Bostonian who spoke good French and expressed admirable sympathy with Canada's aspirations, Cartier ran headlong into the obstinate principles of William Seward, who was convinced that American industries would need protection to recover from the Civil War. In addition, Seward desired to promote commercial depression in the Canadas to further the aims of Manifest Destiny. Cartier returned empty-handed, and with his fears for the safety of Confederation fully justified. When the treaty came up for renewal in 1866, the Americans refused to sign.

By the close of 1864, the Southern Confederacy had determined to force the Union into a war with Britain, What better time to act than at the very moment when the politicians of British North America were meeting at Quebec to discuss their own union, and three weeks before the U.S. presidential election.

On October 20, Cartier received a telegram from J. Gregory Smith, the Governor of Vermont, informing him that a large body of Confederates based in Lower Canada had crossed the border and raided the town of St. Albans. The Confederates – less than twenty-five of them, all dressed in plain clothes – were led by a twenty-one year old Kentuckian, Lieutenant Bennett Young, supposedly a theology student at the University of Toronto. Bennett and his crew had robbed the bank of $210,-000, killed one man and injured twenty others, before putting St. Albans to the torch. Cartier immediately took the telegram to Spencer Wood and interrupted the Governor General, just sitting down to a leisurely breakfast.

Monck straightaway ordered the arrest of the raiders, and the Canadian militia was able to reach the border area just in time to prevent an American posse, ten miles deep into Canadian soil, from taking back the Confederates they had captured. Five days later, when Seward asked for extradition of the raiders, Cartier met with Monck and then arranged a meeting with McGee, McDougall and the American Consul in Montreal to discuss that possibility and plan some means of preventing future border incidents. In that meeting Cartier promised that Canada's government would do everything in its power to enforce strict neutrality, but nothing more. The onus was put back on Washington.

The next day, Cartier ordered the raiders transferred to the Montreal jail, and had a meeting with Sir John Michel, Commander-in-Chief of the British forces in North America. On October 27, Michel wrote to the

Colonial Secretary that Cartier had decided not to press charges, as the evidence was too imperfect to make a conviction likely. He fervently hoped that the whole affair would cool off as quickly as possible.

Washington's demands became more insistent, and on October 31, Monck informed the British Legation in Washington that when "proofs required by the treaty of extradition have been made in the case of these men, the necessary warrants will be issued for their delivery to the authorities of the United States."[81] But Washington stalled, and the situation became more serious, Cartier realized that the whole affair would have to be deflated slowly. He arranged that the case be brought before his friend Charles-Joseph Coursol, the Montreal Police Magistrate, Taché's son-in-law and later M.P. for Montreal East. Three other prominent Lower Canadian lawyers, William Kerr, J.J.C. Abbott (former Solicitor-General in the Macdonald-Sicotte ministry and later Prime Minister of Canada) and Rodolphe Laflamme (whose law clerk was a young man named Louis Riel) were induced to act as defence lawyers for the Confederates. Abbott in particular was able to cool off passions by indulging in a long and tedious cross-examination of the witnesses.

While Abbott rambled on, Cartier hurried to Washington to argue Canadian neutrality in front of Lincoln and Seward. Seward appeared pleased with Cartier's actions and told him that "Canada has acted throughout like a good and friendly neighbour."[82] When Cartier returned to Montreal, Abbott requested a thirty-day delay to obtain material to prove that the raid has been a planned act of war, and as such, not subject to the terms of extradition. His request was granted without too much difficulty, and Abbott went about gathering his evidence. More time was bought when the case was resumed. After further ruminations, Abbott decided that perhaps the best course was to challenge Coursol's jurisdiction, that, as an extradition matter, the case could not be handled by a mere magistrate. Coursol quickly agreed, and on December 13, instead of binding them over to a higher court, he set the prisoners free on this technicality, to the delight of a largely pro-Southern Canadian press.

The whole St. Albans affair was an important and intricate episode in the movement towards Confederation, and it has still not been wholly explained, perhaps because Cartier's responsibilities as Attorney-General have not been adequately considered. It is entirely possible that Cartier stage-managed the whole trial, and without the consent of the Governor General. In fact, seven years later, the Lightning Striker was called up to justify his conduct at Westminister.[83] Delay was a wise course of action – extradition of the Confederates as common criminals would have seriously jeopardized the neutrality of British North America. Delivering the raiders into the hands of Seward would have meant favouring the North, recognizing it and not the Confederacy as the only official belligerent. But favouring the Confederates too much – and appeasing Canadian public opinion – might have led to a war between Britain and the United States, which of course was the plan of the raiders in the first place. Delay, combined with the appearance of fumbling, was surely the best tactic, so that a decision could be held off until the victory of the North, now becoming inevitable.

When Coursol let them go, the released prisoners had the money kept as evidence restored to them, and additional ready cash was waiting for them at the Bank of Ontario, which had extended its closing hours for their benefit.[84] They quickly disappeared into the woodwork, probably with the connivance of one of Cartier's friends, Guillaume Lamothe, Chief of Police of the City of Montreal, who held off further warrants for the Confederates until they had made good their escape.

On December 19, Cartier issued a reward note of $200 for information leading to the re-arrest of the fugitives, and he of course had to disavow publicly Coursol's interpretation of the case. Coursol was suspended until an investigation could be made, and Police Commissioner McMicken – who, ironically, had been involved in repatriating Confederate soldiers – was sent to patrol the border with some militia units. By this time it was too late and most of the raiders escaped. Five were chased to New Brunswick, re-arrested, and finally taken before the proper authority, Judge Smith of the Superior Court, who gave them thirty days to establish that they were belligerents.

By this time, the Canadian Assembly has passed a new and comprehensive alien act, and voted a restitution of $69,000 to the Vermont banks, so that Washington's anger had cooled considerably. Even though Lieutenant Bennett Young had produced his orders at the first trial, Judge Smith ruled that the raiders could not establish their belligerent status, probably because the Confederate bureaucracy was in a shambles, and he threw the case out of court for lack of evidence. Wishing to keep the Confederates in jail for their own good, Cartier immediately had them re-arrested and charged with common assault, for which they were convicted and imprisoned.[85]

Governor General Monck, who had vouched for Coursol to Seward, had been placed in a bit of an embarrassing position, but the affair was over, and the Northern armies were nearing Appomattox. The Lightning Striker had done his work well, or at least adequately. What could have been a prolongued and dangerous public trial that would have led to a worsening of border relations was over and done with. The whole St. Albans affair was beneficial to the Confederation movement. It frightened the British and finally convinced the Colonial Secretary, Edward Cardwell, to throw his energies behind the project, and the construction of the Intercolonial Railway.

The American press were outraged, the *New York Times* declaring that "we were never in better conditions for a war with Britain." Although Lincoln threatened to terminate the Canadian transit privilege through Maine, and although Seward warned the British government that the Rush-Bagot Treaty respecting armed ships on the Great Lakes might be abrogated, their own cooler heads prevailed, and the incident blew over.

The general impression in the United States at the close of the Civil War was that peace at home meant war with Great Britain. Lee's surrender on April 9, 1865, followed by Lincoln's assassination, on Good Friday, April 14, meant even more uncertainty for the politicians of British North America. Who could augur the future?

Canadians were relieved to see the end of the conflict, but for pragmatic politicians like Cartier, the end of the war was a mixed blessing. The war had given them precious time and an excuse to hurry the Confederation settlement, but now, with union on the verge of being achieved, they knew that the dangers were greater than ever. The Reciprocity Treaty would be cancelled – of that Cartier had no doubt – commercial depression was setting in, and Fenian raids still menaced the border settlements. Relations between Britain and the United States had been severely strained by the war – the British declaration of non-belligerency especially angered Seward. At the beginning of the conflict in 1859, the army of the Union States was small and ill-equipped. By 1865, the United States possessed a navy that rivalled Britain's and a superbly equipped army second to none, a force that could have walked into British North America and captured it with hardly a shot. All that the Americans needed was an excuse, or a series of small incidents that could turn the tide in favour of war.

Cartier and Macdonald wisely conjectured that a weary though victorious North would not commit any acts leading to a war with Britain until their position in the South had been consolidated. They reckoned on a two-year breathing space, and more or less demanded Confederation from the Colonial Office within that period of time. In fact, they were given a five-year lease on life, until, in 1871, with the signing of the Treaty of Washington, they were forced to mortgage the future of the new Dominion to prevent the resurrected American colossus from swallowing them up in one large gulp.

13   "In every meeting, every discussion, every negotiation that took place in those days, Cartier played a predominant and decisive role. His situation was unique. He was the leading representative, the mouthpiece, the acknowledged chief of Lower Canada and the French Canadian Nation. His duty was to safeguard special interests, force the recognition of certain principles, obtain guarantees, and consequently, to make a system of government prevail."

Thomas Chapais

On January 19, 1865, the Parliament of United Canada went back into session. Much had happened since that momentous day eight months before when the great coalition was finally formed to work for Confederation.

Cartier must have felt a sense of *déjà vu* as he took his place on the ministerial front benches at Quebec. Much had been accomplished since 1858, when, as Prime Minster, he first set the wheels in motion that led to Charlottetown. Much, too, had been explained, over and over again, and now it had to be done again, before a furious, almost rabid opposition, who claimed all along that the people had not been consulted on such a momentous decision as the creation of "new nationality."

Dorion and the Lower Canadian *Rouges* clearly wanted an election to test support for Cartier and the new scheme of union, but Cartier wisely refrained from falling into that trap, realizing that popular sentiment for or against Confederation had not yet crystallized. The electorate could prove to be fickle. In addition, not enough support from the Catholic Church had surfaced to make the project a *fait accompli*.

While Cartier lay low, Macdonald travelled the length and breadth of Ontario, whipping up support for the movement in drawing rooms and opera houses and smoke-filled halls, mining the same vein so profitably exploited by George Brown, playing on prejudice and telling the people what they wanted to hear, that French Canadian "domination" would be eliminated by Confederation. On December 19, he had written to Cameron, the Grand Master of the Orange Lodge, that

If the Confederation goes on, you, if spared to the ordinary age of man, will see both local Parliaments and Governments absorbed in the General Power. This is as plain to me as if I saw it accomplished now – of course it does not do to adopt that point of view in discussing the subject in Lower Canada.[86]

These calming words, words that had to be uttered, had their effect, and when Macdonald rejoined Cartier in Quebec, he was able to report that Upper Canada was secure.

On the opening day of Parliament, Taché moved the Seventy-Two Resolutions in the Legislative Council, and straightaway struck the keynote of the whole scheme, that if Confederation were not carried, "we would be forced into the American Union by violence, and if not by violence, would be placed upon an inclined plane which would carry us there irresistibly. In either case the result would be the same. In our present condition we would not long continue to exist." [87]

Debate began in the Assembly on Monday, February 6, Macdonald moving the resolutions and speaking until eleven that night. Cartier followed the next day, with a carefully crafted speech designed to allay the fears of the French Canadians, and neutralize and blunt the full force of the attack he expected the *Rouges* to mount. It was not Cartier at his best, but now he could well afford to pull in his claws, sheathe his thunderbolts, and watch the opposition dissipate their rage.

He reviewed the progress of the Confederation movement since 1858, explained yet again his reasons for opposing Rep by Pop, and then laid his cards on the table:

> He was accused of being opposed to Upper Canada's rights, because during fifteen or twenty years he had to oppose his honourable friend the President of the Council (Hon. MR. BROWN). His honourable colleague took the ground that representation should be arranged by population in each section of the province. He (Hon. MR. CARTIER) had resisted that position, believing that the moment such a principle was applied, his honourable friend, who, no doubt, wanted to maintain the peaceful government of the country, would have been disappointed in his wish. It would have given rise to one of the bitterest struggles between the two provinces that ever took place between two nations. He did not mean to say that the majority from Upper Canada would have tyrannized over Lower Canada, but the idea that Upper Canada, as a territory, had the preponderance in the Government by a large number of representatives, would have been sufficient to generate that sectional strife to which he had alluded. In 1858 he first saw that representation by population, though unsuited for application as a governing principle between the two provinces, would not involve the same objection if other partners were drawn in by a federation. In the struggle between two – one a weak, and the other a strong party – the weaker could not but be overcome; but if three parties were concerned, the stronger would not have the same advantage; as when it was seen by the third that there was too much strength on one side, the third would club with the weaker combatant to resist the big fighter. (Cheers and laughter.) [88]

Elaborating on Taché's initial argument, he noted that Confederation was being forced upon British North America: "either we must obtain British North American Confederation, or be absorbed in the American Confederation." [89] He then reviewed the arguments he had put before the Maritimers, that Canada lacked "the maritime element":

> Twenty years ago our commerce for the year could be managed by communication with Great Britain in the summer months only. At present, however, this system was insufficient, and for winter communication with the sea-board we were left to the caprice of our American neighbours, through whose territory we must pass. He had also alluded to the bonding system, which if the Americans were to withdraw, Canada would be left in winter without any winter harbours. Canada, having two or three elements of national greatness – territory and population – wanted the maritime element; and as he had said, – the Lower Provinces had this element and a sea-board, but not a back country or large population, which Canada possessed, – and for the mutual benefit and prosperity of all the provinces, all these elements ought to be united together. [90]

Turning to his own province, Cartier praised the clergy's loyalty to the Crown since the Conquest, and then criticized the *Rouges*, "the French Canadian annexationists," for their republican ideals. Finally, he took on the American Constitution, and in words that have been graphically illustrated since, noted that its one great flaw was

> the absence of some respectable executive element. How was the head of the United States Government chosen? Candidates came forward, and of course each one was abused and villified as corrupt, ignorant, incapable and unworthy by the opposite party. One of them attained the presidential chair; but even while in that position he was not respected by those who had opposed his election, and who tried to make him appear the most corrupt and contemptible being in creation. Such a system could not produce an executive head who would command respect. Under the British system, ministers might be abused and assailed; but that abuse never reached the Sovereign. [91]

When Brown rose to speak the next day, Cartier constantly came to his defence when he was attacked by dissident Grits and *Rouges*. Cartier himself would have need of defence. On Monday, February 20, Henri Joly, a prominent *Rouge* from Lotbinière, put the whole discussion on a lower plane by charging Cartier with treason to his people:

> Thanks to his energy, to his intimate acquaintance with the strong and the weak points of his fellow countrymen, the Attorney-General for Lower Canada has succeeded in attaining an elevation which no one can dispute with him – that of chief of the French Canadian nationality. To attain this eminence, he has crushed the weak, cajoled the strong, deceived the credulous, bought up the venal, and exalted

the ambitious; by turns he has called in the accents of religion and simulated the clamour of interest – he has gained his end. When Lower Canada heard of his alliance with the President of the Council,* there arose from all quarters one universal cry of indignation. He managed to convert the cry of anger into a shout of admiration. When his scheme of Confederation became public, a feeling of uneasiness pervaded all minds; that instinct forewarned them of impending danger. He has hushed that feeling to a sleep of profound security. I shall compare him to a man who has gained the unbounded confidence of the public, who takes advantage of it to set up a Savings Bank, in which the rich man deposits his wealth, and the day labourer the small amount which he has squeezed out of his wages, against a day of need – both without a receipt. When that man has gathered all into his strong box, he finds an opportunity to purchase, at the cost of all he holds in trust, the article on which he has long set his ambitious eye; and he buys it, unhesitatingly, without a thought of the wretches who are doomed to ruin by his conduct. The deposit committed to the Attorney-General is the fortune of the French-Canadians – their nationality. That fortune had not been made in a day; it was the accumulation of the toil and the savings of a whole people in a whole century. To prolong the ephemeral existence of his administration for a few months, the Attorney General has sacrificed, without a scruple, this precious trust, which the unbounded confidence of his fellow-countrymen had confided to his keeping.

HON. MR. CARTIER – And what have I received in payment for that?

MR. JOLY – A salary of five thousand dollars per annum, and the honour of the position.

HON. MR. CARTIER – That is not enough for me.

MR. JOLY – I am well aware of it; that is why the honourable member is desirous of extending the circle of his operations. But he will not long enjoy the fruits of his treason; by crushing the power of the French-Canadians he has crushed his own, for upon them his existence depends. Does he believe in the sincerity of the friendship of the Liberals of Upper Canada? They fought with him too long to allow of the existence of any sympathy between them and him, and now he has lost even their respect. They consented to ally themselves with him in order to obtain their object – representation by population; but when they no longer stand in need of him, they will throw him aside like a worn-out tool.[92]

Cartier now had to tread very carefully indeed, for Joly's speech contained some half-truths that were being echoed across the whole of the

* George Brown

province by the *Rouges*. Their attack was becoming more and more focused on his personality, and even some members of his own party were sharpening their knives. It fell to Langevin to defend his leader, and this he did, both in the Confederation Debates and in private. Gélinas of *La Minerve* expressed this uneasiness in a letter to Langevin:

> One mustn't be persuaded that only the understanding and assistance of the English is necessary to give victory to the plan proposed by the conference. I would not keep from you the fact that there exists among our warmest and most devoted friends a certain malaise. A great deal of caution as well as a great deal of zeal will be necessary to keep us all under the same banner. Don't always put your trust in Cartier, for he is surrounded by flatterers who are far from expressing the feelings of the majority . . . we must take care.[93]

Cartier sensed the rising forces of faction, and it angered him. Another friend of Langevin wrote that he had found Cartier "in an infernal mood, as if it were my fault that Confederation was going badly- . . . Keep up your courage, Mr. Minister; be even-tempered, and safe from the gathering storm."[94]

Langevin's chief duty now was to convince the Catholic clergy of the need for Confederation. Through his brother, the Bishop of Rimouski, he eventually convinced the hierarchy that it was the lesser of two evils – Confederation, or Annexation and Annihilation – and that it would lessen civil strife. Perhaps Langevin and his brother did their work too well. More than ten years later, a Quebec priest was accused of advising his flock that "the place on high is *Bleu*, while the other is *Rouge*."[95]

Cartier had a rougher time of it. On February 26, Vicar-General Cazeau wrote to Father Truteau, the Administrator of the Diocese of Monteal, that he had severely lectured Cartier on a speech he had made in the Assembly, in which Cartier claimed

> that the ecclesiastical authorities were favourable to the Confederation project. To that he pleaded guilty. It happened that Monseigneur de Tloa [the Administrator of Quebec] had explained to him as well as to the Prime Minister, Sir E.P. Taché, that, without being enthusiastic about Confederation, he had resigned himself more to it than to representation by population, which was becoming inevitable. Monseigneur Lynch, the Bishop of Toronto, told him the same thing, and he believed that Grand Vicar Raymond of Ste. Hyacinthe gave him the same impression. As for the other ecclesiastical heads of the province, who hadn't expressed an opinion, he doubtless looked upon their silence as acquiescence, and believed it reasonable that, if they had been opposed to the project, they would not have let the opportunity pass to proclaim this in any possible way.[96]

Fortunately for Cartier's whole gamble, the Church eventually came out solidly for the new union. Without the recommendation and advice given by priests in practically every parish throughout the length and breadth of French Canada, it would have been impossible to carry off.

The project adopted by the Quebec Conference was finally seconded by the Union Parliament. At 4:30 in the morning of March 11, 1865, the main vote was taken and passed. The English members immediately burst out with "God Save the Queen." The French, led by Joseph Cauchon, buzzing on his comb and paper, tried mightily to drown them out with a voyageur song, and then the whole congregation, grown weary of endless debate and stale invective, spilled out into the narrow slushy streets of Quebec, and home to bed.

The tally was 91 to 33, yet twenty-one of the opponents to Confederation were French Canadians. Cartier was able to muster twenty-six supporters – a close vote, but a final one.

Again, the vivacious Frances Monck has recorded Cartier's sense of delight at his victory; it is obvious he was quite taken with her: "Mr. Cartier was very amusing; he abused Colonel Gordon for being so *cold* to the Quebec ladies. He said 'his face was like marble and his lips moved not,' when they were trying to attract him. Cartier and some others go home on the twelfth about Confederation. He says that he and I must *correspond* when he goes to England. He says he is going to hunt out 'Lady Flora Macdonald,'* and go down on one knee before her as he does to me! Captain Eliot made me ask Cartier his character and favourite occupation. He said, '*the activity of the heart.*' What does that mean? . . . The thing he hates most in the world is 'a comp*etee*tar' as he pronounces it."[97]

Cartier did not have long to savour the sweetness of that victory; soon after the vote, the Legislature appointed Cartier, Brown, Macdonald and Galt as its representatives to discuss with the Imperial Government

1. Upon the proposed confederation of the British North American provinces, and the means whereby it would be most speedily effected.
2. Upon the arrangement necessary for the defense of Canada in the event of war arising with the United States and the extent to which the same should be shared between Great Britain and Canada.
3. Upon the steps to be taken with reference to the Reciprocity Treaty and the rights conferred by it upon the United States.
4. Upon the arrangement necessary for the settlement of the North West Territories, and the Hudson's Bay Company's claim.
5. And generally upon the existing critical state of affairs by which Canada is most seriously affected.

---

* one of Queen Victoria's Maids of Honour, with whom he had "breakfasted" at Windsor Castle on his last visit.

Cartier and Galt left first, accompanied by Brydges and a reporter from *La Minerve*. On April 6, they took a special Grand Trunk train to Portland, and then on to Boston, where the three boarded the steamer *Asia*, bound for Liverpool.

The *Asia* stopped at Halifax, where Cartier and Galt were treated to a torch-light parade and a banquet at Temperance Hall. Leonard Tilley, who had foolishly gone to the polls over Confederation and had been defeated, welcomed the two and predicted that the electors of New Brunswick would soon repent and re-elect the Unionists. Cartier told the gathering that the Canadian government would continue to press the issue of union, and fight for the Intercolonial Railway, and that he believed the British Government were now convinced that Confederation was an absolute necessity.

While in London, Cartier and his three colleagues were constantly wined and dined, and he met with the Queen, who spoke to him in French, and the Prince of Wales, who had fond remembrances of his visit to Canada seven years previously. The Queen asked him about the Victoria Bridge: "How many feet is it from shore to shore?" He replied, "When we Canadians build a bridge, and dedicate it to Your Majesty, we measure it not in feet but in miles." She was so pleased that the two talked about Grand Trunk affairs for over an hour.[98]

The delegates were invited to countless banquets with bankers and railwaymen – as Cartier later told Monck, he "did not dine at home more than twice the whole time I was in London"[99] – they took an amusing side trip to the Derby, pelting the other coaches with shots from their peashooters, and they met the novelist Charles Dickens and the poet Robert Browning at a literary dinner. But most of their time was spent in discussion with Gladstone and his cabinet, and as Cartier has predicted, an agreement was eventually drawn up outlining a common policy for the success of Confederation.

It appears that Cartier's special charge was to convince the Imperial Government to replace the Lieutenant-Governors of both Nova Scotia and New Brunswick, on the grounds that they had prejudiced the whole scheme.[100] In this he was successful.

Cartier had only been back in Montreal three weeks when two of his dearest friends and mentors, A.N. Morin and the Prime Minister, Sir E.P. Taché, died within a few days of each other. Taché's death especially filled Cartier with a sense of heavy despair. He was now so much more alone in power, and so much less insulated from the demands of his restless party. A little more than three months later, on November 8, his brother and old law partner Damien died at the House of the Seven Chimneys. Yet McGee's words at Quebec – "We are in the rapids and must go on"[101] – still stirred his voyageur's soul. He was tired, and went on a steamer trip to the Saguenay. As he wrote Macdonald, "The trip did me a great deal of good, particularly to my sight. My eyes wanted a little rest." [102]

The problem of a successor to Taché as head of the coalition government was a touchy one. George Brown correctly argued that he, Macdonald and Cartier were regarded as separate party leaders and when Macdonald suggested Cartier as Prime Minister, Brown would not agree. A compromise was reached with the elevation of Sir Narcisse Belleau, a mild-mannered *Mauve*, as figurehead Prime Minister, while the triumvirate of Cartier, Brown and Macdonald remained intact.

The Legislature of United Canada assembled for its last session on August 8, 1865. One very interesting visitor at Quebec that summer was Lieutenant-General Ulysses S. Grant of the United States Army. "The Lion of Vicksburg" and the victor of Appomattox was on holiday in Quebec with some of his staff, yet found time to visit Governor General Monck at Spencer Wood, the viceregal residence outside Quebec. Grant came with some cheering news, that Cartier, present at a meeting, quickly communicated to the French Consul. The United States, said Grant, would make a deal. As long as Britain did not support French imperialism in Mexico, Canada would not be molested.

Although Grant must have known that Britain had little intention of joining or supporting the Latin American adventures of the French, his strategist's mind grasped that possibility. So he proposed a trade-off that Cartier must have accepted with a sigh of relief. The future of Confederation now seemed secure, or at least probable. What Grant was saying was that the American people considered reconstruction more important than yet another war. His overtures at Quebec meant that powerful interests in the United States, who were then backing him for the Presidency after Andrew Johnson, were now becoming reconciled to the existence of another sovereign nation, sharing the North American continent. Grant's proviso seemed to be that if Britain would eventually withdraw her troops from North America, Canada would be spared. Although Grant was surrounded by flatterers and heavily influenced by Sumner, it was apparent that the United States genuinely wanted a period of security and self-containment. Cartier knew that Sumner could not be trusted, yet Grant's message sparked a ray of hope in his troubled mind.

In late January 1866, Cartier travelled up to Ottawa on business. On the train he met Thomas Chapais, his wife and little boy. Seventy years later, in a reminiscence published in the *Journal de Québec*, the little boy told of his meeting with his father's political chieftain:

At Montreal, someone came into our carriage. My father got up to meet him, introduced him to my mother as "Monsieur Cartier," and made a place for him on the bench where our luggage was stretched out, beside my box of cakes and sweets. Trains had no dining cars in those days, and I was the greediest child in the world. I was also quite

argumentative, though today (1938) even my enemies willingly testify to my moderation . . . We had by this time travelled a long way,
and I went for a little walk in the corridor to stretch my legs. Suddenly hunger or greed drove me back to my seat. Alas! . . . my box of
goodies was gone! . . . "Where did you put it?" they asked me. –
"Here, here – Then it must be still there – No it isn't – Look over
there – It's gone; someone has stolen it."

Monsieur Cartier pretended to sympathize with me in my cruel
loss – "A while ago," he said, "I saw the boy who sells oranges and
sweets pass by . . . Maybe he took your box." I was furious and wanted
to get my box back, so I went out to look for the little thief. Then I
became suspicious. What was the meaning of those mocking glances
between my parents and their companion? . . . I turned around and
went back. – "Monsieur Cartier," I said, "I think you stole my box. –
Never! – Yes, you're a thief! . . . I'm going to tell everybody on the
train; you're a thief!"

Then I had a temper tantrum, whining and crying.

Monsieur Cartier was a tease, and he had pinched my treasure to
see how I would react . . . To console me, he called for the food seller,
who of course was innocent, and bought me some treats which he
stuffed in my pockets. By the time we got to Ottawa, we were the best
friends in the world.

That illustrious statesman must have often recalled this incident:
he was certainly quite used to being called a thief by his political foes,
but by the son of one of his ministerial colleagues . . . . ?[103]

Eighteen months later, in a letter to the boy's father, Cartier asked to be
remembered fondly to his "little travelling companion."

Cartier's spirits brightened considerably when, in June of 1866, the
seat of government was moved from the cramped quarters of Quebec
into the great gothic halls of the newly-completed Parliament Buildings
at Ottawa. They were his work, this "Westminster in the Wilderness,"
his more than anyone else's, and they were magnificent. George Brown
saw them as "fit for the British, French and Russian empires, were they
all confederated."[104] For Cartier, they were a symbol of design put into
action, of a great work given shape.

He had fought hard for this dawning day, and had many great battles
still before him. *Yet it had been done!* His people would survive within
a new nationality! And the constitution now proposed would ensure a
continuation of their potent influence. Cartier knew that federal politics
would forever centre around Quebec, the pivotal province of the new
Dominion. Joseph Howe of Nova Scotia saw it too, and did not like what
he saw. In his *Botheration Letter* No. 2, the crusty old warrior concluded that

Ever since the Union of the Two Provinces, the French Canadians, by sticking together, have controlled the Legislature and the Government of Canada. They will do the same thing in a larger Union, and, as the English will split and divide, as they always do, the French members will, in nine cases out of ten, be masters of the situation. But should a chance combination thwart them, then they will back their Local Legislature against the United Parliament.[105]

Precisely. It was a perfect defensive position for the French Canadians, yet it was more. Cartier knew that this state of affairs would benefit the greater nation, because the existence of French Canada would ensure that the country would never be able, even if tempted, to abandon its larger nationality for a mess of Washington pottage.

"The new constitution recognizes the French Canadians as a distinct and separate nationality. We constitute a state within a state. We enjoy the full exercise of our rights and the formal recognition of our national independence.

14

Our religious institutions are subject to the government of Lower Canada. Our vast natural resources and our educational institutions, in which lie the future of our country, we also control. We have in the hands of our own administrators all that is most dear and precious to us, and we must profit from our own good fortune."

La Minerve, July 1, 1867

With Confederation less than a year away, the politicians of British North America began to retreat back into their home grounds and constituencies to keep up the spirit of the movement and organize their parties and financial supporters for the coming federal and provincial elections. Cartier spent countless afternoons and evenings at banquets and celebrations and investitures and dinner parties, everywhere preaching the success of the project, the future delights of a provincial legislature, and the sure survival of French Canadian nationality.

George Brown had resigned from the ministry at the close of 1865, ostensibly because of differences with Macdonald and Galt, but really because of the political demands of the soon-to-be-born Province of Ontario. Richard Cartwright later wrote that "if Mr. Brown had remained in the Cabinet and had not voluntarily thrown his cards on the table, nothing could have prevented the initiation of Confederation from having been entrusted to Mr. Brown and Sir George Cartier instead of to Sir John Macdonald." [106] Cartwright was imagining things; Brown was not acceptable to French Canada, and Macdonald was. Brown was first and foremost a newspaperman, unsuited to the daily rigour of law-making and drafting. Unlike Macdonald, he was not used to the long-term in politics. It was not his life's work, and it may be that he found working with Macdonald and Cartier, instead of against them, was a colossal bore, and damaging to his political credibility. He was so much happier back at the *Globe*, thundering at the iniquitous ministry, giving the Grits their daily dose of political medicine.

Alexander Galt wrote to his wife:

It is a great relief to me that he is gone. He was absurdly jealous, opposing everything I brought up, so that my patience has really surprised me. His resignation really occurred on the question of whether his policy or mine should prevail on the Reciprocity question, and the Council unanimously approved of my views, his own friend and follower Howland refusing to go with him. He was very much mortified at this & at Howland not being selected to go with me to Washington, and he finally resigned. [107]

But now, as the scenery of the political stage began to be shuffled about, it was Galt's turn to resign. Galt was unsure of his place in a post-Confederation ministry. In addition, he had promised the Protestant minority in Lower Canada that their educational privileges would be extended with the new order of things. When Catholics in Upper Canada began to demand the same privileges, ones that George Brown would never consent to, the government had to back off, and Galt forced by principle to resign.

The whole issue of the protection of minority education, and the right of those minorities to appeal provincial grievances at a federal level, was a political powderkeg that could have delayed Confederation by years. Cartier and Macdonald were forced to postpone implementation of federal educational support guarantees. It was a hard decision, yet the only possible course to take. It led to the resignation of Alexander Galt from the ministry, and was to come back to haunt Canadian governments on more than one occasion.

The wheels of fortune were turning. In New Brunswick, they were even pushed. As a result of some ham-handed manoeuvring by Governor Gordon, who did nothing less than force his government out of power, Tilley's pro-Confederation forces had returned victorious. Fenian border raids in that province and in the Canadas came at an opportune time for "loyal" politicians supporting Confederation, and took much of the sting out of opposition criticism.

By the late summer of 1866, Cartier could afford to relax, and let the dogs of dissent howl themselves hoarse. He hosted a few dinner parties for intimate friends and political colleagues, and in September, left the heat of Montreal and took a leisurely boat trip down the St. Lawrence with his wife and girls. A week later, he took his daughters down to the House of the Seven Chimneys to visit their cousins, then out to his country home, "Limoilou," named after the explorer Jacques Cartier's estate in France.* Limoilou was situated east of the city in the village of Hochelaga. Built with a view of the river, the house was situated on that road Cartier had walked along thirty years before, when he had returned from exile and was lying low in a still unfriendly Montreal. Now, just as Cartier's political deeds were bearing fruit, so too was the garden at Limoilou, and some of the trees he had planted when he bought the property a few years earlier were laden that autumn with ripe plums and pears.

Among those who were intimate with Cartier at this time was the Cuvillier family, and here a shadowy figure appears in his usually straightforward life. Cartier and his wife had not been on the best of terms for some time. She was a Fabre, from a family of *Rouges*. Although one of her brothers became Bishop of Montreal, another, Hector Fabre, was one of Cartier's bitterest political enemies.

Hortense Cartier appears to have been a witty, spirited woman, but perhaps understandable in a wife whose husband put so much into his work, travelled so often, and wrote little in the way of personal correspondence, she grew over the years to become malicious and sharptongued. It appears, too, that she committed an act of betrayal for which Cartier never forgave her. Verbal tradition in the Cartier family says that she foolishly told her brother Hector what had transpired at a political meeting in her home in Montreal. Cartier found her out, and from that time forward, their relationship foundered on the rocks.

Among Cartier's political mentors was Augustin (Austin) Cuvillier, nephew of his great-uncle Joseph. Cuvillier had served under de Salaberry at Châteauguay as Captain of the 5th Batallion of Militia, and was decorated for bravery. He was an importer and wholesaler of, among other things, hardware, dry goods, coal, chocolate, wines, liquors, tea, coffee, spices, furs, books and horses. In 1817, he was the only French Canadian founder of the Bank of Montreal. Cuvillier became M.P.P. for Huntingdon, broke with Papineau over the Ninety-Two Resolutions, and in 1841, on Robert Baldwin's motion, was first Speaker of the new Union. He died in 1849, having witnessed the victory of the Reformers in securing responsible government. Cuvillier's son Maurice was in Cartier's class at the Collège de Montréal, and it is quite possible that the young Cartier met and was quite taken with Maurice's sister Luce, who was three years younger.

---

* The house was demolished and the site is now occupied by oil refineries and storage tanks.

Luce Cuvillier, 1871 (Notman).

During his rise to power, Cartier continued to have intimate commercial and political dealings with the father and son, who were loyal and prominent *Bleus*. He doubtless continued social relations with the family, and when his marriage took a turn for the worse, Luce Cuvillier may have become his mistress, and Limoilou their love nest.

Luce was a sophisticated, intelligent woman, interested in politics, and very widely read, but because of her spirited ways and European manners, she was regarded as something of an oddity by the more strait-laced citizens of Montreal. In short, she was a character. She was an admirer of the life and works of the notorious French novelist Aurore Dupin, Baroness Dudevant, whose pen name was "George Sand." Sand was a lover of many men, in particular the poet Alfred de Musset and the composer Chopin. Her 1855 biography, *Histoire de ma Vie*, was a *succès de scandale* in both the English- and French-speaking worlds. A catalogue of Cartier's library[108] indicates that the works of George Sand were not unknown to him, and if he played Chopin to Luce's George Sand, it is indeed unfortunate that Luce did not write her own scandalous biography. She was, however, content to imitate George Sand's mannerisms at least – it is said she smoked cheroots and wore trousers when gardening at her own country place, located less than half a mile from Limoilou.

The evidence is thin but convincing. Various bills remaining show that the two helped each other out with their respective agricultural enterprises, and Cartier was supplied by Cuvillier and Company with such delights as grain, hay, ditching, carpentry, fruit trees, and several cases of claret and champagne. Luce travelled about with her niece Clara Symes, only daughter of a wealthy Montreal lumberman, and they undoubtedly met Cartier at various functions in Quebec City, Ottawa, and possibly London or Paris. She and Clara were often guests at Cartier's dinner parties, where, with Cartier's daughters Josephine and Hortense, they added their brilliant wit to the conversation, and generally brightened up the Montreal and Ottawa *soirées* for which Cartier was so famous. They moved in high circles. On August 26, 1872, Clara Symes married the Duc de Bassano, Napoleon III's Lord High Chamberlain.

It is difficult to determine whether their relationship was above or below board, whether or not it was kept as a family secret between the Cartiers and the Cuvilliers. We may never know.

The most damning piece of evidence that the relationship may have been below board, is Cartier's witty and high-spirited Last Will and Testament, written on November 10, 1866. He expressed a wish first, "to be buried in the Church of the Parish of Saint-Antoine de Chambly, where lie several generations of my family, on both the paternal and maternal side, that is to say, *du côté Cartier et du côté Paradis.*"*[109] If

* Literally, "on the side of Paradise"; a pun on his mother's maiden name.

the public felt strongly about it, he would not object to a state funeral in Notre-Dame, as long as the Superior of Saint-Sulpice sang the service. He wanted three masses a year, on the feast days of Saint-Georges, Saint-Etienne and Saint-Jacques, and left Luce £ 150 to have twenty-five masses said in the Saint-Sulpice Seminary, asking her to do all she could "to give good counsel to my two daughters hereafter named-. . . being convinced, from all that I know of you, your wisdom and prudence, that you have proven in the education of your niece Miss Symes, who was entrusted to your care, that your judgment with respect to my daughters could be highly useful to them."[110] The executors of the will were Cartier's brother Antoine-Côme, his law partner Pierre Pominville, the Superior of Saint-Sulpice and Maurice Cuvillier. Cartier concludes, in what he told Pominville was "the testament of a madman," with these words:

> I forbid either of my daughters to marry any member or relation of the Fabre family, on the paternal or maternal side, and if one or either of them does this, she will lose the legacy I am bequeathing her and her descendants, by this, my Last Will and Testament. If one of them does this, she will forfeit her legacy, which will go to her sister and her sister's descendants.
>
> If both do this, the legacy to them and their descendants will pass to my brother Antoine-Côme Cartier, and to my two sisters.[111]

His partner Pominville tried to get Cartier to change the will, but failed, and its provisions became public knowledge after Cartier's death. It is no wonder that Cartier's wife never returned to Canada after he died. She passed away in the South of France in 1898; Luce Cuvillier in Montreal in 1900.

At the beginning of October 1866, the Cabinet delegated Cartier, Macdonald, Langevin, Howland, McDougall and Galt to press for the adoption of Confederation at Westminster. On October 30, the City of Montreal held a banquet to honour Cartier before his departure. Among those present were Sir John Michel, Commander of the British Forces in North America, Mayor Starnes, Brydges, Rose, McGee, Maurice Cuvillier, and hundreds of friends and associates. As the toasts began, Thomas D'Arcy McGee rose

> to pay my own tribute to our host, a man who has done so much to make the Confederation of the provinces of British North America possible. One of the main obstacles to this union has arisen from the conflict, real or imagined, between racial interests, religions and languages, existing in Canada today. And this conflict could not have been avoided except by the utmost firmness, and a great deal of mutual liberality, and by a large amount of impartiality in the administration of the country, and it is above all to the Hon. Mr. Cartier that

we are indebted for the happy consequences of this enlightened and far-seeing administration.[112]

When Cartier rose to speak, the gathering erupted in one long ovation. They stood up, then climbed on their chairs, waving handkerchiefs and shouting *Vive Cartier* for ten solid minutes until Cartier begged them to stop. He gave them what they wanted to hear – the history of his life in politics, and the story of the Confederation movement, his story. Then he told them of Jacques Cartier, and the discovery of Canada, then of the French and English, and of their mutual Norman blood. Finally, he praised the balance and elegance of the British Constitution, and at the same time downgraded the "extreme democracy"[113] of the Americans.

They cheered him again at the Montreal station when he left for England for the conference at Westminster. The Vermont Central Railway, mindful of the comfort of the Chairman of Canada's Railway Committee, gave Cartier a special car, divided into a living room and sleeping compartments. He sailed from Boston on November 14, and ten days later arrived in London, where he met up with the other Canadian delegates, and the contingents from New Brunswick and Nova Scotia, who had been in London for over a month.

Most of the sixteen delegates stayed at the Westminster Palace Hotel, and there, on December 4, they began their *in camera* sessions to draft an act for the consideration of the Parliament of Great Britain. Governor General Monck and the new Colonial Secretary, Lord Carnarvon, joined them, and on Tupper's motion, seconded by Tilley, Macdonald was elected Chairman of the Conference. A few nights later, the Chairman fell asleep in his hotel room and let his newspaper fall against the candle, lighting himself and the hotel on fire. He woke up, cried out for help, and Cartier and Galt quickly arrived on the scene in their nightshirts and put out the blaze with jugs of water. The Chairman spent Christmas in bed recovering from his burns.

By Christmas Eve, the delegates had succeeded in drafting sixty-nine resolutions, based upon those agreed upon at Quebec. A legend from this Conference states that many, including Galt and Macdonald, wished to change the basis of union from a federal system to a single unitary state, and that Cartier, at the eleventh hour, threatened to pull out if this were done. The subject did come up outside the conference, when Monck, at Macdonald's suggestion, broached the subject with Carnarvon, but it is doubtful whether the Maritime delegates, jealous of their own local interests, would have supported this proposal. Besides, Macdonald knew Cartier better than to have seriously attempted such a last-minute betrayal; his little intrigue must have been made to cover some angle or other.

While the British North America Act was being drawn up by the law officers of the Crown, Cartier attended his usual round of banquets and functions. In fact, he may have attended too many of them, leaving the faithful, unsociable Langevin to do the hard slogging, the detailed work. Langevin sat in his room, chafing. On January 24, while Cartier was in Rome having an audience with the Pope, Langevin wrote to his mother that "It is true that Cartier is there, but between us, often when he is *there* he is not *here*."[114] Galt whined to his wife that "our friend Cartier devotes himself so much to society that we do not get much work out of him,"[115] and Belleau described to Chapais how "friend Cartier is out every evening with Princes, Dukes, Lords, MPs, Countesses, Duchesses, Marquesses, etc, and is not tired of it."[116]

He was filled with the smooth success of it all, and enjoying himself immensely. Yet he had at all times one eye on the future. There would be a transcontinental railway built through territory that would be acquired from the Hudson's Bay Company, and a number of Princes, Dukes, Lords and MPs were beginning to express some interest in the capitalization of the road.

On January 30, Cartier was present at a banquet given to Lord Monck by the City of Portsmouth. In replying to a toast, Cartier expressed his hope that the Imperial Parliament would approve Confederation:

> Those who read the American newspapers must have seen that our project of Union does not please them. And why? Because in the United States it is well understood that we are going to assure forever the stability of British domination over us. When the project comes before the Parliament of Great Britain, I hope that it will not be discussed as a party matter.
>
> One remembers that when those provinces that would eventually form the United States began their revolution, the French Canadians did not wish to heed the voice of Washington that called on them to embrace the cause of revolution; at that juncture, England owed them, in all truth, the retention of Canada. Their number has since grown, and their loyalty has not diminished.[117]

Two weeks later, Carnarvon presented the British North America Act to the House of Lords, where it was passed easily. By March 8, the Act had sailed through the Commons, and on the 29th, was given Royal Assent. While waiting for the Bill to go through, Cartier and the other delegates attended the wedding of a quite recovered John A. Macdonald to Susan Agnes Bernard, in St. George's Church, Hanover Square. She was the sister of Major Hewitt Bernard, Secretary to both the Quebec and London Conferences.

Cartier remained in London to watch the progress of the Intercolonial Railway Loan Act, that would guarantee £ 3 million toward the completion of a steel link between the soon-to-be united provinces of British North America. Soon after the passage of the Act, he travelled again to

Paris, and then on to Rome, possibly in company with Luce Cuvillier. Back in England in April, he boarded the Allan Line *Hibernian* at Liverpool, and after a heavy crossing, arrived back in Canada by May 16. Thousands were on hand to greet him as he came down the gangplank at Quebec, and in the towns and villages of the south shore, and when his special train arrived at Bonaventure Station in Montreal, a vast crowd of 10,000 people, led by the Mayor, presented the conquering hero with an address of welcome and escorted him home, home at last.

Monck called on John A. Macdonald to form the first ministry of the Dominion of Canada. Cartier chose the Militia and Defence portfolio because, as he explained to Tupper, it was the most difficult post to fill. He would hold this office until his death.

One small matter clouded the accomplishment of Confederation for Cartier. The Governor General's first official act on July 1, 1867, was to announce that the Queen had been pleased to confer the honour of Knight Commander of the Bath (K.C.B.) on Macdonald, and create Cartier, Galt, Tilley, Tupper, Howland and McDougall Companions of the Bath (C.B.s). Langevin was not mentioned. Cartier, as well as Galt, felt that their services had been at least as significant as Macdonald's, and took the drastic step of declining the honour.* As Galt wrote to his wife, "It is an ungracious and most unusual thing to refuse an honour publicly conferred, but if Lord Monck is an ass, I cannot help it."[118] Cartier seriously believed that the lesser honour, and Langevin's lack of recognition, was a shameful insult to the French Canadians, whom he represented. Tupper took the initiative, and wrote to the new Colonial Secretary, the Duke of Buckingham,

> for the purpose of communicating my views upon the desirability of submitting to Her Majesty the propriety of conferring upon the Hon. Mr. Cartier, the Minister of Militia, as high a mark of the Royal favour as that bestowed upon Sir John A. Macdonald. Although I had the honour of proposing the latter gentleman as Chairman of the Conference of B.N.A. delegates, held here in 1866, I think it but right to inform Your Grace that but for the patriotic devotion of Mr. Cartier to the great project of confederation, and the courage with which in the face of great difficulties and dangers he pursued that policy to the end, the union could not have been accomplished. I rejoice that it was the Royal pleasure to confer deservedly a distinction so high upon Mr. Macdonald, but I regard it as a great misfortune that a million of Catholic Frenchmen, than whom Her Majesty has no subjects more loyally devoted to her throne and person in any portion of her empire, should feel that one of their own race and religion, whose standing was equally high in Canada, and whose claim to Royal favour was as great,

---

* Cartier, Macdonald and Galt had previously declined Knighthoods, on the occasion of the 1860 visit of the Prince of Wales.

should not have been deemed worthy of the same gracious consideration.

Tupper finally made the point that

> Mr. Cartier's acceptance of an inferior distinction would undoubtedly have destroyed the great influence which he wields amongst his countrymen and impaired the power he is now able to exert so beneficially in the service of his sovereign. I may also add that the liberty I have taken in bringing this matter under the notice of Your Grace is inspired by no personal consideration and is entirely without the knowledge of Mr. Cartier.[119]

As a result of Tupper's fine work, Cartier was awarded a Baronetcy, an even higher title than Macdonald's, and one matching the honour that had been given to Louis-Hippolyte LaFontaine. Galt was appeased with a K.C.M.G.,* and Langevin's services finally recognized with a C.B.

It was an indication of Cartier's lack of wealth that, when he was created a Baronet, he was forced to borrow the money to pay the fee. The motto or device Cartier chose for his coat of arms was the phrase, *"Franc et Sans Dol"* – Frankness without Deceit.

It had been a long and hard fight for the politicians of British North America. That "antiquated piece of mid-Victorian plumbing" that was their constitution was full of flaws and imperfections, and failed to consider problems that those men never dreamed would exist, yet it was a workable document, and now they would turn to explore its uses, test its faults, and carry it west to a promised land.

Far up the Great Lakes, past where the bush thinned to prairie, men were waiting, buffalo hunters, sons of the voyageurs, waiting for the new order and the new law. And over those plains and hills, and through tangled mountain gorges to the delta of the Fraser, and across the island-strewn gulf to Victoria, the way was prepared, the thought broadcast, and the will and desire made ready.

---

* Knight Companion of the Order of St. Michael and St. George. On the subject of honours, Bonaparte once exclaimed, "Toys! You call these decorations toys! It is with such toys you govern men!"

PART THREE

ALL ABOARD
FOR THE WEST
(1867-1871)

"Confederation was not mere colonial politicking on the fringes of the known world. It was one of the great national unions of the nineteenth century; it was central to the balance of power between Europe and America, and all the passions of its era, national, imperial and ultra montane. It could not be carried without violence, nor expanded without force."

W.L. Morton

And when 'gainst the emprise
Arose those enemies
Whose house is hell with chambers
full of death,
Who knit their hands and weep,
And curse us in their sleep,
And drink the wine of madness
with their breath,
He wrung the secret from their minds,
And cast their schemes unto
the shuddering winds.

1

Charles Mair, *In Memory of*
Thomas D'Arcy McGee

When the great work had been accomplished, Cartier had less than eight years to live, but in that short period of time he would pack as much work as most men do in their lifetimes. He had been deeply involved in the Confederation settlement; in fact, it could be said to be his work more than any other's. Now he would give the young Dominion of three and a half million souls the cornerstones on which to build a transcontinental nation, by presenting to Parliament the four legislative bills that were to expand its horizons and ensure its survival. The Act providing for the transfer of the Hudson's Bay Company territories to Canada, the Manitoba and British Columbia Acts, and the Canadian Pacific Railway Bill were largely his creations; he almost singlehandedly drew them up and drove them through the Commons.

Like a Napoleon overextending himself deep into Russia, Cartier would stretch his lifeline of political support to the uttermost, and leave the new Province of Quebec to embark on the rockier roads of federal politics. There was no longer a Taché to smooth troubled waters, yet his awesome political machine would hold together long enough to give him what he wanted, to re-establish the ancient kingdom of the voyageurs, and make his city of Montreal once again the home base of a continental trading system.

Cartier was the political strong arm not only of the French Canadians, but of the northern continentalists, locked in combat with the United States. What had made him such a powerful individual was his brilliant use of capital, both political and financial, his employment of French

Canadian votes and British (Grand Trunk) money. He was the embodiment of three continuing desires: that of the French Canadians for cultural sovereignty, that of Montreal for economic ascendancy, and that of British financiers connected with the Colonial Office for Grand Trunk solvency and material expansion. He made their desires his own, and like a nova, an exploding star, he burned himself out in their accomplishment, in ensuring that a steel life-line would be thrown from one ocean to the other.

In pursuit of these goals, Cartier had to fight not only against apathy, commercial depression and small-mindedness at home, but also against British reticence, in the persons of Cobden, Bright and the Little Englanders, and against American expansionism, the dangerous continentalism of Secretary of State Seward, the new Czar of Alaska. It is no remarkable coincidence that Seward and the Russian Minister signed the agreement for the purchase of Alaska at 3 o'clock in the morning of March 30, 1867, a day after Queen Victoria had given Royal Assent to the British North America Act, Seward's $7 million "Folly" was not purchased for its furs or fisheries, and few Americans dreamed of future riches. It was bought purely and simply as a flanking action, and cheap at the price, to annex the entire west coast of North America, to nip Confederation in the bud. According to Dr. Helmcken of British Columbia, Americans in that colony were boasting how they had "sandwiched British Columbia and could eat her up at any time."[1]

The creation of a new power centre in North America, with a monarchical system to boot, had insulted the United States of America to its very core. The creation of the Dominion of Canada was, to some, a violation of the Monroe Doctrine of American hegemony in North America, and if the new nation expanded, it could threaten the mind of the Republic with "otherness," with an alternative to its great principles as well as its economic might. The ripe plum that promised sooner or later to drop into American hands was now threatening to turn into a very large and independent pumpkin, weighing heavily over the Yankee head. Alaska was step one in a fight to clip the wings of the young Dominion. Alaska, said Charles Sumner to the Senate of the United States, was "a visible step in the occupation of the whole North American continent."[2]

Alexander Morris M.P. expressed the sentiments of most Canadians when he said that "Canada is bound to the North-West by the ties of discovery, possession and interest. The country is ours by right of inheritance." But the Canadian expansionists had little time to lose. The northern and central American states, with three-quarters of the population, and fresh from a Civil War that had defeated the southern cotton-producing states, were turning their energies toward the northern third of the continent, to the fur wealth of Rupert's Land and the Pacific colonies of British Columbia and Vancouver Island.

Cartier was the central figure in the cold war for control of what is now Western Canada. Still flushed with success from Confederation, and a hard-fought victory in the fall elections of 1867, he threw himself into his militia work, having every reason to fear a drift into war with the United States.

After an incredible orgy of spending, producing and destroying, a sweet and longed-for peace had descended on the war-weary United States. But now came the period of Reconstruction, when the virtual control of government lay in the hands of the "robber barons" and their lobbyists. The power of the American railway builders was especially potent, and would prove extremely dangerous for the young Dominion. Congress was their bear garden. Their reach extended into every dark corner of the federal and state governments, and few were untainted by bribery or payoff. It is said that Jay Gould, "the Mephistopheles of Wall Street," and one of the more flagrant of the Robber Barons, once turned up at the State House in Albany toting a satchel containing $500,000 in greenbacks, all to help oil the wheels of legisation. According to William Seward, political parties were nothing more than "joint stock associations, in which those who contribute most direct the action and management of the concern." [3] The war years had interrupted America's spirit of unbounded development, but now the country – its economy consolidated and its south made subservient – began to put itself back together again, and looked outward for new fields to conquer.

On March 6, 1868, the State Legislature of Minnesota passed the following resolution:

> That we regret to be informed of a purpose to transfer the Territories between Minnesota and Alaska to the Dominion of Canada, by an Order in Council, at London, without a vote of the people of Selkirk and the Settlers upon the sources of the Saskatchewan River, who largely consist of Immigrants from the United States; and we would respectfully urge that the President and Congress of the United States shall represent to the Government of Great Britain, that such action will be an unwarranted interference with the principle of Self-Government, and cannot be regarded with indifference by the people of the United States. That the Legislature of Minnesota would rejoice to be assured that the cession of North-West British America to the United States, accompanied by the contruction of a Northern Pacific Railway, are regarded by Great Britain and Canada as satisfactory provisions of a Treaty which shall remove all grounds of grievance between the respective countries. [4]

Behind this motion, forwarded to Senator Alexander Ramsey of Minnesota but then shelved by the Committee on Foreign Relations, were the beginning eddies of a maelstrom that would propel Cartier into the centre of a political power struggle between the two great nations of the

English-speaking world. On his shoulders, as Minister of Militia, rested the responsibility for the defence of Canada. He and Macdonald, believing that the interests of the Dominion and the Empire largely coincided, often relied on the advice, and even the dictates of Whitehall. This, along with Cartier's continuing Chairmanship of the Railway Committee, ensured continual close contact with the makers of British imperial policy.

As the drama for possession and control of the west unfolded, the Parliament of Canada gave almost unanimous approval to Cartier's masterful Militia Bill. In a five hour speech to the Commons in March, 1868, he outlined the one hundred and one clauses of his great act. It provided for a voluntary force of 40,000 men and a complete reorganization of the provincial units, at an annual cost of $900,000, and was so innovative and well thought-out that the Leader of the Opposition, Alexander Mackenzie, offered no opposition, seconding Cartier "for any expense necessary to defend the country and the honour of the British flag." [5]

It was all very well to defend the infant Dominion with guns and fortifications, but to stand effectively on guard for Canada, to ensure its survival, it was absolutely essential to create a viable transcontinental nation, a whole state with a will to live and the frontier to sustain that will. And it was necessary to fight the United States every inch of the way. The Americans expected it, the British knew it, and Cartier felt it in his bones, because if the battle were won, it would mean the sure survival of the French Canadian people. If it were lost, first the English, and then eventually the French Canadians, would be assimilated into the North American melting-pot.

The battle, too, had a very special meaning for the Empire builders of Great Britain – the Hudson's Bay Company men, the Grand Trunk interests, the bankers, and Colonial Office bureaucrats. To establish their hegemony over the northern part of the continent and give themselves a safe land route to the Far East, to link up their Empire on which the sun never set, they threw their diplomatic cunning and financial muscle behind the new Dominion, and in doing so chained the American colossus within its own boundaries.

The first casualty of the battle was Thomas D'Arcy McGee. The United States government had done little to curb the power of the Fenian Brotherhood, an organization dedicated to freeing Ireland from the yoke of England. Through border raids into British North America, the Fenians hoped to force Britain out of Ireland, and it suited the U.S. State Department to turn a blind eye to their skirmishing. In the early morning of April 7, 1868, McGee was assassinated by a Fenian bullet, as he prepared to open the door of his lodgings in Ottawa. He was only forty-four and at the height of his powers. Like Cartier, McGee was a former rebel who had made his peace with the British Crown. The

Fenians killed him because of his power and influence with the Irish Catholics, not only in Montreal but throughout Canada. In Parliament the next afternoon, Cartier hailed his friend as a great patriot, and proposed a state pension for his widow and daughters, as well as a civil funeral paid for by the state. Cartier was one of the pall bearers as McGee's coffin was carried into Notre Dame Cathedral. The new nation had a martyr, the most eloquent of its founding fathers.

The Saint-Jean-Baptiste celebrations of that year saw Cartier at his patriotic best, defining and celebrating the new nationality. In the hall of the Ottawa branch of the Society, surrounded by friends and under an arch of maple leaves, he praised the loyalty and virtues of the French Canadian people. "What," he said, "is more painful to us than the memory of the Conquest? Yet the Conquest spared us the misery and shame of the French Revolution. The Conquest succeeded in giving us the noble and free institutions we possess today, and under which we live contented and prosperous, for we are 'men of faith and progress'." Noting that those who had emigrated to the New England states had kept alive their nationality and customs, he praised the vitality and survival instincts of his people: "It is said that only the French refuse to be americanized in that great Republic, where so many Europeans, of diverse origins, have come to blend their names, their labours and energies."[6] Yet emigration from Quebec was draining its life blood. The good land had given out, and the mill towns of New England were attracting a surplus population that Quebec and Canada could not afford to lose.

Cartier kept himself well informed of the situation through his own intelligence network. On May 7, 1869, a Grank Trunk Railway customs officer wrote him from Coaticook on the U.S. border that

> altho' the departure of rather a large number of our french canadians, mostly young men, has taken place since the beginning of April, yet a strong return-immigration has set in – Those returning seem to be in *good* position, and have already purchased land in this and the adjacent townships. From all the information I make it my duty to collect, from those returning, I find that a large return of our own population may be expected next fall – from Springfield, Lowell and other New England towns. I have no hesitation in arriving at the conclusion that, as soon as *full work* is commenced on the Intercolonial R.R., a very large and immediate return will take place . . . I am still and always remain firmly convinced that our salvation so far as Quebec is concerned, is, if we work to retain the French Canadian element, fostering of Manufacturers & above all a *Homestead Law*.[7]

The fact of the matter was that the French Canadians were bursting the bonds of their native province, and looking for new lands to colonize. The region of the Saguenay was being opened up more and more to settlers, yet Cartier was straining for further fields to conquer, new lands for the multitudinous sons of Quebec, and the fields that came to mind were the great plains of the NorthWest, already the home of a "Little Quebec" in the Red River settlement.

A year earlier, George Brown's successor William McDougall, one of the two Grits in the coalition cabinet, had presented the Government's resolutions for the acquisition of the North-West. Rising to support the resolutions, Cartier noted that the United States had eagerly purchased Alaska; he harangued his fellow M.P.s:

Are we going to be small and mean, when it is a question of a bagatelle of five or six million dollars to extend our Dominion as far as British Columbia? Since the United States have become a nation, their policy has been one of aggrandisement by the acquisition of new territory. Now, when it is known in Europe that we have acquired such vast territories, which represent millions of acres of land, you will see a great stream of emigration directed towards this country.[8]

By the summer of 1868, McDougall and Cartier were preparing to travel to England to negotiate with the Hudson's Bay Company. Before sailing, Cartier joined Macdonald, Tupper and John Sandfield Macdonald in Halifax, where the four succeeded in pacifying Joseph Howe, who was seriously threatening to take Nova Scotia out of Confederation. Better terms were guaranteed to that province, and Howe was rewarded for his sensible patriotism by being made President of the Privy Council, from which lofty perch he could keep a closer eye on Upper Canadian trickery.

Cartier and McDougall arrived in London on October 12, on a mission that was to last six months. McDougall fell ill soon after their arrival, and Cartier carried most of the weight of the negotiations. McDougall, the Minister of Public Works, was no diplomat. He merely represented Ontario's insistence on the transfer of the North-West; Cartier was the master of the situation. Only Cartier fully realized the significance of the acquisition of the territories, their long-term advantages. His prestige, influence, knowledge of diplomacy, of what Britain and the Grank Trunk interests wanted, carried the day.

It had to be done quickly. The Disraeli government was tottering and American claims for the territories were becoming more insistent. In fact, as Sir Stafford Northcote, the Governor of the Hudson's Bay Company hinted to Cartier, certain Americans were also in London negotiating to purchase the Hudson's Bay Company.

American sabre-rattling had promised a dangerous time for the young Dominion, but what was worse, there appeared to be traitors within the gates – Cobden and Bright and the whole anti-colonial, free trade school were quite prepared to appease the United States by sacrificing Canada on the altar of peace. The problems created by British support of Canada were more than Bright could bear, and his feelings were nourished by shrewd Americans like Henry Adams, who advised him that "England can do much to remove danger, but the essential point is that she should without delay sever her political connection with Canada and all her territory on our continent. This is the key of the difficulty. If after that concession to us, we still make war, we should hurt ourselves more than you."[9]

At first, Cartier's negotiations in London went well, Buckingham had prepared the groundwork with a special land act, forcing the Hudson's Bay Company to deal outside the courts. During the negotiations, Cartier spent some time renewing old acquaintances, particularly Watkin – now Sir Edward Watkin, M.P. – knighted for his involvement in the accomplishment of Confederation – still at the helm of the Grank Trunk. Cartier was wined and dined, week after week, by the princes of the Empire. English newspapers were full of the success of the mission, when suddenly the roof fell in; Disraeli's government was defeated in the House. One of the casualties was Watkin, who was defeated in the ensuing election, and later deposed from the presidency of the Railway. Cartier wrote Macdonald that

> The principal causes of his defeat are first, that a few days before the election, he went to lay the cornerstone of a Roman Catholic Church and proposed the health of the Pope at the lunch which ensued, and the second that he incurred the ire of Mr. Bright and some of his friends (Bright's friends) for not having supported Bright and his motion in favour of Nova Scotia against the Confederation . . . You may judge what sort of liberalism the pretended "Liberals" are made of here.[10]

In the same letter, he noted that Bright was "full of American ideas and sympathies."

On Disraeli's defeat, the Hudson's Bay Company immediately upped its demands for the territory to $5 million, a sum that the Americans would have paid three times over. Yet there was more than just cash at stake, there was principle and common sense, and the whole delicate structure of negotiations had to be rebuilt brick by brick. The new Gladstone government was cool toward the delegates. On one occasion, Cartier protested a charge of $4,000 made by the British for equipment damaged by the Canadian militia, which led the new Governor General Sir John Young to complain to Cardwell that "the two you had on a visit are about the least reasonable of all. Cartier as a Frenchman imbued with the modes and habits of French thought looks to H.M. Govnt. for everything. McDougall, whom I have never seen, is reckoned a difficult person to deal with. I do not wonder they pressed you."[11] Young's obvious dislike of Cartier, and his prejudice against the French, was to lead to trouble after the Red River rebellion, and indirectly, to Riel's death

many years later. Cartier also ran into difficulties with the "Little En-
glander" John Bright. As he explained in a letter to Macdonald, "Bright
with his anti-colonial ideas seems to think that it would be well if the
H.B. territory were to go to the United States. I had to argue a great deal
against the current of his ideas in my last interview with him." [12] But
the hardest nut of all to crack was the new Colonial Secretary, Lord
Granville, known as "Pussy" for his suave and diplomatic manner.

Cartier was weary, but up to the task. At a dinner promoted by the
Great Western Railway Company, he impressed the financiers by declaring that "Canadians desire to be a power on the American continent,
and to make their influence felt from the Atlantic to the Pacific." [13] The
new Prime Minister, the great and hoary William Ewart Gladstone,
soon mellowed with regard to the wishes of the Canadians. At a banquet
of the Colonial Society, he complimented them on having "assured the
presence here this evening, of representatives of the great British family
of Nations." He then turned toward Cartier, and described him as "a
man who seems to be legion in himself, and displays no less warm a
sympathy, particularly to the origins of his race and the traditions of his
people, and who, superior to any of his predecessors, is eminently fitted
to represent that spirit of fraternity which should unite the English-
speaking nations throughout the world." A strange, convoluted tribute,
but Cartier was equal to it. "I am," he said simply, "a British subject,
like all who surround me; the only difference is that I speak French." [14]

It appears that this banquet was chiefly designed to demonstrate imperial solidarity to the American Minister, Reverdy Johnson, who
marred the evening when he facetiously suggested that the colonies
might find themselves transferred from the Union Jack to the Stars and
Stripes. Granville dismissed the suggestion with jocular scorn, and both
Gladstone and Cartier ended the occasion by proposing toasts to the
Empire, to the accompaniment of great applause.

By the middle of March, 1869, the negotiations had succeeded. For
£ 300,000, the Hudson's Bay Company agreed to surrender all their
interests in the North-West, with the exception of one-twentieth of the
fertile belt and 45,000 acres adjacent to their trading posts. Cartier
spent several days at Windsor Castle as a guest of the Queen, and again
breakfasted with his friend, the witty Lady Flora Macdonald. On April
1, he boarded the *North American* for home. After five months away
from his native land, he found himself hailed as a conquering hero.
Addresses of welcome were presented to him by Mayors and party faithful, and when his train chugged into Bonaventure Station, a partisan
crowd of 6,000 was on hand to greet him.

On May 28, 1869, in the Parliament of Canada, Cartier presented the
resolutions ratifying the bargain he had made in their name, concluding
with the words, "The British North America Act will soon apply to a
chain of provinces, extending from the Atlantic to the Pacific. I hope we

shall then no longer hear of annexation." [15] But annexation was still very much on the minds of the Americans, and the great territories would have to be brought under the direct control of Ottawa. Within two weeks, Parliament had passed "An Act for the Temporary Government of Rupert's Land," providing for a government by Lieutenant-Governor and Council, seated at Fort Garry, effective December 1. Except for laws inconsistent with the British North America Act, all laws in the territory were to remain in force until the Canadian government had decided how the territory might best be governed.

To appease Ontario, William McDougall was chosen as the first Governor. A tall, heavily-built, almost elegant man, McDougall had proven to be moody and uncomfortable in the coalition cabinet, and chafed under the rule of Macdonald and Cartier, without the sustenance of George Brown. He wanted out and Macdonald and Cartier were quite happy to oblige him.

In early October, he and his retinue left Ottawa to begin the long journey to the heart of the continent. They travelled by train to St. Paul, Minnesota, then by river boat, north toward the new seat of government. The party included a Captain D.R. Cameron, his wife (who happened to be Charles Tupper's daughter), and the Civil Secretary-designate, J.A.N. Provencher, former editor of *La Minerve* and a nephew of the former Bishop of Saint-Boniface. Cameron and Provencher were doubtless chosen to balance out McDougall's style of politics, and prevent him from committing any rash acts. Cameron, well known to the Minister of Militia, was to develop a police force in the new territory.

On October 30, at the American border near Pembina, William McDougall, Lieutenant-Governor-designate of the North-West Territories, was stopped by an armed band of men and told to go no farther.

"Old Red River is going to the Devil faster than ever, and God only knows what is to become of us if the English Government or some other friendly soul does not take us by the hand."

2

A.G.B. Bannatyne to
"Old Bear" Ellice, 1863

Seven years before Confederation, on June 10, 1860, a dark, intense sixteen-year-old Métis youth from the Red River sat with his classmates at the year-end ceremonies of the Collège de Montréal, watched the choir sing "O Canada, Mon Pays, Mes Amours," and listened as

George-Etienne Cartier, the author of the song, a former graduate and the political leader of French Canada, spoke to the students about their future.

The boy was of mixed blood – one-eighth Métis – the eldest son of a wool miller and fur trader, who had once studied for the priesthood in Quebec. His maternal grandmother was the first white woman in the North-West. The father, a proud and far-seeing man and a recognized leader of his people, had long desired to start a textile mill, and in 1857, encouraged by Monseigneur Taché, nephew of Cartier's great colleague, Sir E.-P. Taché and the new Bishop of Saint-Boniface, he travelled east to solicit support from the Masson family, seigneurs of Terrebonne, north of Montreal. Madame Masson was a generous woman, and gave him enough to buy a milling machine, but funds could not be raised for a building to house it, even if the huge contraption could be dismantled and dragged across the Prairie to Saint-Boniface. So the father's great commercial dream failed, and he spent the rest of his life doing odd jobs around the Cathedral at Saint-Boniface and for the Hudson's Bay Company.

But for his eldest son there was hope. The Massons agreed to sponsor the boy's education, and on June 1, 1858, he and two friends left Saint-Boniface and travelled south and east by ox cart, steamboat and train the fifteen hundred miles to Montreal. It was an overwhelming experience for the fourteen-year-old – the great cities, the speed of the train, the lakes you could not see across, the first taste of an orange – all new, and followed by the austere, frugal life at the Collège, under the watchful eyes of the Gentlemen of Saint-Sulpice, the drilling, the examinations, the thoughts and words of civilization, so much more difficult than in the little school by the Cathedral at home.

It was expected that he would enter the priesthood, but in spite of his quick acceptance of the school and his high marks, there was a streak of moodiness, compounded by pride and a hot temper, which made this possibility less and less likely. And as he listened to Cartier speak of destiny and nationality, memories of home and of his father's failure stirred new emotions within him. He would not enter the priesthood. His name was Louis Riel and he was to be the hero and martyr of his people.

Four years later, he learned of his father's death in far way Red River. The shock of this news put him into a profound depression. He brooded, wrestled with his new responsibility as head of the family, made himself ill, refused to go to lessons. He wrote long, introspective, melancholy verse, and then, inspired by Cartier's recent defence of minority rights in the Confederation debates at Quebec, wrote several poems in praise of Cartier's stand, and sent them off to his new father, his hero, urging Cartier to "work for us who are your brothers, crush every obstacle before you, defeat your enemies and their noxious schemes, close your ears to the vulgar spite of those who are carried away by their own foolish ideas."[16]

On March 8, 1865, without warning, and with just four months to go before his own graduation, Louis Riel packed his belongings and left the Collège de Montréal to make his fortune in the business world. We know that one of his first steps was to ask for an interview with Cartier, who was a friend of his benefactors, the Massons. There is no record of the interview between the fifty-one year old politician at the height of his powers, and the nervous twenty-one year old, stricken with hero-worship, but it is quite possible that at that meeting, Cartier, desirous of ensuring a strong French Canadian presence in the west, and well informed of American moves in that direction, saw in this idealistic and tormented young man some hope for the future of the west. Perhaps he also saw in Louis Riel echoes of his own youth, and of the son he never had.

There is no proof to this effect, but Cartier may have briefed Riel on the government's plans for the North-West and suggested that Riel work for him as an active intelligence gatherer, or at the very least, that Riel live in the United States, to try and understand the expansionist forces that were already threatening French influence in the Red River. Whether there was any agreement, formal or informal, between the two, we may never know, but later events suggest that there was more going on between Cartier and Riel than mere adulation and inspiration. Cartier may have left the choice open for Riel. The young man was obviously desperate, casting around for a profession and a purpose, and there would be very few outlets for his energies when he returned to the Red River, as Cartier knew he must.

Cartier was at that period trying to build new political alliances in Lower Canada in anticipation of the Confederation settlement and a new provincial order in Quebec. One of his chief opponents, a man worthy of respect, was the *Rouge* lawyer, Rodolphe Laflamme, a former editor of *L'Avenir* and law partner of Joseph Doutre, Cartier's old duelling companion. Laflamme was only moderately anti-clerical and anti-confederate, but he was a strong French Canadian nationalist, and the kind of man who could test Riel's principles, just as Rodier had inspired Cartier thirty years before. Cartier may have recommended Riel to Laflamme, who in any event took the youth into his law office.

Riel soon became bored and impatient with the intricacies of the profession, and as a contemporary said, "carried his office in his hat and met his clients on top of Mount Royal."[17] Standing on its summit, with the city of Montreal, its red brick and balconies and blue-grey spires spreading out around him, and its rivers encircling him like a mother's arms, he felt like a king without a country. His clients did not yet exist, for Riel was a dreamer, and his dream lay hidden somewhere in that blue and orange sunset haze, northwest up the Ottawa.

And now this city was painful to him, hurtful to his pride. He had been in love; he and Marie-Julie Guernon had secretly signed a marriage contract. But Marie's parents objected to their daughter marrying a Métis, so a frustrated and disappointed Louis Riel climbed the mountain one last time to see into his dream. But he was too angry and too much awake and alive to dream. The words of Cartier had begun to take effect. There may have been further meetings. At any rate, sometime soon before or soon after July 1, 1867, Louis Riel boarded a Grand Trunk passenger train, and left Montreal for the west.

He travelled directly to Chicago, and stayed for a time with some French Canadian expatriates, including the poet Louis Fréchette, an often violent opponent of English Canada. He then worked for a time in St. Paul, Minnesota, soaking up the climate of American expansionism, before returning home to Saint-Boniface on July 28, 1868. "It was early in the morning," he wrote, "when I saw my birthplace again; a Sunday, before sunrise. It was a beautiful day. I saw my very dear mother, brothers and sisters that very same day." [18]

Why the delay in returning directly home to his beloved mother, and why did he remain in St. Paul when he was so near home? He knew his family were suffering. He no doubt sent some of his earnings in St. Paul home, but the answer is possibly that he was supplying the Minister of Militia with intelligence, and getting paid for his services. Cartier needed to know more about events in St. Paul, Minnesota, a hotbed of annexationist sentiment and headquarters for the American drive to take over the Canadian North-West. It is known that Riel went to work in Gilbert Lachance's dry-goods firm, [19] but he probably met, and may even have worked for a trader named Norman Kittson, a Quebecker from Chambly, who was the Hudson's Bay Company agent in St. Paul. Kittson, who was bought out by the Company in 1862, had established a trading post at Pembina in 1844, and soon threatened the Company's monopoly of Red River trade. He was doubtless well acquainted with Louis Riel's father, who at that same time had been the leader of an agitation for free trade in furs. In 1849, a five-year old Louis had watched, wide-eyed, as his father and his friends organized a petition, and successfully demanded the release from prison of William Sayer, an independent trader. When the courthouse was surrounded by 400 armed Métis, the Company gave in to their demands, to great whoops and shouts of "le commerce est libre."

Kittson may have been an intelligence gatherer himself. He was certainly a link between the Canadian government and Hudson's Bay Company officers such as Donald Smith. It is reasonable to suppose that Company officials were invited to provide such a service for the Canadian government, especially since the backers of the Company were also the backers of the Grank Trunk Railway, whose solicitor was the Minister of Militia of the Dominion of Canada.

Inspired by a speech of William Seward in 1861, who predicted that St. Paul would be the centre of a great North American power, the citizens and merchants of the city – originally called Pig's Eye – were intoxicated by its future promise as the great and glorious entrepôt of northwest trade. The good free land in the United States had just about disappeared, but there were millions of acres of rich black earth in the Red River and across the Hudson's Bay Company domain – the so-called last, best west – soon to be deeded over to the new upstart Dominion of Canada. The word "Dominion" itself rankled the citizens of St. Paul; it smacked too much of British domination.

In 1859, just over a year after Louis Riel had left for college in Montreal, a friendly, likeable American named James Wickes Taylor arrived "to do business" in the sleepy Red River settlement. Unknown to the farmers and Hudson's Bay Company factors who met him, Taylor had just been appointed special agent of the United States Treasury, Secret Service Branch, and directed to report on the situation and to work for the annexation of the territory to the United States. There was little to be done for the present, as the populace consisted of a few Selkirk settlers, Métis boatmen, hunters and farmers, and the fur traders of the Company. There were only a handful of buildings across the river from Saint-Boniface, on the site of present-day Winnipeg, but Taylor knew the people would come, knew the land would be settled and the town built at the junction of the Red River and Assiniboine trails. It was only a matter of time, and time, for Taylor, should not be lost. Now sporting the nickname, "Saskatchewan," Taylor reported to his Treasury masters that the colony was ripe for American occupation, and that, in the event of war, the State of Minnesota could, with no trouble at all, "hold, occupy and possess"[20] the entire Red River settlement.

That the colony was ripe for American occupation was obvious to every interested politician on both sides of the border, as well as to the administrators of the Hudson's Bay Company, and the mandarins of the British Foreign Office. At the slightest excuse, on the least pretext, the United States could have walked into the Red River and taken it without a shot. There were international checks and balances to prevent the likelihood of this happening, and the United States was, on the whole, weary of war; yet the purchase of Alaska was a clear enough warning of American intent. Unless Canada could get the Red River territory and lay hold on it, unless she could extend her reach from there across the continent, she was doomed to languish, without spirit and without a frontier, in a backwater of North America.

Fronting for "Saskatchewan" Taylor in the U.S. Congress were Senators Zachariah Chandler and Joseph Howard of Michigan, General N.P. Banks of Boston, and Senator Alexander Ramsey, former Governor of Minnesota. Backing them up was, of course, the ubiquitous Bill Seward, Lincoln's Secretary of State, who declared to a Boston audience in 1867,

"I know that Nature designs that this whole continent, not merely these thirty-six states, shall be sooner or later, within the magic circle of the American union."[21]

In 1866, General Banks had presented his notorious bill for "the admission of the States of Nova Scotia, New Brunswick, Canada East, Canada West, and the organization of the Territories of Selkirk, Saskatchewan and Columbia." The bill was written by none other than James Wickes Taylor. Behind all this ranting and huffing was the Americans' real fear that unless the Red River were won, the whole future economy of their own North-West might be jeopardized. For twenty years, American promoters had tried to sell the idea of a railway from New York to the Columbia River. Such a line would have great economic advantages as well as interesting political and strategic possibilities. Hopefully, part of it could be built through British territory – up the valley of the South Saskatchewan – but if it were laid down along the border, it could tap the trade of the British North-West and challenge the commercial hegemony of the Hudson's Bay Company. It could lead to settlement, and when enough American voices could be raised in the name of "Liberty," to political control over the territory. If it were not built, the British and Canadians would surely construct a line that, because of its closer route to the sea via Montreal, and to the Far East via British Columbia, would itself tap the trade of the American North-West.

It is therefore not too difficult to comprehend why the Northern Pacific Railway, chartered in 1864 and endowed with a large block of territory, was of very special interest to the U.S. State Department. To promote the project and raise funds for the line, its directors induced Jay Cooke, boy wonder, financial genius and wizard of the Civil War bond selling campaign, into their scheme. Cooke, at the urging of the State Department and led on by his nose for a profit, soon developed an acute political interest in the Red River. In 1870, he wrote to a friend regarding James Wickes Taylor,

> I should like to be one of a number to employ his services wholly in manipulating the annexation of British North America, Northwest of Duluth, to our country. This could be done without any violation of treaties, and brought about as a result of quiet emigration over the border of trustworthy men with families, and with a tacit, not legal understanding with Riley [Louis Riel] and others there. The country belongs to us naturally, and should be brought over without violence or bloodshed.[22]

To assist him in this worthy endeavour, Cooke hired Taylor as his press agent and lobbyist, so that in the person of Taylor, the U.S. government's interest and the Northern Pacific Railway's interest were one and the same, for the aggrandizement of the American Empire.

The intent of the American promoters of the Northern Pacific was made quite clear in a report of the U.S. Senate Committee on Pacific Railways, dated February 19, 1869:

> The line of the North Pacific road runs for fifteen hundred miles near the British possessions, and when built will drain the agricultural products of the rich Saskatchewan and Red River districts east of the mountains, and the gold country on the Fraser, Thompson and Kootenay Rivers west of the mountains. From China (Canton) to Liverpool is fifteen hundred miles nearer by the forty-ninth parallel of latitude than by the way of San Francisco and New York. This advantage in securing the overland trade from Asia will not be thrown away by the English, unless it is taken away by our first building the North Pacific road, establishing mercantile agencies at Puget Sound, fixing mercantile capital there and getting possession on land, and on the ocean, of all the machinery of the new commerce between Asia and Europe. The opening by us first of a Northern Pacific railroad seals the destiny of the British possessions west of the ninety-first meridian. They will become so Americanised in interests and feelings that they will be in effect severed from the new Dominion, and the question of their annexation will be but a question of time.[23]

Taylor furthermore felt that "we have only to deposit an open basket under the tree, and the ripe fruit will speedily fall."[24] Some Canadians held the same opinion: as early as 1865, George Shepherd, ex-editor of the Toronto *Globe*, wrote to George L. Becker of the St. Paul and Pacific Railway,

> Renew reciprocity, & you postpone annexation indefinitely. Refuse reciprocity – or insist upon conditions with which a colony cannot comply – & you ensure annexation within a brief period. On this point I am positive. To you in the North-West the matter has a significance apart from commercial considerations. For reciprocity will help the Confederation scheme; and that involves the erection of a British province at your very doors. Defeat reciprocity, & the Red River country will drop like a ripe plum into your hands.[25]

Such "ripe fruit" theorizing led to an overconfidence in some Americans that proved their undoing. Cooler heads in the United States knew that Britain would almost certainly go to war to preserve a possible overland route to the Far East. Lincoln knew it, and after 1869, Ulysses S. Grant and his Secretary of State Hamilton Fish knew it as well. Yet still in the back of their collective consciousness, the Americans remained believers in the Ripe Fruit Theory, that sooner or later, by some natural process, some osmosis, the northern half of the continent would fall into their lap. To further this end, they studiously avoided war, but rather tried to exploit their great economic and cultural influence to bring the upstart young Dominion to its knees.

Their plan, as it evolved, was probably this – exploit Canadian sectional differences; use American settlers present in the Red River and British Columbia to demand democratic rights, annexation and statehood; and finally, destroy the one politician who could be said to hold the key to the mint, the political kingpin of Canada, Minister of Militia and Chairman of the Railway Committee, Sir George-Etienne Cartier.

When Hamilton Fish learned of Canada's successful negotiations to purchase the Hudson's Bay Company, he changed tack, and put "Saskatchewan" Taylor to work. On May 15, 1869, Taylor wrote to Norman Kittson urging that the Hudson's Bay Company should press for railroad communication between St. Paul and the Red River. With his real purpose being counter-intelligence, Taylor asked for a position as a Company intelligencer or go-between, and obliquely suggested that the Hudson's Bay Company could be offered $5,000,000 if it went along with American plans for annexation of the Canadian North-West.[26]

Taylor soon learned that there were two groups in Canada vying for control of the North-West; roughly speaking, the English from Ontario and the French from Quebec. The new territory would obviously attract a large number of settlers from an Ontario ripe for expansion. Yet Quebec itself also wished to guard its influence in the North-West as an outlet for its surplus population, and the Port of Montreal, suffering from its failure to capture the trade of the American midwest, wanted to ensure the bulk of North-West traffic for itself.

The clerical nationalism and railway economics of Montreal were no psychological match for the out-and-out imperialist nationalism of Ontario, epitomized by a group of young men calling themselves "Canada First." The acquisition of the North-West had been their Holy Grail, their lode star. Begun initially as a literary coterie of such men as the sentimental and romantic Charles Mair, author of *Tecumseh*, and other epics now largely of interest for their historical value alone, Canada First rapidly emerged as a full-blown nationalist movement. William McDougall, long an advocate of the annexation of the North-West, saw possibilities in the group, and persuaded Mair to write a history of Rupert's Land. Just before he and Cartier left for London to negotiate for the territory, McDougall suggested that Mair visit the Red River himself, and gave him a sinecure as paymaster of a work gang.

Mair arrived in the Red River a few months after Louis Riel's return. He immediately struck up a friendship with a young doctor from Kingston, a friend of McDougall's, the shy giant John Christian Schultz, who had recently purchased control of the newspaper, *The Nor'Wester*. Living first at Dutch George's Hotel, Mair eventually moved in with Schultz. "The change was comfortable," he assured his brother, "from the racket of a motley crowd of half-breeds, playing billiards and drinking, to the quiet and solid comfort of a home." [27]

The two began to engage in land speculation, and dreamed of the money they would make with the flood of immigration. Schultz decided to go to Toronto and Montreal to ship up some trade goods, and while he was away, Mair took the time to write glowing letters to his brother in Ontario, long epistles describing the territory and its fertility, letters that were printed with great effect in the Toronto *Globe*. So obviously a square peg in a round hole, Mair and his remarks to his brother on the morals of Métis women and the laziness of Métis men, were soon found out by the citizens of the colony. He became the laughing stock of Red River when Mrs. Bannatyne, wife of one of the early traders, confronted him with a *Globe* letter and went after him with a horsewhip. And when Mair and some friends began to pace out lots and stake land in Saint-Norbert, they were warned away by an angry group of local Métis.

When Schultz visited Ontario that winter, he carried a letter of introduction from Mair to Colonel George T. Denison, a fiercely pro-British, anti-Yankee swashbuckler whose book, *Cavalry Tactics*, had recently won an honourable mention in the Czar of Russia's competition. Denison was itching for a war with the Americans as a drastic method of forging Canadian nationality, and, interested in Schultz's account of the dangers in the Red River, promised him all the support he could muster in Ontario.

That spring, McDougall, while still the Minister of Public Works, had sent out a party of surveyors to take the measurements of the soon-to-be transferred territory. The Hudson's Bay Company protested that they had not been consulted beforehand, but then allowed the work to proceed. The Métis farmers, alarmed by the brashness of the newcomers and fearful that their long river farms would be parallelled and squared out to an inrush of settlers, began to grow angry and restless. Among them was a young man with time on his hands, and his own ideas of nationality, French and Indian ideas. Louis Riel was more than just alarmed, he was enraged, and the presence of men like the surveyors in the Red River only heightened his anger. These newcomers patronized his people, and swaggered over their land.

Cartier may have warned Riel about McDougall, or Ontario's special interest in the territory. At any rate, when he learned about McDougall's appointment as Governor, Riel saw the writing on the wall, and determined to take action. His people were receptive to being organized. In 1867 and 1868, a plague of grasshoppers, laying as thick as snow on the ground, had infested the Red River, eating away everything that was green. The buffalo had practically disappeared, and Métis hunters found even the lowly rabbit scarce. His people had starved. And now this new plague of English, threatening to turn into a swarm! It was more than he or his people could bear.

Besides the surveyors, there was another significant figure visiting the Red River in the autumn of 1869. In early October, Riel received a note from none other than Joseph Howe, the doughty old warrior from Nova Scotia who had just made peace with the Dominion and had been sent out by its cabinet. Howe asked for a meeting, but Riel, busy organizing men to stop the surveyors, refused to have anything to do with him – perhaps because Howe was accompanied by a party of Canadian businessmen. As President of the Council and newly-designated Secretary of State for the Provinces, Howe joked that he was in the Red River to see if there were any jobs for Nova Scotians. If Riel heard his joke, he probably did not appreciate it. Howe was there ostensibly on a fact-finding mission, preparing the way for the new Lieutenant-Governor, yet strange to say, he refused to see Schultz or any of the Canada Firsters, which enraged them. But Howe was interested in bigger game. In fact, that summer, he had been finding out American intentions with regard to the Northern Pacific Railway.

By some coincidence, Howe was an old acquaintance of James Wickes Taylor, and Taylor had been in Ottawa sounding out the Canadian government's plans for their own Pacific railway. Through Taylor, Howe made contact with Senator Ramsey and travelled to St. Paul to meet him. When he and Howe sat down to feel each other out, to find out the intentions of their respective governments, Ramsey suggested that he and his associates wished to build a railway north from St. Paul to Fort Garry, and thence west to Puget Sound on the Pacific, in other words, largely through British territory. They hoped, he said, for a reciprocity treaty with Canada, land grants and a subsidy from the Canadian government. But the railway Ramsey spoke of to Howe was not Jay Cooke's Northern Pacific, the real contender, but the St. Paul and Pacific, a moribund line owned by Dutch investors, that Cooke may have been using as a smokescreen for the real thing. Ramsey and Cooke were certainly not putting all their cards on the table at this early date.

Howe – a wily old fox – listened noncommittally, and then proceeded on a tour of inspection of the few completed miles of the St. Paul and Pacific. He then told Ramsey that, frankly, a cash subsidy was impossible, but that, as a Canadian line north of Lake Superior might be impossible for many years, Canada would probably make land grants available to see the territory developed. This gave Jay Cooke all the ammunition he needed, and quietly and carefully, he prepared his assault on the Dominion of Canada. Canada would be persuaded of the need for the railway they were prepared to build, and Cartier would be ham-strung by public demand for a cooperative venture to open up the North-West. Canada was already trapped by a thousand miles of rock and muskeg, and would have to abandon a railway north of Lake Superior in favour of an easier, American route. Jay Cooke had a lot of cards up his sleeve, and was one of the finest bluffers in the United States. He was to force

Cartier into a game that both men lost, and both men won.

That October, Howe left St. Paul and travelled on to the Red River, where he found few facts, but reassured those in authority that their interests would be protected after the transfer. He forbade the surveyors to proceed further, and left the inhabitants with the suggestion that, if they had grievances, they should air them as Nova Scotia had done. On the way back to St. Paul, Howe met up with McDougall and his retinue, told him what he had learned, especially of the hatred of the Selkirk Settlers toward the Canadian party and Canada Firsters, and then wearily returned to an Ottawa soon to be enveloped in a hornet's nest.

Riel soon heard of Howe's suggestion, but decided to take the hint one step further. By a resistance, armed if necessary, he would force the Canadian government to grant his people acceptable terms for their entry into Confederation, terms that would guarantee their lands and their religion, and a promise that no more surveys would be taken without their permission. They wanted nothing less than a Parliament, because they feared that unless they had democratic representation right from the start, their majority voice would be submerged by the Canadian party. Bishop Taché held the same fears. On October 7, he wrote to Cartier from Saint-Boniface protesting the composition of the proposed Governor's Council, because, as he saw it, "the names placed before the public up to now, for administrators, are all english and protestant, with the exception of M. Provencher. I dare say that such choices are not only regrettable, but alarming." [28] Taché wished, for the sake of his flock, to have the people of Red River negotiate their own entry into Confederation.

Whether or not the Bishop – or even Cartier, *via* the Bishop – gave them his tacit approval, Taché's assistant, Abbé Ritchot, did. On October 16, 1869, at Ritchot's house in Saint-Norbert, the Métis decided to organize their own provisional government, formed in the manner of the buffalo hunt, quasi-military, with a president, council and soldiers.

The "National Committee" elected John Bruce as their President, but the real power behind the Committee was its Secretary, twenty-four year old Louis Riel, son of their old leader, now a pale, striking figure, with curly brown hair and a drooping moustache, a man of action who would soon lead them to victory. Métis scouts sent out by the Committee watched McDougall as he moved northward with his sixty wagons, Red River carts packed with baggage and 300 Enfield rifles.* On October 30, on orders of the National Committee, a Métis patrol stopped McDougall, Cameron and Provencher at the border, and refused them entry into "the Territory of the North-West." The Red River Rebellion had begun.

---

* Cartier advised McDougall to take the rifles, but the latter wisely left them at Georgetown so that they would not fall into the hands of the Métis.

3   "The choice of Lieutenant-Governor was
most unfortunate. Had Canada desired to stir
up trouble in the North-West she could not
have chosen a more suitable man."

G.F.G. Stanley

By November 1, Riel found that he could easily muster about 600 men.
An early winter had released most of them from their jobs. His troops
needed provisions, so Riel decided on the spur of the moment to capture
Fort Garry. Before leaving their headquarters at Saint-Norbert, he and
Abbé Ritchot erected a wooden cross to show their belief in divine sup-
port, and spent some time in prayer.

The Fort was taken without a shot, and a convention called of all the
settlers in the Red River. It was a disastrous meeting that ended in
deadlock, the French remaining firm and the English protesting that
the proper course was to lay their grievances before McDougall.

McDougall was in trouble, and as he sat in the U.S. trading post at
Pembina, his blood boiling, he could almost hear the derisive laughter of
his colleagues back in Ottawa. Ever since he had obtained notoriety with
his desperate "Look to Washington" speech, in which he advocated
annexation as one antidote to French power, his political career had
been built on such tactics, and on his continued advocacy of the expansion of Ontario into the North-West as a way of counter-balancing
French influence. Now he was bogged down on a cold flat plain seventy
miles from his kingdom, his dream rudely shattered.

The St. Paul *Press*, whose reporter had covered the whole procession,
gleefully informed its readers that "A King without a Kingdom is said to
be poorer than a peasant. And I can assure you that a live Governor with
a full complement of officials and menials from Attorney-General down
to cooks and scullions without one poor foot of territory is a spectacle
sufficiently sad to move the hardest heart." [29]

It is tempting to think that Cartier, through Riel, may have meddled
in the events leading up to McDougall's disgrace, since McDougall was
such a foe of what Cartier stood for. It was certainly in the interests of
Cartier and the French Canadians to see McDougall embarrassed. Cartier feared the man's attitudes, his conception of the future of the Dominion. He rightly suspected McDougall of anti-French and pro-Ameri-
can sympathies. McDougall had been in friendly correspondence with
Seward, had been present at Gettysburg when Lincoln made his famous
address, and was firmly pro-Northern during the Civil War, to the extent of sending to Washington a Canadian who had invented a highly
destructive cannon shell that could have aided the Northern armies.
Cartier may have protested against the choice of McDougall as Governor of the North-West, fearful of the damage he might do to the French
and Métis cause, as well as to the fabric of the Dominion, but probably

agreed on the grounds that McDougall's departure would remove one more thorn from the Ministry's side. In fact, for Cartier's purposes, it may have been a heaven-sent opportunity to damage McDougall's political career, and it is entirely possible that the Lightning Striker unsheathed two or three of his thunderbolts to influence the events that led to McDougall's discomforture at the hands of the Métis, although McDougall proved to be his own worst enemy.

McDougall was fully aware that his commission allowed him to assume power only on the appointed date of the transfer, based on the Queen's proclamation, but by November 29, he had still heard no word that the tentative date of December 1 had become official. Foolishly, yet deliberately, and urged on by Charles Mair, Dr. Schultz and their cronies in the Canadian party, with whom he was in secret communication, McDougall informed his government that he would issue a proclamation on December 1, and occupy the territory. That bitterly cold day, he crossed the border, pulled a small Union Jack from his greatcoat, proclaimed the North-West as Canadian territory and himself as Governor, and hurried back to his cabin in Pembina. Copies of the Proclamation were printed up by Schultz and distributed that same day in the Red River. And on that day, McDougall issued to the surveyor Colonel Dennis, in the Queen's name, a commission as a peace officer, to "raise, organize, arm equip and provision"[30] a police force to disperse or arrest the rebels. Then he reported what he had done to his superiors back in Ottawa. On December 1, the cabinet met in Ottawa, although for what reason we do not know; probably the question of the delay of the Queen's proclamation was discussed. On December 5, John A. Macdonald, still ignorant of the latest events in the Red River, informed Sir John Rose, Canada's confidential agent in London, of some of the government's intentions: "Captain Cameron will also form a body of mounted Police, and it is hoped, will be able to employ the services in that Corps, of some of the French half-breeds. You need not be surprised to see Riel, the Secretary of the Convention, one of his officers."[31]

On December 6, McDougall received a diplomatic pouch from Ottawa. In it he read with disgust and not a little amount of trepidation two letters, one from Howe, dated November 19, warning him that "as matters stand, you can claim or assert no authority in the Hudson's Bay Territory, until the Queen's proclamation, annexing the country to Canada, reaches you from this office,"[32] and the other from his Prime Minister, condescending, but to the point: "Never forget," said Macdonald, "that you are now approaching a foreign country, under the government of the Hudson's Bay Company . . . You cannot force your way in . . . This man Riel, who appears to be the moving spirit, is a clever fellow, and you should endeavour to retain him as an officer in your future police." Macdonald then told the impulsive McDougall not to be so impulsive: "Our Lower Canadian colleagues are intensely disgusted at the actions of the French priests as described by you. I hope you will allow no impatience at their factions and irrational conduct to induce you to hold out any but conciliatory language to them."[33]

McDougall must have been astounded. What exactly was happening? Why was Macdonald being so careful to warn him now? Was he being set up and deliberately embarrassed by Macdonald and Cartier? His suspicions were probably confirmed a few days later when Macdonald replied to his letter of November 29: "A proclamation such as you suggest . . . would be very well if it were sure to be obeyed. If, however, it were disobeyed, your weakness and inability to enforce the authority of the Dominion would be painfully exhibited, not only to the people of Red River, but to the people and Government of the United States." Macdonald also warned him of the legal point, that if he were refused entry into the country, there would exist a state of anarchy: "In such a case, no matter how the anarchy is produced, it is quite open by the law of nations for the inhabitants to form a government *ex necessitate* for the protection of life and property, and such a government has certain sovereign rights by the *jus gentium*, which might be very convenient for the United States, but exceedingly inconvenient to you."[34] This little lecture in international law did not, however, make matters any better for the hapless McDougall. Because of a simple delay, possibly deliberate, he had allowed himself to be trapped. And now he learned that, when the cabinet had heard of his expulsion from the territory, they had instructed Sir John Rose, Canada's agent in London, to hold back the £ 300,000 owing to the Hudson's Bay Company, and had informed the Colonial Secretary, Granville, that Canada would not accept the transfer until peaceful possession could be guaranteed. Although at first annoyed, Granville finally saw the point, that any loss of life in the Red River could lead to deep hostilities that might mar Canada's future success, and that the Americans should not be given either opportunity or excuse to interfere in the colony, or take sides with the Métis.

In early December 1869, the Métis majority on the Convention gave Riel the power to form a Provisional Government, and on December 10, their flag, with *fleur-de-lis* and shamrock on a white background, was raised over Fort Garry. More than sixty of Dennis' "police", including Mair and Schultz, were easily rounded up by the Métis sharpshooters, and imprisoned in the Fort.

McDougall realized the game was up, and his political career in tatters.After failing to receive a reply to his overtures to Riel, and with the weight of his colossal blunder sitting heavily on his shoulders, the Governor wearily loaded up his belongings. Leaving Provencher and Cameron to wait out the winter in Pembina, he beat a retreat back to Ottawa to resign his commission.

Cartier's only recorded comment on the subject of McDougall's embarrassment comes to us from Sir Stafford Northcote, Governor of the

Hudson's Bay Company. According to Northcote, "Sir G. spoke of the 'interregnum' and volunteered the observation that Canada was to some extent responsible for what had occurred, because they had made a blunder in appointing McDougall." [35] Yet Cartier may have been making a private joke – for the Lightning Striker's purposes, the appointment and subsequent discomforture of McDougall were not blunders in the fullest sense of the word. The events of that autumn not only tempted the United States to intervene, but woke the British government from their lethargy and ensured an earlier start on the Pacific Railway. They effectively removed from the political stage an avowed enemy of French Canada, and let to what Cartier had wanted all along – the early establishment of a bilingual province in the Red River to balance out Confederation, a province that was to be led largely by his own hand-picked men.

"Donald Smith was not only an old trickster, he was a Hudson's Bay Company man." 4

Louis Schmidt, 1871

As the year 1870 began, the Red River was a potential powderkeg. Cartier knew that the Dominion of Canada was fully backed by British arms and was not overly concerned. Although Rupert's Land had not yet been officially transferred to the Dominion, an armed provisional government, friendly to French Canada at least, and operating without the opposition of the Hudson's Bay Company, was firmly in the saddle. Cartier's main concerns were railway and fortification guarantees, and Britain was proving reluctant to open her purse strings. Perhaps by tempting the Americans to intervene in the affairs of the Red River, he and Macdonald were trying to force the American hand and convince Britain that Imperial Sovereignty in the North-West was seriously threatened, that a railway would have to be built as soon as possible to counteract American expansionism.

There was one more element in Cartier's game. As Macdonald told Granville, "the French are earnestly bent upon the establishment of a French and Catholic power in the north-west to counteract the great preponderance of Ontario." [36] Using his utmost ingenuity and cunning, Cartier was now fighting to ensure some continuing French influence in the old kingdom of the voyageurs.

Early in 1869, Cartier had brushed aside Archbishop Taché's warnings about the explosive situation in the Red River, saying that he was "perfectly well informed" – probably by the Hudson's Bay Company – but now with Riel in control it was time to cool matters off, and he eagerly accepted Taché's offer to return from the Vatican Conference to smooth the waters. Meeting the prelate's train at Montreal, he confessed that "the Government has made many mistakes, and we cannot be surprised that the population should make some mistakes on their side. Assure them that the disposition of the Government towards them is such that they may rely on us with perfect sincerity." [37]

Bishop Taché was only one of a host of diplomats, politicians and secret agents who were preparing to swarm into the Red River to pay homage to its twenty-six year old monarch, Louis Riel. James Wickes Taylor again entered the Métis kingdom. The old trader, A.G.B. Bannatyne, suggested that, on the advice of William O'Donoghue, a Fenian who had come to Saint-Boniface to study at the seminary, Taylor offered Riel $150,000, a position, and arms and men if necessary, if he would work for the annexation of the territory to the United States. [38] To Riel's lasting credit, he always refused the blandishments of the Americans. His loyalties were to his people, and to French Canada.

The situation was becoming more serious. Charles Tupper arrived in Fort Garry in January, and rescued his daughter from the clutches of the buffalo hunters. He sized matters up, but took no action except to explain to Abbé Ritchot that they could expect no help from the United States.

Cartier and Macdonald decided to send two official parties to the Red River to cool off the passions of the Métis. The more visible group was composed of Colonel Charles de Salaberry, an old north-west hand and son of the hero of the 1813 victory over the Americans at Châteauguay, and the beloved Grand Vicar J.-B. Thibault, a twenty-seven-year veteran of the western mission. Both men were highly respected by the Métis, and it was hoped that they would be able to calm their fears and explain the true intentions of the Canadian government. They partly succeeded in accomplishing this, but the real success was engineered by the able and resourceful Donald A. Smith, Resident Governor of the Hudson's Bay Company in Montreal, and its chief administrator in Canada.

Donald Smith, later Lord Strathcona, was one of the great shadowy figures on the political landscape of the day. A good friend of Cartier, and a constant visitor at the Saturday night *conversationes*, this bushy-browed Scot had become, by late 1869, the controlling shareholder of the Hudson's Bay Company. During the uncertainty and panic surrounding the transfer of the territory to Canada, Smith had purchased some large blocks of stock from nervous British investors. Grand Trunk Railway interests held most of the remainder of the shares – the Railway's President Richard Potter was on the Hudson's Bay Company Board – so that Smith's interests and Canada's were one and the same. With the Red River Transportation Company, he and his friends Norman Kittson and Jim Hill had a virtual monopoly of Red River trade that they were later able to parlay into successful control of the Canadian Pacific Railway.

Cartier knew by this time of the extent of Smith's investments, and when the shrewd Scot offered to serve as the government's agent in the Red River, he and Macdonald eagerly accepted. They gave Smith authority and funds to "construct a golden bridge"[39] that would allow Canadian sovereignty to pass into the Red River. From this period on, Donald Smith was the most active and effective behind-the-scenes agent for the expansion of the Canadian empire.

On January 5, 1870, Riel invited Thibault and de Salaberry to speak to the Métis Council. They were listened to politely, thanked sincerely, and dismissed graciously. Donald Smith's money, £ 500 of it, had more effect, and some of the Métis withdrew their support from Riel and the Provisional Government. Riel was getting too big for his boots; he had failed to dampen the annexationist propaganda of the Americans, a mistake that alienated some of his more influential followers. The chief American propagandist in the Red River at that time was Colonel Enos Stutsman, a retired Civil War officer who had been born without legs. Stutsman impressed the Métis because he could gallop a horse full-tilt in spite of his handicap. On January 7, Stutsman, on instructions from Taylor, issued a newspaper that called itself *The New Nation*. It proclaimed its policy at the outset:

> The United States Republic offers us today that system of government which would best promote order and progress in our midst and open up rapidly a country of magnificent resources. But in our present dependent position what we need in that direction, and hence we will hold it to be our duty to advocate, is Independence for the people of Red River as a present cure for public ill. Our annexation to the States will follow in time and bring with it the advantage this land so much requires.

Riel did nothing to suppress the newspaper until March. By that time it had done its damage, but to the advantage of Canada. Defections in Riel's ranks finally convinced him to listen to Donald Smith's advice, and he proposed a mass meeting to put his case and Canada's before all the people. So it was that on January 19, 1870, one thousand settlers, Scots from Kildonan, St. Andrews and Headingly, and Métis from Saint-Boniface, Saint-Vital and Saint-Norbert, gathered to hear Louis Riel and Donald Smith argue for their future.

For two days they stood listening in the parade ground of Fort Garry and stamped their feet in the bright sunshine and twenty-below-zero cold. When the meeting adjourned, they had agreed to hold an election to choose forty representatives, evenly divided between French and English, who would sit again on January 25 to consider the Canadian case.

In Winnipeg, the Americans packed the nomination meeting and elected Robinson, editor of *The New Nation*, as chairman. The meeting was declared a "primary," in the American style, and Alfred Scott, a Yankee bartender in O'Lone's Red Saloon, was declared elected on a show of hands. To the loud protests of the fur trader A.G.B. Bannatyne, Scott's opponent, the meeting was adjourned and the "election" not contested because there was no machinery to do so. In the French villages, three Métis who had been cultivated by Donald Smith were elected in opposition to Riel.

By January 29, six of the new convention members appointed to draft a new Bill of Rights had completed their work. After several days of amicable debate, agreements were reached on a franchise, bilingual courts, representation in Ottawa and the need for improved transportation. However, on February 3, Riel proposed an amendment for immediate provincial status, which was not adopted. Furious when he was defeated, Riel paced the floor and insulted his opponents. The meeting adjourned in disarray. Smith was then brought before the convention and asked by a cooled-off Riel whether, as Canadian Commissioner, he could guarantee that the Bill of Rights would be granted by the Canadian government. Smith tried to persuade Riel that, as far as he could guess, the articles would be adopted by Parliament. When hard-pressed, Smith could not give a firm answer – he could only promise British justice. This the convention had to accept.

There remained the question of who would govern the territory until the transfer could be accomplished, but with the blessings of gruff old Governor Mactavish of the Hudson's Bay Company, dying of tuberculosis, who growled from his sick bed, "Form a Government, for God's sake, and restore peace and order in the settlement,"[40] a provisional government was finally established on February 10. The rejoicing was universal, all except for the poor tag ends of the Canadian Party, languishing in the Fort Garry dungeon, who listened to the cannonades, the shouting and the carousing, and watched a stunning display of fireworks, originally brought from Toronto to celebrate the establishment of McDougall's government, but stolen from the warehouse of Dr. John Christian Schultz.

Schultz had escaped from Fort Garry on January 23, and was making his way over the snows to Canada. Charles Mair and a hot-headed, wiry Ulster Orangeman named Thomas Scott had escaped two weeks before Schultz, and on February 18, attempted an armed expedition against the Fort. It was unsuccessful, and although Mair was able to escape, Scott and forty-seven others were captured.

On March 4, Riel made the most difficult decision of his career. Although Donald Smith had been quite careful not to recognize it in writing, the Provisional Government led by Louis Riel appeared to be the *de jure* as well as the *de facto* government of the territory. It operated with the tacit approval of Governor Mactavish, and since the territory had not yet been officially transferred to Canada, it existed at the Company's and Donald Smith's pleasure. Yet the Hudson's Bay Company and its controlling shareholder turned away when Riel, on the advice of a government tribunal, ordered the obstreperous Thomas Scott shot for insubordination and for striking a guard.

Until this action, the Provisional Government had worked well; the Canadians had become more pacified and resigned to Riel's power, and the settlement was eagerly anticipating the spring, and with it, the transfer to Canada. Riel's decision made he and Scott into symbols, martyrs to the cause of racial strife. The final bullet that put Thomas Scott out of his misery opened the old wounds that had been so carefully healed by Cartier and Brown before Confederation.

For Riel, it was a political step, "to intimidate the conspirators . . . to be sure that our attitude was taken seriously," [41] yet neither he nor even Donald Smith realized at the time what a serious political blunder was the execution of Thomas Scott. Macdonald's political opponents in Ontario were to seize upon the "murder" for political ends, and destroy the carefully-placed veneer of cooperation that had covered Confederation for the past three years.

It is quite probable that Donald Smith assured Riel that, in the opinion of the Hudson's Bay Company, the Provisional Government was the only legitimate authority during the "interregnum"; certainly James Wickes Taylor had this impression, and reported it to his masters. [42] Smith had at the very least promised Riel that he would take no steps forcibly to upset the government. Riel, in his own opinion, probably believed he was following the law of nations, probably thought he was within his rights to order Scott's execution. But British sovereignty of a kind was still legally active, and at a time when the Americans were seriously threatening to annex the North-West, and Fenians were menacing the Red River, and when Macdonald and Cartier needed all the national unity possible to prepare for Canada's great leap across the continent, it was a disaster of the worst possible proportions.

Donald A. Smith (Notman).

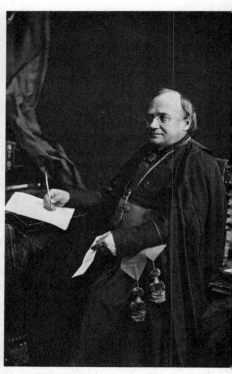

Bishop Taché (Notman).

William McDougall (PAC).

Colonel and Mrs. Wolseley (Notman).

"I have always feared the entrance of the
North-West into Confederation, because I
have always believed that the French-Canadian element would be sacrificed; but I tell
you frankly it had never occurred to me that
our rights would be so quickly and so completely forgotten."

Bishop Taché to Cartier, Oct. 7, 1869

After accepting Cartier's apologies for asking him to return from the
Vatican, and discussing the rebellion with the cabinet, Archbishop
Taché left for the Red River on the evening of February 17, 1870. With
him he carried an understanding from Cartier that the rebels would be
pardoned, as well as a letter from Sir John A. Macdonald promising a
"general amnesty" if the Hudson's Bay Company government were restored before the transfer.

Arriving at his Bishop's Palace at Saint-Boniface on March 8, Taché
was placed under a precautionary guard – possibly willingly – to convince the Canadians that events were out of the Church's control. The
following week he met Riel, and publicly assured the Métis leader that
an amnesty would be granted. Riel appeared overjoyed, proclaimed his
loyalty to the Crown and explained that his whole aim had been to
"arrive at an understanding with the Canadian authorities before entering Confederation."[43]

The Fenian annexationist O'Donoghue was disgusted, all the more so
when Riel took over *The New Nation* and fired Stutsman, its editor.
Full of his loyalty, Riel proceeded to raise the Union Jack over Fort
Garry, and when a furious O'Donoghue tore it down, Riel stationed a
guard under the flag with orders to shoot anyone who tried to remove it.
His statements and actions at this juncture bear a striking similarity to
Cartier's expressions of loyalty after the 1837 Rebellion in Lower
Canada. Bishop Taché's return, and the welcome understanding from
his hero Cartier, certainly had a moderating influence on the Métis
leader. Success was in sight.

On March 22, Riel's Council authorized three men, Abbé Ritchot,
Judge John Black and the Yankee bartender Alfred Scott to "proceed to
the City of Ottawa, and lay before the Dominion Government the ac-
companying list of propositions and conditions, as the terms upon which
the people of Assiniboia will consent to enter into confederation with
the other Provinces of the Dominion." Any arrangements the three
made would have to be ratified by the Provisional Government.

Ritchot, Black and Scott left the next day. Two weeks later, the new
American Consul, James Wickes Taylor, left the Red River and followed them to Ottawa. On April 8, following the letter of Macdonald's

terms of amnesty, Riel surrendered Fort Garry to the Hudson's Bay Company.

Taylor delayed leaving until he could meet with a delegation of Northern Pacific Railway promoters, including ex-Governor Marshall of Minnesota, who had come to Winnipeg. Taylor introduced them to Riel, and Riel again refused a large sum of money – Taché swore it was the colossal amount of $4,000,000[44] – as well as men and arms to repel Canadian troops. Learning of Riel's obstinacy, Jay Cooke realized that some other approach would be necessary, and accordingly wrote to his brother, "In your talk with the President [Grant] & Secretary [Hamilton Fish], tell them the shortest solution of this matter would be the Fenians, & if they say so, I will send for some of the leaders, & have the whole matter attended to in quick time."[45]

The three Red River delegates were quite unprepared for the violence of their reception in Canada. The news of Thomas Scott's execution had reached Ontario, and it greatly cheered Colonel Denison and the Canada First movement, who had been

> much depressed at the apathy of the public, but when we heard that Schultz and Mair, as well as Dr. Lynch, were all on the way to Ontario, and that Scott had been murdered, it was seen at once that there was an opportunity by giving a public reception to the loyal refugees, to draw attention to the matter, and by denouncing the murder of Scott, to arouse the indignation of the people, and foment a public opinion that would force the Government to send up an armed expedition to restore order.[46]

On March 26, the Toronto *Globe* and Montreal *Herald* published a grisly account of Scott's trial and execution. The Orangeman's death was ideal political capital, and by the beginning of April, the Liberals Edward Blake and Alexander Mackenzie began to press for an official statement from the government. Mackenzie, the Liberal leader, publicly spoke of murder and treachery in the Red River and demanded that there be no dealings with the traitors.

When Mair and Schultz arrived the evening of April 6, 1870, the Mayor of Toronto stood in front of his City Hall and told an enormous crowd of partisans, Orangemen all, that the names of "those gallant men who stood up for British supremacy in Red River" would live in history. Schultz described the situation in Fort Garry as "simply this, that the Fenian flag floated from its flagstaff. The rebels hold high revelry within its walls, and Canadians lay in dungeons within it . . . It was from Ontario this movement to add Red River to the Dominion commenced; it was in Ontario this expression of indignation was expressed; and it was to Ontario the Territory properly belonged."[47]

As the tocsins of war drummed in the ears of the listeners, a resolution was adopted declaring that it would be gross injustice to the loyal inhabitants of Red River, humiliating to our national honour, and contrary to all British traditions for our Government to receive, or treat with the emissaries of those who have robbed, imprisoned, and murdered loyal Canadians, whose only fault was zeal for British institutions, whose only crime was devotion to the old flag.[48]

Cartier and Macdonald watched the reports from Toronto with disgust and not a little trepidation. As Ritchot, Black and Scott drew closer to Canada, Cartier warned them of the demonstrations being held in practically every town and hamlet in Ontario. Denison protested to Macdonald, then to the Governor General Sir John Young; and, with Hugh Scott, Thomas' brother, successfully applied in Toronto for a warrant for the arrest of Abbé Ritchot and Alfred Scott. While Judge Black travelled safely through Ontario, the forewarned Ritchot and Scott journeyed south of Lake Ontario, and on April 11, were escorted to Ottawa from Ogdensburg on the St. Lawrence by Police Commissioner Gilbert McMicken, an expert on Fenian counter-espionage. While Ritchot stayed at the Bishop's Palace, Scott installed himself at the Albion Hotel, where he got roaring drunk and staggered around bragging he was Louis Riel's Secretary.[49] When he got sober, he met with Taylor and filled him in on the details of the negotiations that followed.

The next day, de Salaberry introduced Ritchot to Cartier, who fully aware of the political dangers that he, and more especially Macdonald faced, urged the bearded priest to hold off discussions until tempers in Ontario had cooled. That night, through his Deputy Minister Major Futvoye, he warned Ritchot of the warrant for his arrest, and promised assistance were bail necessary. On April 14, Ritchot and Scott were arrested. Major Futvoye accompanied Ritchot to court, where Judge (later Chief Justice) Thomas Galt, Sir A.T. Galt's brother, released them, declaring that the Toronto magistrate had no jurisdiction. They were re-arrested on an Ottawa warrant, let go on bail, and then nine days later, Police Magistrate O'Gara cleared them for lack of evidence, to the cheers of partisan Catholic sympathizers outside the courtroom.

On February 23, Macdonald had written to Sir John Rose,* Canada's agent in London, the witty remark that "everything looks well for a delegation coming to Ottawa, including the redoubtable Riel. If once we get him here, he is a gone coon. There is no place in the ministry for him to sit next to Howe, but perhaps we may make him a Senator for the Territory."[50] He wrote this before he learned of Scott's death, and now he found that Riel's confidant and confessor was very much alive and kicking. Abbé Ritchot was a hard bargainer. On April 26, at a meeting in Cartier's house, he forced the government to recognize the delegation as an official one, although Cartier may have threatened to resign from the ministry if this were not done. By the end of the month, the newly-

---

* Rose had just received a knighthood for his sterling services to the Empire.

legitimized trio had squeezed from the cabinet a promise of separate schools, 1,400,000 acres of land for the Métis, and the granting of provincial status.

By April 28, Macdonald perhaps wisely took to the bottle, leaving Cartier to complete the negotiations. As Cartier worked on the final draft for the admission of Red River as a province, the outrage in Ontario knew no bounds. A satisfied, almost delighted James Wickes Taylor wrote to his chief, U.S. Secretary of State Hamilton Fish, that "there seems a gloomy prospect for the Ministry unless Joseph Howe and the Eastern Provinces can interpose for the adoption of a moderate measure."[51] But Cartier persevered in cabinet, and on May 4, the Manitoba Bill was presented for first reading in the Commons. "Manitoba," he declared, "is the key to the territories of the North West. There are beyond its boundaries vast regions out of which later may be created provinces, and it is necessary that its political machinery should be as perfect as possible. The Indian name which has been given it, and which is very euphonious, means 'The God Who Speaks.' Well, may the new province always speak to the inhabitants of the North West the language of reason, truth and justice."[52] The bill provided for a province of 11,000 square miles, represented by two senators and four federal M.P.s. Manitoba was to be officially bilingual, and separate schools were guaranteed. With great pride, Cartier told his constituents that "we have given Manitoba a government based on Quebec's, and I am happy to say that its inhabitants are satisfied."[53]

Two days later, while seated at his desk in the Parliament Buildings, Sir John A. Macdonald was stricken with a serious attack of "biliary calculus." He passed a small gall-stone, but the excruciating pain knocked him out for more than a month, most of which he spent on a litter in the Speaker's Office. On recovering, Macdonald took the steamboat to Charlottetown, where he recuperated for three months while Cartier, as Acting Prime Minister, steered the Manitoba Bill through.

Macdonald's convenient indisposition cooled off many overheated passions; the Liberals and the Orangemen knew they had nothing to gain from attacking Cartier on the matter, and in spite of McDougall's protests over the death of Scott, and Mackenzie's laughter at the Lilliputian scale of the province, the Bill was passed with an overwhelming majority.

On May 12, the Manitoba Act received Royal Assent, but this was not enough for the tenacious Abbé Ritchot, who still demanded an official written expression of the amnesty he said he had been promised by all and sundry, including the Governor General.[54] An exasperated Cartier informed the dark, bearded priest that any crimes requiring amnesty were committed before transfer of the territory to Canada; therefore the question of amnesty properly belong to Her Majesty the Queen. He again led Ritchot to the Governor General, who promised that a document would be forthcoming; Cartier then urged Ritchot to send a petition to the Queen, which was immediately done. Yet Ritchot felt he could not dare return to the Red River without something in black and white, and kept at Cartier like a terrier. Cartier urged him to consider the political realities of Canada, to "keep quiet and not rack my head about anything . . . the men with whom I am dealing know something about business."

Ritchot was skeptical. "Who will govern the country, pending the arrival of the Lieutenant-Governor?" The Minister of Militia, echoing old Mactavish and Donald Smith, replied, "Let Mr. Riel continue to maintain order and govern the country, as he has done up to the present moment." [55]

Ritchot finally realized Cartier's position, that any Canadian commitment on amnesty would be either foolish or extra-legal, that it would be better to be as quiet about it as possible until the flames of passion in Ontario had cooled, or the Queen had made her decision. Macdonald was in serious political trouble in Ontario. Colonel Denison, a Conservative Orangeman who wielded a heavy block of Toronto votes, was now stumping the province, displaying in Orange Lodges and at "indignation meetings" a piece of rope he alleged was used to bind the wrists of Thomas Scott, rope he said he would personally deliver to the Acting Prime Minister, Sir George-Etienne Cartier. Throughout Toronto, large placards on fences and walls implicated Cartier with Riel by asking. "Shall French rebels rule our Dominion?"

Although Macdonald had been seriously ill, he could not have been indisposed at a better time, for Cartier was able to blunt the attacks on the government and prevent the wholesale defection of the Orange Order. To appease Ontario's imperial instincts and demands for action, and give Canadian militiamen a chance to earn decorations in the field, the Minister of Militia agreed to send a military force to Manitoba. *Le Canadien* sneered, "Will Monsieur Cartier send his compatriots to do battle against the people of Prince Edward Island and Newfoundland who do not wish to enter his happy Confederation? . . . Canada is visibly marching toward annexation with the United States, sooner than our Canadian politicans would have us believe, something which, fearful only of losing power, they seek desperately to avoid." [56]

Cartier refused to deliver a force composed entirely of Canadian militiamen, and fortunately he was able to persuade the British government to supply an imperial contingent, on the condition that they arrive simultaneous with the Canadian administration. This was agreed upon so that, this time, the transfer of power might be made with a minimum of difficulty. The new Lieutenant-Governor was to be Adams G. Archibald, M.P. for Colchester, a Nova Scotian Father of Confederation, a fluent French-speaker and one of Cartier's warmest personal friends; and the military force that would travel to the Red River would be as balanced as possible – the 60th Rifles, and two equal contingents of Ontario and Quebec militia.

On June 8, after discussion with the Cabinet, the Acting Prime Minister completed and delivered to the Governor General a secret memorandum, outling the reasons for the Red River Rebellion, and recommending that total amnesty should be granted by the Queen to all those implicated in the troubles.

He had always believed that the Queen would act for amnesty, and repeatedly promised friends and colleagues that an amnesty would be forthcoming. It was not. Unfortunately for Cartier, he was always suspected of having given Riel a firm promise. Sir Stafford Northcote noted a fault of Cartier's that may have got him into this difficulty. On May 1, he dined at Cartier's house, and reported, "Our host was very agreeable and lively. He has the happy quality of being always thoroughly well satisfied with himself, and this makes him very good humoured with other people. But he is much more than good humoured. He has the great merit of being thoroughly honourable and loyal. Everyone says that once he has given his word he is quite sure to keep it if he can. The misfortune is, that being very sanguine he sometimes makes promises which he cannot perform."* Northcote noted further that Cartier was "behaving remarkably well at the present crisis, taking the whole responsibility of negotiations upon himself, but refusing to supplant Macdonald. Sir J. Young told me that the other Ministers had asked Cartier to take the Premiership, but that he had refused to do so, and had kept the Cabinet together."[57]

As late as February 15, 1873, shortly before his death, Cartier was still working for Riel's amnesty, and reminded Macdonald from London that "no promise was made of an amnesty. Always bear in mind that throughout we stated that the amnesty was not a question for us but for the Queen."[58] Unfortunately for Cartier, and without his knowledge, he was betrayed by none other than the Governor General of Canada! Sir John Young added a reservation to Cartier's Cabinet Memorandum, noting that while it was "entitled to all the consideration due to the writer's long experience and high political standing in British North America," it was "not to be regarded as a Minute of Council nor as the expression of the opinion of the United Cabinet."[59]

* Northcote's view tallies somewhat with Lady Macdonald's: she called Cartier "the fairest of men. He always seems to me full of life and pleasant chattiness but extremely egotistical. He must be clever and powerful, but somehow I don't think he is a favourite. I mean in Public Life. Still his honesty must be respected and a certain plainness that is akin to strength – to that strength, I mean that moral strength which satisfies the people even when qualities which please are wanting." (Lena Newman, *The John A. Macdonald Album*, Montreal, 1974. p. 89)

Not content with having stabbed Cartier in the back, Young twisted the knife. In the diplomatic pouch following the Cabinet Memorandum, he attached a petition from one of the more rabid members of Canada First, Dr. Lynch. Lynch stated that to pardon Riel would be "injudicious, impolitic and dangerous," and threatened that the Canadian Party in the Red River might, "in that wild spirit of justice called vengeance, take the life of Riel," [60] with disastrous consequences.

Lynch's petition was forwarded to "Pussy" Granville with neither explanation nor the sort of qualifications made with Cartier's memorandum. This deliberate misrepresentation by the Queen's Representative in Canada was nothing more than an act of treachery and betrayal of Young's own duty, of Cartier, one of his chief ministers, and of the French Canadians. It was an act of irresponsible government, because, in spite of Cartier's assurances to Ritchot, an amnesty was not forthcoming from the Queen of England.

"We will have that country in spite of traitors in the Cabinet, and in spite of a rebel Minister of Militia."   **6**

Colonel George T. Denison

On the clear, bright morning of June 17, 1870, Abbé Ritchot and an eager young man named Joseph Dubuc stood on the upper deck of Norman Kittson's little steamer *International* as it puffed down the Red River toward Fort Garry. Dubuc had been Louis Riel's best friend at the Collège de Montréal. He had just been admitted to the bar and was a great admirer of George-Etienne Cartier. Six months earlier, Riel had invited him to the Red River, explaining that he was "all alone directing the business of the country and watching out for the intrigues of my enemies. I need an educated right-hand man, trained in the law, energetic, determined. I know you; and if you could find it in your heart to join me, you would render an immense service to our dear Métis people." [61]

When Dubuc replied that he could not afford to come out, Riel wrote advising him to go to Ottawa and meet Ritchot. On May 16, the Abbé told him that "we will need educated men to defend the rights of the Métis," [62] and promised to pay his way to the Red River. Before leaving, Ritchot introduced Dubuc to his hero Cartier. According to Dubuc, "Sir George was greatly in favour of my idea of going to Manitoba, and gave me words of welcome and encouragement." [63] It is probable Cartier did more; he may have introduced Dubuc to Joseph Royal of *La Minerve*. After gauging the effects of Charles Mair's letters in the *Globe*, Cartier probably wanted someone to do the same in a French Canadian newspaper. Dubuc's letters to *La Minerve*, written over the next year, transformed public opinion in the province of Quebec. They were translated and printed in the *Globe* as well, again with great moderating effect. For example, on July 2, 1870, Dubuc was to declare that "Riel has never said nor has given to say that he desired independence . . . He has had nothing to do with annexation. He is a lover of British institutions."[64]

News of Ritchot's return had flashed through the settlement like a prairie grass fire, and from the first hamlet north of the border all the way to Fort Garry, every family rushed to the water's edge and waved to the priest and his companion. On their arrival at the Fort, Ritchot and Dubuc were greeted by a large and friendly crowd, and warmly embraced by Riel, who led them up from the wharf to the booming of a twenty-one gun salute.

Riel seemed greatly excited. He paced the floor and begged Ritchot and Dubuc to tell him everything. They talked until late that night. The next day, Ritchot wrote to Cartier with the news that, as the Minister of Militia had predicted, Riel was satisfied, and that all would go well, "provided always that the amnesty reaches us in good season."[65] Cartier had no reason to believe it would not.

On June 24, the Red River Assembly met, and with great cheering and rejoicing, voted to accept the Manitoba Act. The new Governor would be officially welcomed on his arrival. Riel was pleased with Cartier's choice; he adjourned the meeting congratulating his people for "the happy issue of their undertakings. I congratulate them on having trust enough in the Crown of England to believe that ultimately they would obtain their rights. I must, too, congratulate the country on passing from under this provisional rule to one of a more permanent and satisfactory character. From all that can be learned, also, there is great room for congratulation in the selection of Lieutenant-Governor which has been made."[66]

But all was not well. In Ontario, there were continuing expressions of a different kind of loyalty, and the campaign against Riel continued unabated. On July 5, Cartier wrote to Bishop Taché with some disturbing news:

> In one of your letters to Mr. Howe, you remarked that you had written him more than 6 (?) times and haven't received a reply. Mr. Howe is under the impression that several of your letters have been intercepted . . . I feared the interception of my letters and took advantage of good Father Ritchot to tell you in person what I wouldn't have liked to put on paper.

Cartier continued by reclarifying his own views on the question of amnesty:

If the Amnesty depended on and was the responsibility of the Canadian Government, composed as it is of heterogeneous elements, it would be in great danger. But I repeat it is fortunate that it is Her Majesty, in Council with her ministers, who will have to rule on this question. Already Her Majesty, by the Proclamation of December 6 last which she caused to be issued by Sir John Young, has, in so many words,* promised an Amnesty. This fact was mentioned in Father Ritchot's Petition to the Queen . . . Now I must suggest to you that the best means of obtaining this Amnesty is for the entire population of the Red River to accept the new order of things. It will be good of Your Grace, the Anglican Bishop, all those who figured in the Provisional Government and all the notables of the Red River, to give a fine welcome to Mr. Archibald, your new Governor, and to the military expedition. Perhaps the Queen will await this result before making known her decision. The expedition is an expedition of peace, and the battalion from Quebec is composed of a great number of your friends, including Father Royer.

Then, remembering the rebellion of his youth, Cartier argued:

It will be a great mistake and an error of judgment if the French Métis, on the arrival of the Governor and the troops, leave the English Métis and the Scots alone to make all the demonstrations of loyalty. This will place the French Métis in the same false position as the Lower Canadians were put after the political troubles [of 1837]. The French Métis must show themselves more loyal than anyone.[67]

Cartier's letter showed how fragile the whole situation was, and Bishop Taché felt a gnawing anxiety grow within him. As if by instinct, he knew that he must return to Ottawa to speed up the matter of the amnesty. When Taché arrived and entered Cartier's office, the Minister of Militia was just on his way to inspect the troops at the Niagara Camp, and he urged the Bishop to accompany him, so that he could introduce Taché to the Governor General in person. Cartier first telegraphed to the invalid Macdonald in Prince Edward Island:

Will further explain to Governor on Thursday at Niagara urgent reasons for carrying out our view in the matter. Do not be uneasy, will act cautiously. Kind regards to Lady Macdonald. Continue resting yourself to be yourself again.[68]

Then the two boarded the Toronto lake steamer at Prescott, but at Kingston, Commissioner McMicken came on board and informed Cartier that Toronto was seething with rebellion. Colonel Denison had got wind of Taché's presence in Ontario, and had burst in on the Adjutant-General of the Toronto garrison, threatening to storm the armories if

* "pour ainsi dire."

the troops of that city were intimidated into giving Cartier and Taché a guard of honour. This was revolutionary rhetoric, and extremely dangerous, expecially to Sir John A.'s political future. Cartier felt that, with a provincial election in the cards, discretion was the better part of valour. He advised Taché to travel south to Lake Ontario *via* Buffalo, and meet the Governor General in Hamilton.

Sir John Young arranged to meet the Archbishop, but after a painfully short discussion, he coldly dismissed him with these words: "See Sir Georges Cartier; he knows my views upon the subject, and he will tell you all." [69] Back in Ottawa, Cartier was troubled by reports of a mass meeting at the St. Lawrence Hall in Toronto, attended by William McDougall and Colonel Denison. Denison was now concentrating all his attacks on Cartier, calling him "a traitor in 1837. He was often called a loyal man, but we could buy all their loyalty at the same price of putting our necks under their heels and petting them continually." [70] At Denison's urging, McDougall wrote a book on the rebellion, in which he accused Cartier of having taken charge of the Manitoba Act "on behalf of the priesthood," to establish Manitoba as a "French Catholic Province." [71]

Cartier racked his brains. Something had to be done to save the skin of the ministry and prevent a total polarization between Ontario and Quebec. One side had to yield. Riel had to go.

Macdonald, absent in Prince Edward Island and unable to defend himself, was losing a lot of political ground over the whole issue. Mackenzie and Blake were seriously contending for the loyal British vote, and the Honourable John Hillyard Cameron, one of Macdonald's oldest cronies, was voted out as Grand Master of the Orange Lodge for having defended Ritchot in Parliament. The *Globe* gloated over "the position occupied by Sir John A. Macdonald in his humiliating subservience to Sir G.E. Cartier," [72] while in Quebec, the French Canadians watched the racial cauldron seethe, and held their breath as Colonel Garnet Wolseley and his soldiers paddled, portaged and slogged their way to the Red River.

Early in August, Bishop Taché left Montreal to return to Manitoba. He was accompanied by Joseph Royal and Marc Girard, two of Cartier's hand-picked men. Royal had been with Cartier since the 1850s. He had begun work as his law clerk, but in 1857, at Cartier's urging, he went to work as an editor of *La Minerve*. Royal was called to the bar in 1864, then went back into Cartier's firm. But he discovered that his first love was journalism, and in 1867, founded the influential journal, *Le Nouveau Monde*. Marc Girard was an old Cartier family friend. A lawyer from Varennes, he had persuaded Cartier to run in his first election in Verchères in 1847. Both men were, like Cartier, graduates of the Collège de Montréal.

Joseph Royal's first duty was to tell Riel that Cartier was of the opinion that the amnesty was *"une affaire décidée,"* a sure thing, and to advise him to "go away from the country for five or six years, so as to let the excitement pass away." [73] As Cartier's agent, Royal soon made his presence felt in the province. He founded the very influential newspaper, *Le Métis,* and by the autumn of 1870, was in charge of a Métis cavalry patrol, looking for Fenians along the American border, no mean feat for a man who had rarely ridden a horse. The following spring, he and Joseph Dubuc opened a law office in Winnipeg. [74]

Meanwhile Louis Riel awaited the military force with increasing apprehension: he had received advance reports on the conduct of the troops, and was especially worried about how the Ontario militia would behave. And it was apparent now that Governor Archibald would not arrive before Colonel Wolseley. On August 23, Taché, Royal and Girard reached Saint-Boniface. When Riel heard Cartier's advice that he should not be anywhere near Fort Garry on the arrival of the troops, he was angry and bitter, but realized that it would be wise to play a cautious game. The next day, Bishop Taché stood in his broad hat and rain cape by the gate of Fort Garry and watched – with very little emotion showing through his lozenge-shaped spectacles – as Wolseley's regulars, soaked to the skin but eager for action, rushed into the Fort, raised the Union Jack, and fired one single cannon salute, that Louis Riel heard at his back as he rode south to the safety of the United States.

The Red River Expedition was the last act of British arms on the North American continent, and an inglorious end to a noble tradition. Against the advice of the Canadian cabinet, and, in particular, the Minister of Militia, Wolseley's troops were issued warrants for the arrest of Riel, Lépine and O'Donoghue. Elzéar Goulet, a member of the court martial which had tried Thomas Scott, was chased by some soldiers and civilians into the Red River and stoned to death; François Guillemette, who had given Scott the *coup de grace* with a revolver, was killed near Pembina; and André Nault, Riel's uncle, was chased like a rabbit across the U.S. border, stabbed and left for dead on a desolate stretch of prairie. The Métis of the Red River, who had expected a peaceful and orderly military reign, found themselves mistreated and dealt with like victims of an invading army.

Bishop Taché was outraged, and wrote Cartier a letter full of bitterness and fury. Cartier too was angered and concerned when he heard of Wolseley's conduct, but his return letter shows a touch of sadness rarely seen in his correspondence:

> I cannot help but see from your last letter how much your good heart is bleeding with sorrow since the arrival of the military expedition. Wolseley's stupid proclamation, the murder of Goulet and other facts and circumstances must have been more than enough to fill your soul with sadness. You must have seen from the papers of Montreal and

elsewhere how much Wolseley has been blamed for his proclamation. We have let them know in England what we think of it.

Cartier followed by apologizing for the delay of the amnesty, and advised Taché to be moderate, and prepare for the coming elections: "I will write a word to our friend Girard regarding the choice of two Senators from Manitoba."[75]

Wolseley was furious that Riel had escaped, but his anger stemmed not only from the fact that he had lost his prize, but from something more. Before leaving for the Red River, he had solicited the position of Lieutenant-Governor from Sir George-Etienne Cartier. For obvious reasons, Cartier turned him down, and although Wolseley went on to win great victories in the service of the Empire, becoming Field Marshall and Viscount, he never forgave the Minister of Militia's insult. On his return to England, he published his opinions of Canada in *Blackwood's Magazine*, and was particularly scathing toward Cartier, comparing him to Molière's *bourgeois gentilhomme*:

The only man of really statesmanlike ability in the Canadian Ministry is the Premier Sir John A. Macdonald. Unfortunately for the country, he was just at this critical moment struck down by severe illness, and the general management of affairs devolved upon Sir George Cartier, the leader of the French Conservatives. In early life he had played a minor part in the Canadian rebellion of 1837, when he had actually borne arms against the British Crown – a crime which, in the opinion of his political opponents, his subsequent loyalty has not sufficed to wipe out. This tended to prejudice many against him; for it was considered natural that, having been once himself a rebel, he should sympathise with rebellion wherever he met it. That "foul dishonouring word" is, however, regarded very differently by a man of neither birth, wealth, nor position, when seeking for political notoriety, and when he has succeeded, and is in the Ministry also. But this well-known truth was forgotten, and he was generally regarded as a partisan, and anxious to play into the hands of Messrs Riel, Ritchot and Co.

Such character assassination by a prominent soldier of the Empire was bound to hurt Cartier's reputation in the railway circles of England, because *Blackwood's* was (and still to some extent is) the cultural voice of the Empire. Wolseley continued, damning Cartier with faint praise:

Sir G. Cartier, although a poor debater and of very ordinary ability, is a creditable specimen of Canadian public men. His greatest enemy dares not question his honesty. Others have become rich in the management of public affairs; but he is still, comparatively speaking, a poor man. He is a firm friend and a good hater. His ordinary promise is more to be relied upon than the oath of many of his contemporaries, and he is a hardworking public servant. To accuse him of condescending at times into the lowest depths of jobbery and political trickery, is merely to accuse him of being a Canadian politician. In England we are prone to grumble at the misdeeds of Downing Street; but only purity and virtue emanates from that dingy locality when a comparison is instituted between the political morality of England and that of Canada; and the latter is in its turn little short of perfection when judged side by side with the corruption pervading every department of political and municipal government in the United States.[76]

Wolseley should have been grateful to Cartier, whose refusal to grant him the office of Lieutenant-Governor allowed the soldier to find fame in fields of Empire more receptive of his obvious talents. After his inglorious exploits in Manitoba, this soldier of Empire finally found glory as commander of the Nile expedition, formed to relieve General Gordon at Khartoum.

Back in Manitoba, the Métis, at the urging of the Fenian O'Donoghue, agreed to send a petition to the President of the United States asking him to intercede on their behalf with the Queen of England. O'Donoghue, still smarting from the flag war with Riel, was chosen to deliver the message, but unknown to Riel, he added a paragraph asking Ulysses S. Grant to grant them a government based on the principles of "life, liberty and the pursuit of happiness." O'Donoghue was welcomed ardently by the people of St. Paul, and with Senator Ramsey's assistance, sent to Washington and given an audience with President Grant. Grant, with other matters weighing heavily on his mind, was polite to the Fenian, but not overly sympathetic. He had more serious problems to contend with, including an upcoming high-level conference with Great Britain that would clear up the grievances that had arisen between the two countries during the Civil War period.

By October of 1870, Cartier had got word to a well-guarded Riel, hiding in the home of a priest, Father LeFloche, that it would be advisable to lie low and wait. Riel had lost a lot of influence among his fellow Métis, but he could do nothing but believe and trust that Cartier would deliver the amnesty and restore peace to the settlement. This was his only hope. On this account, he refused to stand for the new provincial Parliament, in spite of being urged to do so by all his friends and associates.

The election was a victory for the Métis, half of whose members had served in the conventions under Riel. Girard, Dubuc and Royal were elected by acclamation and Donald Smith defeated Dr. Schultz in Winnipeg. In addition, Adams Archibald, who had arrived ten days after Wolseley, soon made his moderation felt, and went a long way toward undoing Wolseley's damage.

Archibald wisely chose as members for his first Legislative Council two Métis, two Selkirk settlers, and a Hudson's Bay Company man. The

Ontario Orange firebrands were enraged, calling the new government an act of betrayal, and blaming Archibald, the "tool of his master in Ottawa, Sir George Cartier." [77] They had a point: the first (acting) Premier of Manitoba was Henry J. Clarke, a Roman Catholic lawyer from Montreal. Cartier had sent him to the Red River the year before to take charge of the police.* The first Speaker of the Manitoba House was Joseph Royal; he was eventually to become Lieutenant-Governor of the North West Territories. Marc Girard served on Archibald's first Executive Council, was one of the first Manitoba Senators sent to Ottawa, and in 1874, served as Premier following Clarke. Joseph Dubuc, the first Provincial Secretary, became Solicitor-General, and eventually Chief Justice of Manitoba. Cartier chose his men well.

A heaven-sent opportunity for Riel to earn his amnesty came when "General" O'Donoghue and thirty other Fenians crossed the border from Pembina and proclaimed a new Provisional Government. Because of the upcoming Washington Conference between Britain and the United States, Hamilton Fish advised James Wickes Taylor to warn Archibald about the raid, and thereby preserve U.S. neutrality. Riel wrote to Archibald proclaiming his loyalty, and although O'Donoghue was quickly rounded up by the American police, he was soon released. Riel made his point, however, and on October 8, Lieutenant-Governor Archibald crossed the river to Saint-Boniface and asked the Métis to supply the government with a mounted patrol to watch for movements along the border. He spoke with their leaders, and without any introduction, strode over to one of them, a nervous young man with a mop of black curly hair and a drooping moustache. After murmuring a few words to Louis Riel, Archibald shook hands with him and departed.

The news of Archibald's brave gesture flashed throughout the settlement, and almost as quickly to Ontario, where protest and indignation meetings began anew. Although the military expedition had cooled the tempers of Ontario considerably, its citizens would not let the execution of Thomas Scott be forgotten; yet, there were some rays of common sense driving away the clouds that had hung over the Red River for the past two years. "You can hardly hope," wrote Archibald to Joseph Howe, "to carry on Responsible Government by inflicting death penalties on the leaders of the majority of the electors." [78]

The Protestants of Ontario wanted Riel hanged, even though Ogle Gowan and D'Arcy Boulton, two prominent leaders of the Orange Lodge, came out for Cartier, deploring Mackenzie and Blake's attempt "to make political capital out of our Brother's murder by arousing the passions of Orangemen on the eve of a general election against a government

---

* On January 25, 1871, Clarke wrote Cartier: "I can only congratulate Manitoba on having Sir George to fight her battles and lead her on again and again to victory. Our triumph has been most complete. We will have a majority of at least six in the legislature." (ANQ, Chapais Collection)

arc Girard (PAC).   Joseph Dubuc (PAC).

Mr. John K. Nucke, a gentleman farmer asks his steward (Hincks) about a
road to the lake (the C.P.R.). E. Jump (PAC).

that has no power whatever to deal with the crime."[79] Just before the Ontario election, Blake put a motion before the legislature, demanding that Scott's executioners be brought to justice. The Premier, John Sandfield Macdonald, argued that such a motion was *ultra vires*. His stand probably caused him to lose the election. By the spring of 1871, the new Premier, Edward Blake, passed the same resolution, and, at his instigation, the province of Ontario offered a $5,000 reward for Riel's head.

Again through his old law clerk Joseph Royal, Cartier advised Riel to exile himself.[80] But there was still no amnesty. Perhaps Riel understood why, but Taché was furious, and told Cartier that he had "spared neither pain, nor fatigue, nor expense, nor humiliation to re-establish order and peace, and it has come to this, that I am to receive from my people the cruel reproach that I have shamefully deceived them."[81] Cartier finally and with great difficulty convinced the prelate that, with a federal election in the offing, an amnesty was politically impossible, and Riel's exile was the only way out. Archibald had written to Cartier urging this course of action. He believed that since the Métis had unanimously voted to protect him if he remained, some lawless thugs or American adventurers or agents, lured by Blake's reward or a desire to promote civil war, might try to capture Riel, and bloodshed would surely result. Taché softened. "You must remember," he implored, "that this man is poor; his mother is a widow with four young girls and three young boys, and she has no means of support especially when her eldest son is away." "That is true," replied Sir George, "we will see about that."[82]

On Cartier's advice, the government of Canada, through its Secret Service fund, paid out over $1,000, to which was added £600 from Donald Smith and the Hudson's Bay Company. Taché gave the money to the families of Riel and Ambrose Lépine, and urged them to "disappear for a time; do not leave even a pretext to those who are assailing you so unjustly. They want to accomplish evil ends, to disturb the country, to ruin it if possible."[83] He advised them to be true patriots, and act for the common good.

Riel's boyhood hero, Sir George-Etienne Cartier, a loyal rebel who had himself gone into exile, was now asking him to do the same. On February 23, 1871, Louis Riel said farewell to his family, boarded a private carriage, and, guarded by Archibald's police, travelled that night through to the United States border, and thence on to the anonymity and relative safety of St. Paul, Minnesota. Exile was a cage for Louis Riel, and after bouts of paranoia and insanity, compounded by the death of Cartier two years later, he was secretly admitted to an asylum in Quebec. He emerged blasted clean and filled with new visions, bright delusions, and finally returned home to deal with some unfinished business, and face the federal hangman at last.

A month after Louis Riel's temporary exile began, Cartier stood in his office with his good friend, the newly elected member for Selkirk, Donald A. Smith, fresh from his victory over Dr. Schultz. When the session bells rang, Cartier escorted Smith down the corridors and into the Commons chamber, and introduced him to the Speaker, while the opposition benches buzzed with murmurs and little ripples of ironic applause – they had already decided to call him "the Member for H.B.C." When Smith looked confused about where to sit, some opposition members shouted to him to sit on their side. He didn't appear to understand the joke, and headed their way, but Cartier rescued him in the nick of time and led him by the arm to his seat, grinning all the while. This time, the House broke up with laughter and genuine applause.

"The eagle would not do well to fatten the lion's cub." 7

J.G. Blaine, U.S. Senator, 1866

In spite of Canada's narrow escape, Rupert's Land was now secure within the Canadian Confederation, and Cartier turned more and more of his remaining energy toward fixing the national presence in that great empty empire. There was still a lot of fight left in the American expansionists, and he knew that they were capable of a continuing effort against Canadian influence in the west. Even though President Grant wanted to go to the bargaining table, there were other Americans who could not reconcile themselves to Canada's existence. One of them, Senator Zachariah Chandler, had stood up on the floor of the United States Congress and suggested that "if Great Britain should acknowledge her wrong and cede all her interests in Canada in settlement of the *Alabama* claims, we will have perpetual peace . . . we cannot afford to have an enemy's base so near to us. It is a national necessity that we should have the British possession." [84] Even after the scattered provinces of British North America had gained their own independence, there were still many vociferous and influential Americans, like Chandler, who scarcely recognized the existence of the Dominion of Canada as a sovereign nation, who saw it as nothing more than a violation of the Monroe Doctrine, and a menace to American security. The Wolseley expedition to the Red River was more than some Americans could bear, and President Grant was determined to effect a treaty that would remove British troops from North America. Then perhaps Canada would come to its senses and join the union.

There were other U.S. grievances. After the cancellation of the Reciprocity Treaty in 1866, the two sides fell back on the 1818 Fisheries Convention, where Americans could only fish in British waters under licence. In just three months in 1870, British cruisers under Admiral Fanshawe captured 400 violators of that Convention. The Canadian government, wishing compensation for the damages caused by the Fenian raids that Seward had encouraged, were determined to use the fisheries card to get action. Sir Edward Thornton, the British Minister in Washington, reported this as such to Granville, noting that "Cartier, Tupper and Hincks plainly betrayed that they wished to drive the American fishermen off the field . . . I anticipate retaliation." [85] In addition, Hincks had slapped a protective tariff on U.S. imports in an effort to bring the Americans to the bargaining table.

Early in 1869, the American Ambassador in London and Lord Clarendon came to an understanding that claims between the two nations since 1853 should be settled by a joint commission. The U.S. Senate disagreed, and Sumner demanded the staggering sum of $8 billion (or failing this, cession of the Dominion of Canada) as reparation for "war prolongation" by Great Britain. Fortunately for Canada, President Grant and his Secretary of State, Hamilton Fish, had been steadily undermining Sumner's position as Chairman of the Senate Foreign Relations Committee, and eventually a commission was agreed upon. Sumner, who along with William Seward, was an arch-propagandist of "Manifest Destiny," had steadfastly refused to go along with Grant's management of America's foreign affairs. And affairs they were. A decade earlier, William Seward had complained that "The policy which the United States actually pursue is the infatuated one of rejecting and spurning vigorous and ever-growing Canada, while seeking to establish feeble states out of decaying Spanish provinces on the coast and islands of the Gulf of Mexico. I shall not live to see it, but the man is already born who will see the United States mourn over this stupendous folly." [86] But times had not changed, as Seward and Sumner discovered. Earlier in the year, the President had secretly allotted $150,000 out of the Secret Service Fund to prop up Senor Baez, the notorious dictator of the Dominican Republic. Then, without informing the Senate, Grant had tried to annex the tiny country. Sumner, furious with Grant, and quite unwilling to go along with his little breach of protocol, found it easy to turn around and demand outrageous concessions from Great Britain. The Dominican Republic was nothing to Sumner. He was after a bigger prize – Canada.

Sumner's intransigence once again demonstrated to Canadian politicans the continuing danger from south of the border. It was more than exasperating to them that some Americans would not recognize the four-year old Dominion as an established fact, but the forthcoming negotiations in Washington provided a heaven-sent opportunity to fix this fact once and for all in the minds of even the most ardent annexationist.

The period of Macdonald's recuperation in the summer of 1870 had been a time of hard work for Cartier, but he delighted in this sort of positive political action. He had no sooner passed the Manitoba Act and dealt with Abbé Ritchot's demands for the amnesty of Riel, than a new and exciting political challenge presented itself.

On February 2, 1870, the *British Columbian*, a New Westminster newspaper, argued that "of all the conditions usually attached to a union of this colony with Canada, that of early establishment of railroad communication from sea to sea is the most important. If the railroad scheme is utopian, so is Confederation. The two must stand or fall together." Six weeks later, on March 12, the Legislative Council of the Colony of British Columbia, pressured by the Lieutenant-Governor, Anthony Musgrave, agreed to petition the Dominion of Canada for admission into Confederation.

For the privilege of extending control over the continent, Canada would be asked to assume the Colony's crippling debt of over $1 million, undertake a public works program, build a carriage road and begin construction of a transcontinental railway within three years. To put their case to Canada, the colonists overlooked such rabid pro-Canadians as Amor de Cosmos (formerly just plain Smith from Nova Scotia, but now "the Love of the Universe"), and instead sent Dr. R.W.W. Carrall, a Canadian merchant from the Cariboo; Joseph Trutch, a British civil engineer from the Fraser Delta; and, Dr. John Sebastian Helmcken of Victoria, formerly an annexationist worried that Confederation would favour the mainland and leave Vancouver Island in a backwater, but now a cautious supporter of union.

A railway to the Pacific Ocean! To that "west beyond the west!" This was the grand design that the Chairman of the Railway Committee had been waiting for, a project that, when completed, would guarantee the survival of the Dominion, and not incidentally for Cartier, the survival of the French Canadians.

On June 6, 1870, the British Columbia delegates arrived at the Privy Council chambers to find Cartier "in his shirt sleeves, hard at work." [87] He welcomed them with open arms, and got them some sherry. Soon they were joined by the two other members of the cabinet's committee, Sir Samuel Leonard Tilley of New Brunswick and Sir Francis Hincks, the new Finance Minister, fresh from his exile as Governor of the Barbados and British Guiana. They all agreed to meet the next afternoon. When the delegates returned to the government buildings, they "found Sir G. Cartier engaged and continued so for half an hour longer. He then excused himself in a most merry way, took us to wine and himself to a sandwich likewise, not having had time to take anything before. It is astonishing how Sir G. works . . . " [88] Soon they got down to business around a table in the cabinet room to discuss British Columbia's terms, and in particular, the colony's crippling debt. Cartier "conceived the brilliant idea of our giving up lands for the Railway and for the Govt. to compensate the colony therefore and in this way make up the sum required." The delegates became more and more delighted. "With regard to the Railway," [89] reported Helmcken, "the Committee were enthusiastically in favour thereof. *They do not consider they can hold the country without it.*" [90]

The delegates got all they wanted and more. They were amazed at Cartier, who urged them to ask for a railway begun in two years and completed in ten. When they protested that a railway to the foot of the Rockies, and a colonization road to the coast would be enough, Cartier smiled benignly and said "No, that will not do; ask for a railway the whole way and you will get it." [91] It soon became apparent to them that he was prepared to stake his career, and the country's future, on this promise. Helmcken was amazed by Cartier's drive: "morning, noon, night brings no cessation." [92] He was burning himself out for the survival of his country. He found time to lecture Helmcken on a new kind of nationality and a new kind of patriotism, in this, his most daring utterance: "I am to tell from Sir George Cartier that it is necessary to be Anti-Yankee. That we have to oppose their damned system – that we can and will build up a northern power – which they cannot do with their principles." [93]

On receipt of the signed terms back in British Columbia, Musgrave wrote delightedly to a friend,

> I have the terms agreed on by the Canadian Gov't, forwarded officially by Sir John Young, and although modified in some respects to suit Canadian reasons, they are outstandingly better – even Helmcken says – than what we asked for. And the Railway, Credat Judaeus! is *guaranteed* without a reservation!! Sir George Cartier says they will do that or 'burst.' [94]

Yet there were difficulties ahead for the Lightning Striker. The first rumblings of discontent over Cartier's bargain came from the Ontario caucus of the Liberal-Conservative Party, still angry over his handling of the Red River crisis. But here Cartier was in his element, threatening them as he had often threatened the cabinet or the House of Commons. Dragging an awed Trutch into the caucus meeting, Cartier argued before the skeptical politicians that the terms agreed upon by the British Columbia delegates and the cabinet committee were absolutely necessary to ensure the completion of Confederation. To ease their financial worries, he declared that the railway would not be built by the government, with borrowed money, but by a private company, aided by land grants. Moreover, as Trutch witnessed it,

> He told them that if they shrank from their engagement with B.C., he and his friends from Quebec would vote alone in fulfilment of the Treaty he had made and if defeated in this matter he would dissolve

the House – but that the union with B.C. on the terms arranged should be carried, and he would see it done.

Trutch had been Cartier's house guest during the negotiations. He had seen Cartier at close range, and was astounded:

> But for the pluck and determination of the "lightning striker" (Cartier) they would have given in, the measure would have been defeated, and the Gov't broken up. We must all remember in B.C. that to Sir George Cartier and his followers in Lower Canada we owe the position we are now in and especially the Canadian Pacific Railway.[95]

The bargaining completed, Cartier advised Helmcken, Trutch and Carrall to return home as quickly as possible, and approve the agreements in their own legislature before he presented his own bill in the Canadian Commons.

"The present ministry manifest a very hostile disposition to the United States – their persecution of independent members, like Messrs. Galt and Huntington, is quite remarkable."

8

"Saskatchewan" Taylor to
Hamilton Fish, May 4, 1871

The second hurdle was Parliament, and the timing was right. Macdonald was at this moment in Washington bargaining with the Americans for nothing less than recognition of Canada's transcontinental status. Cartier submitted his Act for the admission of British Columbia into Confederation on March 28, 1871. Right at the beginning of his speech, he sarcastically noted "the absence of the hon. member for Shefford [Lucius Seth Huntington] on this occasion. That gentleman often complained that this country was advancing too slowly, and said that the Dominion would advance more rapidly if placed on an independent footing."[96]

It is ironic, yet quite significant that Cartier should have singled out Huntington for comment. Two years later, Huntington was the man who would release the documents of the "Pacific Scandal" that drove the Macdonald ministry out of office. Cartier knew better than most members of that Parliament where Huntington's principles lay. Under the guise of "independence," he was an annexationist, who stood to make a fortune out of international railways. A former Solicitor-General in the Macdonald-Dorion ministry, Huntington was a director of two small lines near the American border – the Southeastern Counties Junction and Stanstead, Shefford and Chambly Railways – that Cartier knew were linked with the Vermont Central Railway to take western trade out via Boston. Allied with Huntington were, among others, the Honourable John Young, a member of the Montreal Harbour Board and a small-time railway promoter who had been Commissioner of Public Works in the J.S. Macdonald Ministry of 1861. Young had been involved with Galt in the promotion of the St. Lawrence and Atlantic Railway, and as early as 1854, along with Morin, Galt and the American railway promoter John Alfred Poor, had unsuccessfully petitioned for a railway charter to build a line to the Pacific Ocean, via the Ottawa Valley and the South Shore of Lake Superior. Another ally was Senator Asa Belknap Foster, from Waterloo, Quebec, an American-born railwayman who had begun his career as a contractor for the Vermont Central Railway. And very much in the background, though not out of sight, was that versatile chameleon, Sir Alexander Tilloch Galt, whose recent speech in Sherbrooke advocating "commercial independence" had caused a minor sensation. Galt, planning his own little railway and sorting out a string of bad debts, and a ruined bank, sat nursing his wounds in the Eastern Townships, perceptibly changing colour.

Backing Galt this time were the Rouges of the *Institut Canadien*. Through their newspapers, *Le Pays* and *Le Canadien*, Dorion, Doutre and Laflamme hammered away at Canada's links with Britain. An eighty-four-year old Louis-Joseph Papineau surfaced and demanded the annexation of Canada to the United States, and the poet Louis Fréchette, with whom Louis Riel had stayed while in Chicago, returned to Quebec and harangued the pious in every parish he could visit on the benefits of union with the United States. Cartier's own brother-in-law Hector Fabre was prominent in the movement, organizing annexation conferences in Montreal and Quebec City.

The government knew what to expect from Huntington and his friends. In late 1869 and early 1870, Macdonald had received three letters outlining the views of John Young on the subject of Canadian independence from Great Britain. On November 19, Brydges of the Grand Trunk Railway had noted from New York that

> John Young is here, going to everyone he can get at, distributing pamphlets containing his own and Huntington's speeches at Waterloo and elsewhere. He tells people in the most emphatic way that the feeling in favour of independence, as a prelude to annexation, has attained enormous growth – that the leading men of the country, outside of the Government, are all rapidly taking that view – and that all that is necessary to fan this feeling into open action, is for the United States to withhold reciprocity for a short time longer. About this there is no doubt, and it is dangerous.[97]

Four days later, Hugh Allan, the Montreal shipping magnate, gave Macdonald the same news:

He was to go to Boston on Saturday to enlighten Mr. Sumner who is to bring the subject up in Congress. The people there believe that he is a very influential man in Canada, and has long been a member of the Government of Canada. He urges them not to grant reciprocity, as the refusal of it will precipitate the result he wishes. They believe in him, and I think we will not get reciprocity at present. [98]

Young was obviously confusing the Americans with his name, not minding whether people thought he was Sir John Young (Lord Lisgar), the Canadian Governor General.

Brydges was on a fact-finding tour of the United States for the Grand Trunk Railway, who wished to extend their lines west to Chicago. He had first visited Jay Cooke in Philadelphia, and then ex-Governor Smith of Vermont, President of the Vermont Central and Northern Pacific Railways. On January 25, he reported some bad news:

There is no doubt whatever, from what he tells me, that the Government are assisting the Northern Pacific to go on with their work, in the hope that it will have an effect in maintaining the present attitude of Riel and his party.

Governor Smith is counting upon some more material aid from the Government, so as to ensure the speedy prosecution of the works.

I am quite satisfied from the way Smith talks to me, that there is some political action at the bottom of this, and that the United States Government at Washington are anxious to take advantage of the organization of this Northern Pacific Railway to prevent your getting control for Canada of the Hudson's Bay Territory . . . . The Minnesota people are letting the insurgents in Red River understand that their only hope of getting railway communication will be through United States sources. [99]

In reply to Brydges, Macdonald stated:

It is quite evident to me, not only from this conversation, but from advices from Washington, that the United States Government are resolved to do all they can, short of war, to get possession of the Western Territory, and we must take immediate and vigorous steps to counteract them. One of the first things to be done is to show unmistakeably our resolve to build the Pacific Railway . . . The thing must not be allowed to sleep and I want you to address yourself to it at once and work out a plan. Cartier and I will talk it over after Conference with you, and push it through. [100]

The plan the three worked out, to trap the Americans before they themselves were trapped, is perhaps the most interesting and intricate story in Canadian history. Cartier was at the very centre of it.

When Huntington returned from the United States in 1870, he introduced a resolution in Parliament demanding a customs union or *zollverein*,* in other words, unlimited reciprocity with the United States. He criticized the tariff walls erected by Hincks – a protective tariff set up to prevent the dumping of surplus American goods – as suicidal for Canada. Galt did not support him directly, but moved an amendment proposing commercial independence from Great Britain.

In a fierce debate, Cartier scornfully asked "What will be the consequences of industrial reciprocity? The exclusion of English goods, and higher prices for commodities. We will have to resort to direct taxation to defray our expenses. The Canadian people will never consent to the demands of such a scheme. Moreover, the factories of Canada will lose the advantages they now possess; the price of our man-power and labour will rise; and eventually the largest manufacturing industries will be all concentrated in the United States." A customs union, he concluded, would lead to a political union, "that is to say, to our annihilation as a country." [101]

To some extent, Huntington's resolution was intended to smoke out Macdonald on what the government planned to ask for in Washington, but Huntington and Galt were mauled in debate, and the measure defeated by a two-to-one vote. As Macdonald later wrote to Rose, "Galt is down so low that there are 'none so poor as do him reverence' . . . He is finally dead as a Canadian politician. The correspondence between Cartier and himself,† in which he comes squarely out for independence, has rung his death-knell, and I shall take precious good care to keep him where he is." [102] The great question of free trade versus protection was to arise over and over again in the years to come, as Canada desperately struggled to build a solid industrial base, generally under Conservative leaders, or a prosperous raw material export base, under Liberal leadership. The arguments of that debate in the spring of 1870 are still very much with us today.

Macdonald was to repeat Cartier's arguments, under the umbrella of "The National Policy," with great political success during the prosperous days of the late 1870s and early 1880s, but in the first few years of Confederation, there was a deep sense of gloom and pessimism among some Canadians over the increasingly stagnant economy of the Dominion.

The country needed a little more time to find its boundaries and consolidate its gains, for it to harden "from gristle into bone," [103] and the Liberal-Conservative Party felt that it was surely foolhardy to speak of

* the name of the customs union of the German states.

† Cartier offered the post of Finance Minister to Galt if he would abandon his ideas of "commercial independence." Galt declined. The letters between them were made public in the Commons, *Debates*, Feb. 21, 1870.

a customs union while the United States still coveted Canada so ardently. The last British troops were about to leave the country, and Cartier's militia was still in the embryonic stage. To turn around and cut the economic umbilical cord with Great Britain (which is what free trade would have meant) would be not only foolish but suicidal.

The official Canadian representative on the Washington Commission was a brilliant first stroke. The newly-recovered Prime Minister, Sir John A. Macdonald, was there in Washington to add a bit of local colour to the proceedings, to dazzle and bedevil the Americans. As Hincks said, the negotiations would be "a game of brag, and by bragging high you must win." [104] Macdonald was determined that Canada would not be put off in a corner and her claims ignored. The danger was that the United Kingdom, now menaced in Europe by the Franco-Prussian War, might be willing to purchase peace with the United States by selling out Canadian interests. Macdonald drove a hard bargain with both sides, but especially with Britain. On April 16, he wrote Cartier that he had warned Lord de Grey

> that as there was an anti-Colonial party in England so was there an annexation party in Canada, and if we were told that England was afraid or unwilling to protect us in the enjoyment of our undoubted rights, not from fear of the American Gov't or the American people, but from fear of the Gloucester Fishermen, that party would gain great strength in Canada and perhaps imperil the connection with the Mother Country. – That, in case such connection was severed, the consequences in any opinion would be annexation to the United States . . . that we must be either English or American, and that if protection was denied us by England we might as well go while we had some property left us with which we could make an arrangement with the United States. [105]

A high brag, but it had its effect, and woke the British from their indifference and apathy toward Canada. Cartier read Macdonald's letter to the cabinet, and replied that the cabinet had agreed to recommend that the fisheries were to be exchanged only for a reciprocity treaty. The letter did not reach Macdonald in time, and he signed away the fisheries for cash for a period of twelve years. This may have been planned as a means of covering both angles, and to allow Macdonald leeway in negotiations. What the Maritimes would regard as a sell-out would be blamed solely on Macdonald – because of the delayed letter, the cabinet's hands would be clean, and Macdonald was fully prepared to take the brunt of the criticism. He was able to argue successfully that he never would have signed away the fisheries if he knew a united cabinet was opposed to the measure, and on his return to Ottawa, held off comment on the Treaty until the *Globe* came out solidly against it, whereupon he too complained of a British sell-out.

The Treaty of Washington was signed on May 8, 1871. Although a cash settlement was negotiated for the fisheries, and the Portland, Maine, bonding agreement renewed, there was no agreement on reciprocity – the U.S. was still determined to rebuild its war-shattered industries, and starve Canada into submission in the process. Nor were Canada's claims for damages arising from the Fenian raids entertained. Yet out of all this came a new measure of peace and safety, and above all, recognition. Even such a minor concession as perpetual rights of navigation for Canada on the Stikene and Porcupine Rivers through the Alaska Panhandle, was a recognition, in law, by the United States, of Canada's presence, her *de jure* existence, as an independent, separate political nation state.

There were other benefits for Canada, negotiated behind the scenes. In agreeing to support Britain, and dropping her damage claims for the Fenian raids, the Dominion received a loan guarantee of $2.5 million and a promise that further support would be given for the construction of a railway to the Pacific Ocean. As President Grant concluded in his State of the Union address in December, 1871, "the disappearance of these issues leaves the two governments without a shadow on the friendly relations which it is my sincere hope may forever remain equally unclouded." However, no one knew better than Cartier and Macdonald, that this idyllic state of affairs could be upset easily by a mere change of administration in Washington, and as they prepared for their bold leap across the continent, they knew they would have to safeguard their fragile nation with all the cunning they could muster.

Some Americans were delighted with the Treaty of Washington, confident that it now allowed them free rein over the continent. Sumner's propaganda organ, the New York *Herald*, was jubilant over the "humiliation" of Great Britain:

> In this Great Treaty of Washington we have the virtual recognition from England of our "manifest destiny." So far as human foresight can fathom the events of the future, it is the "manifest destiny" of these United States to occupy and govern the North American continent and the islands thereof, and England, in the reciprocities of this treaty, if she does not accept this idea, ceases to resist it. She abandons the idea of war, and consents to a settlement of the great question through the moral agencies of peace.[106]

But England had not stopped resisting the idea. If the United States had used force in an attempt to conquer Canada, then, in the words of Newcastle, the bricks of Boston and New York would soon have fallen on the heads of the inhabitants.

Canada was now one year away from a federal election, and her government, led to a large extent by Cartier, was committed to continue the impetus of Confederation, and finally put to rest the myth of manifest destiny. The North-West, after a disastrous transition, was secure, and British Columbia was preparing to enter the Dominion.

Cartier shrewdly presented the British Columbia Act as a complete package, meaning that it was a party measure, and he would brook no opposition from his own members. He reminded Parliament that it was "in the nature of a treaty, and consequently the Government would insist upon the adoption of those terms as adopted in British Columbia – that the amendment of one paragraph or one item of those terms would defeat the whole project." [107] He had left very few loopholes, if any. A firm enough bargain had been negotiated, and Parliament was being asked to rubber-stamp it.

With not a little understatement, Cartier remarked that

> Item eleven, relating to the construction of the Pacific Railway, would no doubt provoke discussion . . . Starting from Lake Nippising it would connect with the Ontario system of railways and with the Quebec system of railways through the Ottawa Valley. They were prepared to give it to any company which would undertake the construction of the line, with a capital of twenty-five millions of dollars, which with interest at five per cent, would represent $1,500,000 per annum. The hon. member for Sherbrooke [Galt] had recently remarked that the certain increase of receipts from customs and excise was at the rate of five per cent per year. At that rate, taking the customs at $10,000,000, the increase would be $500,000, and on excise, taking the receipts at $5,000,000, $250,000. That would give a total from these two sources alone to meet $1,500,000 per annum, a sum of $750,000. [108]

Therefore the tariff walls that Hincks had finished building would match half the cost of the railway, and there would be no increase in taxation.

The Liberal Reformers made a valiant effort to properly criticize the bill, but Cartier was too well armed with answers. Their leader, the cool, taciturn Alexander Mackenzie, objected to the ten year "promise" that had been made to British Columbia. Cartier countered that

> in past years even when the country was new and with comparatively few resources she had built 2,000 miles in eight years. Had Canada been ruined by those works, had her agricultural interests suffered on this account? And in addition to this, Canada had built the Victoria Bridge at Montreal, itself equal to 500 miles of railway, and other large bridges in different parts of the country. Had Canada suffered from building those works? [109]

He lashed out at the opposition, saying that they had been

> sufficiently unpatriotic to represent the country as that it would never attract immigration, and he quoted from the proceedings of the House

of Representatives of the State of Minnesota speaking of the Canadian line as practicable, and the territories of the North West and British Columbia as fertile, and the most valuable of the continent; and yet men in this country, the leaders of their party, did their utmost to decry their country . . . . It was absurd to speak of building a line to the Rocky Mountains only, a vote could not be obtained for such a purpose, but when it was proposed to extend the line to the ocean, the question assumed a very different aspect. Many great works had been accomplished in England, but what were any of these compared with the scheme now proposed, and he could say that already there was a movement in England to assist the measure, and there would doubtless be capitalists to take the matter in hand, and everything was in favour of the successful construction of the road.[110]

The House approved the bill in principle, and the next day, April 1, 1871, it was passed and given Royal Assent. On that day, an enlightening exchange took place betwen Sir Charles Tupper and Lucius Seth Huntington. With reference to the railroad the Americans were planning, Tupper argued that if the Canadian Pacific line were built, "the Northern Pacific road would either be abandoned or become a branch of the Canadian Pacific. It could never compete with our line, running as it did through a much less fertile country than our North West, and lying between our line and the Central Pacific route."[111] Huntington countered by referring to rumours "that the Government had been greatly influenced by the presence of Capitalists and Contractors who were opposed to the Northern Pacific Railway, and who thought that if the Canadian Government would decide definitely to construct the Canadian line, it would operate strongly against the Northern Pacific."[112] What Huntington neglected to mention was that, in favouring Montreal, the Canadian Pacific would also damage the exports of the Port of Boston. Boston was the home of Charles Sumner, the American ex-Secretary of State, and it was a terminus of the Vermont Central Railway, whose lines Huntington's little railways connected with. And the president of both the Vermont Central and Northern Pacific Railways was a man named J. Gregory Smith, a constant and generous contributor to the campaign funds of Lucius Seth Huntington.

The scramble for charters was about to begin, and the businessmen and politicians of the Canadas, backed by British and American and even Canadian capital, frantically prepared their paper railway lines for the consideration of Canada's Railway Committee. And south of the border, the tycoons and their shadowy minions planned their attack on the Chairman of that Committee's great dream – a Canadian Pacific Railway.

The events that followed make the average Victorian melodrama – the leering villain with the black moustache tying a beautiful young girl to the railway tracks to force her to hand over her farm comes to mind –

look thin and unconvincing. The temptation is there – will the Lightning Striker and his hung-over sidekick Old Tomorrow rescue lovely Miss Canada from the clutches of Hamilton Fish?

The actual events of the next two years would prove infinitely more complex, as four railway rings, two in Canada and two in the United States, battled for and against the Canadian cabinet's decision – Canada's largesse – for permission to tap the greatest agricultural frontier left in the world, by means of a pair of parallel steel lines shooting west from the shores of Lake Nipissing. The elements of a melodrama were certainly all there – the scheming villains, the blackmailers, the bumbling fools, the rascals, the wise old counsellors and the virtuous patriots – but what took the events of 1871-73 out of the melodramatic mould was the steadily unfolding epic of nationality that involved a hero of the Odyssean cast – George-Etienne Cartier – in his last great trials.

"Cut her adrift, eh? How dare you!" (PAC).

236   Grand Trunk Advertisement.

PART FOUR

PANDORA'S BOX
(1871-1873)

"The success of the Northern Pacific opens
up to us, within a comparatively short period, a prospect whose vastness it is utterly
impossible to exaggerate. It is a prospect to
which all interested in Montreal should direct their attention with great earnestness,
and we may venture to remark that it is one
which is attracting the serious notice of others than Canadians. The people of Boston are
very anxious to secure for themselves better
routes to the West than those which they at
present have, and which by their inferiority
to those of New York have greatly retarded
the progress of the great New England city,
which was once much more important than
her present prosperous rival. Ex-Governor
Smith of the Vermont Central, who is also
largely interested in the Northern Pacific, is
we understand most anxious to get to Montreal . . . . It is no secret that he looks upon
the parts of the route from Boston to the Pacific via Montreal, Ottawa and Lake Nipissing as making up one complete line shorter
than any other, which is possible; and that
his influence, as well as that of the eminent
financial promoter of the Northern Pacific,
will be given to forward every part of the
grand design. There are other developments
which may grow out of the realization of
these projects to which we need not here al-
lude, but among them will doubtless, hereafter, be some question of additional facilities
for crossing the St. Lawrence."

Front page editorial in the
Montreal *Herald*, October 2, 1871

"Henceforth we shall rank among the nations."

George-Etienne Cartier, May 17, 1867

British Columbia became the sixth province of the Dominion on July 20, 1871. In just four short years, Canada had seen the spirit of its Founding Fathers, the dream of dominion from sea to sea, fulfilled; it then had to become a consolidated, vital governing force, a cautious but effective rival to its great neighbour to the south.

For Cartier and the Quebec wing of the party, Macdonald's one-year absence had been salutary. It had allowed the Lightning Striker free rein to confound the opposition with his blunt and forceful lawmaking, and aggressively push through the difficult Manitoba and British Columbia Acts without too much of the kind of opposition niggling that Macdonald seemed to attract. Macdonald had emerged from his recuperation and his attendance at the Washington Conference with his political reputation intact. He had avoided the dangerous Riel episode, the Orange Order had cooled off, and now Old Tomorrow was back in harness, ready to run the country while Cartier steered the railway into being.

It was to take Cartier almost a year – one that was the most critical of his life – to hack through the jungle and pass his Canadian Pacific Railway Act. And at the end of that year, he was to fight the hardest election battle he had ever fought, and retire to England to die, while a scandal broke about the heads of his colleagues.

The events leading up to what was called "the Pacific Scandal" have never been adequately explained. Canada's planning for construction of a Pacific railway, to open up a new route to the Far East, which passed through some of the richest agricultural land on earth, was of more than passing interest to powerful men on both sides of the Atlantic Ocean. That it would probably put an end to American dreams for total control of the continent was known by all engaged in trying to build it or trying to stop it. American involvement in the Red River had shown Cartier what to expect, and he was prepared for the worst – financial pressure, espionage, diplomatic outrages, party strife – a Pandora's box of trickery and chicanery, as powerful interests in the United States tried to force the Canadian Pacific off the tracks.

The railway had to be built to fulfil the outrageous bargain Cartier had arranged with British Columbia. He know that it would be a hard promise to live up to, but Cartier had seen a lot of railway promises broken – the Grand Trunk, for which he was the solicitor, was a glaring offender. Yet above all, the railway had to be built to keep Canada in a competitive position with the United States. Twenty years earlier, Cartier had read the prophetic words of T.C. Keefer, in his great work, *The Philosophy of Railroads*, that

> we are placed beside a restless, early-rising, "go-ahead" people – a people who are following the sun Westward, as if to obtain a greater portion of daylight: *we* cannot hold back – we must tighten our own traces or be overrun – we must *use* what we have or *lose* what we already possess – capital, commerce, friends and children will abandon us for better furnished lands unless we *at once* arouse from our lethargy; we can no longer afford to loiter away our winter months, or slumber during the morning hours. Every year of delay but increases our inequality, and will prolong the time and aggravate the labour of what, through our inertness, has already become a sufficiently arduous rivalry: but when once the barriers of indifference, prejudice and ignorance are broken down – no physical or financial obstacle can withstand the determined perseverance of intelligent, self-controlled industry.[1]

The railway had to built; the challenge of our national survival demanded it.

Cartier's particular railway was not built. It came to a grinding halt a few months after his death in 1873, in the great world-wide commercial depression that followed the collapse of Jay Cooke's banking house in Philadelphia and New York. Yet Cartier had succeeded in constructing the idea that did more to mould our nation than anything that followed it, the idea that fixed, permanently and indelibly, our national nervous system.

There has always been an air of mystery about the Pacific Scandal that brought down the Macdonald government in 1873. The most common historical interpretation has been that Cartier, his judgment muddled by Bright's Disease, cracked under the strain, and sold Sir Hugh Allan – whom he knew was backed by American financiers – the Presidency of the C.P.R. and a controlling interest in its stock. This, as we shall see, is nonsense.

Cartier's role in the whole affair surrounding the awarding of the C.P.R. contract has remained shadowy because he was in England seeking medical aid when the scandal broke, and he died before he could return to Canada. He kept no papers regarding the matter, or if he did, they may have been burned by Macdonald to protect secrecy when the scandal broke. No Cartier letters have surfaced to explain his position, apart from one written from England to Macdonald, congratulating him on having done "the right thing." Most of what we know about the scandal comes from the evidence gathered by a Royal Commission in late 1873, and since it lacks Cartier's testimony, or the evidence of men like Senator Asa B. Foster and Lucius Seth Huntington, M.P. – both of whom refused to testify – the report is a pile of bones without flesh and blood.

Yet we know Cartier's principles, his almost monomaniacal concern for the survival of the French Canadians, his awesome political ability, the power and effect of his lightning strikes, the way his mind worked. With this knowledge, and a careful study of the events of the scandal and the incredibly complicated intrigues of the American railway barons and their Canadian friends, the clouds of mystery surrounding those events can be blown away. For the man at the centre of the scandal was the Chairman of the Standing Committee on Railways, and the key to the mystery was his presence at centre stage.

As Canada began life as a nation, geography was our problem. Railways were our solution. But whose railways? Apart from Hudson Bay there were two principal economic outlets from the heartland prairies of northern North America – the St. Lawrence valley, and the valleys of the Missouri and Mississippi Rivers. The St. Lawrence was many thousands of miles closer to the market of Europe, and its railways and canals poured out the produce of its Empire in a constantly growing stream through the port of Montreal. Yet the St. Lawrence was closed by ice for five months of the year. Although Canada had managed to obtain and keep the privilege of exporting, in bond, through the ice-free harbour of Portland, Maine, that privilege could have been revoked at any time, trapping the country, as Keefer said, in "apathy and ice."

Geology conspired against us. The Canadian Shield to the north of Lakes Huron and Superior, a thousand miles of granite and bottomless muskeg, stood like an impregnable fortress in the way of any railway running from Montreal to the Pacific. On the other hand, a small gap in the Appalachian Mountains continued to bleed away much of Canada's produce, carried by the Erie Canal, the Hudson River and the New York Central Railway down to the port of Montreal's great rival, New York City.

Yet our geography blessed us. A land-hungry and war-torn Europe lost no time in discovering that the Canadian Prairies were rich, far more so than the American plains immediately to the south. They were not as dry, and with more summer daylight, had a longer growing season. In fact, it was then known – and widely broadcast – that an acre in Manitoba could grow twice as much as an acre in Minnesota. The first railway to reach those Prairies stood a good chance of being enormously profitable to its shareholders, not only by the sheer volume of trade it would carry, but from the immigrants it could attract and transport to the lands granted to aid its construction. In addition, the St. Lawrence valley pointed straight to Europe, and the route through Canada was by far the shortest route between those future granaries and the factories of that continent. Cartier was determined to have it built, but by 1871, a cold war was already in progress to determine who would benefit from the riches of that "Great Lone Land."

Jay Cooke, the original "Tycoon," "boy wonder" of the American financial world, had eagerly agreed to take up the cause of his friends in the American State Department. A blond, youthful looking giant in a flowing beard, Cooke was perhaps the first modern American, a red-white-and-blue huckster who could sell anything he put his mind to, with a dedication bordering on religious fervour. His first bond issue, for the State of Pennsylvania, was oversubscribed, and his reputation, due in part to his own successful self-promotion, grew to the extent that he was the only choice for the job of raising the Civil War bond issue. By the end of 1863, Cooke was selling $2,000,000 worth of bonds a day, at a ½ per cent commission, and earning enormous profits. But he was not one to rest on his laurels, and entered into a second career of banking and land speculation that led him naturally into railroads. In 1869, he and a group of prominent Republicans engineered Ulysses S. Grant's rise to the Presidency. The "Lion of Vicksburg" and the conqueror of Lee diminished in office, becoming a little man, terrified by his wife and controlled by a "kitchen cabinet" composed of men like Jay Cooke's brother. His cabinet was no better; Grant appointed two friends from his home town.

Financial recession must follow war, yet the Robber Barons and their government managed to hold off the inevitable by inflation, by floating the American economy on a sea of so-called "Greenback Dollars." The printing presses were busy in the service of a progressive Republican bourgeoisie who controlled, from the northern states, practically all the manufacturing in the country. The tariff was raised for their benefit, and reciprocity with Canada cancelled. The war-weary soldiers of the Union and the Confederacy were bought with free land in the west.

This was the age of the new alchemists, financiers able to turn water into gold – by watering down stocks, by excessive capitalization – a feat pioneered by the original Robber Baron, Commodore Vanderbilt of the New York Central Railroad.

The Republican Party was their private club. Universal manhood suffrage required a sophisticated political machinery; the party supplied it perfectly. Grant's National Campaign Committee had mastered the fine art of political extortion. For example, employees of the New York Customs House were fired unless they contributed 6 per cent of their salaries to Grant's electoral campaign.

Money literally poured in from the railway companies to oil the machinery of government. In most cases this money had already been "loaned" by the government to financial cartels known as "Railway

Rings." Under the Pacific Railway Act, $54,000,000 in 6 per cent, thirty-year government bonds, as well as 22,000,000 acres, were granted to the Union Pacific and Central Pacific Railways to aid them in constructing a transcontinental line. The U.S. government was overgenerous – the companies easily raised their own money by going into a town and threatening to bypass it if funds from prominent citizens were not forthcoming. The Central Pacific Railway cost $79,000,000 to build, yet $36,000,000 of this total lined the pockets of the railway ring, who spent none of their own money to build the line. The profit was funnelled out through the owners' construction company, which had the sole right to build the line, and back into banks and insurance companies.

Much of the capital subscribed to construct the American lines came from the surplus funds of European financiers. It has been estimated that, by 1873, U.S. railroads were capitalized to the extent of $3 billion, half of it from Europe. Yet there were dangers; the prosperity of the United States was vulnerable to the whims of Europe.

The Northern Pacific Railway was incorporated in 1864 by Boston and Vermont interests, but it was not until 1869 that Jay Cooke made it his own. When he and his lobbyist "Saskatchewan" Taylor got involved in its affairs, Cooke to raise more European capital that he could change from gold to paper, and Taylor to pry the North-West loose from Canada, the Northern Pacific was bound to flourish, especially on paper. Cooke, who had of course already bought up land in St. Paul by the late sixties, was soon promoting the railway and the land with his usual ballyhoo, prompting some wags to speak derisively of "Jay Cooke's Banana Belt."

Yet in a tight money market, the Northern Pacific was doomed from the start if it did not run north through the richer lands of the Canadian Prairies. Only one line could be successful, and Cooke wanted nothing more than to sabotage or delay the Canadian Pacific Railway, which would greatly increase his chances of raising money in Europe. But like all great financiers, he knew he could not lose in the long run. If he could not persuade Congress to back the line, or if Cartier and the Canadians insisted on a Canadian line entirely through British territory, then he could make an enormous profit out of stock manipulation alone. But if the Canadian railway and the Canadian government, or even Canada itself, could be sabotaged, then so much the better.

Although Jay Cooke and Company advertised lavishly in Europe, and opened a branch in London to interest the English Rothschilds, the Northern Pacific was in trouble from the start. The Germans and Dutch were not interested, and a crash on the Vienna exchange in 1870 made money tight all over Europe for Cooke's salesmen. Of course, the line was capitalized excessively – at $100,000,000 – and the inability of Cooke's men to sell bonds only diminished confidence in the line further. To add to Cooke's woes, the Franco-Prussian War had further cut off funds, as well as the flow of immigration that would have sustained the construction of the railway in stages.

Initially, Cooke's main ally in promoting the Northern Pacific was J. Gregory Smith, the line's president and head of the Vermont Central. We have already seen how Brydges of the Grand Trunk had sounded out Smith and communicated his own fears to Sir John A. Macdonald. Smith was backed by a group of Boston businessmen who hoped to tap the trade of the North-West and carry it out through their own city, via Vermont and Canada. Boston itself was trapped in a backwater between New York and Montreal, and wanted a bypass to the west without having to go over the tracks of the Grand Trunk or Commodore Vanderbilt's New York Central.

Smith reckoned at first without Cooke's treachery. It is apparent, if other men behind Cooke are examined, that Jay Cooke was also planning to swindle Smith and the Bostonians, and take western trade out through St. Paul and Chicago, down to Pittsburg and his home town of Philadelphia, using the Pennsylvania Railroad of his friends Cass and Scott. Although he later pretended otherwise, Cooke had no intention of passing through Eastern Canada to Montreal or Boston, and was merely using Smith as a decoy. His friend Scott of the Pennsylvania Railroad, now promoting the Kansas Central and Kansas Pacific Railways, was locked in battle with Collis P. Huntington of the Union Pacific over land rights, and losing. Scott needed a new route west, and Jay Cooke's Northern Pacific promised to be the only profitable alternative. Northern Pacific trade would of course feed down through Philadelphia over the tracks of Scott's Pennsylvania Railroad.

Brydges and the Grand Trunk directors went along with Smith and the Bostonians, as much out of curiosity as anything, curiosity about what was really behind the American proposals. As early as 1863, Brydges visited St. Paul, Minnesota, at the urging of the Duke of Newcastle, who realized that the Americans would eventually have to be headed off at the Red River pass. On December 24 of that year, Brydges wrote James Wickes Taylor that, with respect to a St. Paul-Fort Garry railway, "negotiations, which are now in progress . . . will result in the actual construction of that line before very long, and that steps will immediately be taken to continue the line across to the Pacific coast."[2] British investors were at the time reluctant to support the scheme, and the formation of the Northern Pacific the following year showed that the Americans were planning to fight the Grand Trunk every inch of the way, to prevent the Canadian line from building anything west of Chicago and Milwaukee, least of all to the Red River. To capture and retain control over the export trade of the North-West, Canada's own transcontinental railway would have to go north of Lake Superior, or else see that trade siphoned off down the Mississippi or out through Philadelphia.

By 1870, the Grand Trunk was making a good profit out of its lines through Windsor and Sarnia, with connections to Chicago and Milwaukee, and had temporarily lost interest in a Pacific Railway. In fact, while profiting from its U.S. connections, the Grand Trunk was now embarking on an extensive scheme of re-financing and modernization. In 1869, it had borrowed £ 100,000 from Hugh Allan to purchase 600 freight cars, and become heavily involved in buying track from Casimir Gzowski's Toronto Rolling Mills. Cartier may have urged the Grand Trunk directors not to prejudice the Pacific Railway by pressing too heavily for a line through the U.S. to Fort Garry. In any event, with their solicitor Cartier in power, they were almost certain to be awarded some share in the Canadian Pacific.

About one-third of the Grand Trunk's earnings came from the American Mid-West, and the company was successfully advertising its straight and fast through-connection with American trains bound for California. Its freight service was doing so well that, for five frantic weeks in 1870, it was actually forced to suspend hauling to Portland because there were not enough steamships to take away cargo. The directors even considered building a line of steamships, in opposition to the Allan Line of Montreal, a possibility that did not sit lightly with its owner, Sir Hugh Allan. After years of debt, the Grand Trunk Railway was at last able to give its shareholders something more than promises.

Although the Grand Trunk would have nothing to do with a line north of Lake Superior, at least not for the moment, their manager Charles Brydges probably agreed, at the urging of his friend Cartier, to play along with the Americans, keep his ears open, and if possible, help sabotage the Northern Pacific and Jay Cooke's schemes against Canada's railway to the west.

We have already seen how Cooke and Ramsey had sounded out Joseph Howe on the possibilities of a route south of Lake Superior in the autumn of 1869. Cartier knew that the Americans were in favour of this plan for two reasons: first, as the money market stood, the only way Jay Cooke and Gregory Smith could raise cash was by linking their scheme with Canada's. But Canada's was to be a subsidized railway; theirs was not, and European financiers would not touch it. As the Lightning Striker realized, the real danger lay in the fact that, if Canada were to build its own line entirely through its own territory, as he intended that it should, it would kill the Northern Pacific's chances. Cartier knew all along that he and Macdonald were in for heavy weather from the Northern Pacific financiers.

Secondly, if on the other hand, Canada were to cooperate with the Americans in a line south of Lake Superior, the end result would be that the United States would siphon off trade that by all rights should have gone to Montreal, and destroy Canada's western thrust, as well as damaging Canada's influence in its new territories, perhaps irreparably. The only way out of this dilemma was to draw out the American schemes by pretending to go along with them, and then expose their dangerous plans to the Canadian public. This was probably their initial strategy, and it was a partial success.

It would appear that Cartier's friend Adams Archibald, Lieutenant-Governor of Manitoba, was chosen to be the first to let out the bait, first to get the nibble. On January 3, 1871, he suggested to "Saskatchewan" Taylor, now no longer a secret agent of the U.S. Treasury, but the American Consul in Winnipeg, that the two countries cooperate to take a railway from Sault Ste. Marie south of Lake Superior to Fort Garry. Taylor, probably after consultation with Jay Cooke, proposed an International Pacific Railway, constructed in sections. Archibald, doubtless briefed by Cartier to try and bring the Americans out in the open, suggested to Taylor that Jay Cooke and the Northern Pacific go to Ottawa and make a definite proposal to the Canadian government. Cooke wisely did not.[3] He realized the game was getting more complicated, and wanted to retain the element of secrecy and surprise.

But Cooke knew all along that he was playing with fire and lightning. In the spring of 1871, George B. Sargeant, one of his London agents, wrote Cooke that he was "fully satisfied that we are to have competition from the Canadian N.P. [the C.P.R.]. The scheme will pass in some way or other; it will have the guarantee of the *Dominion* which will give it great strength and will induce Barings to bring it out here, I am told."[4] All the participants knew the game was for high stakes. For Cartier and Macdonald, it involved nothing less than national survival. For Brydges' Grand Trunk Railway and Donald Smith's Hudson's Bay Company, for Cooke and J. Gregory Smith and Hamilton Fish, it meant tapping the wealth of the last great agricultural frontier left in North America, and the richest.

2   "The public be damned!"

Commodore Vanderbilt
of the New York Central
Railway

With the Grand Trunk's graceful, though temporary exit from the race, with the passage of the British Columbia Act, and with Cartier's railway bill forthcoming, the scramble for charters began in earnest. The parliamentarians and financiers of Canada lost no time in presenting their proposals to the Standing Committee on Railways, and voting themselves and their friends the right to raise money as companies. This was basically all a railway charter entailed; then after companies had established themselves, the cabinet would decide which company it would allow to go ahead with a particular route, if at all.

Cartier sat back to watch the fools rush in. One of the first was Alfred Waddington – "Old Waddy" – a seventy-five year old Don Quixote from Victoria, B.C. Waddy had made a fortune in the Fraser and California gold rushes, but had caught the transcontinental railway fever, and spent most of his gold in preliminary surveys and travels in Europe and America to promote his dream. He and his Sancho Panza, William Kersteman of Toronto, made little headway until, by no chance at all, they met a young Chicago publisher and entrepreneur – Jay Cooke's secret agent – twenty-seven year old George "Washington" McMullen.* McMullen was the black-sheep son of a Methodist minister from Picton, Ontario, and as he later related it, he had "visited Ottawa in March, 1871, on a Chicago delegation connected with the enlargement of the canals, and while there met the late lamented Mr. Alfred Waddington and Mr. William Kersteman, who were agitating the subject of a Canadian Pacific R.R., and who introduced the matter to my notice, with a view to organize a Company to build the proposed road." [5] McMullen involved the two in a syndicate, and they visited Ottawa again to put their case before the government. A few weeks later, McMullen continued, they saw Macdonald and Hincks, with little success, then "Mr. Chas. M. Smith, of Chicago, who was my colleague in this matter, received a letter from Sir Hugh Allan, stating that Sir Francis Hincks had requested him to communicate with us in order to effect a union of Canadian and American interests in the Pacific Railroad Company that was to be formed." [6]

The reason for the government's apparent change of heart was that it had discovered that, behind McMullen and Charles Mather Smith, a Chicago banker, lurked the bigger fish it was still trying to lure out: namely William B. Ogden, an original member of the Northern Pacific ring; General George W. Cass, President of the Pittsburg, Fort Wayne and Chicago Railway (part of the Pennsylvania Railroad); T.A. Scott of Philadelphia, the controlling shareholder in the Philadelphia and Erie and Pennsylvania lines; J. Gregory Smith of Vermont; Jay Cooke; and, by inference, Hamilton Fish and the U.S. State Department. The prospect of an international railway dangled by Archibald and Hincks was beginning to bring the developers to the surface.

Earlier that year, the government had received other nibbles from the Americans. Cyril Graham, a special Hudson's Bay Company Commissioner travelling in the United States, wrote Hincks that he had been approached by some financiers who intimated to him that they were prepared to "abandon the Western Section of the Northern Pacific Road, carrying it through Canadian territory, if the Canadians would

* the meeting may have been orchestrated by J.W. Taylor, who met Waddy in Ottawa at about the same time.

abandon their Eastern Section, and carry it through United States territory by the Sault Ste. Marie."[7] In May of 1871, Sir John Rose wrote Macdonald that he was being approached in London with the same suggestion, and out in Winnipeg, "Saskatchewan" Taylor was hard at work promoting that possibility. Taylor and J. Gregory Smith got a charter from the Manitoba government for a line from Winnipeg to the Dakota frontier, but on Cartier's advice, the line was later disallowed by the Governor General. In his July 4 speech to some citizens of Winnipeg, Taylor praised Canadian-American harmony and suggested that the people of Manitoba should press for an immediate railway connection with Minnesota instead of waiting for the C.P.R., just as Montrealers had got a line to Portland, Maine before waiting for the Intercolonial Railway to link them to the Maritimes.[8] Taylor had swallowed Archibald's bait, and was now bringing the possibility out into the open.

And now Old Waddy had brought Jay Cooke out of his lair. On June 17, Ogden wrote to Cooke, urging him to take steps to "control the project,"[9] and very shortly afterwards, Cooke went ahead, and through McMullen, made contact with Sir Hugh Allan. Although Sir John A. Macdonald later protested that "Hincks made a mistake and acted without authority,"[10] it is likely that Cartier advised Hincks to see Sir Hugh Allan and persuade him to begin dealing with the Americans. It was another way to smoke out enemy intentions. As Allan modestly related it, he was "very reluctant to go into it at all." But Hincks pressed the matter and Allan agreed. Hincks then suggested that he put himself "in communication with those parties who have applied to us; you can make your own arrangement with them. You will find those gentlemen at New York, and you will find them more likely to take it up than the people in England, because they have already commenced two railways across the Continent, and are about commencing a third. They are much more likely to undertake it than our own people, who do not know anything about it, and who would be afraid of so large a sum."[11]

Although Allan did not realize it then, he was being pushed by the Hyena Hincks because the Canadian government needed a further sounding board to ascertain American plans and nip them in the bud. Allan was the perfect choice. He was regarded in some circles as an avaricious man, he was known to have dealt with J. Gregory Smith in the promotion of the Northern Colonization Railway, and he and his cronies were unfriendly toward Cartier and the Grand Trunk Railway.

Macdonald, in his later testimony to the Royal Commission, vigorously protested that Hincks acted on his own in dealing with Allan, and that no member of the government knew of McMullen's links with the Northern Pacific. Balderdash! Macdonald was unwilling, at this early date, to let the cat out of the bag; his testimony provides a stunning view of his mastery of political understatement:

At that time it had not occurred to me, or I think to anyone, that these American gentlemen were in any way connected with the Northern Pacific Railway. That had not occurred to any of us. It certainly had not occurred to me, and the reason why I thought that the action of Sir Francis Hincks was premature, was that I thought that the true plan would be to endeavour to get up a strong Canadian company, in which would be represented the capital of the different sections of the Dominion, and after a body of Canadian capitalists was so formed, they might extend to the United States, or to England, and I thought that it would frustrate that policy, to have communication in the first place with Americans.[12]

Yet by allowing Americans to come into the picture through Sir Hugh Allan, Macdonald was providing himself with a sure-fire weapon to use in the upcoming federal elections. After the Red River troubles and the Canada First demonstrations, he had lost a great deal of the so-called "loyal" vote in Ontario. Now he could lure the Americans in, then expose them, and by exploiting anti-American sentiment, protest that the railway should be pre-eminently a Canadian (and an Imperial) project. He and Cartier would shame the country into proceeding with the line, and easily persuade British politicians and capitalists that, without Imperial support, the Grand Trunk would languish and the west would be lost to the United States. But Old Tomorrow and the Lightning Striker reckoned without Allan's brash foolishness in dealing with the Americans, and while attempting to trap Jay Cooke, got partly ensnared in a web of their own making.

The newly-knighted Sir Hugh Allan was the wealthiest man in Canada, and a large part of his fortune was due not only to his native business sense, but his fairly comfortable relations with the party of Cartier and Macdonald. He and Cartier were the two most prominent men in Montreal. They often had dealings on political and financial matters, and worked out mutually beneficial agreements through the intermediaries of party and business; yet they were not friendly, and rarely met, and lately had just about come to blows. Needless to say, Allan was a regular, quiet and generous contributor to the Liberal-Conservative Party and *La Minerve*, as well as being part-owner of the Montreal *Gazette*.

Back in 1819, Allan's father, Captain Alexander Allan, began the first regular passenger service from Britain to Montreal with his brigantine, *Jean*. Hugh, the second son of the family, was packed off to Canada in 1826 to learn the family business. He served as a clerk in a drygoods firm, then in a shipping office, where he rose to be partner, and then owner. The family line prospered in the timber/immigrant trade, ferrying a large part of the 500,000 Britons who came to Canada between 1840 and 1850. By 1853, he obtained ship-building and trans-atlantic mail contracts from the Canadian government, and his profits led him into an incredible variety of businesses. He was president of sixteen corporations, vice-president of six. Apart from shipping, his interests ranged from telegraphs and navigation to coal and iron, tobacco, textiles, sewing machines, cattle, rolling mills, paper mills, railway cars and elevators. By 1871, his net income, in today's terms, was an estimated $2,000,000 per annum. He was, of course, a thrifty man. There is a story that once Allan was a guest at Earnscliffe, and over supper Lady Macdonald asked him for a donation for her church fund. When he hesitated, she joked, "You can't take all your money when you die." Sir John A., his ear cocked, added, "It would soon melt if he did."

Something had to be done with all this money. With some of it, Allan built "Ravenscrag," the largest mansion in Montreal. Government bonds swallowed the rest, and in 1864, he obtained a charter for the Merchants' Bank, later absorbed by the Bank of Montreal.

The Lightning Striker and the Laird of Ravenscrag had not yet quarreled openly, even though Allan was not above exploiting divisions in Cartier's party for his own ends. We have already noted Cartier's delay in granting government support to the Quebec North Shore and Northern Colonization Railways. The lines, now almost wholly controlled by Allan, would have diverted Ottawa valley trade north of Montreal to Quebec City. And Quebec City was the kingdom of Joseph Cauchon, Cartier's chief rival within the party. Despite Allan's protestations to the contrary, he was intensely interested in a transcontinental railway, and realized that the Ottawa valley would be its first leg to the west. To exploit Montreal-Quebec City differences, Allan appointed Cauchon President of the lines, thereby forcing a quarrel between the two French Canadians. Although Cartier was able to whip Cauchon into line over Confederation by delaying the railway, and to neutralize him politically by making him the first Speaker of the Senate, Allan's sortie into the backrooms of Quebec politics had created a great deal of ill feeling between the Laird and the Lightning Striker.

Cartier was the kind of person who never forgave what he considered to be a betrayal. Allan feared the Minister of Militia's wrath, and more especially, Cartier's Grand Trunk connections, realizing that if the Grand Trunk wished to develop a steamship line to compete with the Allan Line, it would be assured of government contracts. He also knew that the Grand Trunk would be favoured in any contract to build a railway from Montreal to the terminus of the Canadian Pacific Railway on Lake Nipissing, and might even be awarded the transcontinental line itself.

Cartier held in his grasp the power to break Allan, and this power did not sit lightly with the Laird of Ravenscrag. He had worked diligently and soberly all his life to reach his position of wealth and independence, and was enraged when he paused to realize that his position depended on the largesse of one man, Sir George-Etienne Cartier. Cartier was above personal bribery, and could always turn elsewhere for campaign funds.

Elsewhere meant the Grand Trunk Railway and the Hudson's Bay Company. Allan knew that if he were to withdraw his support from the party, the British imperialists of the Grand Trunk would come to Cartier's rescue. He chafed under the realization that the Grand Trunk would start to build their own ships if his Northern Colonization Railway took away their business. And the Grand Trunk was coming more and more into Canadian hands: Brydges, Senator Ferrier and William Molson were now controlling shareholders, backed by Lord Wolverton and the Barings. And now the Hudson's Bay Company were getting into the game; in 1870 a consortium led by George Stephen of the Bank of Montreal and David Torrance (Alexander Galt's cousin) established a steamship company called the Dominion Line, and soon began to threaten his monopoly of trans-atlantic trade.

Almost by instinct, Allan knew he must destroy Cartier's power, or tie him firmly to his own interests, to eliminate all the nagging uncertainty of being self-made, but not secure. He was growing restless, tired of paying for government handouts. He was not satisfied with his present boundaries, and began to look for bigger game. If Commodore Vanderbilt and Jay Cooke could make state legislatures eat out of their hands, why could he not do the same? With Alexander Galt now in opposition, Cartier had lost a great deal of support in English Quebec, and with the federal elections less than a year away, he was ripe for attack.

Cartier knew Allan was restless – the Franco-Prussian War had cut into his profits; he had begun to agitate for the completion of the Northern Colonization Railway, and was demanding better service from the Port of Montreal. In July of 1870, Cartier had given the Allan Line a very favourable twenty-one-year wharfage lease, but this was only a bone for the terrier to gnaw. So when Sir Francis Hincks suggested that some prominent Americans were interested in building the Pacific railway, Allan knew that he had found a way out of his little empire.

Like a man who has just seen the light, Allan boldly and joyfully leapt from his own little kingdom into the bearpit of American railway politics. They were waiting for him with open arms, and it is a wonder that they did not eventually tear him apart, but the bears of Boston and Philadelphia were, like him, looking for bigger game. They would destroy him as they had destroyed other men. If he ever had a chance of building the Canadian Pacific Railway, he would lose it now. He was to be nothing more than their Trojan Horse.

3   **"There is nothing in Canadian railway history that approaches in deviousness the story of the Vermont Central."**

G.R. Stevens

On July 13, 1871, Sir John Rose, the former Finance Minister and Canada's business agent in London, wrote Macdonald that, as requested, he had been investigating the Northern Pacific's prospects of success. He reported wryly that "from what I now hear I fear it would not rebound to the credit of Canada to be identified in any way with the undertaking now in progress. Statements were made in reference to its resources and prospects which I am told can never be fulfilled." [13] Cooke knew that he was in for some heavy weather, but tried to keep up morale for the benefit of his beleaguered bond salesmen. On August 8, he wrote to his brother Henry Cooke, that "Canada will build to Sault Ste. Marie to meet us – This is a grand thing for N. Pacific & disposes of all those Morton Rose & Co. stories set afloat in London about rival Pacific Road. Hincks & Macdonald are cordially *with us*." [14] Six weeks later, he wrote blithely to Puleston of his London branch that "the Canadian government is extremely friendly to the connection of our roads at Sault Ste. Marie, and they will do all they can to connect with us at Manitoba and other points. I have no doubt whatever that arrangements can be made by which the Hudson's Bay people, headed by Sir Stafford Northcote, can have an interest in our road and in its direction." [15] Cooke may have fooled his brother and his dealers, but he never fooled himself. He was in trouble, and knew that he would have to use other, more subtle weapons to sabotage the Canadian Pacific.

Rose's letter pleased Cartier, and the information in it tallied with what he had been able to learn through his contacts in the Grand Trunk and Hudson's Bay Company. It was apparent that Jay Cooke's paper railway would have no chance of success. The European money markets would not be interested in a competitor to Canada's line, backed as it would be by all the resources of Ottawa and Westminster. Cooke – knowing that he had been bamboozled – would now concentrate his efforts on sabotaging the C.P.R. But how? What would be the Americans' game and where would they attack next? It did not take Cartier long to pinpoint where. He himself would be the chief object of the attack. Now, instead of being the Lightning Striker, he would play at being the Lightning Rod.

Cartier realized the threat came not just from Jay Cooke's Northern Pacific or from Sir Hugh Allan's Northern Colonization line, but also from a number of small border railways in the Eastern Townships and eastern Ontario – milk, butter and cheese lines – controlled, he knew, by what appeared to be one more railway ring, centred around J. Gregory Smith of Vermont. In his history of the Canadian National Railways,

n. John Young (PAC).

J.J.C. Abbott (PAC).

The Eastern Townships Railway Ring

nator A.B. Foster (PAC).

Lucius Seth Huntington (Notman).

G.R. Stevens has quite rightly called Smith's railways "a maze of cross-transactions – loans and borrowings, mortgages and leases, transfers and re-transfers of assets, abandonments and reclamations, capitalization of debt and discount allowances, options and escape clauses. Not a trick or twist of financial manipulation was overlooked. Peter was robbed to pay Paul, who in turn had his pocket picked by Peter." [16]

Cartier knew from Brydges that the Vermont Central had over-reached itself from buying up lines to Ogdensburg and New London, Connecticut, and was now desperately trying to reach more capital in conjunction with the Northern Pacific. The Barings had always refused to support the Vermont Central, arguing that it was too speculative. [17] Yet they and the Grand Trunk were very much aware that J. Gregory Smith's railway could turn out to be a very dangerous competitor, dangerous for the Grand Trunk, and dangerous for the City of Montreal. Some ten years previously, on May 11, 1860, Cartier had stood up in the Assembly and argued that "we haven't yet attained our goal, which is to divert the commerce of the Great Lakes from American routes and direct it toward the St. Lawrence. This commerce continues to pass through New York and Pennsylvania and all we see of it is traffic destined for Ogdensburg and Oswego." [18] The times had not yet changed, and the threat to Canadian commerce was, if anything, more serious than in 1860. Ogdensburg and Oswego were still draining life blood from the body of Montreal, and threatening to take even more; in October of 1869, Barings had been approached by a group calling themselves "the Oswego Transcontinental Railway Convention." Barings replied to their query, stating that "500,000,000 bushels of American wheat could annually find a market in Europe at the present cost of production, if adequate facilities existed for its transportation to tide-water." [19] The Vermont Central wanted to provide this transportation.

By the early 1870s, the Vermont Central owned, leased or controlled some 773 miles of track in Canada, along the border, and down to Boston and New London. Its Canadian lines were the following:

The Montreal and Vermont Junction Railway – Saint-Jean to the border – president, the Honourable John Young.

The Stanstead, Shefford and Chambly Railway – Saint-Jean to Waterloo – managing director, Senator Asa B. Foster; director, Lucius S. Huntington.

The Southeastern Counties Junction Railway – Saint-Jean to Richford, Vermont with branches – managing director, Senator Asa B. Foster; director, Lucius S. Huntington.

The Massawippi Valley Railway (under construction) – Stanstead to Sherbrooke, with a branch line to Derby, Vermont – president, Sir Alexander Tilloch Galt.

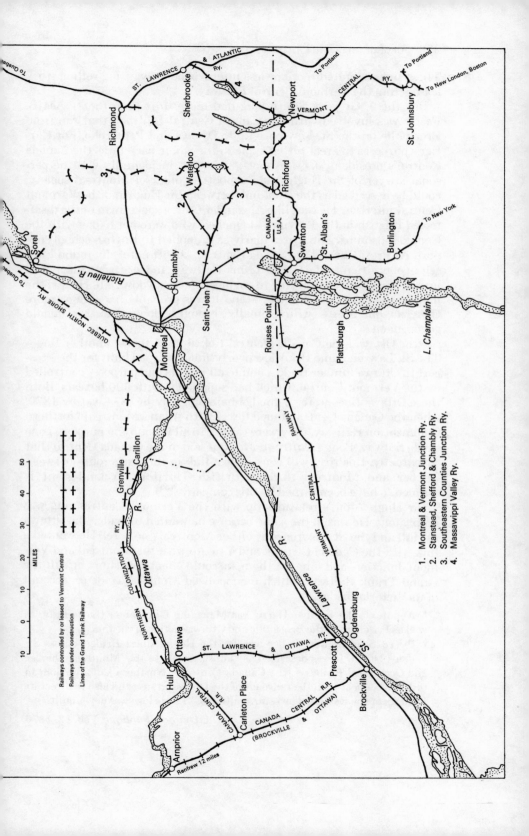

MILES

0   10   20   30   40   50

Railways controlled by or leased to Vermont Central
Railways under construction
Lines of the Grand Trunk Railway

1.   Montreal & Vermont Junction Ry.
2.   Stanstead, Shefford & Chambly Ry.
3.   Southeastern Counties Junction Ry.
4.   Massawippi Valley Ry.

These lines operated more or less interdependently, using rolling stock leased from the Vermont Central Railway.

But the J. Gregory Smith ring had more to it than that – Asa B. Foster was involved with the Canada Central Railway, that ran from Brockville on the St. Lawrence up to Ottawa and Pembroke. For Cartier's purposes the real rotten apple in the whole barrel was the Canada Central's president, J.J.C. Abbott,* who not incidentally was the personal lawyer of Sir Hugh Allan. Abbott, a pillar of Montreal society, could be described as the chief link between Sir Hugh and the Vermont Central interests. He was, like Alexander Galt, a spokesman of the disaffected English in the Province of Quebec, who were not happy with the Confederation bargain, particularly as it applied to English school support. As President of the Canada Central, Abbott naturally found himself in opposition to the Grand Trunk Railway, and was particularly and intimately involved in trying to engineer Cartier's downfall. He was the man in the middle – the fixer – and it was probably his actions more than anyone else's which finally brought down the Macdonald government.

Near Ottawa, the Canada Central linked up with yet another line – The St. Lawrence and Ottawa, a poorly-financed road built for the Prescott to Ottawa lumber trade – and to all intents and purposes controlled by the Vermont Central, which had supplied it with 500 boxcars. Both these Ottawa lines were to amalgamate officially in 1874, yet by 1870, when the Canada Central joined forces with Allan's Montreal Northern Colonization Railway, they were (again, to all intents and purposes) one single railway. Poor's *Railroad Manual* said of the Canada Central that "eventually, this road will constitute a link in the great route between Quebec and Montreal through British Territory. A land-grant is claimed to have been earned by this company." [20]

Sir Hugh Allan's relationship with the Vermont Central ring was ambiguous. He was in the game because he wanted to bridge the Ottawa at Hull and the St. Lawrence at either Montreal† or Sorel. He wanted a link with the Canada Central, and a tie-up with the Montreal and Vermont Junction, and if he got them, he could effectively short-circuit the Grand Trunk Railway, which monopolized Montreal trade on account of its Victoria Bridge.

* Abbott's older brother Harry was Managing Director of the railway, as well as President of the Brockville and Ottawa section of the line.

† By 1875, plans were under way for the Royal-Albert Bridge, across St. Helen's Island. It was described as "indispensable to the 'Montreal, Quebec and Occidental Railway' [the Canada Central – Northern Colonization] in order to connect with the railroads of the United States, and also to direct its traffic over the Eastern Townships railways." The bridge was never built.

L'Opinion Publique, Feb. 12, 1876

The St. Lawrence and Ottawa's managing director was an American engineer and friend of J. Gregory Smith named Thomas Reynolds. For the past two Christmases, Reynolds had sent six bottles of the best "Old Jamaica" to Cartier. Reynolds and his cronies were asking the Canadian government for a charter for a company they called "The St. Lawrence International Bridge Company,"[21] and their intention was, not unexpectedly, to build a bridge between Prescott, Ontario and Ogdensburg, New York. Of course, waiting eagerly at Ogdensburg was J. Gregory Smith and his Ogdensburg and Lake Champlain Railway, another section of the Vermont Central. Smith's plan was simple – to divert western trade away from Montreal by means of this bridge, and take it down through Boston and New London. His involvement with Sir Hugh Allan's railway was merely a smokescreen for this plan, and it is entirely probable that through his friends Abbott, Reynolds, Foster, Young and Huntington he intended to go along with Allan, then sabotage him, and bring down Cartier and the Canadian government at the same time.

It is apparent the whole strategy was hatched in early 1871. On January 9, Gregory Smith wrote Jay Cooke that he "had here to see me the gentlemen who control the Canada Central interest (the charter running from Montreal to the Sault Ste. Marie). I have from them a very favourable proposition and one which if we are in condition to accept will as it seems to me aid us much in working up our enterprize in England."[22] The gentlemen Smith refers to were likely Abbott and Reynolds, and their proposition probably was made without Sir Hugh Allan's knowledge. He was to be the Trojan Horse; they and Gregory Smith would be the Greeks inside it.

Their ring was forged with the purpose of working for an international railway using the Vermont Central, the Canada Central and the Northern Pacific Railways. Their primary aim was to replace the Canadian administration, and particularly the Grand Trunk man Sir George-Etienne Cartier, with a government more amenable to a bridge across the St. Lawrence at Ogdensburg.

The map reproduced here is from the Annual Report of the Vermont Central Railway, published in Boston on October 2, 1872. Its intent is to show "the exact relations of the Vermont Central Railroad to Boston and New England on the one hand, and to the St. Lawrence and Ottawa valleys, the Lakes, the grain fields of the North-West, and the Northern Pacific Railroad, on the other." What it in fact illustrates is the grave danger Montreal and the Grand Trunk Railway faced in this dirty game. Cartier knew more than any other man, that if his government were defeated and the Ogdensburg Bridge were built, the trade of Montreal would literally go down the drain, and with it, the viability of both the Grand Trunk Railway and the Dominion of Canada.

By the summer of 1871, the plot began to thicken. In early August,

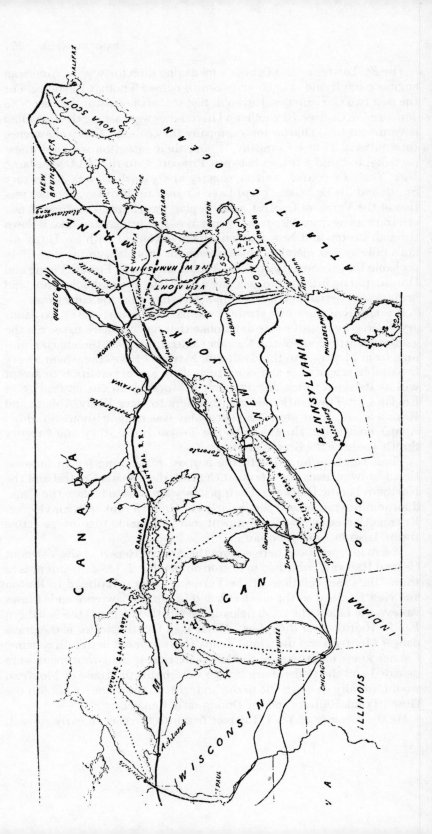

Hincks travelled down to New York and met "two prominent railway bankers,"[23] perhaps Scott or Cass of the Pennsylvania Central, or possibly even Jay Cooke himself. Hincks advised them to come out into the open, and deal directly with Allan instead of through McMullen. The Americans, rightly divining Hincks' intentions, refused to be drawn out and continued to insist that McMullen act as their intermediary.

While Hincks did the work of drawing the Americans out, the Chairman of Canada's Railway Committee laid low. In August, he spent two weeks in Rimouski, supposedly for a rest, but he found most of his time taken up with mending political fences and receiving a steady stream of callers.[24] By the end of the month, he had returned to Montreal, and on September 3, held a magnificent garden party at Limoilou for the officers of the militia units around Montreal. One of the tents set up behind the house contained a large picture of Jacques Cartier, suspended above the refreshment table.[25]

In early September, McMullen met with Allan in Montreal. They concluded a tentative arrangement whereby Allan would work for the charter in exchange for the financial backing of Jay Cooke and Associates. To reassure himself about the government's plans, McMullen met Macdonald briefly in a council room and at Bonaventure Station. All Macdonald would say was that he had no objection to them going ahead with their project to obtain the charter, but that the government could not entertain it seriously until after the beginning of the next parliamentary session the following spring.

McMullen and Allan then asked for and were granted a meeting with the cabinet that October. The conference was decidedly cool and short, with only Hincks appearing to favour some form of American participation in the building of the railway. According to McMullen, Hincks told him at this meeting that the Grand Trunk Railway, represented by Cartier, was extremely jealous of Sir Hugh Allan. A broader hint could not have been given to the Americans. If they wanted to make any headway, they should concentrate their campaign on Cartier. Cartier would draw the fire.

Cartier knew very well that Jay Cooke was beginning to run short of capital; and through Rose and the Grand Trunk, he had learned that the Barings and other British investors were now quietly and deliberately withdrawing their funds from American railroads. The Tycoon wanted some of this money back, and here in the cabinet room sat Cooke's minions, ready to deal.

Cartier said little, but sat back and sized up the intent of the delegation he knew were out to destroy the Canadian Pacific Railway. Sir Hugh Allan appeared brash and confident. Watching Allan speak, Cartier knew he would have to tread a very fine line to delay giving him any firm promise until after the next federal election. He would stay out of the whole discussion, bide his time, and wait to see what the Americans would do next.

Macdonald straightaway asked Allan if he and his friends had any proposition to make. Sir Hugh wondered in reply whether "the Government were in a position to entertain a proposition if he made one?" [26] Macdonald said no, not at the moment; and that was the end of the meeting.

Allan seethed with anger. He had expected some small glimmer of support, some softening from either Macdonald or Cartier, not the embarrassing stony silence they received. Now he would have to wait. It was apparent that the government wished first of all to pass Cartier's railway bill. The Laird's timing was bad, and seven months seemed like a long time to wait, so shortly after the meeting with the cabinet, Sir Hugh Allan sailed for England to test the availability of British and European capital.

With Allan away, the Siamese Twins sat down to consider how the situation could best be used to their political advantage. With great satisfaction, they watched as the rumours began to circulate concerning Allan's dealings with prominent American capitalists. While Cartier set to work drafting his railway act, Macdonald, anxious to rebuild his shattered party in Ontario, hastened off to Toronto. Sandfield Macdonald's defeat as Premier in December did not augur well for the upcoming federal elections, and Sir John A. realized that there was much work to be done. As he later described it, "a feeling of fear arose in Ontario, especially in Toronto, that the Pacific Railway might get into American hands and under American control, or might get into American and Montreal hands, and that in the construction of the Board the interests of Ontario might be forgotten or neglected." [27]

There were other reasons why Macdonald thought his party was in grave danger. Richard W. Scott, a tough old Ottawa lumber baron, had been appointed Speaker of the Ontario House by J.S. Macdonald, but on Macdonald's defeat, Scott, always a loyal Tory, had defected over to Edward Blake and the Liberals and taken with him most of the English Catholic vote in the Ottawa valley. This was hard enough for Old Tomorrow to bear, but Scott's motive for defection was worse. He was heavily involved with Foster, Reynolds and Abbott in the Canada Central Railway, and defected as revenge for the provincial government's decision to delay support for the railway.

In Toronto, Macdonald worked diligently, and soon the railway interests, Tory and Grit together, were convinced that *they* would get the C.P.R. charter. In this he was aided by old friends such as Senator David L. Macpherson, a member of the Grand Trunk Board as well as a partner in Gzowski's Toronto Rolling Mills (he and Gzowski were engaged in constructing the Grand Trunk's Buffalo-Fort Erie International Bridge); and, Frederick W. Cumberland, Managing Director of the

Northern Railway, both of whom tested the waters for Macdonald, and courted and canvassed the newspapers.

On November 4, Allan was in London, and he wrote McMullen's colleague C. Mather Smith that he had found "considerable interest manifested here by the moneyed men in our scheme of a Dominion Pacific Railroad, and if we desire to raise funds here to carry on the work I have no doubt they can be obtained." [28] But on his return to Montreal, he discovered to his chagrin that his involvement with the Americans was public knowledge. And what was worse, Hincks told him that, because of this, the government would have to make a show of advertising for tenders for the railway. This was a deep blow for Allan – he had lost the advantages of secrecy and was in for some heavy weather from his backers. But he refused to see the writing on the wall, refused to see that his game was just about over, refused to take into account that neither Cartier nor an irate public would ever allow American control, much less American influence in the railway. He had some explaining to do to his American backers, and in late December, journeyed down to New York to meet the railway ring.

By Christmas, the unfortunate Allan had signed a firm contract with the Americans. Two paper companies, the Canada Pacific Railway Company, and the Canada Land and Improvement Company were set up, the majority of the stock to be held in trusteeship in Jay Cooke's New York bank. Jay Cooke and his associates subscribed $5,500,000; Allan with Smith and McMullen plumped for $4,500,000. This was only a tentative agreement, and no money was to be deposited until construction of the road began. In defending his actions before the 1873 Royal Commission, Allan stated that he favoured the American scheme,

> because it not only gave us such a Pacific Railroad as we might desire, but also the advantage of a direct connection with the States of Northern Michigan, Wisconsin, Minnesota, and Dakota, the traffic and produce of which would naturally find its way to and from the seaboard through Canada, as being much the shortest, and consequently the cheapest route, even for the traffic of New York and Boston. [29]

Allan apparently never considered why the railway bankers of New York and Boston were so interested in sending the produce of the west out through Montreal, instead of out through their own ports. He arrived back in Montreal on Christmas eve, and after sizing up the situation, wrote to McMullen, home for the holidays in Picton, Ontario, that

> A good many rumours are afloat, regarding railway matters, and I have good reason to believe that Mr. Brydges is using all the influence he can with Cartier to thwart our views. Not that he has any proposal to make, but he wants to stop the Pacific Railroad altogether. A party in the interests of the Hudson's Bay Co., consisting of Donald A.

Smith, D. McInnes, G. Laidlaw, G. Stephen, Daniel Torrance of N.Y., and one or two others, have given notices in the *Official Gazette* that they will apply for a charter to make a railroad from Pembina to Fort Garry. That is the only one that affects us.[30]

This was a further blow for the Laird. The Hudson's Bay Company, through its Grand Trunk connections, probably Cartier, had got wind of Allan's scheme, and were being pressed into service to thwart him.

But there were now bigger fish in the game. Daniel Torrance of New York, brother of David Torrance, a cousin of Sir Alexander Galt, and Vice-President of the New York Central Railway, was involved with the Hudson's Bay Company and Toronto interests who planned to head Allan off at the Red River pass. Commodore Vanderbilt of the New York Central had rightly suspected a squeeze from Montreal and Philadelphia interests, and he was an adversary to be reckoned with. Moreover, the Grand Trunk had extensive cooperative contracts with Vanderbilt, and freight crossing the new Fort Erie-Buffalo Bridge would go on to New York City over the Commodore's New York Central tracks.

Allan began to realize the trouble he was in, and he began to backtrack carefully, feeling out the opposition and closing in on the one man who still stood in his way, the Grand Trunk's solicitor and Chairman of the Standing Committee on Railways, Sir George-Etienne Cartier.

On the last day of the old year 1871, Allan called on the president of the Grand Trunk to wish him the compliments of the season. Brydges had been expecting him. When Allan asked him to join the railway project, Brydges knew immediately that Allan had backed himself into a corner, and Brydges began to bluff. "His terms are very high," Allan wrote McMullen, "but as they possibly include more than himself, we may have to concede them. He thinks, however, that the Government will not have the courage to go into the scheme at all, and will shirk it till after the elections."[31] Whether Brydges' "terms" had anything to do with the presidency of the proposed line, or running rights on Grand Trunk lines, or access to the Victoria Bridge, or even with the admission of British capital into the project, we do not know. What we do know is that Allan partly believed Brydges' bluff, and asked McMullen to hold, out of his own $1,450,000, the sum of $200,000 to help bring Brydges around. What we can be sure of is that Cartier and the Grand Trunk knew they had Allan where they wanted him. In a sense, they had given him a choice – he could still have abandoned his American friends, and received the contract. If he did not, then the power of the Canadian and British governments, the Hudson's Bay Company, the merchants of Toronto, the Grand Trunk Railway and even the New York Central Railway would be arrayed against him. Yet Allan had sighted his Holy Grail, and urged on by his newfound friends, princes far wealthier than he was, he ignored the storm warnings and ploughed blindly ahead.

On New Year's Day, 1872, Allan attended the Governor General's levee at Rideau Hall, where he exchanged mild pleasantries with Sir Francis Hincks, and suggested a position for Hincks' son in the future Pacific railway. Cartier was not there. In December, while travelling home from Quebec City to Ottawa, he caught a chill, and spent most of the holidays in bed. His legs had become swollen, and although he passed it off as a touch of the gout, Cartier was experiencing the first symptoms of Bright's disease, or nephritis, a kidney ailment that was incurable. Within ten months, the pain and swelling would become so unbearable that he would be forced to go to England for medical treatment. Less than a year and a half from that New Year, he would be dead.

"For a mere population of 16,000 whites, 1,000 Chinese and 45,000 Métis, they want to build a Pacific Railway costing at least twenty-five million dollars."

4

Le Canadien, 1872

For the first few weeks of 1872, Cartier recuperated, working in front of a fire with his legs up on a stool, while the first blizzard of winter whipped through the streets of Ottawa. Thomas Vincent, his faithful major-domo, kept the house in order and cared for his master while Lady Cartier and his daughters holidayed in the South of France. His house, a modest building located on the corner of Metcalfe and Maria (now Laurier) Streets, south and east of the Parliament Buildings, was demolished after the turn of the century.*

By late January, Cartier felt well enough to take the train to Montreal to begin preparations for what would be his last political campaign. As Cartier's train ploughed slowly east through snowdrifts, Macdonald was busy criss-crossing the Province of Ontario, lashing out at the Grits and overseeing stage two of the plan to befuddle Jay Cooke – the formation of a rival consortium, based in Toronto – the Interoceanic Railway Company of Canada, president, Senator David L. Macpherson, a member of the Grand Trunk Railway Board.

The presence of the Prime Minister in Toronto after a long absence excited feelings of warmth and generosity among his political cronies, especially with a railway in the offing. Macdonald told them all of the debts he had incurred during his recent period of illness, and of his history of financial troubles. Three years previously, he had been heavily indebted to Alexander Galt's Commercial Bank. Galt never pressed him to repay, but when Sir Hugh Allan's Merchants' Bank took over the

* The site was occupied by the old Ottawa Y.M.C.A.

failing Commercial in 1869, Allan had handed him a claim for $79,-590.11 owing, with no hints of how the debt could be postponed. Allan, he told them, had hoped to hold him on some sort of financial leash, but he would have none of it. The Laird could have claims on Macdonald's party, but not his person. His friends listened sympathetically when he told them how, by handing over all his savings and mortgaging his property to the hilt, he had been able to emerge proud, but virtually penniless.

Now, to Macdonald's boundless delight, Senator Macpherson brought together some Toronto and Hamilton colleagues who collected a "testimonial fund" of more than $67,000 to help the Prime Minister live in the style to which he was accustomed. His gratitude to those good burghers knew no bounds.

In Montreal and Quebec City, it was a different story. With six months to go before the federal election, Cartier was becoming increasingly disturbed by two very sinister developments in the province, developments that were to make a nightmare of the remainder of his political career. As if to compound his physical suffering, he learned what he had expected to learn, that Sir Hugh Allan was now blitzing the province, throwing his money around, and, in his flawless French, haranguing anyone who would listen, politicians, priests and newspapermen alike, on the benefits of his North Shore and Northern Colonization railroads. Newspapers, presumably blessed with Allan's largesse, were now demanding that the lines be completed, and daring to suggest that, because of his Grand Trunk connection, Cartier was opposed to the lines being built. It was argued far and wide that without a railway running along the north shore of the St. Lawrence, the area would continue to be isolated for up to six months of the year, the valley of the St.-Maurice would remain closed for colonization, and the town of Trois-Rivières would languish in a backwater. To Cartier's increasingly vociferous critics, the Grand Trunk benefited only Montreal and the Eastern Townships, then largely English-speaking. The proposed North Shore railway would not only add to the prosperity of Quebec City and the whole north shore, but would have its terminus in Montreal East, Cartier's own riding. In actual fact, Allan was less interested in the Quebec-Montreal line than in the Montreal-Ottawa section, which he saw as the first leg of his transcontinental railway.

And now, when Cartier needed all the political support he could get, certain elements in the Roman Catholic Church were conspiring against him. Cartier's relationship with the Church had never been the best. Although he had remained a loyal friend of his old teachers in the Sulpician Order, and had been able, through his colleague, Sir Hector Langevin – brother of the Bishop of Rimouski – to keep ecclesiastical influence in political affairs at a minimum, he was now caught up in a struggle between warring factions within the Church itself.

Since the 1830s, two radical (and radically opposed) nationalist movements had been battling it out in French Canada. Much of Cartier's political success was due to the fact that he and his party had been able to sit firmly straddled on the broad fence between these two often hysterical movements, so alien to the broad mass of the people. On the one hand were the heirs of Papineau – ultra-democratic, anti-clerical, left wing, annexationist – inspired by the French and American revolutions and European nationalism, and determined to give Quebec a popular republican government. On the other hand were the Ultramontanists or "Ultras," later called "Castors"* – radical Catholics horrified by the revolutions of Europe and Garibaldi's attacks on the papacy, and determined to preserve French Canada's religious and racial purity, to ensure the supremacy of Church over State.

By 1870, the two groups had reorganized to attack not only each other, but the centre, and Cartier, who embodied the liberal centre. Within the Church itself, the more moderate elements, Cartier's allies, were under siege by Bishop Ignace Bourget, the passionate, shrewd old Bishop of Montreal, and the inspirational fountainhead of the Ultras. Under Bourget, the Roman-minded Jesuits soon clashed with the Sulpicians, the original founders of the diocese, and builders of all the parish churches of Montreal, over the division of the diocese into several new parishes. The quarrel was taken through the courts and as far as Rome, before the Bishop was defeated.

Cartier's law firm represented the Sulpicians; after the London Conference in 1867, he had personally travelled to Rome to discuss the matter with the Pope.

One cleric, the pot-bellied and energetic Curé Labelle, a notorious influencer of politicians, promised Bourget that he would apply pressure to Cartier through his party members in the legislature:

As for our Legislature, I am sure that a law can be passed favouring the division of the Diocese of Montreal, and passed even in spite of Cartier. If he wants to stick a log in our cartwheel, that is his business, but he will be broken . . . Cartier will pass the measure. If he does not, well then he will be attacked on a matter of public interest.[32]

But Cartier wouldn't budge, and the case never came before the Provincial Parliament of Quebec.

Polarization between the *Rouges* and the Ultras had come to a head in the infamous "Guibord Affair." In November, 1869, as Joseph Guibord, a printer and prominent member of the radical *Institut Canadien* lay on his deathbed, a priest demanded that he renounce the *Institut*. He refused, and was denied the last rights. Bishop Bourget refused his body Christian burial in consecrated ground, with the result that Guibord's corpse was buried temporarily in the Protestant cemetery.

* "Beavers"

Guibord's wife, backed by Joseph Doutre, Rodolphe Laflamme and most of the *Rouges*, sued the Parish of Notre Dame. A liberal judge decided for the widow, and ordered the parish to provide burial and pay the court costs. The Court of Appeals overturned the verdict, but Doutre eventually took the case to the Privy Council in Great Britain, and won, the court deciding that the ecclesiastical sentence on Guibord was invalid.

On November 16, 1875, the corpse was finally exhumed and, under the escort of more than 1,000 militiamen, was taken and buried under tons of cement and scrap iron in a part of the Catholic cemetery already deconsecrated by Bishop Bourget. During all this turmoil, the Bishop got little help from Cartier, who refused to be drawn out into the open. In 1871, Cartier had narrowly missed Church censure when the government of New Brunswick passed a law abolishing separate school support in that province. Under great pressure for federal action to disallow the law, Cartier could only state that the constitutional responsibility for education rested with the provinces – "*dura lex, sed lex*" – the law is hard, but it is the law. Privately, however, he told his Church critics in no uncertain terms that to infringe on provincial rights might set a precedent that could be turned against Quebec in the future. Bourget was forced to concede this, and because he was as much a nationalist as a cleric, he did not press the matter, but rather attacked Cartier along different lines.

For the provincial election of 1871, Bourget's followers formulated what they called the "*Programme Catholique*." The *programmists* supported the Liberal-Conservative Party as "the defender of social authority" and "the only one offering serious guarantees to religious interests"[33]; but – and this was where the attack came – the group would not support any candidate, even if he were in Cartier's camp, who refused to support the principles of the *Programme*. The unanimity of the *programmists* was weakened by a letter from Archbishop Taschereau in *Le Journal de Québec*, affirming that the *Programme* had been issued "without the consent of the bishops."[34] Cartier personally refused to support the group, and since papal infallibility did not extend into the political sphere, they elected only one member in the elections of June, 1871. Cartier wisely abandoned his Montreal provincial seat – under the law of the day, he could hold a seat in both Parliaments – and he ran in Beauharnois, where he was easily elected. As he had foreseen, the three Montreal seats were swept by the *Rouges*, who gained overall, including the seat of Arthabaska, won by a young moderate *Rouge*, Wilfrid Laurier.

The Ultras' attempt to drive Cartier's party right, or rather, heavenward, was parallelled by a *Rouge* shift into the centre. Both were serious developments, and the provincial election bode ill for the federal election the following summer. Some of the more moderate *Rouges*, seeing their chance at last, founded a new party, the *Parti National*, to try and exploit the Holy War between Bourget and Cartier. Young patriots and nationalists as well as practising Catholics, who deplored the *Rouge* party's drift toward annexationism and anti-clericalism, made up the heart of the new party. At its founding meeting in January, 1872, the *Parti National* came out for decentralization and provincial rights, a secret ballot, a protective tariff and an end to the Pacific Railway. Unfortunately, by early 1872, the new party had been infiltrated by some of the old *Rouges* as well as the English-speaking free traders, lovers of the United States, John Young and Lucius Seth Huntington, who saw in the *Parti National* one more method of defeating Cartier and promoting their own little railways. To that end, they gladly went along with the innocents Laflamme, Jetté and Laurier in their espousal of protection instead of commercial independence. Some of the electorate would be fooled.

> **"Our friends there are fighting the battle with great vigor and in a most resolute manner, but they do earnestly desire that we should keep entirely out of sight and perfectly quiet."**
>
> **J. Gregory Smith to Jay Cooke,**
> **March 14, 1872**

5

While Cartier huddled before the stove in his office that bitterly cold winter of 1872, the rotund Reverend Antoine Labelle, Bourget's political jack-of-all-trades, was busy carrying out his promises to the Bishop to bend Cartier to the ecclesiastical will. An Inquisition was out of the question, but there remained means just as effective. In early January, he organized a party of eighty two-horse wagons to cut wood near his home town of Saint-Jérôme in the Laurentians, for delivery to the poor of Montreal. At a banquet in his honour following the delivery of the firewood, Labelle – now called *"le roi du nord,"** spoke passionately to his friends, reminding them of the great natural riches to be found in the mountains north of Montreal, resurces that the city could profit from. He concluded his inspirational address by asking the gathering to subscribe a million dollars to the Northern Colonization Railroad, a line, said Labelle, that Cartier was delaying because he wanted to give a monopoly to the Grand Trunk.[35] Cartier and his friends attempted to head off the *curé* by the establishment of the Montreal and St.-Jérôme Colonization Railway, directors Starnes, Stephen, Ogilvie, Cuvillier and others, to bring firewood down to Montreal. The village council of

* "King of the North"

Saint-Jérôme refused to subscribe to the line, stating that it had "no reason to withdraw its confidence from the President and Directors of the Montreal Northern Colonization Railway Company as at present constituted." [36] Allan had done his work well.

There was an unholy alliance in the making. Allan had successfully conscripted the Ultras into his fight against Cartier. They were willing allies; Bourget found in Allan a kindred spirit, and together they conspired to effect the downfall of the Member for Montreal East.

This time, it was Cartier who could see the writing on the wall, and it is probable that he and Sir John A. met and adopted a campaign strategy reminiscent of their pre-Confederation days. Macdonald would continue to dangle the bait of the railway before the good burghers of Toronto; and to exploit the anti-French, anti-Catholic bias of the Canada First movement, he would let out a rumour that Cartier was tired of working with Macdonald and was trying to establish a coalition with the Liberal leader, Alexander Mackenzie. Cartier fed the fires of speculation by remarking, off the cuff, to a colleague, "Did you see how I praised Blake this evening? I covered him with roses. I just about made advances to him. In these times of crisis, it's the only way I can make Macdonald see reason." [37] Allan reported to McMullen, "in strict confidence," that

> there are symptoms of coolness between Sir John A. and Cartier, arising from the coquetting of the latter with Blake and Mackenzie, to form an alliance and carry the elections next summer, with a view to leave John A. out in the cold. This would not be so favourable to us, but I am going to Toronto on the 7th inst., to look after our interests. [38]

So far, so good. Cartier, on the other hand, was in deep trouble. The provincial elections had shown him that it would be a mistake to run again in Montreal East.

The Siamese Twins had to use all their cunning to get up a plan that would allow them to emerge from the elections relatively unscathed. Outside Montreal, Cartier's members were out of danger, but in the city, Bourget and Allan had done their work all too well – Cartier's campaign was in deep trouble. Curé Labelle was busy contacting all the *Bleus* in the Montreal area, sowing the seeds of pessimism. To Luc Masson he wrote that Cartier's "popularity hangs only by a thread. Even his friends find him more at fault than he is." Another seat could easily be found outside Montreal, but Cartier had done this in the recent provincial election, and to retreat federally, as well, would only show to the electors of Quebec that the Minister of Militia was on the run. There was a medical consideration as well. A campaign outside Montreal would be hard on legs that could hardly support him at times. Better to stand in Montreal, and draw all the opposition fire to himself. He could not campaign effectively at any rate, but by staying close to his office where the very serious work of the day could be done, Cartier would be making the best of a bad situation.

He would almost certainly be defeated, but he would go down bravely, and lull the Americans and the opposition into a false sense of security. There was a railway to be built, and all his waning energies would have to go into ensuring its success. Another seat could be found afterward; a bye-election could be won.

There were two other factors to be considered. The first was the increasing world-wide recession. Daily, it was becoming more unlikely that funds for a railway could be obtained, even with British government support, even by Jay Cooke himself. Cartier had been informed that the Barings were rapidly withdrawing capital from the United States, so certain were they that a railway bust was imminent. He realized, with some disappointment, yet with a certain amount of wry amusement, that any railway company chartered by his Committee and his government would have very little hope of getting off the ground for many years to come. What was important for Canada was to show *resolve* to build the railway, a firm enough intent to hold off the Americans, satisfy British Columbia, and give the country a national purpose. Sandford Fleming's surveys had shown the sheer magnitude of the project and its incredible difficulties. This and the worsening financial situation combined to show Cartier and Macdonald that their railway was only in its very early stages, and that they could afford to sit back, profit from the charter scramble, and watch the developing proceedings with some sense of irony. There would be an explosion – of this they had no doubt – but when it was all over, the Grand Trunk Railway and Hudson's Bay Company could pick up the pieces.

The other factor that neither of them dared fully to consider was the state of each other's health. Macdonald had just narrowly escaped death from a gallstone; Cartier's worsening condition could mean the end of their partnership. Their actions over the next year would show that this fear was always looming in the background. They would have to move fast to scuttle the Americans, and use all their cunning and grasp of the subtleties of political life to play the game and win. Even if they lost all the battles, they knew that they must win the war, if they had not done so already. So to tighten the screws on Jay Cooke and kill the idea of an International Pacific Railway, Macdonald cabled John Rose to "make known that Dominion is about to construct Pacific Railway through British Territory"[39]; British Territory alone.

Events were almost out of their control. The fuses had been lit and they could only wait for the explosion and see what remained when the smoke cleared. Whether Cartier realized it or not, his political usefulness was almost at an end. His Pacific Railway Act would give future governments virtually total control over any railway financing. Allan would find it very hard indeed to hide any form of American influence in the company he was about to propose.

The railways that Cartier had spread out over the land that he had brought together were now out of his hands. His store of thunderbolts was dangerously low, but he knew he had used them wisely and well, and now there were younger politicians ready to flesh out the skeleton of the nation. Best of all, he had given his people the chance to work out their own survival on an equal footing with the English. So like an ironic Napoleon before a papier-mâché Waterloo, he sat in his tent and pored over his maps, waiting for his comic defeat.

The redoubtable Sir Hugh Allan was continuing to find his way barred and his efforts blocked by Canadian and British financiers. By the end of February, 1872, Brydges was still refusing to join him, and in fact, "making a strong attempt, by exciting national feeling," [40] to establish a purely Canadian company. Brydges was appealing first and foremost to a developing Canadian loyalty, and having great success in subscribing stock by calling attention to the enormous profits that would leave the country if the line were given to Sir Hugh Allan. On March 11, Brydges wrote to Senator Macpherson, making the important point that any American money in the C.P.R. would only be recirculated funds from England and Europe. He gave Macpherson his opinion that

> I have no belief myself in any line of railway running to Fort Garry, for a very long time to come, through British territory. What I believe in, and what I think must be done in the first instance is to make a connection between Fort Garry and Lake Superior in British territory, a railway west from Fort Garry, built in sections, and not attempted too fast, and a branch down to Pembina to meet the United States system of railways, which will certainly get up to that point during the present year. That would give a rail connection in Winter, and by Lake Superior, water connection would be had throughout the Summer during the season of navigation, which, for the next 10 or 15 years will be all that can possibly be wished. [41]

But Brydges' sensible proposals – which were adopted eventually because they offered the easiest and most economical construction of the line – were lost in the maelstrom. Sir Hugh Allan was still after Senator Macpherson to join his project; and Macpherson was still tightening the screws on Allan, who was becoming panicked. "He has been applied to by our opponents," wrote Allan to C. Mather Smith, "and uses that as lever by which to obtain better terms from us. He insists on getting $250,000 of stock, and threatens opposition if he does not get it. You will remember he is one of those I proposed as a Director. I will do the best I can, but I think that McMullen, you and myself, will have to give up some of our stock to conciliate these parties." [42] According to Macpherson's later testimony to the Royal Commission, [43] he declined unconditionally to

D.L. Macpherson (PAC).

Sir Francis Hincks (Notman).

C.J. Brydges (Notman).

Sir John Rose (Notman).

act with Allan. Allan, he said, was surprised at his "narrow views" and remarked that he should be more "cosmopolitan."

Allan would not heed Macpherson's warning, and as the Laird became more desperate about prospects in Canada, his game now turned to blackmail and bribery. He would, he knew, catch a few fish with the cash he had at his disposal. One of these fish might even be induced to commit a crime or make the mistake of signing his name to piece of paper linking himself with a bribe. He still believed that Jay Cooke was a fountain-head of wealth, and that with American support, all things were possible. And as he continued on his nefarious way, his correspondence with Smith and McMullen grew ever more optimistic about success. In a letter to Smith on February 28, his fantasies exceeded all reasonable bounds:

PRIVATE   MONTREAL, 28th Feb., 1872

DEAR SIR, – It seems pretty certain that, in addition to money payments, the following stock will have to be distributed: –

Hon. D.L. Macpherson	$100,000
Hon. A.B. Foster	$100,000
D.A. Smith	$100,000
C.J. Brydges	$100,000
J.J.C. Abbott	$50,000
D. McInnes	$50,000
John Sheddon	$50,000
A. Allan	$50,000
C.S. Gzowski	$50,000
George Brown	$50,000
A.J. Hincks	$50,000
H. Nathan	$50,000
T. McGreevy	$50,000

To meet this, I propose that we give up of our stock as follows:

C.M. Smith	$250,000
George W. McMullen	$250,000
Hugh Allan	$350,000

Please say if this is agreeable to you. I do not think that we can do much less, and may have to give more. I do not think we will require more than $100,000 in cash, but I am not sure as yet.

Who am I to draw on for money when it is wanted? And what proof of payment will be required? You are aware I cannot get receipts.

Our Legislature meets 11th April, and I am already deep in preparation for the game. Every day brings up some new difficulty to be encountered, but I hope to meet them all successfully. Write to me immediately.

Yours truly   HUGH ALLAN[44]

It must have been obvious to Allan that Macpherson, Brydges and Donald Smith, tied as they were to the Grand Trunk and Cartier, could never be "influenced" by Allan's promises. The other names in his letter, with the exception of Allan's brother and the Canada Central men Foster and Abbott, are simply ridiculous. What was Allan's game? Was he trying to turn around and swindle Jay Cooke? He *is* lying in his letter to Mather Smith. The question is, why?

Why would Cass and Ogden and Jay Cooke, let alone McMullen and Smith, trust this man Hugh Allan enough to hand over thousands of dollars in cash with neither promise of success, nor even receipt? The answer, of course, is that they knew that they could blackmail Allan himself, at any time, by threatening to pull the financial plug, or by leaking incriminating documents to the Canadian press. This would have had the effect of completely destroying Allan's credibility in Montreal and in the English and European money markets. They had Allan where they wanted him, on a very tight leash indeed.

In all likelihood, Cartier, Macdonald, Brydges and Macpherson met in early March to plan their strategy. They knew Allan was in over his head, and threw him a lifeline. To their disgust and dismay, he refused. As Allan wrote McMullen,

> Mr. Macpherson, Toronto, and Mr. Brydges, here, have both notified me today that they decline to join us in the Canadian Railway scheme. Their reasons are, that the Company is too largely American, and that they want to see it in the hands of Canadians. They tried to detach me from the company we have formed, and get me to join them, which, of course, I declined. I don't know what they can do against us, but I intend going to Ottawa on Monday, 11th. inst., and will then try to find out something about it.[45]

Not only was Allan a drowning man, but it was apparent – even in New York – that Jay Cooke was sinking fast. The following day, Macdonald wrote to Sir John Rose in London, asking him to confirm rumours the Cabinet had heard concerning the finances of the Northern Pacific:

> I should like to know how the railway stands in the English market, as to its bonds and general credit. There is a general impression, I find, at New York, that the whole thing must end in a fiasco, which may perhaps be disastrous, even to Jay Cooke & Co. I would be very sorry if this should be the case – at all events until they have finished the railroad connecting Duluth with Pembina. After that, we Canadians can afford to view any further western extension with considerable philosophy.
>
> You are quite right in your mode of dealing with the matter with Mr. McCulloch.* While we wish it to be known that we are going to

* Of Cooke's London branch; McCulloch had been courting Rose all along.

build a railway of our own, we do not in any way desire to prejudice the fortunes of the Northern Pacific. The more modes of communication there are across the continent, the better for the whole continent, and you can assure anyone who speaks to you on the matter that we would rather aid the progress of the Northern Pacific than impede it. They, on the other hand, however must not by assuming to be the Canadian road, prejudice our enterprize.[46]

Reading between the lines, Rose took the hint and proceeded to downplay Canada's previously heated opposition to the Northern Pacific, in hopes that the American government would try to restrain Cooke's activities, and the British government, pleased by a calming of the waters, might now guarantee the loan Macdonald had extracted at the Washington Conference. To Cartier's boundless delight, the Gladstone government agreed on March 16 to guarantee a loan of £ 2,500,-000 for the construction of railways and canals in Canada. It was not the £ 4,000,000 they had hoped for, but the railway to the Pacific could now be seriously, if slowly, undertaken.

Another joyful tiding was Rose's report that the Northern Pacific was a dismal failure on the London money market. The financiers knew that the contractors of the line were refusing bonds for payment and insisting on cash. They knew that, although the U.S. Congress had granted $53.5 million to the Central Pacific and Union Pacific, they were in no hurry to extend the same generosity to the Northern Pacific. In fact, the only buyer of Northern Pacific bonds in London appeared to be the firm of Jay Cooke and Company.[47]

The American government itself did not curb Jay Cooke, but on February 12, Gregory Smith's partner General Banks, Representative of the State of Massachusetts, got up in the House and moved that the Northern Pacific be investigated to see if it was fulfilling its charter and continuing to act in the best public interest.[48] The Vermont Central ring were now aware of Cooke's real plan, his intention of siphoning off North-West trade and draining it out through his home town of Philadelphia, instead of taking it through Canada and Vermont to Boston.

While the American dogs fought over their bone in the House of Representatives, a Canadian cur, Sir Hugh Allan, handed the Government his preliminary draft charter of the "Canada Pacific Railway Company," his still tenacious proposal to build a railway across the continent.

6

"You must be very cautious in anything you
do because the greatest jealousy exists in
Canada against the Northern Pacific."

Jay Cooke to "Saskatchewan" Taylor,
March 23, 1872

With the coming of spring, Cartier's condition had improved slightly,
and between bouts of working on the Pacific Railway Act, he took great
pleasure in purchasing more fruit trees from Cuvillier and Company,
having them planted in the garden at Limoilou, discussing horticulture
with Luce, and visiting his family at the House of the Seven Chimneys.

Back in his Montreal house on April 5, he was faced with the delicate
task of explaining to a large delegation of lawyers, city councillors, and
other prominent citizens of Montreal East, his views on the Northern
Colonization and Quebec North Shore Railways. The group arrived at
Rue Notre-Dame after lunch, and Cartier listened skeptically as their
leader, Jean-Marie Papineau, explained that they had come to ask him
to give the railways "the powerful benefit of your influence to assure its
success. We represent the electors who believe in your spirit of cooperation." Cartier thanked them and replied that he, too, was interested in
the line, and that it was "destined to form a link in the great Pacific
railway, over which, I hope, we will travel before long."

Realizing that many of those present were under Allan's influence, he
very carefully warned them that, for the line to succeed, "it will be
necessary to curb our zeal and not abandon ourselves to oratory." "It is
above all important," he continued, "not to excite the prejudice of those
who are prepared to fight us, not to create irritation or hostility among
the different sections of the city, because we have to deal with everyone
fairly and make the best of the present state of affairs." [49] For those
sympathetic to his pre-election dilemma, he was explaining his painful
position. For the rest, including the absent Sir Hugh Allan, he was warning them to hold off or the whole Pacific line might be placed in jeop-
ardy. If they acted well, they would get their railway; if not, they might
not.

In spite of Cartier's promise that the terminus of the C.P.R. would be
in Montreal East, and in spite of his declaration that, although he had
links with the Grand Trunk, he was also in favour of the Northern
Colonization Railway, the delegation went away from this painful
meeting unsatisfied and distrustful. Allan's money and Bourget's radical
persuasion were turning the electors of Montreal East away from
Cartier.

That weekend, as he travelled to Ottawa, the warm spring weather
evaporated. On April 11, the day of the opening of Parliament, raw
winds from up the Ottawa beat against the windows of the frame shan-
ties of the town, and blew down the streets so recently hard ice tracks

and now dangerous rivers of mud. Cartier and his daughters got into a carriage and slithered the few short blocks to the Hill where they joined with the other Windsor-uniformed gentlemen and crinolined ladies to hear Sir John Young, Lord Lisgar, read the Speech-from-the-Throne.

It was a short speech, but one that proposed nothing less than a completion of the skeleton of Confederation. Along with trade union legislation and electoral redistribution, it called for ratification of the Treaty of Washington, a Dominion Lands Act giving free homesteads to *bona fide* settlers in Manitoba and the North-West, and incorporation of a Pacific railway company.

While debate began on the legislative program, and the wheels of government began to roll, Allan's efforts intensified, in direct proportion to the coolness emanating from both the Canadian government and the boardrooms of New York and Philadelphia. The Laird called on Macdonald once again, and again came away empty-handed, with a warning that Canada would not hand over her Pacific Railway to the Americans.

The Prime Minister was now confident that Allan would come over, and wrote to Rose that he would soon be "obliged to abandon his Yankee confrères." [50] All seemed well in Ontario for the summer elections; it was a far cry from the disaster that awaited Cartier in Montreal.

On April 26, Cartier strutted around his office and regaled a number of M.P.s, civil servants and junior clerks with the nature of the measure he was about to propose to Parliament: "Here," he bellowed, "is a bill that has attraction for a man!" Holding the printed act above his head, he filled them all with his infectious happiness: "Here are ideas! We are going to tie the oceans together . . . More than that, we are going to bring together the China of Asia and the Lachine of Montreal.* A hundred victories carried over the opposition please me less than the mere presentation of such a bill. This bill is my pride and joy." [51]

At that very moment, Macdonald sauntered in, with his hands in his pockets, and catching the mood of the moment, smiled and said, "Well, ready? Let us have another field day." He cocked his head, turned around, and marched down the hall swinging his arms like a toy soldier. Cartier fell in behind him, followed by the members, and together they trooped down the corridors of Parliament to the House of Commons.

The Chamber was full. At the appointed time, a smiling Cartier rose from his seat, pointed at a small set of papers on his desk, and "begged leave to introduce a small Bill under a modest and humble title. It was a Bill respecting the Canadian Pacific Railway. (Hear, hear) . . . To a great extent this measure is an enabling Act, empowering the Government to make agreements with companies incorporated, or hereafter to

---

* In 1535, his ancestor Jacques Cartier, searching for the passage to China, had been stopped by the rapids at Montreal, which La Salle later called Lachine (China), George-Etienne Cartier was now fulfilling Jacques Cartier's dream, 337 years later.

be incorporated, for the purpose of building a railway from Lake Nipissing to the Pacific coast." [52] As Cartier explained it, the government
intended to have strict control, by this Act and previous railway acts,
over the financing and construction of the line. Control would be exercised largely through Orders in Council by the cabinet, without going
before the Commons. The company, and therefore the cabinet, would
have strict control over any branch line either to or from the United
States. *This was the key to Cartier's whole plan.* Although he did not
elaborate, this provision would effectively bar the Northern Pacific or
the Vermont Central from tapping any of Canada's North-West trade.

Parliament was asked to approve a land grant of fifty million acres,
given in alternate blocks twenty miles deep on each side of the road, and
a cash subsidy to the line of $30,000,000. According to Cartier, this sum
could be raised easily through bonds and land sales, without any increase
in taxation.

George W. McMullen, watching Cartier from the visitor's gallery,
realized the game was up. Or was it? He slipped out to the nearest telegraph office and wired Jay Cooke that it was imperative they should
have an immediate meeting of their "Canadian Railway project association." [53] McMullen knew that if the Canadian cabinet were to have strict
control over branch lines (the Pembina-Fort Garry line was of course
the important one) then the present Canadian cabinet would have to be
replaced with men more receptive to their own proposal. The Vermont
Central ring had reached the same conclusions.

On June 1, 1872, after a long though not particularly bitter debate,
Cartier's bill received third and final reading. The opposition appeared
to agree in principle with the carrying out of the "bargain" made with
British Columbia, yet did not feel that the length of time nor the cash
subsidy were realistic, and objected to the cabinet being given the power
to control the destiny of the railway. Yet the bill was so airtight that no
amendments were seriously considered. It was a masterpiece of law-
making, and when the Speaker signalled unanimous passage of the act at
two o'clock in the morning, a delighted Cartier rose from his seat and
crowed, "All aboard for the West!" The House rose as one man and gave
him a long and grateful cheer.

After receiving the congratulations of his colleagues on both sides of
the House, Cartier slowly made his way down the corridor to his office.
There he greeted his assistant Benjamin Sulte, told him the good news,
and sat down wearily at his massive black walnut desk. He opened a
drawer, drew from it a sheaf of papers, placed the Pacific Railway Act on
top of them, and told Sulte that they were the laws he had succeeded in
passing. Apart from most railway acts put through the Parliament of the
Union, they included all the Dominion railway acts, the British Columbia and Manitoba Acts, the Bill for purchase and transfer of Rupert's
Land, Canal Acts, Steamship Acts, Militia and Fortification Bills, acts

for the reformation of Quebec law and land tenure, all in all, acts for the creation and survival of the Dominion of Canada, acts that make him, more than any other of the Fathers of Confederation, the greatest of the founders.

He ordered Sulte to take away his acts and have them bound. Now he was alone. With a dying man's sense of destiny, he had passed his life's work into the bound pages of history. Standing up and hobbling over to the window, he cranked it open and felt a rush of cold air, but fresher now. Across the Ottawa, under the full moon, above the timber rafts moored with their lanterns twinkling over the swirling black river, above the few glowing lights on the Quebec shore, rose the Gatineau Hills, sleeping etherial half-mountains, rock of the Shield, ground down by ice. The wind dropped, and he heard the roar of the Chaudière, imagined la Chasse-Galérie, the flying canoe, with the devil steering in the stern, and heard those voyageurs sing the old song of the lumberjacks, a shanty his father had often sung:

> Voici l'hiver arrivé,
> Les rivières sont gelées,
> C'est le temps d'aller au bois
> Manger du lard et des pois!
> Dans les chantiers nous hivernerons!
> Dans les chantiers nous hivernerons!

Then from up the Ottawa, from north and west where the Métis waited for the railway, where the voyageurs once reigned, the wind came up again. He breathed in deeply, shut the wind out, walked down the back stairs, and woke his driver to take him home.

7   "I got pecuniary assistance where I could. In Canada we have not the same organization that they have in England. We have neither a Reform Club nor a Carleton Club to manage elections, and the leaders have to undertake that for themselves. I found, as the contest went on, that it was getting more severe; representations were coming to me from all parts of Ontario that the Opposition, to use a general expression, had two dollars to our one."

Sir John A. Macdonald,
to the Royal Commission, 1873

With the passage of the Canadian Pacific Railway Bill, Cartier and Macdonald were prepared to throw Allan one more life line. They realized that the Americans had given him just enough rope to hang himself, but that he might try and drag Cartier down with him. Their strategy now was to suggest to Allan, through his lawyer Abbott, that an amalgamation of Toronto and Montreal interests might be given the contract, and that Allan would be president of the line if he agreed to abandon his American contacts. They would first promise to try and get him a majority of the directors, and then later trap him by insisting on broader representation from all parts of the Dominion.

Parallel with the formation of Allan's Canada Pacific was Macpherson's Interoceanic, composed of Toronto and Grand Trunk interests. While Abbott and Macpherson argued over the composition of the proposed combined board, Cartier met with Allan and gave him the news he had long hoped for, that because of his long interest in the Pacific railway, Cartier saw no reason why Allan should not be offered the presidency, and he would do his best to ensure that this be done. Cartier made no promise that Allan would definitely be president, but the Laird immediately wrote McMullen bragging that he had "got the whole arranged through my French friends by means you are aware of, and we have now the pledge of Sir G. that we will have a majority and other things satisfactory. I have told you all along that this was the true basis of operation, and that anything else was powder and shot thrown away, and I think so still."[54]

By the middle of June, after a short but whirlwind session, the House was dissolved. The Members of Parliament trudged home to their constituencies to do battle in the July to September elections, and spend the money that was being lavishly spread about for their benefit. Cartier had two months to prepare his groundwork, but it was not a very pleasing prospect. Allan and Bourget had done their work well, and the Great Depression of the 1870s was beginning to make itself felt. Quebec's fragile economy, firmly tied to lumbering and agriculture, suffered first. The grain and timber markets of Europe had dried up, and as countless New Englanders flooded into the American West to homestead, their places in the mills and factories were taken by the surplus population of Quebec.

A Quebec friend of the Liberal leader Alexander Mackenzie wrote him that

The country is in a very bad condition. Labour cannot be procured; a vast acreage is under grass instead of cereal; farms are for sale everywhere; the young are leaving the country in hordes, for the United States. No mere Act by the Local Parliament at Quebec will remedy this state of things. The next five years will strain confederation to its utmost tension, for the people are heart and soul dissatisfied and talk "strange theories." . . . The approaching elections will turn this province of Quebec upside down. Everything is in confusion. The priests have begun to denounce John A. and Cartier for their action on the

New Brunswick School Bill. Sir Hugh Allan has declared war against Brydges on the Railway question. Local issues – peculiar to Quebec – are springing up everywhere. The "National Party" is very strong and aggressive. In a word Quebec is a camp divided and sub-divided. We are certain to win at least ten or a dozen seats. In case Cartier procures a majority, it will be only a nominal one, a piece of rubble-work, that will go into fragments at the first blow of the hammer.[55]

Although Mackenzie's correspondent was being a trifle optimistic, his view of the economic situation was correct, and his opinion that Cartier was in trouble was being echoed throughout the province.

No one realized his predicament more than Cartier himself, yet to his friends, he appeared to be more concerned about his railway work than about re-election. One of his friends, Charles LeBlanc, Sheriff of Montreal and a director of the Northern Colonization Railway, was particularly worried by the early rumours of defeat, and acted as a link between him and his disaffected supporters. LeBlanc's testimony before the Royal Commission is of great interest:

I now remember that in two instances in the month of June, 1872, Sir George Cartier said, with those energetic words that he generally used, something about the Pacific Railway Company, and that he would never, as long as he would be in the Ministry, consent to any American Company having the contract for building the Pacific Railway; that there were enough of Canadian Companies who were able to do the work, and that he would resign his place in the Ministry if the contract was given to any such company; and he added that he hoped his friends would see that the two Companies, meaning that of Sir Hugh Allan and that of Mr. Macpherson, would be amalgamated, and that they would be able to carry the whole matter through without any trouble . . . .

Question – What do you mean by "those energetic words" you refer to. Give as near as possible the very words he addressed to you when speaking of the Pacific Railway?

Answer – The words he used were, as near as I can remember, as follows: – "Aussi longtemps que je vivrai et que je serai dans le Ministère, jamais une sacrée compagnie américaine aura le contrôle du Pacifique, et je résignerai ma place de ministre plûtot que d'y consentir."* . . . .

Question – Were you on such intimate terms with Sir George that would have induced him to speak more particularly to you than to the others?

* "As long as I live and as long as I am a member of the Ministry, never will a damned American Company have control of the Pacific. I will resign my place as a Minister rather than consent to it."

Answer – I suppose I was the most intimate with him. I was one of his most intimate friends in Montreal – I mean outside of politics. Every since we were at college we have been personal friends. I may add that he placed great confidence in me at many times.

Question – You mentioned that there was another occasion on which Sir George spoke to you personally on this subject; was it in the same spirit?

Answer – Yes, this was [on August 18, 1872] It was at his own place at Long Point [Limoilou]. I was down there, as his nomination was to take place the next day, and he wanted to see me, and we had a very long conversation that afternoon. He repeated those very words to me, that it was not necessary to look to foreign companies to build the Pacific Railway, as we had men in the country who could do the work; and he added that we should try to have an amalgamation made between the two companies – that of Sir Hugh Allan and that of Mr. Macpherson – and also said that he could not say as to what the Government would do.[56]

It was apparent, from LeBlanc's testimony, that Cartier and Macdonald were holding their cards quite close to their chests. Cartier was becoming increasingly exasperated with Sir Hugh Allan, and furious at what he considered to be the Laird's stupid toying with the future of the country. Allan was revealing himself to be nothing more than a greedy, ungrateful fool, who moreover had probably left himself open to blackmail. The government, at Cartier's instigation, had recently given him favourable wharfing privileges, the Montreal-Liverpool mail contract, and a chance to extricate himself from the tentacles of his American friends, with honour if not safety. What was Allen after; what more did he want?

Also enlightening is the testimony of the Honourable Gédéon Ouimet, Provincial Secretary of Quebec and M.P.P. for Two Mountains, located on the route of the Northern Colonization Railway, and that government's representative on the railway's board of directors. We have no proof Ouimet was paid off by Allan – it is certain that Allan did not insist on receipts for the thousands of dollars he was quietly paying out through the province to ensure the defeat of Cartier, or rather, the victory of men of both parties loyal to the Northern Colonization:

> I was in communication with Sir Hugh Allan as a Director of the Northern Colonization Railway. I may add that Sir Hugh Allan appeared to favour me with his confidence. I endeavoured to induce my friends from the Province of Quebec, who were members of the House of Commons, not to lose sight of the interests of our Province, and to favour the Northern Colonization Railway; and if that influence was favourable to the Pacific Railway, with a view to its union with the Northern Colonization Railway. I induced them to give it.

McMullen was not present at the hearing, but had charged that Ouimet had received the sum of $6,000 "for aid rendered at Ottawa." Ouimet strenuously denied the allegation, even though he appears to have given a great deal of aid to what was essentially Allan's cause: promotion of the Northern Colonization as a foot in the door to get the Canadian Pacific contract. Ouimet continued his testimony, stating that he had remarked to Cartier that it was

> unfortunate that his Government had not settled this question of the contract of the Pacific Railway before the elections, because, I added, that this question would militate against him in the Province of Quebec, and particularly in Montreal East. I said to him, also, that Sir Hugh Allan had told me that he owed his commercial prosperity in a great measure to the Conservative party, and that I thought that Sir Hugh or his Company would aid him by influence or otherwise in his election. Sir George thereupon said that he could not entertain much hope that Sir Hugh Allan or his Company, meaning the Montreal Ocean Steamship Company, would come to his assistance, but as for himself (Sir George) he had several times put his portfolio in danger to maintain or obtain the subsidy for the Allan Company. Sir George told me this in that energetic language which he ordinarily used, and which is well known to those who were familiar with him. I had the honour to occupy myself in the election of Sir George at the last elections, and, notwithstanding that his friends urged him to let us make his election on the basis of the railway policy, and particularly the Pacific, he would not consent, saying, that he would conduct his election on his own personal merit.[57]

Et tu, Ouimet!

Whether or not he was bribed by Allan, Ouimet's defection from Cartier's ranks of "moutons"* shows the long-delayed erosion of Cartier's solid bloc of Quebec support. The bloc had remained together long enough to ensure the survival of Confederation. Now, with the approaching end of their leader's life and work, they were beginning to follow a natural law of politics, and falling apart, jockeying for future leadership, testing new avenues of financial support. They would regroup later with a new leader, new energies, but for the moment, they were in a state of frenzied anarchy.

South of the border, the Great Depression was beginning to make itself felt, and in the fifty-two-room palace of "Ogontz" outside Philadelphia, Jay Cooke watched the news from the European money markets with displeasure. Business was turning sour, and the Tycoon was beginning to lose money and momentum. Both the Vienna crash and the Chicago fire had hurt him. Grain could not be sold in Europe, and his

---

* "sheep," a name for the more docile of Cartier's followers; the modern equivalent would be "trained seals."

Northern Pacific Railway was being effectively attacked by his enemies as a "South Sea Bubble." It had been badly managed by the Boston-Vermont clique and ex-Governor Smith. After voting himself a $20,000 a year salary, Smith had spent all his time in the east worrying about his lines in the Eastern Townships and along the Canadian border.

Smith was forced out of the Presidency and General Cass put in his place. Yet matters had not improved, and Cooke began to grow restive. Sir Hugh Allan was running into trouble with the wily Cartier, backed, he knew, by the British government. He also knew the British were out to get him in other ways: despite his efforts at promotion, he could not raise a single penny in the British money market. Moreover, the London branch of J.S. Morgan, acting behind the American bankers Pierpoint Morgan and Anthony Drexel, had wrestled away his monopoly on government financing, a monopoly that had been the foundation of his prosperity.* Back in the United States, some investors who had purchased Northern Pacific Railway bonds and shares were now desperately trying to unload their holdings to others in the Northern Pacific group at cost plus interest.

Unknown to all but his closest associates, Cooke had started to bail out, and convert his paper holdings to gold. By the beginning of 1872, the Northern Pacific was overdrawn to the tune of $1,600,000. A year later, Cooke had managed to extract a further $3,900,000, borrowed, of course, from his Philadelphia bank. The Tycoon, already deep into his swindle, spent a few weeks in the early summer of 1872 relaxing on his island fortress on Lake Erie, discussing religious matters with the impoverished clergymen he and his wife so delighted in entertaining.

Although his own government had wished to bring down the Canadian government and create a more pliable Canadian administration, Jay Cooke had given up on immediate construction of the Northern Pacific Railway. This fact, known to most financiers with any sense at all, had not yet drummed its way into the ears of Sir Hugh Allan, who still went blindly onward, lulled by the sweet sound of American voices, bursting with greenbacks, promising success.

Allan's problem was that he underestimated Cartier. On July 1, believing that Cartier had promised him all that he wanted, Allan wrote to General Cass the letter of an over-optimistic fool:

> On a calm review of the situation, I satisfied myself that the whole decision of the question must ultimately be in the hands of one man, and that man was Sir George E. Cartier, the leader and chief of the French party. This party has held the balance of power between the other factions. It has sustained and kept in office and existence the

* It is interesting to note that the Morgan bank had been members of the International Financial Society, purchasers of the Hudson's Bay Company in 1864.

entire Government for the last five years. It consists of forty-five men, who have followed Cartier and voted in a solid phalanx for all his measures. The Government majority in Parliament being generally less than forty-five, it follows that the defection of one-half or two-thirds would at any time put the Government out of office. It was therefore evident that some means must be adopted to bring the influence of this compact body of members to bear in our favour, and as I soon made up my mind what was the best course to pursue, I did not lose a moment in following it up.

A railroad from Montreal to Ottawa, through the French country north of the Ottawa River, has long been desired by the French inhabitants, but Cartier, who is the salaried solicitor of the Grand Trunk Railroad, to which this would be an opposition, has always interposed difficulties, and by his influence prevented its being built. The same reason made him desirous of giving the contract for the Canadian Pacific into the hands of parties connected with the Grand Trunk Railroad, and to this end he fanned the flame of opposition to us. But I saw, in this *French* railroad scheme, and in the near approach of the general elections, when Cartier as well as others had to go to their constituents for re-election, a sure means of attaining my object, especially as I propose to carry it through to the terminus on the Pacific. The plans I propose are in themselves the best for the interests of the Dominion, and in urging them on the public I am really doing a most patriotic action. But even in that view, means must be used to influence the public, and I employed several young French lawyers to write it up for their own newspapers. I subscribed a controlling influence in the stock, and proceeded to subsidize the newspapers themselves, both editors and proprietors. I went to the country through which the road would pass, and called on many of the inhabitants. I visited the priests, and made friends of them, and I employed agents to go amongst the principal people and talk it up.

I then began to hold public meetings, and attended to them myself, making frequent speeches in French to them, showing them where their true interest lay. The scheme at once became popular, and I formed a committee to influence the members of the Legislature.

This succeeded so well that, in a short time, I had 27 out of the 45 on whom I could rely, and the electors of the ward in this city, which Cartier himself represents, notified him that unless the contract for the Pacific Railway was given in the interests of Lower Canada, he need not present himself for re-election. He did not believe this, but when he came here and met his constituents, he found, to his surprise, that their determination was unchangeable.

He then agreed to give the contract, as required, in this way, that there would be seventeen Provisional Directors, of which Ontario would have eight and we nine, – thereby giving us the control.[58]

But Allan had fallen into a trap, and as the railway proposals went into Cartier's Standing Committee on Railways, and then into the Privy Council Committee, he would soon feel the sting of the Lightning Striker.

By July 4, 1872, both the Canada Pacific and Interoceanic companies had formally applied for permission to build the Canadian Pacific Railway, and just as formally both were turned down. The Committee explained to the Companies that it wished them to amalgamate and form one company.

Allan tried to sweeten the pot by promising the Committee that he would also build an additional line from Nipissing to Ottawa, there to connect with the Northern Colonization Railway, but the Committee received this promise with a deep silence. Now that Allan had been drawn out into the open, Cartier began to tighten the screws.

Allan was enraged. He began to suspect he had been tricked by Cartier. This was confirmed when, in the middle of July, he tried to sound out the Minister of Militia on the government's further intentions. Seated behind his desk in the law office of Cartier, Pominville and Bétournay, Cartier faced the ruddy, white-bearded shipping magnate and announced that he did not now, "nor ever did, intend to deal" either with Macpherson's company or Allan's, "and that he only allowed them to get incorporated as a matter of amusement."

Allan was flabbergasted, and reported the meeting to McMullen, waiting eagerly in New York for further developments:

> He says he always intended that the Government would form its own Company, who will carry on the work *under the orders of the Government according to the views of the Government engineers*, and with money *furnished by the Government*. He says that he and Sir John A. made up their minds to this long ago, but did not tell any of their colleagues.
>
> A kind of negotiation is going on with both Macpherson and myself, relative to the composition of this Government Company, but it has not come to anything as yet. Meantime the period of the elections is drawing near, and unless the matter is arranged satisfactory to Lower Canada, Sir George Cartier's prospect of being returned is very slim indeed. I cannot foresee with any certainty the ultimate result, but the decision cannot be long put off.[59]

Allan was furious, but a long career in business had taught him the value of maintaining his composure. He rose, thanked Cartier for the interview, and drove away to Ravenscrag. The meeting convinced him that this audacious little Frenchman must be destroyed. He had given Cartier a chance to save his seat, and his political skin. He had bought men before. Now he would destroy Cartier by buying off his political support. Back in Ravenscrag, he hit upon a plan.

By selective bribery, he would cause the funds he usually gave the party at election time to be diverted into the hands of his agents, and through them, to the opposition. The opposition in Ontario had already been doused with campaign funds, likely from J. Gregory Smith via Reynolds and the Ottawa and Prescott Railway, or from the lumber barons via Richard Scott and the Canada Central. Allan would do the same in Quebec, with funds promised by Jay Cooke, some of which had already been drawn from Cooke's New York bank. It would be no problem to buy out his own workers – or rather withhold funds altogether until they were attracted to go over to the *Rouges* by the wealth in that camp. The Irish Catholic navvies who worked on the docks or in the Grand Trunk yards were leaderless, and since the assassination of Thomas D'Arcy McGee, easy targets for election dollars.

There was another possibility, another way of getting at Cartier. Surely Sir John A. Macdonald would come to his senses and persuade Cartier that he was harming his political future. Allan immediately telegraphed Macdonald: "It is very important in the interest of the Government that the Pacific question should be settled without delay. I send this from no personal interest, but a storm is raising." [60]

Macdonald probably read Allan's thinly disguised threat with a smile of amusement. So Allan had decided to brew up a storm! It was unfortunate, even sad, that it should come to this. But now the game was becoming deadly serious. A floundering, drowning Allan was more dangerous than the old safe swimmer. But the man had overstepped his bounds and was now seriously blackmailing the government. Cartier would never back down – he would fight the Americans to the death – and unless Allan backed off and supported Cartier's election, there might easily be a ministerial blow-up. The government might fall, but Allan, his financial and personal reputation seriously damaged, would never realize his dream of building the Pacific Railway. Macdonald would see to that, if it were the last thing he did.

The play would have to be acted out. The immediate problem was to try and force an amalgamation of the two companies before Cartier's election. Macpherson was proving to be quite reticent, and warned Macdonald,

It was with some reluctance that I interested myself in this undertaking, and I only did so to defeat what I must call the American Conspiracy, and to aid in securing the Railway, its lands, and all the advantages to accrue from it to our own people . . . I do not believe that his vanity is Sir Hugh's only motive for so earnestly desiring the Presidency. He and Abbott know full well its importance. If his Ring, owing to their electioneering influence, can force Allan upon you now, what will they do when they constitute a Parliamentary phalanx, able under their leader to importune, embarrass and bully the Government from day to day. [61]

But at Macdonald's request, Macpherson agreed to travel to Montreal and beard Allan in his den. Allan said he was willing to entertain the possibility of amalgamation, but only if he were guaranteed the Presidency and he and his "friends" guaranteed over 50 per cent of the stock.

Macpherson refused, and on July 17, Allan again telegraphed Macdonald, "the absence of a settlement is embarrassing our party here, in preparing for the coming electoral struggle."[62] Two days later, Cartier decided it was time to act, and sent a carefully worded telegram to Macdonald, now electioneering in Stratford. Although not in cipher – as some of his telegrams were – it probably contained a password of sorts. He told Macdonald about the meetings between Macpherson and Allan, and suggested that the affair be settled "on account of elections in Ontario and Quebec."[63] He felt now that if Allan could be "promised" his demands, he could be held off until after the election. Then he could be finally and completely trapped by the government's demand that it choose the members of the board and be given full details on the financing of the line. Cartier had outlined this intent in his C.P.R. Act. The government was to have total control over the establishment of the company it chose to build Canada's transcontinental railway.

Allan then wrote to Macdonald outlining his demands, and a few days later visited Cartier, who "granted" them. A dual telegram was immediately sent off to Macdonald, Allan suggesting that he would be satisfied "if the government will pledge itself to appoint directors favourable to me as president and to the allotment of stock as stated in my letter of yesterday." In a postscript, Cartier added, "Matter could be settled at once thus between him and Macpherson. Important it should be settled without delay."[64] After persuading Macpherson to accept the plan, Macdonald wired back to Cartier, in Ottawa, on July 26.

> Have seen Macpherson. He has no personal ambition, but cannot, in justice to Ontario, concede any preference to Quebec in the matter of the P[residency], or in any other particular. He says the question about the P. should be left to the Board. Under these circumstances, I authorize you to assure Allan that the power of the Government will be exercised to secure him the position of P. The other terms to be as agreed on between Macpherson and Abbott. The whole matter to be kept quiet until after the elections; then the two gentlemen to meet the Privy Council at Ottawa, and settle the terms of a provisional agreement.[65]

On July 30, Allan and Abbott came to Cartier's office, and he gave them a copy of Macdonald's telegram. But Allan wanted a further promise in writing from Cartier. Cartier had been waiting for this, and he of course obliged, playing as he always did, like a master. His letter is a masterpiece of legalese, promising nothing but his own "opinion" and "belief":

DEAR SIR HUGH, – I enclose you copies of telegrams received from Sir

John A. Macdonald; and with reference to their contents, I would say, that in my opinion the Governor in Council will approve of the amalgamation of your company with the Inter-Oceanic company, under the name of the Canadian Pacific Railway Company . . .

Upon the subscription and payment on account of stock being made, as required by the Act of last Session respecting the Canadian Pacific Railway Company, I have no doubt but that the Governor in Council will agree with the Company for the construction and working of the Canadian Pacific Railway, with such branches as shall be agreed upon, and will grant to the Company all such subsidies and assistance as they are empowered to do by the Government Act . . .

I would add, that as I approve of the measures to which I have referred in this, I shall use my best endeavours to have them carried into effect.

Very truly yours,
(Signed)
GEO. E. CARTIER[66]

Yet Allan, with only the slightest suspicions penetrating his blinkers, believed that he finally had the government under control. Even ten months after Cartier's departure to England, and two months after his death, Macdonald continued the charade, attributing Cartier's action to his "failing health and waning mental faculties."[67] Yet it is obvious the "promise" to Allan had been planned from the start.

Abbott's testimony before the Commission contained the following delightful view of Cartier reminding Allan of his duties as a Conservative:

We rose to leave, and we were leaving the room when Sir George addressed Sir Hugh on the subject of money . . . He said in an off-hand way, "Are you not going to help us with our elections?" Sir Hugh said he would, or words to that effect, and said, "how much do you want," or "how much do you require?" or something like that. I understood Sir George to say that there would be a considerable sum required, as there was so much opposition on various grounds. Sir Hugh said, as far as I can recollect, "Well, write down what you want." Sir George said very rapidly, "You know you won't lose it all. Our party will make up the greater part of what you give, but we want it now," or something like that. My memory is very imperfect as to the exact phrases used, as I never endeavoured to recollect them until lately, when the matter became the subject of conversation. Sir George then said, "Very well; come back this afternoon. Let Mr. Abbott write a note requesting you to advance this money, and telling you that I will see that you are repaid, and come back this afternoon at such an hour and we will close the matter up."[68]

The damning money letter, later paraded by the opposition as evidence of the "deal" made between Cartier and Allan, is as follows:

PRIVATE AND CONFIDENTIAL   MONTREAL, 30th July, 1872

DEAR SIR HUGH, – The friends of the Government will expect to be assisted with funds in the pending elections, and any amount which you or your Company shall advance for that purpose shall be recouped to you.

A memorandum of immediate requirements is below.

Very truly yours,
(Signed),
GEO. E. CARTIER

NOW WANTED

Sir John A. Macdonald $25,000
Hon. Mr. Langevin $15,000
Sir G.E.C. $20,000
Sir John A. (add'l) $10,000
Hon. Mr. Langevin...$100,000
Sir G.E.C. (add'l) ....$30,000[69]

Cartier very carefully drafted this letter to ensure that only a loan was being asked for, and not a cash grant. By the end of the elections, Allan had "loaned" the Liberal-Conservative Party in the Province of Quebec alone about $300,000 of his own and what he considered to be Jay Cooke's money – all to oil the wheels of Pacific patronage!

Why Cartier put his demands in writing has been an intriguing question. It was done, not absent-mindedly, but to give Allan one final life line. Allan could have easily blackmailed the government or scandalized the public with these letters, but Cartier knew he would not, that if he did, he would irreparably damage his own credibility in the money market. Cartier's mistake was that he considered Allan's situation, but had not entirely grasped the plans of the Vermont Central ring, of which Abbott was a member. Sir Hector Langevin, unaware of Cartier's course of action, refused to give any receipt in writing. It was Cartier's and Macdonald's game alone!

Allan's folly led him even further into a trap. Although he had not received any promises in writing, he tried to sow the seeds of mistrust between Cartier and Macdonald by writing to Macdonald and suggesting that he had struck a bargain with the Minister of Militia. The letter is also dated July 30:

I have this day arranged with Sir George Cartier to the following effect, and we have put the whole in writing –

1. Macpherson's Co'y and mine to be amalgamated partially,
2. Directors to be 17 – Macpherson names *four*, I name *four* and the Government name *nine* favourable to me being President.
4. [sic] My friends to subscribe and have alloted to them 9/17 of the stock.
5. Government influence to be used in my favour, and the Contract in terms of the Act to be given to the amalgamated Company.[70]

Macdonald must have laughed when he received this letter. Of course Cartier knew that Macpherson would not agree to amalgamate on these terms. The arrangement was not worth the paper it was written on. Macdonald wrote back protesting that, as Prime Minister, he must demand that Cartier's "intention" be withdrawn, and that the whole "arrangement" be based on his telegram of July 26. Not wishing to push his luck, a flummoxed Allan agreed, and was thereby trapped:

KINGSTON, July 31st, 1872.

(By Telegraph from Montreal)

TO SIR JOHN A. MACDONALD:

I have seen Sir Geo. Cartier today, you may return my letter or regard it as waste paper, it was not intended as anything official. Your telegram to Sir Geo. is the basis of our agreement, which I have no doubt you will approve of. He purposes to go out of town on Saturday afternoon, and I am persuaded his health will be benefited thereby.

(Signed)
HUGH ALLAN[71]

All he got out of the government was a written promise, politically written so as to be virtually meaningless, that the "power of the Government will be exercised" to secure him the position of president. No agreement was made concerning Allan's percentage of stock. It was a promise of intent only, whose execution in committee could easily be stage-managed to fail, especially after the elections. Even if Sir Hugh Allan were to become president of the *Canadian* Pacific Railway, there was no guarantee that he would have a board sympathetic to his wishes.

Question - You say "signed an agreement." You were aware that any document which Sir George Cartier signed would not bind the Cabinet?

Answer - Yes, I was aware of that.

Question - Then why did you use the expression "signed an agreement?"

Answer - It was the expression used in the hurry of the moment.

Testimony of Sir Hugh Allan, 1873

Sir Hugh Allan had extracted a token pledge that he thought would keep his American associates pleased with the progress he had made. However, his chief worry was how to gain his ends if Cartier's Railway Committee were to insist on a strict accounting of the sources of his funding. It would be impossible to hide from the Committee his links with Jay Cooke. So Allan blithely thought that he could afford to let the Americans go. The government appeared to be reconciled to his presidency, and there seemed to be enough Canadians, bursting with patriotic pride, interested in investing in the railway. At Cartier's urging, additional funds could be extracted from the British money market, this time with the backing and blessings of Whitehall.

But slowly the realization came to Allan that it was he, and not Cartier, who was trapped. And in that curious, fumbling way of his, he panicked. He was not trapped by Cartier; Cartier's hands were clean. He was trapped by Jay Cooke. The whole significance of his colossal blunder came rushing in on him in a blinding flash. Allan's later testimony is revealing:

> It was a very delicate and unpleasant thing for me bluntly to tell them that I would not carry out the arrangement; besides, although I came gradually to know how strongly opposed the government was to the introduction of American capital and influence, and that this feeling had taken possession, to a considerable extent, of the public mind: still I had never been formally notified by the Government that it was their intention positively to exclude foreigners and their capital, in the organization of the Pacific Company.[72]

Allan knew he would have to let Cooke go, but now realized that Cooke knew too much. He desperately feared blackmail, the release of his correspondence with the Americans, a full public enquiry, all of which would destroy the whole enterprise.

Allan rose from his despair not a better man, but as foolish as ever. Instead of straightaway confiding in Cartier, and mending the breach, he decided to try and let Jay Cooke and his associates go slowly, by lying to them, holding them off with promises. Allan had not been guaranteed a majority of the stock, yet on August 6, he wrote to McMullen:

Yesterday we entered into an agreement, by which the Government bound itself to form a company of Canadians only, according to my wishes. That the company will make me President, and that I and my friends will get a majority of the stock, and that the contract for building the road will be given to this company in terms of the Act of Parliament. Americans are to be carefully excluded, in the fear that they will sell it to the Northern Pacific. But I fancy we can get over that some way or other.

This position has not been attained without large sums of money. I have already paid over $200,000, and I will have at least $100,000 more to pay. I must now soon know what our New York friends are going to do. They did not answer my last letter.[73]

When McMullen received this letter, he chuckled, and said to his cousin that "Sir Hugh Allan is a tricky fellow, and not to be depended upon, but I think we have got him so tightly bound by these letters that he dare not go back on us."[74] The following day, Allan wrote a very careful letter to General Cass, saying that

Our opponents are to get the minority of the stock, and they regard us with great jealousy and dislike, in consequence of their defeat, and on that account the Government is obliged to stipulate that no foreigner is to appear as a shareholder, so as to avoid the former cry of selling ourselves to the Northern Pacific, and succumbing to foreign influence. The shares taken by you and our other American friends, will therefore have to stand in my name for some time.[75]

If Allan now hoped that he would be able to hide American influence by putting the shares in his own name, he was fooling himself much more than the Americans.

The Laird had spent much more of his own money than he had expected, and the Americans were holding back their share of the expenses. It is possible that Allan made up his mind to make partial amends with Cartier, in case his worst suspicions were ever confirmed, and accordingly decided to appear with Cartier the next day at an election rally in the Place Saint-Jacques.

Cartier's opponent was Louis-Aimable Jetté, a moderate young lawer and one of the founding members of the *Parti National*. Although he was lawyer for the wife of the unfortunate Joseph Guibord, still later Lieutenant-Governor of the Province of Quebec, and finally Chief Justice, Jetté at age thirty-six was a relative unknown, and on nomination, fully expected to be led like a lamb to the slaughter. To his great delight, Bourget's attacks on Cartier were beginning to take effect, funds were appearing from out of nowhere to pay his canvassers,[76] and the general impression in Montreal East was that Cartier would be defeated. When Cartier discovered that an anonymous donor had deposited $25,000 in Jetté's account[77] – likely J. Gregory Smith *via* Huntington and Laflamme – he knew the election was beginning to get out of control.

Montreal East was a tough, workingman's riding, with a mixture of Irish and French Canadian dock and railway workers, where campaign funds could disappear without a trace, where votes could be bought and sold for the price of a drink. Allan had done his job well, too well, and his repentance came a little too late to help Cartier's election chances. Funds recently supplied to Cartier's campaign committee were not being paid out to canvassers, or were beginning to disappear unaccountably, or were turning up in the hands of the Irish Catholics, most of whom changed their vote to the *Parti National*. In other ridings, Cartier's party was rent down the middle. His good friend Victor Hudon had been tricked out of the nomination in Hochelaga by Louis Beaubien, the provincial member, and not incidentally vice-president of the Northern Colonization Railway. Hudon's defeat was an indication of just how much Northern Pacific and Vermont Central money was beginning to take effect, and how it split the *Bleus*. Even before the nomination, *La Minerve*, liberally doused by Allan, named Beaubien and not Hudon as the government candidate. Hudon was furious, and wrote Cartier, regretting to tell him that "you always have too much confidence in people who do not deserve it."[78]

There was a moody, hostile crowd assembled August 8 in the square, as Cartier, obviously in great pain, was helped to the platform by his election officials. Allan led off the speeches by declaring, in his flawless French, that Cartier was fully behind the Northern Colonization Railway, and was promoting the interests of the riding with his plan for a Pacific railway. Scarcely had Allan begun to speak when the catcalls began. "The contract!" they hollered, "Show us the contract!" Rotten eggs and stones began to fly. An egg narrowly missed the Laird of Ravenscrag, who soon cut his speech short, and sat down out of harm's way. There was a hush as Cartier, grimacing with pain, rose to his feet and reached the podium. To the applause of all his supporters, he told them that his victory would be theirs. He attacked Jetté as a political unknown:

> I have an adversary, but who is he? I scarcely know him. I cannot attack him, because he is without a political past, and consequently escapes praise or blame . . . I am presenting myself before you with twenty-five years of experience, after having occupied important positions in the government of the country for the past seventeen years. My political career is not without fault, but I can tell you, in all sincerity, that I have always worked to obtain for my fellow citizens the greatest happiness and prosperity.[79]

In reply to critics who accused him of selling out the advantages of the Pacific railway, he replied that Montreal would "have the lion's share." The crowd cheered, but soon the catcalls began again. Fistfights broke out in the crowd, and Cartier was constantly interrupted:

> It would be easy to gag those rowdies – one word would do it – but, I repeat, don't attack them – they may get tired of shouting . . . I hope that the explanations I have made and which Sir Hugh Allan will support, will calm your fears and quiet those who speak wrongly about things they know nothing about. The Pacific railway will begin at Nipissing, beside the lake – that is a geographical necessity – but the company will build a line from there to Montreal that will virtually give you the Pacific terminus. Sir Hugh Allan will be in charge of it.[80]

With the last of his election promises, Cartier took his seat, and the first Battle of Place Saint-Jacques began. The two partisan elements in the crowd began to fight it out, but the police intervened before any more damage was done than a few broken noses.

Feeling that discretion was the better part of valour, and wishing to reassure McMullen and Smith, Allan left Montreal soon after, and was absent for three weeks. Cartier, now quite ill, took advantage of Allan's offer to recuperate in splendour at Ravenscrag, where he remained for three days.[81] A week after Allan's departure, Cartier's supporters decided to have another meeting on the Place Saint-Jacques, to repair the damage to their reputation suffered on the 8th.

In the interim, the *Rouge* newspapers printed handbills crying

Shame to the English Baronet!

Electors of Montreal East! The solemn day is at hand: Wednesday the 28th of August will be marked by a glorious victory, the triumph of Monsieur Jetté, the candidate of the people; and a great defeat, the fall of Monsieur Cartier, betrayer of the working class.[82]

La Minerve fought back, pouring scorn on the new party, sneering "scratch a National and find a Rouge." The paper compared the *Rouges* to the Communards, assassins of the Archbishop of Paris:

> Same ideas, same doctrines, same ends. When Rougeism succeeds in making Canada a nation without religion, without spirit, without bravery, it will put the country to the torch. The Rouges of Canada are the Rouges of Paris, as irreligious and as envious.[83]

Cartier's feet had become so swollen that he had great difficulty walking in shoes. But this did not prevent him from travelling down to Saint-Antoine for a holiday and a rest. Something in him realized that he might die without seeing his birthplace again. For two days, he stayed at Saint-Antoine in the new house of his nephew Louis. Then he visited his brother Antoine at the House of the Seven Chimneys, soaking up the sun, receiving the best wishes of family and friends, and letting the old memories of that Eden on the Richelieu flow back, until his mind was full of the singing and carousing of his father's friends, the hot summer days full of the buzzing and chirping of life, the crunch of iron sleigh runners on the river ice, the advice of his kind but sometimes too pious mother.

To his family and friends, he appeared sad and full of suffering, resenting the defections and ingratitude in the party ranks, and disgusted by the riot of the week before. It was hard to leave Eden, but Cartier knew the voters were waiting, ready to see him fight again.

By the afternoon of August 19, an enormous crowd had squeezed into the square, ready to cheer and defend their leader. While some sailors from the Allan Line surrounded the platform, the podium was packed with the dignitaries of the riding, including the former Mayor, William Workman, and Mayor (formerly Judge) C.-J. Coursol, now a member of Allan's provisional board, who presented the candidate. Cartier had hardly begun to speak when he was interrupted by shouts and whoops from the fringes of the crowd, and from up streets radiating away from the square.

"Does someone think I will allow myself to be intimidated," he bellowed across the mass of people. "In the twenty-five years I have been in public life, I have seen other demonstrations of this kind, but they have never prevented me from speaking." He ridiculed Jetté's attacks on Confederation, declaring that it had "put an end to our internecine quarrels, consecrated the rights of the Catholic Church, assured to all French Canadians the free exercise of their rights within the Province of Quebec, and inaugurated an era of prosperity that is our foundation for a future full of promise." He charged Jetté with having ignored the fact that "we form the majority in the Province of Quebec, that we possess a real counter-weight against Ontario in the equality of representation on the Senate, that the Maritime Provinces, allied with us, want the same protection, that all in all we have nothing to fear."

As he began to speak about the New Brunswick schools question, Jetté's supporters, now packing the side streets, started a constant jeering in an effort to drown him out. Cartier's men finally turned on the hecklers, and serious fighting broke out. The police tried to separate the warriors, but not before Jetté's men had been pushed out of the square. The second Battle of Place Saint-Jacques became more ominous when the intruders, better prepared this time, returned from the backstreets armed with clubs, cudgels and even axes, and threw a great volley of stones onto the podium, injuring some of the speakers.

Yet Cartier's supporters had also come well prepared, and dodging Mayor Coursol, who waded right into the thick of the battle, calling for order, they beat back the invaders for a final time. The victors returned in triumph to the square, and setting up a loud cheer, called again for Cartier.

"As you have witnessed with your own eyes," he went on, "we have allowed Jetté to exercise his right of free speech, and you can see how he has responded to our generosity. I am happy to see that the friends of order are on my side – this has been proven once again."[84]

When he had finished his speech, Cartier invited his supporters to accompany him to his house on Rue Notre-Dame, a few blocks away. They carried their crippled leader home on their shoulders, where, flushed by the excitement, and shoeless, but forgetting his swollen legs, he harangued them for another hour, repeating that the C.P.R. terminus would be in Montreal East. "It will be here," he said, pointing across the road to the site of the Viger Station. Legs that had supported Cartier for speeches of thirteen hours and more finally gave out, and he was carried indoors to rest and ramble on, while outside, the faithful guarded him until dawn.

Another late penitent to Cartier's cause was Bishop Bourget, who, alarmed by the riots and realizing that Cartier was not one to forget an insult, visited him the next day. The *modus vivendi* they hammered out, whereby the provincial government would agree to some of Bourget's demands about the division of the parish of Montreal, came too late, and although *La Minerve* reported the Bishop as saying, "I will be pleased to see Sir Georges re-elected," the damage had been done, and *Le National* jeered, "why don't the hypocrites come right out and say that Our Holy Father supports the candidacy of Cartier."[85] Both Allan and Bourget had realized at the last minute that, although Cartier would probably be defeated, his Party would not be, and they feared his wrath if and when he returned to Parliament in a bye-election.

Cartier's troops had won all their skirmishes, but on August 28, lost their Waterloo, lost by a crushing 1300-vote margin, lost in every poll counted. The *Parti National* candidate in Montreal West, the annexationist John Young, also was victorious, yet most other *Bleus* in the Province of Quebec were returned. Cauchon, who had resigned as Speaker of the Senate, was victorious in Quebec City, but in disgust over Allan's defection back to Cartier – and perhaps realizing that Allan had been using him all along – he soon went over to the opposition. Cauchon's campaign was marked by incredible violence, including a gun battle fought in the English cemetery, in which a supporter of the *Parti National* was killed. All in all, the election campaign of 1872, liberally oiled as it was by railway money, was the most vicious ever held in Canada, and the party feeling then engendered took a long time to die down.

When the ballots had all been counted, the party of Cartier and Macdonald found that it had lost seven seats in Quebec and twelve in Ontario, but gained most of them back in the Maritimes and in the new seats of Manitoba and British Columbia, for a not-so-solid majority that would depend on satisfying the desires of the "loose fish." Although Cartier's supporters dropped from forty-five to thirty-eight, they still outnumbered Macdonald's, many of whom were loose fish.

Most Canadians were amazed by Cartier's defeat, but he accepted it stoically, even humourously. What amazed and concerned him more was his illness; he knew it would probably be fatal. He was astounded before the coincidences of that present – the end of his life, the end of his life's work, and his defeat in the most violent election he had ever seen. But as he stood on the Olympus of the dying, smiling at the mortals below, he knew there was still work to be done, matters to be tidied up, a railway company to be wrestled into being. On election day, according to a friend, he acted as if nothing were happening:

> At around ten o'clock, he was dictating a memorandum on Manitoba, when the news came concerning the rout of his supporters. The street was full of people. He rose, went to the window, then shrugging his shoulders, he returned to his daybed, saying, "Well, where were we? . . . continue."
>
> Half dreaming, half smiling, he continued his dictation. It concerned organizing a corps of volunteers for the North-West. This done, at about two in the afternoon, the visitors rushed in. When someone expressed surprise at seeing him work on militia documents at such a moment, he answered him in that dry tone of voice he was known for: "well, there you are. You doubtless would like to see me in tears, or making plans for the inevitable. The best distraction, my friend, is work."
>
> A little after six o'clock, he left for his country house (Limoilou) at the urging of his partner, Monsieur Pominville, whom he took with him. He repeated all the names of those who had come to see him, and, visibly moved, showed his gratitude for their sympathy. This was not only a result of his physical weakness at this time – he hid his emotion less than usual.[86]

The next day, he received the condolences of both Bourget and Abbé Bayle, Superior of Saint-Sulpice. The new Governor General, Lord Dufferin, wrote him the nice compliment that "as to your easily procuring a seat of course there can be no doubt, for I am sure that even your bitterest political opponents will scarcely forgive themselves if their triumph were to involve your exclusion from parliament."[87]

The results of the election saddened, but did not really astound Sir John A. Macdonald, and he poured out his explanations to former Governor General Lisgar, now playing at being an Irish farmer:

> The local [Ontario] Government used all its power, patronage and influence to defeat us. They forced the great lumber merchants [such as Richard Scott], who depend upon them for licences of occupation of

timber lands, to subscribe large sums, and I have reason to believe that the U.S. Northern Pacific Railway also subscribed largely in order to place Mr. Mackenzie at the head of the Government, as he would have handed over our Pacific Railway to them. This nefarious design has, however, been defeated. We are, I think, fixed in the saddle for the next five years, and shall take good care that the Yankees have nothing to say to our Pacific Railway.[88]

Macdonald was obviously delighted at the party's narrow escape from the designs of Jay Cooke, but his feelings welled up angry and bitter when he spoke to Lisgar of Cartier's defeat, and of his sure knowledge that he would soon lose his great and dear friend:

I would not regret his defeat at all, as he brought it upon himself by sheer obstinacy, were it not that I fear it will greatly affect his health. I am sorry to say that he is in a very bad way. His legs are swollen to an enormous extent. It has all the appearance of confirmed dropsy. But still worse, Dr. Grant tells me confidentially that his ailment is what is commonly known as "Bright's disease," which is generally considered as incurable. I do not anticipate that he will live a year, and with all his faults, or rather with all his little eccentricities, he will not leave so good a Frenchman behind him; certainly not one who can fill his place in public life. I cannot tell you how I sorrow at this. We have acted together since 1854, and have never had a serious difference.[89]

Throughout the Province of Quebec, *post mortems* were held to explain the reasons for Cartier's defeat. Cartier himself, apparently bemused, termed it "merely a transient political blunder." Colonel George Denison, a mortal enemy, got in on the act, claiming that it was the militia volunteers, organized by himself and other officers with grievances against the way Cartier was organizing the militia, who had beaten the Minister.[90] Many looked to Sir Hector Langevin, Cartier's lieutenant and obvious successor, for advice. Arthur Dansereau of *La Minerve*, apparently disgusted by the way the election funds had been handled, wrote Langevin that,

In our district, patronage has been offered only to the personal friends of Sir Georges or to those incapable of rendering service. Review those favoured by the government and you will find only loose fish and often enemies. It has come to pass that the friends of the party, always left out, became disillusioned at the last election, not one wanting to work without money. The $25,000 spent to get a minority of 1300 votes remains in the hands of these friends. There is no party spirit left.[91]

Allan's greed had sown a bitter harvest. Langevin himself was exasperated by the election, and especially with some priests who had muddied their boots in the mire of politics. To Abbé Désilet, a *programmist* who implied that Cartier had been struck down by God, he wrote

I am convinced you will not be surprized to find that I do not agree with your conclusions. Any man can make mistakes, and if Sir Georges made one or two, we must recall the long and important service he rendered, and the fact that he did no wrong to our nationality and our influence as a Province in Confederation, and not rejoice in the shock he was given at Montreal.[92]

But the election was over, and soon the wheels of politics began to turn to find another seat for the defeated Lion of Quebec.

Cartier was offered many seats in Quebec, but decided, at Macdonald's suggestion, to try and get a seat in the Red River. Macdonald wrote to Taché, suggesting that the electors of Provencher, now trying to choose between Louis Riel (who in spite of his "exile" was still to be seen around Saint-Boniface) and Henry J. Clarke, might be persuaded to give up their seat to Cartier. On September 7, Macdonald telegraphed Archibald, "Get Sir George elected in your Province – *Do not however* let your late President [Riel] resign in his favour – *That would do mischief in Ontario.*"[93] Neither of the opponents objected, Riel agreeing with Taché that it would be wise to have the government further in his debt. On September 12, Cartier wired Macdonald, "agree with you can't make pledges it is question of confidence in me they must rely on my doing my best for them & their interest."[94] In spite of not getting a definite pledge from Cartier, the electors of Provencher, on September 14 elected Sir George-Etienne Cartier as their Member of Parliament by acclamation.

It must have pleased him to receive the following telegram, signed by Joseph Royal, his former law clerk and Speaker of the Manitoba House:

Winnipeg, 14th September, 1872

To Hon. Sir George Et. Cartier,
Bart., Montreal

Your election in our County is by acclamation, and have reason to hope in the success of the cause trusted into your hands.

(Signed)
LOUIS RIEL
JOSEPH ROYAL
A. LEPINE
JOS. DUBUC

The story in Provencher was much different from that in the Selkirk riding, which included Saint-Boniface, where the election was nothing more than a pitched battle fought with pistols and axe handles. Before the militia could stop them, the rioters destroyed the newspaper offices of *The Manitoban* and Joseph Royal's *Le Métis*. By September 21,

Royal had repaired his press enough to be able to publish Cartier's letter of thanks. The new M.P. for Provencher asked his constituents to believe that, in the face of the most bitter prejudice, the government had been able to give them the justice they demanded and deserved:

> You and your Province have many sincere friends in the different provinces of the Dominion, and especially in the good old Province of Quebec, which has always, and will never cease, to sympathize with you, and which will forever do all in their power for your peace and harmony.

He promised to serve them faithfully as their Member, but regretted to tell them that he found it necessary to travel immediately to Europe "for the sake of my health . . . I pray God that He will bless the object of my voyage, and that He will restore my health so that I can resume my political work in the interests of your constituents, as well as for your province and mine, and for the Dominion."[96] One of his last acts before leaving was to ensure the appointment of his law partner, Louis Bétournay, as Puisne Judge of the Court of Queen's Bench for the Province of Manitoba.

9   "Whoever Allan's associates in the pact may have been, I cannot but think it possible to devise checks to prevent any foreign element exercising an injurious influence."

Sir John Rose to Sir John A. Macdonald, November 7, 1872

The news from Manitoba reached Limoilou on the evening of September 15. It buoyed Cartier's spirits tremendously, and the next day he left to rejoin the government at Ottawa. Met at the station by a huge crowd of M.P.s, civil servants and workers, he was escorted by torchlight parade to the City Hall, where, deeply moved, he told the gathering that, God willing, they would see him back at his old desk in Parliament, working for their well-being.

In Montreal, the partly repentant Sir Hugh Allan found himself in a very delicate situation. To his disgust, he now found that the Interoceanic Company, informed and primed by Macdonald, were demonstrating some unwillingness to amalgamate with him. Macpherson appeared to be dead-set against Allan being President, calling his whole adventure with the Americans, "an audacious, insolent, unpatriotic, and gigantic swindle – the greatest ever attempted in this Dominion."[97] Yet by promoting Allan for the presidency, Cartier and Macdonald had not only held him off until after the election, but had kept him relatively out of danger. The amalgamation game was being played partly to rescue Allan, but also to allow the government time to plan and force through a board of their own choosing. Under the circumstances, Allan now found he could do nothing but go along with Cartier and Macdonald, and jettison Jay Cooke.

But General Cass was a difficult man to persuade. On September 16, Allan wrote McMullen saying that "today I have a letter from General Cass, stating that he is leaving New York for Chicago, there to join Mr. Ogden, and the two are going to Puget Sound. They say no meeting can be held until 15th November, which will not do at all. I hope in ten days or so to have the contract signed, and would like immediately after to go to England to raise the money to build the line. I have disbursed $343,-000 in gold, which I want to get repayed. I have still to pay $13,500, which will close everything off."[98]

The contract was not yet signed, and Allan knew it would not be signed, because the Interoceanic Company was playing the role of the Devil's Advocate, Cartier's role, not wishing to amalgamate until it was satisfied that all American influence had been expunged from Allan's company. What the Interoceanic were in fact doing was providing Allan with an excuse, and a not very subtle one, to abandon Jay Cooke. He would be given the presidency if he played along with the government, even at the risk of blackmail.

Macdonald and Cartier thoroughly discussed the whole blackmail question before Cartier left for England. Their prime political aim was reaffirmed. Their government must continue to show Canada's intention to build the Pacific Railway, whatever the political cost. It was nothing less than a question of national survival. Their government must also be prepared to receive blackmail threats – rumours were circulating in Montreal at that very moment that Allan had bought the Pacific charter from Cartier. They must be fully prepared to be thrown out of office.

As Old Tomorrow and the Lightning Striker sat and talked in Cartier's office, the one, his future clouded over, the other, his store of thunderbolts quite gone, the two realized, almost by instinct, that they had won, that their Confederation was secure.

Let the depression come, let all the dirt and blackmail float to the surface and stink, let Jay Cooke fume and curse. The railway would be built by and for Canadians.

On the evening of September 27, Macdonald and Langevin said what was to be a final farewell to Cartier, as he boarded the Grand Trunk night train to Lévis. The next morning, the rock of Quebec loomed slate-grey and forbidding across the river, but Cartier was thrilled as always to see it. He watched as the boat tender *William* puffed across, stirring up the river mist, straining against the ebb-tide, carrying friends who were coming to give him a send-off. Pierre-Joseph-Olivier Chauveau, the Premier of Quebec and one of his closest friends, was first off the boat to meet him. Then his younger sister Léocadie, then Pierre Garneau, the Mayor of Quebec, and Joseph Cauchon, the political boss of Quebec City – a man to respect but not love, a man who had realized Allan's game too late – many friends, friends in the military, friends in the priesthood, political friends. Now seated on a platform on the station dock, the chill breezes of morning tugging at his overcoat, he listened with emotion as the Mayor of Lévis read an address from the citizens, thanking him for his service to the country and wishing a speedy restoration of his health. "Posterity," concluded the Mayor, "will come to see the era of your presence on the political stage as one of the most important in our history."[99]

These were final words, passing him into history – everybody knew it, and he felt almost naked before their reverent eyes – and as he thanked them, the old political fire was drowned by his tears. He had to stop often to fight them back, but many of his friends could not. He told them that if their wishes and prayers gave him back his health, he would soon return to take his place in the government: "I will be pleased, if the people continue to give me their support, to devote the rest of my life to working for this country and for your well-being."[100]

Then he had to depart. As the *William* made its way back across the St. Lawrence, carrying Cartier toward the Allan Line steamship *Prussian*, the cheers died away on the Lévis shore. Some shafts of sunlight began to break through the low cloud. The artillery band on the deck struck up a fanfare, and far up on the rock the great cannon of the Citadel of Quebec, fired by the men of his Canadian militia, boomed out a seventeen-gun salute. Soon the *William* drew alongside the black-hulled *Prussian*.

Before Cartier boarded the steamer, Mayor Garneau read an address, signed by 1500 citizens of Quebec, wishing him God-speed. In what he probably knew would be his last speech in Canada, Cartier summoned his strength, and spoke to his friends for half an hour. He remembered with affection his years at Quebec City as Prime Minister of the Union, praised their famous hospitality, and wished the city a prosperous future. Interrupted by a blast from the Allan Line steamboat's whistle, he said that "interruptions do not bother me. They tried to interrupt my political career, but I can assure you that the incident in Montreal East disturbed me no more than this interruption just now. I am not easily discouraged."

Again, it was time to depart. "I must now tell you," he said, preparing to board the ship, "with my heart full of gratitude, adieu, or rather, au revoir,"[101] and he turned, and aided by his valet Thomas Vincent, climbed the gangway, and disappeared into the ship.

He intended to return. "If the specialists condemn me," he had said to a friend, "I will return home to die among my own people."[102]

The ocean voyage did him good, and when he reached London, Cartier's condition showed some improvement. He immediately placed himself under the care of Dr. George Johnstone, a Harley Street kidney specialist, and began to follow a strict diet, consisting mainly of eggs and milk. He wrote to Macdonald that the doctor was of the opinion that "my illness must have originated in the cold I caught December last on my way from Quebec to Ottawa . . . He has put me under a strict milk diet. I drink eight or ten tumblers of it every day. In fact, I am living on it."[103]

Cartier soon began to work, and when he could, threw himself into a round of social and private functions, all to upgrade Canada's relations with the Gladstone government, and convince financiers of the attractiveness of the Pacific railway. Lady Cartier and his two daughters, Josephine and Hortense, met him in London, and they stayed together for a time at the Westminster Palace Hotel before moving to quieter lodgings on Wellbeck Street, close to his doctor's office.

Back in Montreal, Sir Hugh Allan lamented Cartier's departure. At least Allan knew where he stood with Cartier. Now he would have to deal with Macdonald, and rely on the Prime Minister's judgment regarding the Americans. Cartier had stood firmly behind the interests of Montreal; Macdonald, although from Kingston, was backed by Allan's Toronto rivals in the railway sweepstakes.

Along with Macpherson, the Provisional Directors of the Interoceanic, as submitted to the Cabinet in their act of incorporation on September 26, included Senators William McMaster and John Carling; Joseph Cauchon (now in opposition to Allan); the Ottawa valley lumber barons Thomas Ryan and David Price (in opposition to R.W. Scott and the Canada Central); the Grand Trunk engineer Walter Shanley, M.P.; David Torrance of the Dominion Steamship Line, brother of the New York Central Vice-President Daniel Torrance; Frederick W. Cumberland, Managing Director of the Toronto Northern Railway; British Columbia M.P. Amor de Cosmos; all in all, a solid phalanx of businessmen dedicated to keeping the line under British and Canadian control. The addition of Torrance to the Board was most ominous to Allan, for it signalled that Jay Cooke, bitterly opposed to Vanderbilt and Torrance's New York Central, would be even more bent on destroying the whole idea of a Canadian Pacific Railway.

No one was more disappointed in the results of the Canadian election than Jay Cooke and General Cass, yet when they learned from McMullen that Allan was now asking for about $350,000 from the ring for promotional purposes, they were highly amused. They well knew that they now had their man trapped, and had decided that, if the Northern Pacific was going to go bust, it was time to sabotage the Canadian Pacific and Macdonald in the process. A more pliable government in Ottawa, one composed of men not like Cartier, men they knew could be persuaded, would be valuable in the future. Accordingly, McMullen was sent to Montreal to begin the stages of blackmail. McMullen explained to Allan that Cooke and Cass were "somewhat startled at the magnitude of the figures," and "proposed to have some reasonable explanation of how the money had been expended before they returned it to Sir Hugh."[104]

McMullen's sinister questions frightened Allan, and his realization that the game was up caused him to approach Macdonald for help. On October 2, Allan wrote the Prime Minister a whimpering letter, explaining that he had all along believed the government had wished him to deal with the Americans. In fact, Sir Francis Hincks had suggested this to him. He explained that, on Cartier's advice, he was now, "gradually and in not too rude a manner," attempting to separate himself from Jay Cooke and General Cass.

Macdonald determined to make Allan crawl, and through Abbott, forced the Canada Pacific Company to write a memorandum to the cabinet declaring that "the organization should be pre-eminently national in its character; and that its means must be drawn first from Canadian and secondly and chiefly from British sources."[105] By forcing this memorandum on Allan, Macdonald effectively insulated the man from attack. Henceforth Allan would keep his mouth shut; his company alone would speak for him.

Also sent to the cabinet was the Provisional Board of Directors of Allan's company, a rag-bag of names, most of whom were party stalwarts, inoffensive to Macdonald. On Macdonald's advice, Allan attempted to field a broad spectrum from across the Dominion. The addition of Edward Kenny and Isaac Burpee from the Maritimes was a political necessity; many of Cartier's friends were included; and, the presence of the ubiquitous Donald A. Smith ensured that the Hudson's Bay Company would be deeply interested in the success of the line.

The cabinet received the Canada Pacific memorandum, and then on October 16, proceeded to give a tongue-lashing to the boards of both companies. While it recognized the Interoceanic's objections to Allan's American friends, it further accepted Allan's lame excuse that he dealt with the Americans believing it to be a wish of the government. Moreover, it recognized that it believed Allan had cut all links with the Americans. The cabinet then threatened that unless the two lines agreed to amalgamate, the railway would be built as a public work. Allan would be nominal president, but a very much chastened one. The real control over the enterprise would remain where Cartier had always intended it to remain, firmly within the hands of the cabinet.

On October 24, with the weight of the cabinet's decision sitting heavily on his shoulders, Allan wrote to McMullen and told him as plainly as possible that the game appeared to be over, and that "the Government seem inclined to exact a declaration that no foreigners shall have directly or indirectly any interest in it."[106] McMullen sent back a vigorous protest, and as the Jay Cooke ring sat down to plan further action, the Canadian cabinet found that it was still juggling two companies. Allan had formally accepted the cabinet's advice and agreed to amalgamation, but the Interoceanic were still holding off, wanting fuller Ontario representation, and determined to make Allan suffer even more. In late October, Macdonald's law partner Alexander Campbell stumped across Ontario, trying to reassure the Interoceanic board members that their fears were groundless, and that representation would match the balance of the Canadian cabinet.

On November 6, McMullen wrote an ominous letter to Allan in which his mockery seems to ooze between the lines:

Since the receipt of your letter, the contents of which surprised me considerably, following so soon after our conversation at Montreal, and in view of the fact that the Government seem so much at sixes and sevens about the whole matter, I have of course communicated the substance of it to my friends. They are anxious to know whether such a decision will be arrived at, after the various pledges made, as will debar our association from participating in the construction of the railway. Whatever skirmishing may be done by way of talk, they can hardly have an idea that you will prove recreant to your business associates, in an arrangement mainly of their own suggestion. (I mean the Government, who first requested you to write to Chicago). However much they may be beset with political problems, I do not believe they could get, in any other way, so difficult a one on their hands as they could by taking such a course. Mr. Ogden and party are now back from Puget Sound, and I shall take an early opportunity of meeting them.[107]

Allan may have shown this letter to the Prime Minister, whose final plan, worked out long before with Cartier, was to have the cabinet draw up its own company and board of directors. It was imperative, for Allan's own safety, that the new company be the government's own, rather than an amalgamation. On November 11, Allan wrote to McMullen saying that

You really know as much about the Pacific Railroad contract as I do, and that is not much. I am assured that the Government have resolved to form a new company, but under what conditions, or who the parties will be, I am ignorant. It is said that the whole matter will be arranged by the end of the month, and if so, we will soon know it. I have not changed my views of what it ought to be.[108]

Allan still wanted more from the government. Two days later, he foolishly wrote Macdonald in terms that narrowly approached blackmail,

"You remember that it was agreed between us that I and my friends should have a majority of the stock. It will be better I think that you should adhere to that agreement, and give me full trust and confidence – it will result all the better for you."[109] Macdonald must have smiled; he knew there had been no agreement, no real contract. Allan tried the same tack with Cartier, and persuaded Senator Asa B. Foster, who desperately wanted a seat on the Board, to telegraph to the absent Minister of Militia:

Sir George Cartier,   14 Nov/72
Care Grant Secretary
Grand Trunk
London

Pacific to be closed next week please telegraph Sir John immediately to provide for me if you do not I fear the result.

A.B. Foster[110]

When Cartier opened Foster's telegram, his explosive laughter must have been heard from one end of the Grand Trunk office to the other.

On November 25, the Interoceanic Company sent the cabinet a memorandum formally declining to amalgamate. In it, the Company turned the screws more fully on Allan, arguing that

No more suicidal policy could be pursued by the people of Canada than to allow their rivals to have such an interest in this national undertaking as would virtually transfer to them the ownership and control of 50,000,000 acres of Canadian territory, would invest them with the direction of the immigration policy, which must be inaugurated for the settlement of those lands; confer upon them the power to influence the construction and progress of the railway; and grant to them, in perpetuity, a monopoly of the traffic over the Canadian, which is the shortest and best Transcontinental route.

Your committee firmly believe that amalgamation means the admission of this rival United States interest into the organization of the Canadian enterprize, and that once admitted and wielded for one object, it would speedily master the divided and weakened Canadian representation. They consider that this danger far outweighs any possible advantage that could result from union with Sir Hugh Allan and his associates.[111]

This memorandum, surely the most succinct and complete denunciation of Allan's betrayal of his country that could have been written, could have been composed by the absent Cartier himself, so brilliantly does it express his principles and explain his fears, and his understanding of the reasons behind American involvement in the whole Canadian Pacific affair. It was, of course, written by Cartier's good friend Senator

Macpherson, a member of the Grand Trunk Railway Board of Directors. It is not difficult to see, in these few words, the great significance of the decision by Cartier, not to give "a damned American company control over the Pacific."

"There are rocks ahead of the most danger- 10 ous character, and I therefore think you must be here without fail."

Macdonald to Langevin, November 28, 1872

The cabinet began to work at the beginning of December. It decided to choose thirteen board members, to match the regional interests as reflected in the cabinet itself. At these meetings, Macdonald probably laid most of his cards on the table, explaining his and Cartier's plans and actions, explaining that the whole charade of amalgamation was an attempt to buy time so Allan could extricate himself from American influence, and so that they might wait until the Northern Pacific had gone belly-up. Macdonald still proposed Sir Hugh Allan as president, and may have defended his choice by suggesting that it might draw blackmail attempts away from the government.

One cabinet member who was terrified by the implications of blackmail, who could not force himself to go along on Macdonald's fishing expedition, was the ailing old Nova Scotian warrior, Joseph Howe. In his letter of resignation, dated December 6, 1872, he explained that he had "come to the conclusion that I cannot defend that scheme, or be a party to arrangements which, I believe, will be a surprise to Parliament and the country, and fraught with consequences deeply injurious to the best interests of the Dominion."[112]

Howe was gone, but the rest of the cabinet played along, rapt with fascination at the intricacies of this colossal stacked-up house of cards. From London, Cartier reported that, although he felt "very tired of living a life of doing nothing,"[113] his health was improving, and that his wife and daughters were enjoying themselves in Paris. In addition, he said he was appearing to have some success in negotiating funds for fortifications at Montreal.* Macdonald wrote him that all was going well, and that he should not "hurry too much about coming out."[114] A few days before Christmas, he gleefully wrote that "We are making the

* After the Treaty of Washington, the need for Canadian fortifications had disappeared, so it is probable that Cartier was hoping to convert this fortification guarantee into a C.P.R. loan. This arrangement was in fact made shortly after his death.

best company we can. The thirteen directors are not all chosen yet, but they will all be settled by New Year's Day."[115]

The timing was crucial. Worried by a silence from south of the border, Macdonald probably now advised Allan to try and draw the Americans out into the open. The day before Christmas, McMullen arrived in Montreal, on an urgent telegram from Allan. There, before the fire at Ravenscrag, Allan informed McMullen that the whole deal was off, that he had written a letter to General Cass to the same effect. McMullen was not amused by this Yuletide present, and, in his own words,

> I protested strongly against such conduct, and referred to the contracts we had entered into, and the long association existing, as well as the uniform good faith evinced by our party, stating that I deemed it only honourable in him to insist on the original agreement, or else to retire himself from the proposed Company. When this was refused, I announced my intention of going to Ottawa to lay the matter before Sir John A. Macdonald. On the 31st December, I had an interview of some two hours duration with Sir John, and placed him in possession of all the facts, and showed him the letters which I had from Sir Hugh in regard to the matter . . . He strenuously denied that the Government had been bribed, and I pointed out that if not, then our Canadian associate must be a swindler in attempting to get refunded nearly $400,000, which he had never laid out. I then requested him to do one of two things – either to allow our original arrangement to be carried out, or else to leave Sir Hugh out of the Government Company, since we did not propose to be a stepping-stone for his personal advancement. Sir John said the Government arrangements had gone so far that he feared they could do neither, and said that from Allan's memorial in answer to the Interoceanic Company, and from his assertions since the Session, they had supposed he had entirely broken with us.[116]

Macdonald almost seemed to be daring McMullen to blackmail the government. He knew of the men behind McMullen, and must have smiled inwardly watching this puppet, whose voice and gestures were being manipulated by those shadowy, substantial men of power, and likely had to keep a very straight face indeed when McMullen claimed that he and his friend Mather Smith had spent a great deal of their own personal time and money to help Allan's cause. So Sir Francis Hincks brought the principals together, and Allan finally agreed to pay McMullen the sum of $40,000, to be delivered if the papers and letters were not released to the press, payable after the opening of the next session of Parliament. McMullen also gave his word that he would deliver the correspondence after that date.

It suited Macdonald's macabre sense of humour to have Allan pay even more for his sins. He hoped that the matter was now closed, yet Macdonald knew in the very depths of his political soul that more was to come, that in satisfying McMullen they were only paying for time. He looked back on McMullen's pitiable little drama with admiration – it had been a fine way of feeling out the government – for Macdonald knew that it was the government of the Dominion of Canada who were really under attack in this deadly game. But where would they strike next?

On December 27, McMullen had been seen having supper with Senator Asa B. Foster in Ottawa's favourite dining room, the Russell House. It is likely this information was passed quickly to the Prime Minister, since the Russell House, with its glittering chandeliers and long, linen-clad tables, was the best listening post in the country, and Old Tomorrow's favourite watering-hole.

On New Years Day, 1873, Jay Cooke's new contact man in Canada, Lycurgus Edgerton, wrote him that "the *opposition* generally, in the Parliament, headed by Hon. John Young, Huntington and others, will coalesce with the Government, in sustaining Allan . . . P.S. Great events, of a political character, are in the near future in Canada."[117] Cooke had known for a year that the game was up. But it suited his sporting soul to see how it would all turn out. And it interested him greatly to imagine what the optimistic Vermont Central ring – including Young and Huntington – had up their sleeves, and whether they would have any success in attaching themselves to the C.P.R. Cooke knew that by releasing incriminating letters, he would not only damage Sir Hugh Allan and the Canadian Pacific, but also the future prospects of his erstwhile colleague, J. Gregory Smith. When they learned of the dealings of the past year, European financiers would shy away from both railways.

Fearful of putting too much of a strain on Cartier's health, and careful to keep his plans out of the mails, Macdonald reported only the cabinet's proceedings to his absent friend. Cartier was pleased with the results:

> It would not have done to have given the contract to Allan's company, since it would not have been united with Macpherson's one. In forming a new company and in excluding members of Parliament, you have done the right thing. Neither Macpherson nor any Ontario man, can find a ground of real complaint with regard to the company to be organized under an Order of the Privy Council.[118]

On January 31, 1873, the cabinet finally completed the draft of the railway charter, an instrument that would lay the ghost of American influence to rest. The board of the Canadian Pacific Railway Company was to be composed of individuals drawn from both the Canada Pacific and Interoceanic companies, and from all parts of the Dominion: Donald McInnes, representing Hamilton interests; F.W. Cumberland of the Northern Railway; Sandford Fleming; Adams Archibald, lately Lieutenant-Governor of Manitoba; Burpee of New Brunswick; Sir Hugh

Allan, and others from Quebec, Beaudry, Hall and Beaubien. On February 14, following the letter of Cartier's Act, the charter was not sent through Parliament as a bill, but rather was issued and granted as a Royal Proclamation.

The great task had finally been completed, and a company established – prepared to bind the nation with two parallel lines of steel, from tidewater to tidewater.

What Cartier and Macdonald had fought for, the firm national decision to build the line, was now fixed indelibly on the political landscape of Canada. The resolution, the decision, had been the important thing all along. It broadcast Canada's desire for nationhood out over borders and oceans. It shouted sovereignty out over the shingle rooftops of Ottawa, away across the bushland, lakes, prairies and mountains, down to the islands in the sea.

Sir Francis Hincks was one of the first to see that although the hard part of the decision had been made, the first problem was emerging. The old Hyena had just endured a humiliating election defeat in South Brant, and had to accept a seat in British Columbia. He was tired of it all, and as he wrote Macdonald,

> The Pacific Railway scheme having now been fairly launched, there is no longer any reason for my deferring my long contemplated retirement from active public life . . . You and I can afford to treat with contempt the gossip of newspaper correspondents, but this is a suitable occasion for me to state that during the term of our political connection, you have invariably treated me with the greatest consideration and confidence, and that I continue to believe that the integrity of our great Dominion depends much on the success of your administration.[119]

Hincks had already been caught out once, and his eye for trouble had told him that now was the time to exit gracefully. Rumours were now rampant in Montreal about shady dealings between Cartier and Allan. The sinister McMullen had sounded out Macdonald; now he was testing the waters of public opinion, releasing a fact here, a letter there, waiting for the right time to spring his bundle to a curious opposition.

More threats came from south of the border, threats embroidered with expressions of hurt and outrage. "Sir Hugh Allan *came to us,*" protested C. Mather Smith to Macdonald, "*We* did not go to him . . . The Government alone had the address of our syndicate, and Sir Hugh's approach could not be viewed by us in courtesy or practically as resting on less than direct authority from the cabinet, and we accepted him as their representative."[120] McMullen again came to Montreal, determined to draw out the government, but Macdonald argued that the whole responsibility for the fiasco rested on the shoulders of Sir Hugh Allan. Allan had dealt with them in the first place; Allan would now have to deal his way out of trouble. Finally, McMullen was promised an additional sum to keep him satisfied for the time being, at least until the end of the coming Parliamentary Session.

On March 1, the grisly charade took a new turn with the departure of Allan, Abbott and Archibald for England to drum up interest in the London money market. Cartier and Rose were advised to prepare to meet the delegation, Rose having been told by Macdonald to be cautious of Allan:

> *Entre nous*, Allan seems to have lost his head altogether. He has made a series of most stupendous blunders with respect to the whole matter, and the Company is not yet out of the troubles caused by his imprudence. He is the worst negotiator I ever saw in my life . . . I fear that Allan's intense selfishness may blind him as to the true interests of the scheme; that is to say, I fear he will be inclined to think more about how much he can make out of the thing, than the success of the enterprise itself. I fear too that he will be attempting to fasten his North Shore Railway and the Northern Colonization scheme upon the Pacific, and if he does he will of necessity arouse the opposition of all those interested in the Grand Trunk Railway.[121]

The trip was a disaster, a fraud – probably everyone but Allan knew it – but it had to be made. They would find no money in England, no real financial support – there was none to be had. But they had to be seen to be trying. The play had to drag on to its ridiculous, inexorable conclusion.

Allan had hardly stepped off the boat before he was informed by Sir John Rose that "our mission has no chance of success."[122] After only a brief, perfunctory interview with Cartier, the undaunted Allan got to work. To his dismay, he found that the Barings and Glyns, backers of the Grand Trunk and the Hudson's Bay Company, had firmly closed their doors to the delegation, and the Rothschilds were unwilling to go beyond passing the time of day. What was now beginning to be called "the Pacific Scandal" was being read about by the bankers in the city daily.

What was worse, the Grand Trunk, always ready to pick up the pieces, let Allan know that they would restrain their opposition if, and only if, he would drop his Northern Colonization Railway scheme and give them the line from Montreal to Nipissing Junction. This the proud Laird of Ravenscrag would never do! Cartier had the last and best laugh as Allan, in desperation, cabled Macdonald and asked him to hold up the Grand Trunk Aid Bill, now on the floor of Parliament. By the time Macdonald had replied that he would do what he could, Allan had given up. The sun seemed to have set on his dreams.

Even with Allan firmly in his place, Jay Cooke's agent was proving to be a problem. What Macdonald did not know, but probably suspected, was the McMullen had already sold his packet to another bidder. In fact, the price McMullen got was $25,000, allegedly paid by Senator Asa B. Foster.[123] Foster probably realized that the letters would blow the whole Pacific project open, but they could be released to the potential advantage of the Canada Central and Vermont Central Railways. On February 3, he wrote ominously to Macdonald that he had "seen all the papers that were shown to you by McMullen and some that were not. I had an understanding with Allan and the Americans that I was to have 3½% interest, and . . . the Americans were to furnish the funds."[124] Foster probably was obliquely suggesting to Macdonald that unless he was made a member of the C.P.R. Board, he would cause these letters to be released. Macdonald did not budge.

Macdonald had played the amalgamation game and had the charter set up so well that he felt the letters could not prove that the government was in the wrong. The letters could do nothing more than discredit Sir Hugh Allan. The cabinet's hands were clean; it had insisted all along that Allan abandon his links with the Americans; only when Allan assured the cabinet that he had done so, was he awarded the Presidency of the Canadian Pacific Railway Company.

There might be other damning evidence, but Macdonald doubted it. He had done everything possible, and had done it brilliantly, to save Allan's skin, cover the government, and prevent the collapse of the Canadian Pacific Railway. What he did not know was that the Jay Cooke ring, now out of the running for the charter, had sold their bundle to the Gregory Smith ring, a rare instance of honour among thieves.

At this point, Allan's Eastern Township friends were determined to exact revenge for the treatment they had received from Cartier and the Grand Trunk, and to ensure that J. Gregory Smith would get his bridge across the St. Lawrence. There is a story that, one damp, chilly night in March of 1873, one George Norris, Abbott's confidential clerk, accompanied by a younger man, entered the Allan Line office using a key, and systematically and rapidly, opened the safe, drew out letter books and dockets, copied them, and then as quickly and efficiently as they had come, the two tidied up, locked the door behind them, and drove away into the night.

The story was probably a neat piece of fabrication by Abbott and his Vermont Central friends. Norris, according to his boss Abbott, was a man "desperately ill from venereal disease,"[125] who stole the documents because he was deranged. In any event, Norris received $5,000 for his exploits or lack of them, paid by the *Rouge* M.P. Laflamme. It is doubtful whether Allan had anything to do with this "theft" of documents from his office. Foster and Gregory Smith and Abbott and Huntington had decided to let their Trojan Horse go, because he was playing along with Macdonald to their detriment, playing both ends against the middle. But they were now where they wanted to be, inside the walls of

Troy, and Allan was just so much excess baggage. What the proud Laird of Ravenscrag had never stopped to realize was that his Northern Colonization Railway would be of no use to the Canada Central and Vermont Central Railways, after a bridge had been built across the St. Lawrence at Ogdensburg.

What Macdonald did not know he feared, and as he prepared for the opening of Parliament, his lack of knowledge numbed him. March 5 dawned cool and bright; its bracing air invigorated even Macdonald. But as he drove with his wife in an open carriage through the streets of Ottawa, heard the boom of the Field Artillery's battery and thrilled at the pomp and circumstance insisted upon by the new Governor General, he found himself impatient with time, restless at the prospect of defending a pedestrian Throne Speech, and nervous about the accusations he knew would surface in the House. He thought of Cartier. Cartier was not there to drink with him, laugh at his stories, or sing him a song. Cartier was not there to draw fire, call in the members, hurl his thunderbolts and marshal the facts. He was probably now suffering horribly. In his place, there was a cabinet and a caucus who would have to be told what to expect, and what to do when the expected came.

The next three weeks saw the usual petty wrangling over details of the government's planned policy, and a little irrelevant fencing. Alexander Mackenzie protested that, while the Liberal Party did not oppose construction of the Canadian Pacific Railway, it must object that the government had not properly averted the dangers of foreign control. If Mackenzie only knew! Macdonald replied that the cabinet had spared nothing to keep "the entire control of this great Canadian enterprise in Canadian hands, and to ensure its being dealt with by Canadian means and Canadian ingenuity and skill, and by Canadian or English capital, or both."[126]

It was obvious to Macdonald that Mackenzie was merely stalling for time, and for the first time he sensed that the opposition had more up their sleeves, that they were putting together what would be their most concentrated attack on his government since Confederation.

The Americans had done their work well. Macdonald knew he would have to tax his political ingenuity and cunning to the utmost to survive the onslaught. But when would it come, and who would be the man to do it?

11 "His yearning after Canada was preying so upon his mind . . . . "

Josephine Cartier to Sir John A. Macdonald, May 22, 1873

To be fair to the Liberals, they delayed lowering the boom until they had learned that the railway delegation in England was having little or no success in tapping the London money market.

On April 2, Macdonald watched with disdain as that annexationist and small-time railway promoter, the member for Shefford, Lucius Seth Huntington, known in the House for his smiling manner and "agreeable" speeches, rose to put the case for the prosecution. What better man to do it! A year previously, Macdonald had suggested to a newly elected member, W.H. Gibbs, that "a party, like a snake, is moved by its tail. The tail of the Grit party is the Annexation section."[127] If any man represented that tail, it was Lucius Seth Huntington. Macdonald listened, scarcely concealing his disgust, as Huntington, in his nasal drawl, without explanation and with only the faintest of smiles playing across his bland face, moved, since he was "credibly informed" and believed that he could "establish by satisfactory evidence" that, since

> an understanding was come to between the Government and Sir Hugh Allan and Mr. Abbott, M.P., – that Sir Hugh Allan and his friends should advance a large sum of money for the purpose of aiding the elections of Ministers and their supporters at the ensuing General Election – and that he and his friends should receive the contract for the construction of the Railway; that accordingly Sir Hugh Allan did advance a large sum of money for the purpose mentioned, and at the solicitation, and under the pressing instances of Ministers; that part of the monies, expended by Sir Hugh Allan in connection with the obtaining of the Act of Incorporation and Charter, were paid by the said United States Capitalists under the agreement with him, that a committee of seven should be struck to enquire into the whole affair.[128]

When Huntington resumed his seat, a pall of silence descended over the House. Macdonald was silent, and his entire caucus sat poker-faced as the eyes of the opposition flickered over them, searching for any sign, any break in unanimity. There was little; they had all heard the rumours. The motion, treated as a confidence vote, was called, and at division, the House split exactly on party lines, 107 Conservatives to seventy-six Liberals. Unfortunately for the Conservatives, their supporters included a large number of lukewarm independents, who, if they were to defect, could easily put Alexander Mackenzie into office.

On adjournment, Macdonald calmly rose, went straight to his office, and shot off a cable to Cartier. Then he began to think, and think fast. What was Huntington's game? Why was he involving his railway crony Abbott in the whole affair? He knew that the Liberals would likely attempt to orchestrate the release of the documents, timing it so as to make the most effective impact on the independents. Delay was surely the best tactic, and the next day, Macdonald brought the first trick out of his well-stocked bag. He moved for a Select Committee to meet behind closed doors, composed of three Conservatives, and the Liberals Blake and Dorion, whom he might be able to trust with the truth. The motion was passed, and Macdonald sat back to see what developed.

On April 10, he wrote Cartier that he was pleased with the vote of confidence, "but Council felt that we could not properly allow it to remain in that position. I accordingly, the very next day, gave notice that I would move for a committee. It was fortunate that we took that course, as we found great uneasiness among our friends . . . It looked so like stifling an enquiry that they were afraid of the consequences to themselves in their constituencies." To Cartier's relief, he noted that "Huntington's motion is, I understand, founded altogether on letters written by Allan to McMullen of Chicago. The imprudence of Sir Hugh in this whole matter has almost amounted to insanity. His language has been as wild as his letters, and, between you and me, the examination must result greatly to his discredit." In an orgy of irony and understatement, Macdonald concluded by saying, "I fear that our friend Sir Hugh is not getting on so well as we would wish with the Pacific Ry. scheme. However he must do his best, and we must trust to luck. I do not see any other rocks ahead."[129]

In reply, Cartier said that he "felt so much relieved in my mind to know that you have had such triumph." Returning the irony, he said that he regarded Huntington's motion as "malicious," that "the *Yankee* [indecipherable] *McMullen* must be at the bottom of the mischief."[130] Cartier knew that the government had very little to fear from the release of any of Allan's correspondence with the Americans, and knew that Allan would damage his own case if any of the money demands cabled in the last election were released.

What he and Macdonald did not fully recognize was Abbott's deep involvement with the Vermont Central ring. They did not know at this point that the money telegrams had been "stolen" and were in Huntington's hands. The only danger, as Macdonald saw it, lay in Sir Hugh Allan's deliberate lies to the Americans in some of his letters, especially his brazen statements that he had "made an agreement" with the government, that he had been "promised" a majority of the stock.

While Cartier waited restlessly for further news, Macdonald tried another trick to confound the opposition and the independents. On his advice, Macpherson stood up in the Senate on April 17 and moved that Allan's charter be withdrawn, for patriotic reasons. Macdonald knew that wavering Ontario Conservatives would not waver so much if they felt that they could convince the cabinet to change its mind. This would keep the fish on the hook for the time being.

By the middle of April, the Commons discovered that Macdonald had neglected to mention that a Select Committee could not take evidence on oath. Furthermore, if Parliament were prorogued, the Committee would also have to suspend operations at the same time. After a few days of wrangling, Macdonald offered to transform the Committee into a Royal Commission, but the opposition, wishing to keep the fight on the floor of Parliament, objected on the grounds that a Royal Commission would be nothing more than a tool of the government. Macdonald then pulled out another trick, and pushed through a special Oaths Bill empowering the Select Committee to examine witnesses on oath. Parliament would not be prorogued; it would simply adjourn and then receive the report in the autumn, when the Committee had done its business.

While constitutional experts tried to decide whether the Oaths Bill was legal, the government got down to some serious business. On May 3, Macdonald introduced a bill, one he had worked on with Cartier, providing for the establishment of the Royal North-West Mounted Police; and on May 17, Tilley moved a resolution that would admit Prince Edward Island, suffering from the impending bankruptcy of its own shore-to-shore railway, into the Canadian Confederation. Once again, a part of British North America was to be "railroaded" into the union. One other measure established a Department of the Interior, to administer the Dominion Lands Act, passed the previous year.

Still playing for time, Macdonald clung to his Oaths Bill, and the Select Committee began its sittings. A few weeks later, he "remembered" that three of the star witnesses, Cartier, Allan and Abbott, were in England, and he then objected that it was unfair to those three to examine the case without giving them an opportunity to reply to the charges. Under the circumstances, he must ask the committee to adjourn until July 2. It could do nothing but accept his recommendation.

Back in England, Allan still would not abandon his search for funding, and kept hounding Macdonald to call off the Grand Trunk. But Macdonald was prepared to deal Allan the final blow. "I have received your letters," he wrote the Laird, "and greatly regret the opposition that you seem to have received from the Grand Trunk Railway Co." He added that he had received a promise from Brydges that there would be "no opposition to the Pacific Railway scheme, but that the Grand Trunk Railway would cordially assist in the project. This, however, was not to extend to the rival lines east of Nipissing, which they felt themselves at liberty to oppose."[131] What Macdonald was finally saying to him was that Allan would find it extremely difficult, if not impossible, to get control of the Montreal-Nipissing section of the line.

Macdonald's hopes for time were fulfilled even further when he received the expected reply from the law officers of the British Crown: the Oaths Act was *ultra vires*, and could not be allowed. There would be a Royal Commission, and the facts would be placed before the people of Canada for their judgment! And the Liberals, knowing now that they had been tricked, would show their hand at last!

Macdonald's worst fears were confirmed on May 15, when Huntington submitted an extensive list of witnesses to be examined before the Royal Commission. In addition, Huntington explicitly charged that Allan had paid the staggering sum of $350,000 to obtain the charter from the government. The news hit Macdonald like a bombshell. Somehow his opponents had got hold of the money telegrams! How else could they know or prove what had happened? Had they been stolen? Had Allan finally realized that he had been played for a fool, and now wanted revenge? Or were Abbott and J. Gregory Smith behind this new development? He and Cartier had not been overly concerned by the possible release of McMullen's correspondence – Allan would suffer more than the government – but now the game was in deadly earnest.

Cartier would be coming home soon. He had written regretting that he could not share "your troubles and your work,"[132] and said that he would be sailing on May 29. Together they could plan a way to extract themselves from this shambles.

Despite Dr. Johnstone's assurances, Cartier continued to grow weaker. He suffered terribly from what he believed were rheumatic pains, and became totally bedridden. He was desperate for news from Canada, and had his family read him all the newspapers for clues as to what was happening in the final days of the session. He noted, with mixed feelings, the death of former U.S. Secretary of State William Seward on April 17. A worthy enemy. On May 13, while visiting the Foreign Office, he had a relapse, and had to be carried back to his lodgings. Four days later, in great pain and suffering, he asked his daughter, twenty-six-year old Josephine, to bring him pen and paper. He began his letter, "My dear Macdonald," but was so weak he was unable to continue. Josephine took down the remainder:

LONDON, 47 Welbeck St., West,
May 17th, 1873

My dear Macdonald, – I am ill in bed since a few days suffering from rheumatic pains in chest. I am so weak I cannot hold a pen and I use Josephine to write for me. I hope to get rid of my pain in a few days and always propose to sail on the 29th of May. Allan communicated to me your last about Grand Trunk and other matters. You did well in writing him thus. I have not as yet got a reply from Lord Kimberley about the extension of the railway building time, but I expect it from day to day. Very likely he is waiting for the opinion of the law officers on the subject. With regard to my disease Dr. Johnstone says I am progressing as well as possible. But the cold weather and the cold wind we are having here since several weeks do not work favourably for me. I presume you have prorogued or you are on the eve of doing so. My kind remembrances to our colleagues and the same from us all to Lady Macdonald. And, my dear Macdonald, believe me, as always,

Yours very sincerely,

P. Josephine Cartier.   G.E. CARTIER[133]

As Josephine later wrote to Macdonald,

Life was ebbing away quietly, and none of us could perceive it. On Sunday night, however, this evil work became conspicuous, and several doctors were called in. All agreed, on Monday night, that another consultation would take place on Tuesday morning at nine o'clock, as danger was imminent. That night he slept, which was unusual of late, and, towards dawn, mamma, who had been at his bedside all night, left the room for a few minutes, with some of the attendants. On her returning, a change had occurred; she gave the alarm. Doctors, clergymen were called, and all was over in twenty minutes. He rallied strength and told us himself, "I am dying."

He was conscious until the end, recognizing them all, and speaking French to them and English to his valet, Thomas Vincent. He did not complain, but was obviously in great pain until he died. He was given the last rites in the presence of his wife and daughters, and at six o'clock in the morning of Tuesday, May 20, 1873, peace finally came to Sir George-Etienne Cartier.

Josephine wrote Macdonald:

The body being embalmed cannot sail before the 29th inst. Thomas, his devoted attendant, is unable to accompany it; in fact the shock was so great that we are all prostrated. All friends in England show us a deep and most heartfelt sympathy; but mamma, my sister and myself intend leaving London after the funeral service, to recover a little before sailing for Canada. Thomas sails on the first week of June. From him you can learn more than I can write today.

Pray accept our united kind regards to you, dear Sir John, and to Lady Macdonald, and also to all the members of the Canadian Cabinet, whom four days ago my poor father still called so fondly "his colleagues," and believe me,

Your most sincere little friend,

JOSEPHINE CARTIER[134]

At two o'clock in the afternoon of May 20, Macdonald was sitting in

Cartier and his daughters outside their Ottawa house. (Notman).

his office preparing for the day's session, when he received a sealed cable from Sir John Rose in London giving him the news that Cartier was dead. That he had expected this news did not make it any less terrible, and Macdonald wept.

The news spread fast. By three o'clock, the galleries of Parliament were packed, and nearly every member in his seat. They watched silently as a pathetic, red-eyed Macdonald took his seat, front row centre, next to a desk whose emptiness now seemed so frighteningly real; and then they listened, as he rose and said:

> Mr. Speaker, I have a painful duty to fulfil to this House. I have received a telegram this morning from Sir John Rose, which I will read to the House.
>
> "Sir George Cartier had a relapse last Tuesday and he died peacefully at six o'clock this morning. His body will be sent by Quebec steamer on the 29th.
>
> ROSE."[135]
>
> I feel myself quite unable to say more at this moment.

Sir John A. Macdonald sank back into his seat and his eyes filled with tears. Now sobbing uncontrollably, he placed his right arm on Cartier's desk and buried his head in his left, while his whole body shook with grief. The House sat stunned until his sorrow fell and he was quiet.

Langevin rose, hardly daring to speak his own feelings. Mackenzie followed, then Cauchon, then Dorion. Then a composed Macdonald spoke again, saying that he intended to make a motion that a grateful country grant Cartier a state funeral. On Friday, May 23, he proposed

> that a humble address be presented to His Excellency the Governor-General that he would be graciously pleased to give directions that the remains of the honourable Sir George E. Cartier be interred at the public expense, and that a monument be erected to the memory of that excellent statesman with an inscription descriptive of the public sense of so great and irreparable a loss and to assure His Excellency that the House would make good the expenses attending the same.[136]

The resolution was adopted, and the Members of Parliament waited for the homecoming of Cartier's mortal remains.

EPILOGUE

"Les quatres saisons de l'année,
Offrent tour à tour leurs attraits.
Au printemps, l'amante enjouée
Revoit ses fleurs, ses verts bosquets.

Le moissonneur, l'été, joyeux s'apprête
A recueillir le fruit de ses labours.
Et tout l'automne et tout l'hiver, on fête.
O Canada! mon pays! mes amours!"

George-Etienne Cartier

Last Rites

Two days after the death of George-Etienne Cartier, a funeral service was held in the French Chapel on Portman Square. Lady Cartier was too ill to attend, but Cartier's two daughters were there, as well as Luce Cuvillier, Lord Lisgar, Sir Hugh Allan, Sir John Rose and Abel Gauthier, the former French Consul at Quebec and one of his dearest friends.

Cartier's body was placed in a sealed coffin, and Rose arranged to have it sent back to Canada on board the old Allan Line Steamship *Prussian*. On the morning of June 8, it was taken off the *Prussian* and placed in a polished elm casket, then, to the booming of the Citadel guns, drawn slowly through the streets of Quebec, past his great-grandfather's old warehouse, up to the Cathedral. Five thousand citizens heard a mass sung by Vicar-General Langevin, and watched as the militia band, playing the Dead March from *Saul* and Mozart's *Requiem*, escorted the coffin back down to the quays, where, at 8:30 p.m., it was placed in a specially-prepared chapel on the deck of the government steamer *Druid*.

Druid sailed slowly up Jacques Cartier's "River of Canada," stopping for a service at Trois-Rivières the next day. On that same day, Lady Dufferin and her children were passing down the river to Quebec. The Governor General's wife described the journey in her journal:

We had a delightful cruise down the river, and an exciting descent of the Rapids. In one place we passed within a few inches of a wreck, and we felt quite creepy. At Montreal we changed steamers. The children were delighted with the grandeur of the St. Lawrence boats, with the enormous saloons and state-cabins. When we were at tea we heard some music – the "Dead March" – being played; and looking out, we saw, passing slowly in the darkness, the steamer with the body of Sir

George Cartier on board; it was a stirring moment – the chapel on board lighted up, the band playing, and bells tolling at sea, answered by bells tolling on shore.

When *Druid* reached the Richelieu, it steamed up and dropped anchor below the House of the Seven Chimneys, where the family and visitors came on board and masses were said. The following day, it passed down the river and headed up toward Montreal. When it neared Longue Pointe at the eastern end of the island, Militia Battery "B", stationed by Limoilou, boomed out a seventeen-gun salute for its late chief.

Cartier's state funeral – held on Friday, June 13 – was criticized as extravagant by the Toronto *Globe*. Certainly, it was fit for a reigning monarch, or at the very least, a Napoleon Bonaparte. An estimated 75,000 people, half of them from outside Montreal, passed by his casket as it lay in state, under a black velvet dome in the Palais de Justice.

At 9:00 a.m. on that beautiful late spring day, the casket was loaded on an enormous twenty-two-foot high funeral car for the procession to the Cathedral. This hearse was, by all accounts, the very epitome of French Canadian funeral art. Draped with heavy black cloth, decorated in panels mounted with silver stars and festooned with Cartier's coat of arms and monogram, it was surmounted with a huge silver cross and drawn by eight black horses.

As the procession left the court house, the Grand Trunk Infantry and the Montreal Field Battery thundered out a volley, which was answered by the guns on St. Helen's Island. Together they boomed away on the minute until the church service two hours later. When the carriage passed the house of Francois-Pierre Pominville, Cartier's law partner, the old man tottered out onto his black-draped balcony, then sank back into his chair with grief. Shortly after, the cross on the top of the hearse was wrenched off by some overhead telegraph wires, but it was rescued before it fell to the ground.

At 11:00 a.m., the pall bearers – Hincks, Sicotte, Galt, Howland, Belleau, Dorion and Doutre – carried the coffin up to the transept of the Cathedral and placed it on an enormous base inscribed with the words,

Homme sincere – A Sincere Man
Homme droit – An Upright Man
Homme firme – A Firm Man
Homme honnête – An Honest Man

and the motto, "Sir George Cartier, L'ami de son pays" – "Sir George Cartier, the friend of his country." Surmounting the pillars around the base was a twenty-six-foot high cross, and below was a bust of Jacques Cartier and the words, "Je revis dans mon descendant" – "I survive in my descendant." As if this were not enough, the casket was surrounded by myriad pieces of statuary, weeping and praying figures, guardian angels, funeral urns and enormous wreathed vases, and the windows of the Cathedral were draped with purple velvet cloth, giving the whole scene – as one participant put it – an air of heavy solemnity. Mass was sung by Cartier's brother-in-law, Monseigneur Fabre.

Sir John A. Macdonald did not feel up to marching in the funeral procession, but he pulled himself together long enough to attend the service. According to Lord Dufferin, "he was in a very bad way – not at all himself – indeed quite prostrate."

Sir George-Etienne Cartier was buried in the Côte-des-Neiges Cemetery, near the grave of Ludger Duvernay. A funeral elegy was read by Joseph Doutre, his old duelling opponent. In 1917, the coffin was moved to a special plot in the new Mount Royal Cemetery.

The Canadian government voted Cartier's widow a $1200 pension, and she and her daughters retired to a villa at Cannes in the south of France. The elder daughter Josephine died there in 1886, Lady Cartier twelve years later, but his daughter Hortense outlived them both. In 1914, she attended a celebration in Montreal marking the one hundredth anniversary of her father's birth, and had some interesting things to say about John A.'s son, Sir Hugh John Macdonald, who had recently had his leg amputated:

> Sir John A. was a frequent visitor at our home, and you know how parents are. They said together, "We will make a closed corporation of Canada. We will marry Hugh to Hortense." But Hugh said, "I wouldn't have her." You couldn't blame him, could you? I trust he will recover rapidly and completely.

After the fall of France in 1940, Hortense Cartier left the villa at Cannes and settled in London, England, where she died the following year at the age of ninety-three. Her body was brought back to Canada by the family in 1952 and reinterred next to her father in Mount Royal Cemetery.

A Postscript on Railways

On Friday, May 23, 1873, two days after the announcement of Cartier's death, the stock of the Montreal Northern Colonization Railway shot up to record heights. A few days later, Royal Assent was given to a bill granting the railway an extension to Hull, making it, because it now was to cross provincial borders, a federal as well as a provincial company. Henceforward, it would also be under the control of the federal cabinet. Joseph Cauchon would have to wait a long time before seeing a north shore line built to Quebec City, and a disappointed Curé Labelle, who wanted the railway to go further north into the Laurentians, saw it diverted west to Ottawa and amalgamated with the Canada Central. Now called the Quebec, Montreal, Ottawa and Occidental Railway, the line was finished in February of 1878. By then practically bankrupt, it was swallowed up by the Canadian Pacific Railway of Donald Smith and his cousin George Stephen.

By August 15, 1873, the Northern Pacific Railway was indebted to the banking firm of Jay Cooke and Company to the tune of $7,000,000. A week later, a government employee in Toronto telegraphed John A. Macdonald, "Geo. W. McMullen is here what is your wish or desire?" Macdonald wired back, "I have no wish or desire except that Mr. McMullen should attend and give his evidence before the Commission."

On September 4, 1873, the Royal Commission began its hearings in the Parliament Buildings in Ottawa, but without the presence of McMullen, Foster or Huntington, Macdonald was unable to bring out the whole story of the Pacific Scandal. Perhaps he did not really want to: Donald A. Smith, whose testimony might have proved most interesting – if he chose to give any – was not called as a witness because of the "distance and subsequent delay" involved in bringing the Member for H.B.C. all the way back from Manitoba. Perhaps Macdonald's political nose – always adept at smelling out the long-term advantage – told him that his fall from power was inevitable, that it would be best to go out of office as quietly and as advantageously as possible, just as he had done so many times before with Cartier. How else can we explain what is probably nothing more than a bare-faced lie, in the following letter written by Macdonald to Lord Dufferin:

> It is too evident . . . from the evidence that has come out before the Commissioners, that Sir Hugh Allan took undue advantage of the failing health and waning mental faculties of Sir George . . . Not until after his death, and the evidence was produced, were any of his colleagues aware of his insane course. As I have already said, it showed too clearly that mind had broken down as well as body. Of course I can say this to you only, as I would rather suffer any consequence than cast reflection on his memory before the public, or say anything that would have even the appearance of an attempt to transfer any blame that may attach to these transactions to one who is no longer here to speak for himself. No member of the Government here knew or had any suspicion of the nature of the arrangement made between Sir George and Sir Hugh Allan, or of the papers signed by the former until they were recently published. I certainly did not.

Now if there is a Heaven, and if Cartier did indeed look down on Macdonald as he wrote this letter, it is quite probable that Cartier forgave him for his excesses. Cartier would have understood that Macdonald, unable fully to prove the circumstances behind the Pacific Scandal, and doubtless wishing – even longing – to go out of power before the depression made its effects felt, might have tried to calm the official waters and keep his reputation intact with a fussy Governor General. He was not called Old Tomorrow for nothing. Nor was Cartier called the Lightning

Striker for nothing; but no thunderbolts rained down on Macdonald's head as he sat hunched over his writing desk, still "in a bad way," shedding a well-oiled tear for his departed friend.

Ten days later, he got the expected reply from Lord Dufferin: "In spite of Cartier's weakness, you have religiously protected the interests of Canada both against the American speculators who addressed you, and against the approaches of Sir Hugh Allan."

On the night of September 17, 1873, President Ulysses S. Grant arrived at Jay Cooke's palace, "Ogontz," outside Philadelphia. The two had a fine meal, and retired to the drawing room where they drank whisky and smoked the private brand of cigars Cooke supplied to the President. Their discussion was not recorded. The next day, the doors on Jay Cooke's banks in New York and Philadelphia swung shut. The great depression that followed was to last until 1879 and bankrupt an estimated 5,000 American businesses. According to an associate of Andrew Carnegie, "you could not even give away a rolling mill." The railway bubble had burst, not only in the United States, but in Canada, and around the world.

On November 5, 1873, the Macdonald government resigned. With Jay Cooke bankrupt, his railway could not threaten the C.P.R., at least not until the return of prosperity. Waiting for that day was Cartier's good friend Donald A. Smith, whose defection from the government's ranks had precipitated Macdonald's resignation. It is most tempting to think that the whole Smith defection was engineered with Macdonald, because five years later both men re-emerged hale and hearty to resurrect the railroad. It certainly allowed Macdonald, Smith and Charles Tupper – who called it "the Pacific Slander" – to exercise their political histrionics to the fullest.

Early in 1874, a Montreal wag calling himself "Alphonzo Stilletto" penned the following little ballad:

> And here, I may tell you, that Sir John is in luck
> Because of the death of Sir George, through whose pluck,
> The *pivot* of action was only himself –
> 'Twas HE that sold all for an ignoble pelf!(?)
> But as to the terms, *not a mortal will know*,
> For *dead men are quiet* with friend or with foe;
> Hence George will remain with his secrets interred,
> And never respond to the charges preferred.

Most Canadians were content to leave it at that, to blame the debacle on a dead man who could tell no tales. Cartier's demise was indeed a convenient one, although I would argue that, had he lived, he would have played the game a little differently, a little more dangerously than Sir John A.

Macdonald was able to extract some revenge on Senator Asa B. Foster.

In 1877, he had a backbencher stand up and charge that "It is a notorious fact that the information used to turn out the late government was furnished by the Hon. A.B. Foster, and everybody expected that the hon. gentleman would receive his reward for the same. And he did. The manner in which the contracts for the Georgian Bay Branch and the Canada Central Railway were let showed it . . . He was the gentleman who furnished the noted letter at the time of the McMullen developments a few years ago." Foster did not reply to the charge; his involvement with the Vermont Central soon bankrupted him; he spent some time in a Vermont prison for bad debts, and died shortly after.

The Northern Pacific Railway was finally completed in 1883, two years before the C.P.R. In 1891, a frail old man in a white beard – the Tycoon himself – made the journey from Duluth to Tacoma as a guest of the railroad. Two years later it was bankrupt again. The Canadian Pacific, on the other hand, was, to all intents and purposes, an unqualified success.

As for Cartier's beloved Grand Trunk Railway, it eventually swallowed up John Young's Montreal and Vermont Junction Railway and Foster and Huntington's Stanstead, Shefford and Chambly Railway. By 1885, the G.T.R. had virtual control of Gregory Smith's Vermont Central, having bought up shares and options to prevent them from falling into more hostile hands. Smith never got his railway bridge at Ogdensburg.

A final, ironic postscript – the Grand Trunk soon found that the Vermont Central was a financial liability, and in 1896, unloaded it to the Canadian Pacific, who were seeking an alternative to the Grand Trunk's line to Portland, Maine. The Grand Trunk, having lost the first race to build a railway to the Pacific, practically bankrupted itself in building the Grand Trunk Pacific, and was rescued by the Borden government, to form the nucleus of the state-owned Canadian National Railway.

The French Canadians and Confederation

Cartier's transcontinental railway policy was ultimately a success, but his desire to provide new areas for French Canadian settlement was not. I suspect his heart was not entirely in it. As late as June 5, 1872, one of Archbishop Taché's agents, J.-B. Proulx, had a frustrating interview with Cartier, and sarcastically reported the meeting as an insult to his intelligence:

> M. Cartier, *ta ta ta, c'est bon, c'est bon,* says we must make Manitoba a French province. The people of Ontario can jump over it and have Saskatchewan, *ta ta ta.*

The policy belonged less to Cartier than to Taché, who wanted French

Canadian expansion to Manitoba to shield the Métis and promote further missionary work. He worked diligently through his brother, who was Deputy Minister of Agriculture, and founded the Société de Colonization de Manitoba, but unfortunately, he ran into opposition from Quebec colonization societies, and in the end, from the Quebeckers' innate fear of the north and their unwillingness to live outside the Province of Quebec. To move to Manitoba was to emigrate, to commit an act of betrayal. The result was that the French Canadian element in Manitoba decreased from 50 per cent of the population at the time of the Red River insurrection, to slightly over 7 per cent in 1891, twenty years later. Marc Laterreur has explained this phenomenon, and argued that English-speaking Canadians must recognize it:

> The Quebec francophone does not wish to be enveloped in the great Canadian whole; he is a citizen of Quebec before Canada. It is high time that English-Canadians lose their illusions and stop dreaming. They must accept – or reject – French Canada as it exists, and not as they would wish it to be; and they must accommodate themselves to what French Canada desires, on the condition that these desires are finally clearly expressed.

Perhaps the one word that can express these desires is "survival." It was certainly an important one in Cartier's vocabulary.

If the British North America Act is ever "patriated" – unilaterally, multilaterally, or as one wag has suggested, by its immediate repeal in the British Parliament – the statements and opinions of the Fathers of Confederation will doubtless have to be examined in the light of modern regional and national needs. A study of Cartier may not be all that relevant when considering the *particularities* of a revised Constitution. Chief Justice Bora Laskin once wrote that

> The intentions of the founders cannot, except by chance, provide solutions for problems of which they never dreamed . . . All the historical interpretations go far afield for their arguments. There is no final certainty as to what the framers meant by the use of these phrases. The records of the time have not preserved all their opinions on all parts. Clear statements of the views of some on particular points have come down to us; of the views of others, nothing is known.

Nevertheless, the *general* desires of Cartier and the other founding fathers are known, and the spirit of compromise with which they framed the Act should be an inspiration to future tinkerers and draftsmen. As Senator Eugene Forsey has declared, "A Canadian Anglo-French partnership was the vision of Cartier and Macdonald. It is not obsolete."

With regard to the attitude of the average French Canadians toward Confederation, J.-C. Bonenfant has written that they generally accepted federalism as inevitable, yet "did not have any elevated theoretical vision about it, and would have been incapable of carrying on any discussion of the majority of problems posed today, problems they never dreamt would exist." But as Ernest Lapointe once said, "the federal power is the child of the provinces, not the father": the French Canadians who voted for Confederation trusted the new system to the extent that they gave over interpretation of Articles 91, 92, 93 and 133 of the British North America Act – definitive articles – to the federal government and its Anglo majority.

Although a young Wilfrid Laurier would call Confederation "the tomb of the French race and the ruin of Lower Canada," Cartier knew that the French Canadians possessed a cultural solidarity that would manifest itself in the political sphere, and rare is the federal government that can stand for long without taking French desires into account. The fusion of the races Cartier called "a utopia, an impossibility," and trusted the English not to abuse the system and threaten French Canadian survival. If they did, he knew that "the mass of the people" would rise up and fight, more than they had done in 1837, when he was a rebel.

The Leopard

One evening in 1871, a young M.P.P. named Wilfrid Laurier, in company with a few of his friends, was waiting for a train in the lobby of the Hotel Victoria in Lévis, across from Québec, when the Minister of Militia walked in the door. They expected him to talk about politics, but "He came up to us," related Laurier, "and began talking to us with great excitement. He spoke to us of his poems; he even sang to us one of his songs, not the one which all the world knows, 'O Canada, Mon Pays, Mes Amours,' but another of which I recall the two last verses: 'Le Léopard me tient mains et pieds Liés'."

The song was 'Un Souvenir de 1837,' written by Cartier thirty-three years earlier when he was in exile with a price on his head. The poetry is of course untranslatable, but I have supplied a rough literal meaning below:

UN SOUVENIR DE 1837

Air: *Combien j'ai douce souvenance.*

Dans le brilliant de la jeunesse
Ou tout n'est qu'espoir, allégresse,
Je vis captif en proie à la tristesse,
En tremblant je vois l'avenir
    Venir.

De longtemps ma douce Patrie
Pleurait sous les fers asservie;

Et, désireux de la voir affranchie,
Du combat j'attendais l'instant
   Gaîment.

Mais advint l'heure d'espérance
Où j'entrevoyais délivrance;
Eh! mon pays, en surcroit de souffrance,
Mars contraria tes vaillants
   Enfants.

Et, moi, victime infortunée
De cette fatale journée,
Le léopard sous sa griffe irritée
Sans pitié me tient mains et pieds
   Liés.

La reverrai-je cette amie
Naguère qui charmait ma vie,
Souvent en moi son image chérie
Fait soupirer dans sa douleur
   Mon coeur.

Adieu! ma natale contrée
Qu'à jamais je vois enchaînée,
Fasse le ciel qu'une autre destinée
T'accorde un fortuné retour
   Un jour!

(In my bright and shining youth, When all is hope and joy, I saw myself
captured by sadness, and trembling, saw the future unfold.
For so long my sweet homeland wept in her chains of slavery, I wanted
to see her free, and waited gaily for the moment of battle.
But came the hour of hope, of glimpsed deliverance, and O my country,
you suffered more – Mars betrayed your brave sons,
And me, the poor, sad victim of this fatal day. The pitiless leopard, with
unsheathed claws, binds me hand and foot.
Will I ever see my love again, she who not so long ago claimed my life?
Often her beloved image makes my heart sigh with sadness.
Farewell the country of my birth, that I still see in chains. Heaven grant
that another destiny brings your fortune back one day!)

When Cartier sang his song to those young men, he knew he was
dying. It therefore assumes a special poignancy. It was, I believe, his
most poetic utterance, and, in those circumstances, his heartfelt hail and
farewell.

George-Etienne Cartier, 1871 (PAC).

BIBLIOGRAPHY

"We have beside us a mountain of Books, Magazines, Pamphlets and Newspapers, that have been accumulating for the past two months, unopened and unread. Like a Turk, in the dim twilight of his Harem, we scarcely know which to choose . . . . "

Joseph Howe, *Novascotian*, May 2, 1833

MANUSCRIPTS

The following collections in the Public Archives of Canada were consulted: Baring Papers; George Brown Papers; Cartier Papers; Château de Ramezay Papers; Galt Papers; LaFontaine Papers; J.A. Macdonald Papers; Tupper Papers. In the Archives nationales de Québec, and at Laval University, the Chapais Papers, Chauveau Papers, Langevin Papers and E-R Fabre Papers, as well as H.B.M Best's thesis, "George-Etienne Cartier" (Laval, 1969) were examined. In Montreal, the Château de Ramezay Collection yielded up some items of interest.

PRINTED SOURCES

Province of Canada: The Sessional Papers, Journals of the Legislative Council, Journals of the Legislative Assembly and Debates (CLA microfilm) were studied, as well as the *Parliamentary Debates on the Subject of the Confederation of the British North American Provinces* (Quebec, 1865).

Dominion of Canada: The Statutes, Sessional Papers, Journals and Commons and Senate Debates were intensively studied for the years 1867-74, and in particular, the "Report of the Royal Commissioners appointed by Commission, addressed to them, under the Great Seal of Canada, bearing Date the Fourteenth Day of August, A.D., 1873," the "Report of the Select Committee on the Causes of the Difficulties in the North-West Territory in 1869-70" (1874), and "Rupert's Land and the North-West Territory" (Cartier and McDougall, Sessional Paper No. 25, 32 Vict. 1869).

Colonial Office Despatches were examined in the *British Parliamentary Papers*. The following newspapers and journals were examined: *La Minerve*, Montreal *Gazette*, Montreal *Times and Commercial Advertiser*, Montreal *Herald*, Montreal *Witness*, *L'Avenir*, *Le Canadien*, *Le Pays*, *Le Nouveau Monde*, *L'Opinion Publique*, *L'Aurore des Canadas*, *La Patrie*, Montreal *Leader*, *Le Journal de Québec*, Quebec *Gazette*, Toronto *Globe*, London *Times*, New York *Times*, New York *Herald*, *Punch in Canada*, *Canadian Illustrated News*, *La Revue canadienne*, *Nor'Wester*, *Le Métis*, *The Manitoban*.

BOOKS AND PAMPHLETS

Allaire, Abbé J.-B.-A. *Histoire de la Paroisse de Saint-Denis-sur-Richelieu*. Saint-Hyacinthe, 1905.

Allin, C.D. and G.M. Jones. *Annexation, Preferential Trade and Reciprocity*. Toronto, 1912.

Angus, H.F. ed. *British Columbia and the United States*. New York, 1970 (reprint).

Appleton, T.E. *Ravenscrag, The Allan Royal Mail Line*. Toronto, 1974.

Archambault, J.-B.-O. *Album-Souvenir de la paroisse de Saint-Antoine-sur-Richelieu.* Saint-Hyacinthe, 1924.

Arion (pseud.) *Alphonzo Stilletto's Poetization of the incipient stage of the Great Pacific Scandal and of the celebrated speech of Lord Dufferin in reply to a health toast at a dinner given by the Halifax Club.* Montreal, 1874.

Auclair, E.-J. *Le Curé Labelle.* Montreal, 1930.

Audet, F.-J. *Les Députés de Montréal (ville et comtés), 1792-1867.* Montreal, 1943.

_____ et E. Fabre-Surveyer. *Les Députés au Premier Parlement du Bas-Canada, 1792-1796.* Montreal, 1946.

Bancroft, F. *The Life of William H. Seward.* 2 vols. New York, 1900.

Barnard, Julienne. *Mémoires Chapais.* 3 vols. Montreal, 1961-64.

Beaty, J. *The History of the Lake Superior Ring.* Toronto, 1874.

Beaudry, J.-W.-B. (et G.-E. Cartier). *Réplique des marguilliers de Notre-Dame de Montréal.* n.p.n.d. (1867?).

Beaulieu, André et Jean Hamelin. *Les Journaux du Québec de 1764 à 1964.* Quebec, 1965.

Béchard, A. *L'Honorable A-N Morin.* Québec, 1885.

Bellerive, Georges. *Délegués Canadiens-Francais en Angleterre de 1763 à 1867.* Quebec, 1913.

Benoit, Dom J.-P.-A. *Vie de Mgr. Taché.* 2 vols. Montreal, 1904.

Bernard, J.-P., ed, *Les Idéologies Québecoises au 19e Siècle.* Montreal, 1973.

_____ *Les Rouges.* Quebec, 1971.

Berton, Pierre. *The National Dream.* Toronto, 1970.

Bertrand, Camille. *Histoire de Montréal, 1835-1942.* 2 vols. Montreal, 1942.

Biggar, E.B. *Anecdotal Life of Sir John Macdonald.* Montreal, 1891.

Boissonnault, C.-M. *Histoire Politico-Militaire des Canadiens-Francais, 1763-1945.* Montreal, 1967.

_____ *Histoire politique de la province de Québec (1867-1920).* Quebec, 1936.

Bonenfant, J.-C. *The French Canadians and the Birth of Confederation.* Ottawa, 1966.

_____ *Les Institutions Politiques Canadiennes.* Quebec, 1954.

_____ *Thomas Chapais.* Montreal, 1957.

Booker, M.A. *Catalogue de la Bibliothèque de feu l'Hon. Sir G.E. Cartier, Baronet.* Montreal, 1873.

Borthwick, Rev. J.D. *History and Biographical Gazetteer of Montreal to the Year 1892.* Montreal, 1892.

Bossé, Evelyne. *Un Grand Réprésentant de l'Elite Canadienne-Francaise.* (J.-C. Taché), Quebec, n.d.

Bourinot, J.G. *Lord Elgin.* Toronto, 1903.

Bowen, F.C. *History of the Canadian Pacific Line.* London, 1929.

Bowsfield, Hartwell, ed. *The James Wickes Taylor Correspondence, 1859-1870.* (*MRSP*, III) Altona, 1968.

_____ *Louis Riel.* Toronto, 1971.

Boyd, John. *Sir George Etienne Cartier, Bart. His Life and Times.* Toronto, 1914; 1917.

Brady, Alexander. *Thomas D'Arcy McGee.* Toronto, 1925.

Brebner, J.B. *North Atlantic Triangle.* Toronto, 1966.

Brown, T.S. *A History of the Grand Trunk Railway of Canada.* Quebec, 1864.

_____ *1837, My Connection with it.* Quebec, 1898.

Bruchési, J. *Histoire du Canada.* Montreal, 1951.

Brunet, Ludovic. *La Province du Canada, de 1840 à 1867.* Quebec, 1908.

Brunet, Michel. *Les Canadiens après la Conquête, 1759-1775.* Montreal, 1969.

_____ *La Présence anglaise et les Canadiens.* Montreal, 1958.

Burroughs, Peter, ed. *The Colonial Reformers and Canada, 1830-49.* Toronto, 1969.

Burt, A.L. *The United States, Great Britain, and British North America.* Toronto, 1940.

Callaghan, J.M. *American Foreign Policy in Canadian Relations.* New York, 1937.

Camillus (Adam Thom). *Anti-Gallic Letters.* Montreal, 1836.

The Canadian Biographical Dictionary and Portrait Gallery of Eminent and Self-Made Men. 2 vols. Toronto, 1881.

Caniff, W. *Canadian Nationality.* Toronto, 1875.

Carbonneau, John. *Grand Trunk Railway.* Island Pond, Vt., 1968.

Careless, J.M.S. *Brown of the Globe.* 2 vols. Toronto, 1959-63.

____ ed. *Colonists and Canadians, 1760-1867.* Toronto, 1967.

____ *The Union of the Canadas: The Growth of Canadian Institutions, 1841-1857.* Toronto, 1967.

Carrier, L.-N. *Les Evénements de 1837-38.* Quebec, 1877.

Cartwright, Sir Richard. *Reminiscences.* Toronto, 1912.

Cauchon, Joseph. *L'Union des Provinces de l'Amérique Britannique du Nord.* Quebec, 1865.

Chambers, E.J. *The Canadian Militia.* Montreal, 1907.

Chapais, Thomas. *Cours d'histoire du Canada.* 8 vols. Quebec, 1919-34.

Christie, Robert. *A History of the Late Province of Lower Canada.* 6 vols. Montreal, 1866.

Clark, S.D. *Movements of Political Protest in Canada, 1640-1840.* Toronto, 1959.

Comeau, R, ed. *Economie québecoise.* Montreal, 1969.

Cook, Ramsay, ed. *Constitutionalism and Nationalism in Lower Canada.* Toronto, 1969.

Corey, A.B. *The Crisis of 1830-42 in Canadian-American Relations.* Toronto, 1941.

Cornell, P.G. *The Alignment of Political Groups in the Province of Canada.* Toronto, 1962.

Craggs, R.S. *Sir Adams G. Archibald.* Truro, 1967.

Craig, G.M. ed. *Lord Durham's Report.* Toronto, 1963.

____ *Early Travellers in the Canadas, 1791-1867.* Toronto, 1955.

____ *The United States and Canada.* London, 1968.

____ *Upper Canada: The Formative Years, 1784-1841.* Toronto, 1963.

Creighton, D.G. *Dominion of the North.* Toronto, 1962.

____ *The Empire of the St. Lawrence.* Toronto, 1956.

____ *John A. Macdonald.* 2 vols. Toronto, 1952-55.

Cross, M.S. ed. *Free Trade, Annexation and Reciprocity, 1846-54.* Toronto, 1971.

Currie, A.W. *The Grand Trunk Railway of Canada.* Toronto, 1951.

Currier, J.E.W. *Index to Railway Legislation of the Dominion of Canada from 1867 to 1897 inclusive.* Ottawa, 1898.

Dansereau, A. *et al. Georges-Etienne Cartier, Etudes.* Montreal, 1914.

David, L.-O. *Biographies Canadiens.* Montreal, 1872.

____ *Monseigneur Alexandre Taché.* Montreal, 1883.

____ *Mélanges Historiques et Littéraires.* Montreal, 1917.

____ *Les Patriotes, 1837-1838.* Montreal, 1884.

____ *Salut au Canada.* Montreal, 1927.

____ *Souvenirs et Biographies, 1870-1910.* Montreal, 1911.

____ *L'Union des Deux Canadas, 1841-1867.* Montreal, 1898.

De Celles, Alfred D. *Cartier et Son Temps.* Montreal, 1913.

____ *LaFontaine et Son Temps.* Montreal, 1907.

____ *Papineau, 1786-1871.* Montreal, 1905.

____ *The Patriots of '37.* Toronto, 1916.

____ *Sir George Etienne Cartier.* Toronto, 1904.

Denison, G.T. *Soldiering in Canada.* Toronto, 1900.

____ *The Struggle for Imperial Unity.* London, 1909.

Dent, J.C. *The Last Forty Years.* 2 vols, Toronto, 1881.

Désilets, Andrée. *Hector-Louis Langevin.* Quebec, 1969.

Dessaules, L.-A. *Papineau et Nelson: blanc et noir.* Montreal, 1848.

____ *Le Principe des nationalités.* Montreal, 1864.

Donnelly, M.S. *The Government of Manitoba.* Toronto, 1963.

Dorion, A.-A. *La Confédération couronnement de dix années de mauvaise administration.* Montreal, 1867.

Doughty, Sir Arthur G. *Elgin-Grey Papers, 1846-1852.* 4 vols, Ottawa, 1937.

Drapeau, Stanislaus. *Biographie de Sir N.F. Belleau.* Quebec, 1883.

Dufferin & Ava, Marchioness of. *My Canadian Journal, 1872-8.* London, 1891.

Easterbrook, W.T. and H.G.J. Aitken. *Canadian Economic History*. Toronto, 1956.
_____ and M.H. Watkins. *Approaches to Canadian Economic History*. Toronto, 1967.
Fabre, Hector. *Chroniques, 1834-1910*. Montreal, 1911.
_____ *Confédération, Indépendance, Annexion*. Quebec, 1871.
_____ *Esquisse biographique sur le Chevalier de Lorimier*. Montreal, 1856.
Farr, D.M.L. *The Colonial Office and Canada, 1867-1887*. Toronto, 1955.
Fauteux, Aegidius. *Le Duel au Canada*. Montreal, 1934.
_____ *Patriotes de 1837-38*. Montreal, 1950.
Filteau, Gérard. *Histoire des Patriotes*. 3 vols, Montreal, 1942.
Foster, J. *Railway from Lake Superior to Red River Settlement considered in a Letter to the Hon. William McDougall, CB*. Montreal, 1869.
Frégault, Guy. *Canada: The War of the Conquest*. Toronto, 1969.
Galbraith, J.S. *The Hudson's Bay Company as an Imperial Factor, 1821-1869*. Toronto, 1957.
Garneau, F.-X. *Histoire du Canada, 1712-1840*. 4 vols. Quebec, 1845-52.
Gérin-Lajoie, A. *Dix Ans au Canada, 1840-1850*. Quebec, 1888.
Gibbon, J.M. *Our Old Montreal*. Toronto, 1949.
_____ *Steel of Empire: The Romantic History of the Canadian Pacific*. Toronto, 1935.
Gilbert, Heather. *Awakening Continent: The Life of Lord Mount Stephen*. Vol. I: 1829-91. Aberdeen, 1965.
Girard, Marcel. *Le Métis Canadien*. Paris, 1945.
Girouard, J.-J. *Patriotes*. Montreal, 1973 (reprint).
Glazebrook, G.P. de T. *A History of Canadian Political Thought*. Toronto, 1966.
_____ *A History of Transportation in Canada*. 2 vols. Toronto, 1964.
_____ *Sir Charles Bagot in Canada*. Oxford, 1929.
Gluek, A.C.Jr. *Minnesota and the Manifest Destiny of the Canadian Northwest*. Toronto, 1965.
Graham, G.S. *British Policy and Canada*. New York, 1930.
Grant, G.M. *Ocean to Ocean*. Toronto, 1873.
Gravel, J.-Y. *Le Québec et La Guerre, 1867-1960*. Montreal, 1974.
Gray, J.H. *Confederation*. Toronto, 1872.
Gore, Montague. *Observations on the Disturbances in Canada*. Montreal, 1969 (reprint).
Groulx, Lionel. *La Confédération Canadienne, Ses Origines*. Montreal, 1918.
_____ *Histoire du Canada Francais*. 4 vols. Montreal, 1950-52.
_____ *Louis Riel*. Montreal, 1944.
_____ *Notre Maître, Le Passé*. Montreal, 1936-44.
Guillet, E.C. *The Pacific Scandal*. MSS in the Toronto Public Library, 1948.
Hamelin, Jean et Marcel Hamelin. *Les Moeurs électorales dans le Québec de 1791 à nos jours*. Montreal, 1962.
_____ et Yves Roby. *Histoire Economique du Québec, 1851-1896*. Montreal, 1971.
Hamelin, Jean; John Huot; Marcel Hamelin. *Aperçu de le Politique Canadienne au XIXe Siècle*. Quebec, 1965.
Hammond, M.O. *Confederation and its Leaders*. Toronto, 1927.
Hannay, James. *The Life and Times of Sir Leonard Tilley*. Saint John, 1897.
Harkin, W.A., ed. *Political Reminiscences of The Right Honourable Sir Charles Tupper*. London, 1914.
Harvey, D.C. *Sir George-Etienne Cartier*. Toronto, 1930.
Hedges, J.B. *The Federal Railway Land Subsidy Policy of Canada*. Cambridge, Mass., 1934.
Helps, Sir Arthur. *The Life and Labours of Mr. Brassey*. London, 1876.
Hidy, R.W. *The House of Baring in American Trade and Finance*. Cambridge, 1949.
Hincks, Sir Francis. *The Political History of Canada between 1840 and 1855*. Montreal, 1877.
_____ *Reminiscences of His Public Life*. Montreal, 1884.
Hitsman, J.M. *Safeguarding Canada, 1763-1871*. Toronto, 1968.

Hodgins, B.W. *John Sandfield Macdonald.* Toronto, 1971.
Horetzky, Charles. *Canada on the Pacific.* Montreal, 1874.
Hornby, Sir Edmund. *Autobiography.* London, 1928.
Innis, H.A. *The Fur Trade in Canada.* Toronto, 1956.
_____ *A History of the Canadian Pacific Railway.* Toronto, 1923.
_____ and A.R.M. Lower *Select Economic Documents, 1783-1885.* Toronto, 1933.
Innis, M.Q. *An Economic History of Canada.* Toronto, 1938.
Irving, L.H. *Officers of the British Forces in Canada during the War of 1812-15.* Welland, 1968.
Irwin, L.B. *Pacific Railways and Nationalism in the Canadian-American Northwest, 1845-1873.* New York, 1968.
Jenkins, Brian. *Fenians and Anglo-American Relations during Reconstruction.* Ithaca, 1969.
_____ *Britain and the War for the Union.* Vol. I. Montreal, 1974.
Josephson, Matthew. *The Politicos.* New York, 1938.
_____ *The Robber Barons.* New York, 1962 (reprint).
Keefer, T.C. *The Canada Central Railway.* Ottawa, 1870.
_____ *The Philosophy of Railroads,* ed. H.V. Nelles. Toronto, 1972.
_____ *The St. Lawrence and Ottawa Grand Junction Railway Company.* Montreal, 1853.
Kennleyside, H.L. *Canada and the United States.* New York, 1929.
Kennedy, W.P.M. *Lord Elgin.* London, 1930.
Kerr, D.G.G. *Sir Edmund Head: A Scholarly Governor.* Toronto, 1954.
Laflamme, J.-L.-K. *Le Centenaire Cartier, 1814-1914.* Montreal, 1927.
Lanctôt, G. *Canada and the American Revolution, 1774-1783.* Toronto, 1967.
_____ *Les Canadiens-Français et Leurs Voisins du Sud.* Montreal, 1941.
Langevin, F. *Monseigneur Ignace Bourget.* Montreal, 1932.
Larsen, H.M. *Jay Cooke.* Cambridge, Mass., 1936.
Lavergne, C.-E. *Georges-Etienne Cartier.* Montreal, 1914.
Leacock, Stephen. *Mackenzie, Baldwin, Lafontaine, Hincks: Responsible Government.* Toronto, 1907.
Lecompte, Edouard. *Sir Joseph Dubuc, 1840-1914.* Montreal, 1923.
Lindsay, Charles. *William Lyon Mackenzie.* Toronto, 1908.
Logan, R.S. *Synoptical History of the Grand Trunk System of Railways.* Montreal, 1912.
Longley, R.S. *Sir Charles Tupper.* Toronto, 1916.
_____ *Sir Francis Hincks.* Toronto, 1943.
Lovett, H.A. *Canada and the Grand Trunk, 1829-1924.* Montreal, 1924.
Lower, A.R.M. *Canadians in the Making.* Toronto, 1958.
_____ *Colony to Nation.* Toronto, 1966.
_____ *Great Britain's Woodyard.* Montreal, 1973.
Mackenzie, Alexander. *The Life and Speeches of the Hon. George Brown.* Toronto, 1882.
MacBeth, R.G. *The Romance of the Canadian Pacific Railway.* Toronto, 1924.
MacNaughton, J. *Lord Strathcona.* Toronto, 1927.
MacNutt, W.S. *New Brunswick: A History, 1784-1867.* Toronto, 1963.
Manning, Helen Taft. *The Revolt of French Canada, 1800-1835.* Toronto, 1962.
Martin, Chester. *Foundations of Canadian Nationhood.* Toronto, 1955.
Masters, D.C. *The Reciprocity Treaty of 1854.* Toronto, 1969.
Maurault, Mgr. Olivier. *Le Collège de Montréal.* Montreal, 1967.
McDougall, J.L. *Canadian Pacific.* Montreal, 1968.
McDougall, William. *Eight Letters to Joseph Howe on the Red River Rebellion.* Toronto, 1870.
McGee, R. *The Fenian Raids on the Huntingdon Frontier, 1866 and 1870.* Huntingdon, 1967.
McNab, W. *Historical Narrative of the Inception and Development of the Grand Trunk Railway of Canada.* Montreal, 1923.
Monck, Frances. *My Canadian Leaves.* London, 1891.

Monet, Jacques. *The Last Cannon Shot: A Study of French-Canadian Nationalism, 1837-1850*. Toronto, 1968.

Montreal in 1856. A Sketch prepared for the Celebration of the Opening of the Grand Trunk Railway of Canada. Montreal, 1856.

Morgan, H.J. *Sketches of Celebrated Canadians*. Quebec, 1862.

Morice, A.G. *A Critical History of the Red River Insurrection*. Winnipeg, 1935.

Morin, Victor. *Vieux Montréal*. Montreal, 1942.

Morris Alexander. *The Hudson's Bay and Pacific Territories*. Montreal, 1859.

—— *Nova Britannia*. Toronto, 1884.

Morton, Desmond. *Ministers and Generals*. Toronto, 1970.

Morton, W.L. *The Critical Years*. Toronto, 1968.

—— ed. *The Journal of Alexander Begg and other Documents of the Red River Resistance*. Toronto, 1957.

—— *The Kingdom of Canada*. Toronto, 1963.

—— ed. *Manitoba: The Birth of a Province*. (*MRSP*, I) Altona, 1965.

—— *Manitoba: A History*. Toronto, 1957.

—— *Monck Letters and Journals, 1863-1868*. Toronto, 1970.

—— ed. *The Shield of Achilles – Le Bouclier d'Achille*. Toronto, 1968.

Neatby, Hilda. *Quebec, The Revolutionary Age, 1760-1791*. Toronto, 1966.

Nelson, Joseph. *The Very Latest Grand Trunk Scheme*. London, 1873.

Nelson, Wolfred. *Wolfred Nelson et Son Temps*. Montreal, 1946.

New, Chester W. *Lord Durham*. Oxford, 1929.

—— *Lord Durham's Mission to Canada*. Toronto, 1963.

Nish, Elisabeth, ed. *Racism or Responsible Government*. Toronto, 1967.

Notman, W. and Fennings Taylor. *Portraits of British Americans*. Montreal, 1865.

Oberholtzer, E.P. *Jay Cooke, Financier of the Civil War*. 2 vols. Philadelphia, 1907.

Ormsby, Margaret A. *British Columbia: A History*. Toronto, 1958.

Ormsby, William, ed. *Crisis in the Canadas, 1838-1839. The Grey Journals and Letters*. Toronto, 1964.

Ouellet, Fernand. *Histoire Economique et Sociale du Québec, 1760-1850*. Montreal, 1966.

—— *Lower Canada, 1792-1841*. (unpublished MSS).

—— *Papineau*. Quebec, 1959.

Parent, R. *Duvernay le Magnifique*. Montreal, 1953.

Papineau, Amédée. *Journal d'un Fils de la Liberté*. Ottawa, 1972 (reprint).

Papineau, L.-J. *Histoire de l'Insurrection du Canada*. Montreal, 1963 (reprint).

Phelan, J. *The Ardent Exile*. Toronto, 1957.

Poor, Laura E. *The First International Railway*. New York, 1892.

Poor, J.A. *Poor's Railroad Manual of the United States for 1873-74*. New York, 1874.

Pope, Sir Joseph. *Correspondence of Sir John Macdonald*. Toronto, 1921.

—— *Memoirs of the Right Honourable Sir John Alexander Macdonald*. Toronto, 1930.

Pouliot, L. *Mgr. Bourget et Son Temps*. 2 vols. Montreal, 1955.

Preston, W.T.R. *The Life and Times of Lord Strathcona*. London, 1914.

Proulx, J.-B. *Le Curé Labelle et La Colonization*. Paris, 1885.

Résumé Impartial de la Discussion Papineau-Nelson sur les Evénements de Saint-Denis en 1837. Montreal, 1848.

Rich, E.E. *The Fur Trade and the Northwest to 1857*. Toronto, 1967.

—— *The Hudson's Bay Company*. 3 vols. Toronto, 1960.

Richard, J.-B. *Les Evénements de 1837 à Saint-Denis-sur-Richelieu*. Saint-Hyacinthe, 1938.

Riel, Louis. *L'Amnistie*. Montreal, 1874.

Robitaille, Amédée. *Sir Georges-Etienne Cartier, Conférence donné au Club Cartier de Québec*. Quebec, 1883.

Rose, G.M. *A Cyclopedia of Canadian Biography*. 2 vols. Toronto, 1888.

Routhier, L'Hon. Sir A.-B. *Conférence sur Sir Georges-E. Cartier*. Montreal, 1912.

Roy, J.-L. *Edouard-Raymond Fabre*. Montreal, 1974.

Royal, Joseph. *Histoire du Canada: 1841 à 1867*. Montreal, 1909.

Rumilly, Robert. *Histoire des Franco-Americains*. Montreal, 1958.
_____ *Histoire de Montréal*. 4 vols. Montreal, 1970-74.
_____ *Histoire de la Province de Québec: Vol.* I, Georges-Etienne Cartier. Montreal, 1940.
_____ *Monseigneur Laflèche et Son Temps*. Montréal, 1945.
_____ *Papineau*. Montreal, 1944.
Saunders, E.M., ed. *The Life and Letters of the Rt. Hon. Sir Charles Tupper, KCMG*. Toronto, 1916.
Savard, Pierre. *Le Conseil-Général de France*. Quebec, 1970.
Schull, Joseph. *Edward Blake*. Toronto, 1975.
_____ *Laurier*, Toronto, 1965.
_____ *Rebellion*, Toronto, 1971.
Secretan, J.H.E. *Canada's Great Highway*. Toronto, 1924.
Séguin, R.-L. *La Victoire de Saint-Denis*. Longueuil, 1968.
Seward, William. *A Cruise to Labrador*. New York, 1857.
Shelton, W.G., ed. *British Columbia and Confederation*. Victoria, 1967.
Shippee, L.B. *Canadian-American Relations, 1849-1874*. Toronto, 1939.
Skelton, Isabel. *The Life of Thomas D'Arcy McGee*. Gardenvale, 1925.
Skelton, O.D. *The Life and Times of Sir Alexander Tilloch Galt*. Toronto, 1920.
_____ *The Railway Builders*. Toronto, 1916.
Sleigh, Lt.-Col. B.W.A. *Pine Forest and Hacmatack Clearings*. London, 1853.
Smith, Goldwin. *The Treaty of Washington*. Ithaca, 1941.
Smith, William. *Political Leaders of Upper Canada*. Toronto, 1931.
Stacey, C.P. *Canada and the British Army: A Study in Responsible Government, 1846-1871*. London, 1936.
Stanley, G.F.G. *The Birth of Western Canada*. Toronto, 1936.
_____ *Canada Invaded, 1775-1776*. Toronto, 1973.
_____ *Louis Riel*. Toronto, 1963.
_____ *New France: The Last Phase, 1744-1760*. Toronto, 1968.
Stevens, G.R. *Canadian National Railways*. Vol I. Toronto, 1960.
Stewart, G. *Canada under the Administration of the Earl of Dufferin*. Toronto, 1878.
Sulte, Benjamin. *George-Etienne Cartier* (Mélanges Historiques, IV), Montreal, 1919.
_____ *Histoire des Canadiens-Français (1608-1880)*. 8 vols. Montreal, 1882-84.
_____ *Histoire de la milice canadienne-francaise, 1760-1897*. Montreal, 1897.
_____ *Le Saint-Jean-Baptiste, 1636-1852* (Mélanges Historiques, XV) Montreal, 1929.
Taché, Mgr. Alexandre *L'Amnestie*. Montreal, 1874.
_____ *Encore l'Amnestie*. Montreal, 1875.
_____ *Sketch of the North-West of America*. Montreal, 1870.
Taché, J.-C. *Des Provinces de l'Amerique du Nord et d'une Union Fédérale*. Quebec, 1858.
_____ *Esquisse sur le Canada*. Paris, 1855.
Taché, L.-H. *Men of the Day: A Canadian Portrait Gallery*. Montreal, 1890-94.
Tassé, Joseph *Les Canadiens de l'Ouest*. 2 vols. Montreal, 1878.
_____ *Le Chemin de Fer Canadien du Pacifique*. Montreal, 1872.
_____ ed. *Discours de Sir Georges Cartier, Baronet*. Montreal, 1893.
Taylor, James Wickes. *Northwest British America and its Relations to the State of Minnesota*. St. Paul, 1860.
Thompson, N. and J.H. Edgar. *Canadian Railway Development from the Earliest Times*. Toronto, 1933.
Thomson, D.C. *Alexander Mackenzie, Clear Grit*. Toronto, 1960.
_____ *Travellers Official Railway Guide of the United States and Canada*. New York, 1869.
Trotter, R.G. *Canadian Federation*. Toronto, 1924.
Trout, J.M. and E. Trout. *The Railways of Canada for 1870-1*. Toronto, 1871.
Tucker, G.N. *The Canadian Commercial Revolution, 1845-1851*. Toronto, 1964.
Tupper, Charles. *Recollections of Sixty Years in Canada*. Toronto, 1914.
Turcotte, L.-P. *Le Canada sous l'Union, 1841-1867*. Quebec, 1882.

———— *L'Honourable Sir G.E. Cartier.* Quebec, 1873.

Underhill, F.H. and C.W. de Kiewiet, eds. *Dufferin-Carnarvon Correspondence (1874-1878).* Toronto, 1955.

Vallée, Jacques, ed. *Toqueville au Bas-Canada.* Montreal, 1973.

Vaugeois, D. *L'Union des Deux Canadas, 1791-1840.* Trois-Rivières, 1962.

Wade, Mason. *The French Canadians, 1760-1945.* 2 vols. Toronto, 1955-67.

Waite, P.B. *The Life and Times of Confederation, 1864-1867.* Toronto, 1962.

Wakefield, Edward Gibbon. *England and America.* London, 1832.

Walker, Charles. *Thomas Brassey: Railway Builder.* London, 1969.

Wallace, W.S., ed. *The Macmillan Dictionary of Canadian Biography.* Toronto, 1963.

Walling, H.F., ed. *Tackabury's Atlas of the Dominion of Canada.* Montreal, 1875.

Warner, D.J. *The Idea of Continental Union.* Kentucky, 1960.

Watkin, Sir E.W. *Canada and the States, Recollections, 1851-1886.* London, 1887.

Whelan, Hon. Edward. *The Union of the British Provinces.* Toronto, 1927.

Whitelaw, W.M. *The Maritimes and Canada before Confederation.* Toronto, 1934.

Willson, H.B. *Friendly Relations.* London, 1934.

———— *Lord Strathcona.* London, 1915.

Wilson, G.E. *The Life of Robert Baldwin.* Toronto, 1933.

Winks, R.W. *Canada and the United States: The Civil War Years.* Baltimore, 1960.

Wrong, G.M. *Canada and the American Revolution.* New York, 1968.

———— *The Earl of Elgin.* Toronto, 1905.

Young, Hon. John. *Letters first published in the "Northern Journal" during 1871.* Montreal, 1872.

ARTICLES

Auclair, E.-J., "Sir Georges-Etienne Cartier à Saint-Antoine-sur-Richelieu," *La revue canadienne,* XIV, 3, 1914.

Audet, F.-J., "Le Barreau et la Révolte de 1837," *MSRC,* 3e Serie, 1937, xxxi.

Bellefeuille, E.L. de, "L'Incursion de St. Alban's," *La Revue canadienne,* II, 6, 1865.

Boissonnault, C.-M., "Les Patriotes à Saint-Denis," *RUL,* VI, 6, 1950-51.

Bonenfant, J.-C., "Les Canadiens-français et la Naissance de la Confédération," *CHAR,* 1952.

———— "George-Etienne Cartier," *Dictionary of Canadian Biography,* X, 1972.

———— "George-Etienne Cartier, Juriste," *Cahier des Dix,* XXXI, 1966.

———— "L'Esprit de 1867," *RHAF,* XVII, 1, 1963-64.

———— "Idées Politiques de George-Etienne Cartier," in Jean Hamelin, ed., *Idées Politiques des Premier Ministres du Canada,* Montreal, 1969.

———— "Sir George-Etienne Cartier," in Laurier Lapierre, ed., *French Canadian Thinkers,* Toronto, 1966.

———— and J.-C. Falardeau, "Cultural and Political Implications of French-Canadian Nationalism," *CHAR,* 1945.

Cartier, G.-E., "Testament de Sir Georges-Etienne Cartier," *RAQ,* XLI, 1963.

Chapais, Thomas, "Cartier et la Confédération," *La Revue canadienne,* XIV, 3, 1914.

Chartier, Emile, "Les Discours de Cartier," *La Revue canadienne,* XIV, 3, 1914.

Cooper, J.I., "George Etienne Cartier in the Period of the Forties," *CHAR,* LXXI, 1938.

———— "The Political Ideas of George Etienne Cartier," *CHR,* XXIII, 3, 1942.

———— "The Social Structure of Montreal in the 1850s," *CHAR,* 1956.

Cook, Ramsay, "Quebec and Confederation, Past and Present," *QQ,* LXXI, 4, 1964-65.

Creighton, D.G., "Economic Nationalism and Confederation," *CHAR,* 1942.

———— "The United States and Confederation," *CHR,* XXXIX, 3, 1958.

De Celles, Alfred D., "La Carrière de Cartier," *La Revue canadienne,* XIV, 3, 1914.

Désilets, Andrée, "La Succession de Cartier, 1873-1891," *CHAR,* XLIX, 1968.

Doughty, A.G., ed., "Notes on the Quebec Conference, by A.A. Macdonald," *CHR,* I, 1, 1920.

Dowden, A.R., "John Gregory Smith," *Vermont History,* XXXII, 2, 1964.

Dubuc, Eugénie, ed., "Correspondance de Sir Joseph Dubuc," *RHAF*, XX, 2-4, 1966-67: XXI, 1, 1967-68.

Duvernay, Ludger, "Lettres, 1837-1838," *CANJ*, 1907-1912, Série 3, vols 5, 6, 7, et 8.

_____ "Papiers Duvernay conservés aux Archives de la Province de Québec," *RAPQ*, 1926-27.

Fabre-Surveyer, E., "Charles-Ovide Perrault (1809-1837)," *MSRC*, 3e Série, 31, 1937.

_____ "Correspondance d'Edouard-Raymond Fabre," *MSRC*, 3e Serie, 38, 1, 1944.

Farr, D.M.L., "Sir John Rose and Imperial Relations," *CHR*, XXXIII, 1, 1952.

Fauteux, Aegidius, "Antoine-Aimé Dorion," *Cahier des Dix*, XXVI, 1961.

_____ "Cartier et les Minorités," *La Revue canadienne*, XIV, 3, 1914.

Forsey, Eugene, "Government Defeats in the Canadian House of Commons," *CJEPS*, XXIX, 3, 1963.

Fraser, Barbara, "The Political Career of Hector-Louis Langevin," *CHR*, XLII, 2, 1961.

Gibson, J.A., "The Colonial Office View of Canadian Federation, 1856-1868," *CHR*, XXXV, 1954.

Gluek, A.C. Jr., "The Riel Rebellion and Canadian-American Relations," *CHR*, XXXVI, 3, 1955.

"Glyns and the Grand Trunk Railway," *Three Banks Review*, LII, 1961.

Gouin, Lomer, "Quebec and Confederation," in G.H. Locke, ed., *Builders of the Canadian Commonwealth*, Toronto, 1923.

Groulx, Lionel, "Le Britannisme des Patriotes," *RHAF*, V, 3, 1951-52.

_____ "Les Idées religieuses de Cartier," *La Revue canadienne*, XIV, 3, 1914.

Hafler, Ruth, "The Riel Rebellion and Manifest Destiny," *Dal. Rev.*, XLV, 4, 1965-66.

Heath, G.E., "The St. Albans Raid: Vermont Viewpoint," *Vermont History*, XXXIII, 1, 1965.

Hidy, R.W. and M.E. Hidy, "Anglo-American Merchant Bankers and the Railroads of the Old Northwest, 1848-1860," *Bus. Hist Rev.* XXXIV, 2, 1960.

Hill, R.A., "A note on Newspaper Patronage in Canada during the late 1850s and early 1860s," *CHR*, XLIX, 1, 1968.

Hutchison, P.P., "Sir John J.C. Abbott," *Canadian Bar Review*, XXVI, 1948.

Ireland, W.E., "Helmcken's Diary of the Confederation Negotiations, 1870," *BCHQ*, IV, 2, 1940.

Jenkins, B., "The British Government, Sir John A. Macdonald, and the Fenian Claims," *CHR*, XLIX, 2, 1968.

Jensen, V., "Lafontaine and the Canadian Union," *CHR*, XXV, 6, 1944.

Kazar, J.D., "The Canadian View of the Confederate Raid on St. Albans," *Vermont History*, XXXIII, 1, 1965.

Laurier, Wilfrid, "Les Discours de Sir George Cartier," *La Revue canadienne*, XXX, 3, 1894.

LeFebvre, J.-J., "La Famille Cartier," *MSRC*, III, 4e Serie, 3, 1965, I.

LeGoff, T.J.A., "The Agricultural Crisis in Lower Canada, 1802-12," *CHR*, LV, 1, 1974.

Lockhart, A.D., "The Contribution of Macdonald Conservatism to National Unity, 1854-1878," *CHAR*, 1939.

Long, M.H., "Sir John Rose and the Informal Beginnings of the Canadian High Commissionership," *CHR*, XII, 23, 1931.

Longley, R.S., "Cartier and McDougall, Canadian Emissaries to London," *CHR*, XXVI, 1, 1945.

Macfarlane, R.O., "Manitoba Politics and Parties after Confederation," *CHAR*, 1940.

Martin, Chester, "British Policy in Canadian Confederation," *CHR*, XIII, 3, 1932.

_____ "The United States and Canadian Nationality," *CHR*, XVIII, 1, 1937.

Masters, D.C., "Toronto vs. Montreal," *CHR*, XXII, 1941.

Maurault, Mgr. Olivier, "Saint-Sulpice et Montréal," *CHAR*, 1956.

Mitchell, Elaine A., "Edward Watkin and the Buying-Out of the Hudson's Bay Company," *CHR*, XXIV, 3, 1953.

Monet, Jacques, "French Canada and the Annexation Crisis, 1848-50," *CHR*, XLVII, 3, 1966.

Morton, W.L. "The Conservative Principle in Confederation," *QQ*, LXXI, 4, 1964-65.

_____ "The Formation of the First Federal Cabinet," *CHR*, XXXVI, 1955.

_____ "The Geographical Circumstances of Confederation," *Can. Geog. Jour.*, LXX, 3, 1965.

_____ "The Meaning of Monarchy in Confederation," *TRSC*, 4th Series, 1, 1963, II.

New, Chester W., "The Rebellion of 1837 in its Larger Setting," *CHAR*, 1937.

Ouellet, Fernand, "Denis-Benjamin Viger et le problème de l'annexion," *BRH*, LVII, 4, 1951.

_____ "M. Michel Brunet et le problème de la Conquête," *BRH*, LXII, 1956.

_____ "Le Nationalisme canadien-français: de ses origines a l'insurrection de 1837," *CHR*, XLV, 1964.

_____ "Papineau dans la Révolution de 1837-1838," *CHAR*, 1958.

_____ et Jean Hamelin "La crise agricole dans le Bas-Canada, 1802-1837," *CHAR*, 1962.

Paquet, G. and J.P. Wallot, "Aperçu sur le commerce international et les prix domestiques dans le Bas-Canada (1793-1812)," *RHAF*, XXI, 1967.

Perrault, Antonio, "Cartier et le Droit civil canadien," *La Revue canadienne*, XIV, 3, 1914.

Pouliot, Leon, "Monseigneur Bourget et la Confédération," *RSCHEC*, 1959.

_____ "Mgr. Lartigue et les Patriotes de 1837," *BRH*, XLIV, 1938.

Prud'homme, L.-A., "Le Conseil législatif de Manitoba," *MSRC*, 3e Série, 25, 1931, I.

_____ "Le Premier Parlement de Manitoba, 1870-74." *MSRC*, 3e Série, 11, 1917, I.

_____ "L'Honorable Joseph Royal," *MSRC*, 2e Serie, 10, 1904, I.

_____ "Sir Joseph Dubuc," *La Revue canadienne*, L, 1, 1914: L, 2, 1914.

Royal, Joseph, "Le Traité de Réciprocité," *La Revue canadienne*, I, 2, 1864.

Rumilly, Robert, "Quand La Société Saint-Jean-Baptiste a-t-elle été fondée?" *RHAF*, I, 1946.

_____ "Monseigneur Laflèche et les Ultramontains," *RHAF*, XVI, 1, 1962-63.

Shortt, Adam, "Austin Cuvillier, Merchant, Legislator and Banker," *JCBA*, April 1923.

Shortt, G.E., "The House of Baring and Canada," *QQ*, XXXV, 4, 1929-30.

Silver, A.I., "French Canada and the Prairie Frontier, 1870-1890," *CHR*, L, 11, 1969.

Smith, Wilfrid, "Charles Tupper's Minutes of the Charlottetown Conference," *CHR*, XLVIII, 2, 1967.

Smith, William, "The Reception of the Durham Report in Canada," *CHAR*, 1928.

Stacey, C.P., "Britain's Withdrawal from North America, 1864-1871," *CHR*, XXXVI, 3, 1955.

_____ "The Fenian Troubles and Canadian Military Development, 1865-1871," *CHAR*, 1935.

_____ "The Military Aspects of Canada's Winning of the West, 1870-1885," *CHR*, XXI, 1, 1940.

Stanley, G.F.G. ed., "Le journal de l'abbé N-J Ritchot, 1870," *RHAF*, XVII, 4, 1963-64.

Storey, N. ed., "Stewart Derbishire's Report to Lord Durham on Lower Canada, 1838," *CHR*, XVIII, 1, 1937.

Sulte, Benjamin, "L'Expédition militaire de Manitoba," *La Revue canadienne*, VIII, 7-8, 1871.

_____ "Sir George-Etienne Cartier," *La Revue canadienne*, X, 6, 1874.

Taché, L., "Sir E-P Taché et la confédération canadienne," *Revue de L'Université d'Ottawa*, 1935.

Tassé, Joseph, "Le Chemin de Fer Canadien du Pacifique," *La revue canadienne*, IX, 6-7, 1872.

Trotter, R.G., "Lord Monck and the Great Coalition of 1864," *CHR*, III, 2, 1922.

Ullman, W., "The Quebec Bishops and Confederation," *CHR*, XLIV, 3, 1963.

Waite, P.B., "Edward Cardwell and Confederation," *CHR*, XLIII, 1, 1962.

_____ "Edward Whelan Reports from the Quebec Conference," *CHR*, XLII, 1, 1961.

_____ "The Quebec Resolutions and Le Courrier du Canada, 1864-1865," *CHR*, XL, 1959.

Whitelaw, W.M., "Reconstructing the Quebec Conference," *CHR*, XIX, 2, 1938.

Wolseley, Garnet J., "Narrative of the Red River Expedition by an Officer of the Expeditionary Force," *Blackwood's Magazine*, Dec. 1870.

Young, Brian J., "The Defeat of George-Etienne Cartier in Montreal-East in 1872," *CHR*, LI, 1970.

REFERENCES

Authors and/or titles are given in the most convenient abbreviated form; full details will be found in the bibliography. Unless otherwise indicated, translations from the French are the author's.

PART I (From the House of the Seven Chimneys)

1 Tassé, *Discours*, 642.
2 Lanctot, *Canada and the American Revolution*, 66.
3 Stanley, *Canada Invaded*, 42; 70-73.
4 Lanctot, 102-3.
5 Chapais, *Cours d'Histoire*, II, 124-6n.
6 *Ibid.*, 21-2.
7 Craig to Castlereagh, Aug. 4, 1808; C.O. 42/136.
8 F. Huot, "Aux Electeurs du Comté d'HAMPSHIRE," Québec *Gazette*, Nov. 9, 1809.
9 *Le Canadien*, Nov. 13, 1806.
10 Quebec *Gazette*, Nov. 9, 1809.
11 Paquet and Wallot, "Aperçu," *RHAF*, XXI, 1967,454.
12 Sir Louis-Hippolyte preferred the capital "F" because it is a more noble way of spelling the name. Who are we to deny him this little vanity?
13 Tassé, 256.
14 Groulx, *Histoire*, II, 141.
15 PAC, Cartier Papers, Rodier to Cartier, n.d.
16 John Palmer, *Journal of Travels in the United States of North America and in Lower Canada*, London, 1818, p. 216.
17 Creighton, *Empire*, 275-6 (trans.).
18 *Précis des Débats de la Chambre d'Assemblée* (Québec, 1834); Wade, *French Canadians*, I, 144 (trans.).
19 Boyd, *Cartier*, 37-8.
20 *Gazette*, Nov. 8, 1834.
21 Filteau, *Histoire*, II, 81.
22 *Ibid.*, 109-10; Wade, 163 (trans.).
23 *La Minerve*, April 27, 1837; Wade, 159 (trans.).
24 Christie, *History*, IV, 373-4.
25 Amédée Papineau, *Journal*, 38.
26 John J. Bigsby, *The Shoe and Canoe*, (London, 1850), I, 206-7.
27 *Gazette*, Sept. 30, 1837.
28 "Camillus" (Adam Thom), *Anti-Gallic Letters*, 118.
29 Boyd, 59-60.
30 In the New York *Albion*, Nov. 25, 1837.
31 Boyd, 62.
32 Ormsby, *Crisis*, 171n; New, *Durham*, 418n.; *L'Aurore des Canadas*, Jan. 22, 1839.
33 Storey, ed., "Stewart Derbishire's Report," *CHR*, 1937, 57-8.
34 Durham Papers, IV, 1, 43-4; Clark, *Movements*, 311.
35 Bonenfant, "George-Etienne Cartier, juriste," *Cahier des Dix*, 31 (1966), 12; *RAPQ*, 1925-26, opp. p. 193.
36 David, *Salut*, 60.
37 Lucas, *Durham's Report*, II, 16.
38 *Ibid.*, 22.
39 Boyd, 69.
40 Creighton, *Empire*, 330.
41 New, *Durham*, 419.
42 Creighton, *Empire*, 330.
43 PAC, LaFontaine Papers, Hincks to LaFontaine, April 12, 1839.
44 Martin, *Foundations*, 162.
45 Château de Ramezay Collection, Cartier to Perrault, May 14, 1839.
46 Leacock, *LaFontaine*, 171.
47 Boyd, 75-76.
48 ANQ, Papiers LaFontaine, Cartier to LaFontaine, Sept. 18, 1842.
49 Sulte, *Mélanges Historiques*, IV, 51.
50 *RHAF*, 10,325.
51 Bonenfant, 11.
52 PAC, Château de Ramezay Papers.
53 *Times and Commercial Advertiser*, April 7, 1843.
54 Tassé, 2-3.
55 Rumilly, *Histoire de Montréal*, II, 302.
56 Keenleyside, *Canada and the United States*, 105.
57 PAO, Mackenzie-Lindsey Papers, W. Gibbons to Mackenzie, Dec. 23, 1851.
58 PAC, LaFontaine Papers, Bouthillier to LaFontaine, Oct. 17, 1845.
59 Papineau to O'Callaghan, May 12, 1846; Wade, I, 256-7 (trans.).
60 *Journal de Québec*, Nov. 13, 1847: Wade, I, 257 (trans.).

61 *La Minerve*, Jan. 17, 1848.
62 *La Minerve*, July 17, 1848; and Susan Robertson, "The Institut Canadien: An Essay in Cultural History," (Unpublished M.A. Thesis, University of Western Ontario, 1965), 46.
63 *La Minerve*, Oct. 3, 1844.
64 Christie, IV, 535; Boyd, 56-7.
65 *L'Avenir*, Aug. 9, 1848.
66 Fauteux, *Le Duel au Canada*, 275.
67 *Ibid.*, 277-8.
68 *Résumé Impartial de la Discussion Papineau-Nelson sur les Evénements de Saint-Denis en 1837*. Montreal, 1848.
69 Wade, I, 167.
70 Tassé, 5-7.
71 *Ibid.*, 13-4.
72 Innis and Lower, *Select Documents*, II, 357: April 19, 1848.
73 *La Minerve*, Feb. 26, 1846.
74 Shippee, *Canadian-American Relations*, 7.
75 Doughty, *Elgin-Grey Papers*, I, 256.
76 Chapais, VI, 8; Wade, 250.
77 Doughty, June 29, 1848.
78 Chapais, VI, 74-75; Wade, 267-8.
79 Chapais, VI, 97; Wade, 269.

80 Boyd, 98.
81 *Ibid.*, 99.
82 *L'Avenir*, March 3, 1849.
83 Doughty, I, 350-52.
84 *Gazette*, April 30, 1849.
85 Doughty, I, 208.
86 Creighton, *Macdonald*, I, 142.
87 *Ibid.*, 142-3.
88 Shippee, 9.
89 *Gazette*, Oct. 11, 1849.
90 *L'Avenir*, Oct. 13, 1849.
91 J.S. Buckingham. *Canada, Nova Scotia, New Brunswick and the other British Provinces in North America*, (London, 1843), 30-37, 138-9.
92 Keenleyside, 106.
93 Tassé, 31-2.
94 Currie, *Grand Trunk*, 18.
95 Stevens, *Canadian National Railways*, I, 256.
96 Hornby, *Autobiography*, 90.
97 *Globe*, Jan. 20, 1860.
98 *Ibid.*, March 26, 1853.
99 Data from Cornell, *Alignment*.
100 *Debates*, Sept. 5, 1854.
101 Doughty, August 20, 1850.
102 Tassé, 46.
103 *Ibid.*, 48.

PART II (Siamese Twins)

1 Sleigh, *Pine Forest*, 127.
2 Tassé, 194.
3 Kerr, *Head*, 125; Head to Lewis, June 15, 1856.
4 *Ibid.*, Head to Lewis, June 15, 1856.
5 Tassé, 65-7.
6 Boyd, 112.
7 Tassé, 60.
8 PAC, Macdonald Papers, Macdonald to Brown Chamberlin, Feb. 2, 1865.
9 Lindsey, *Mackenzie*, 499.
10 PAC, Macdonald Papers, Macdonald to Cameron, Jan. 3, 1872.
11 Sulte, *Mélanges Historiques*, IV, 49.
12 Barnard, *Mémoires Chapais*, II, 163-5.
13 Tassé, 148-9.
14 *Ibid.*, 258.
15 *Ibid.*, 278.
16 *Globe*, May 21, 1856.
17 Tassé, 102.
18 *Ibid.*, 138.
19 Désilets, *Langevin*, 110.
20 Tassé, 491.
21 *Ibid.*, 472.

22 *Ibid.*, 473-4.
23 *British Colonist*, July 6, 1858,
24 Head to Lewis, Aug. 9, 1858; Kerr, *Scholarly Governor*, 191.
25 *Globe*, August 6-7, 1858.
26 PAC, Macdonald Papers.
27 Morton, *Critical Years*, 65 (trans.).
28 Tassé, 158.
29 Trotter, *Canadian Federation*, 5.
30 *Assembly Journals*, (1858), 1043.
31 Tassé, 170-74.
32 ANQ, Papiers Langevin, Sicotte to Langevin, Feb. 25, 1859.
33 *Ibid.*, Oct. 24, 1859.
34 Boyd, 124.
35 Phelan, *Ardent Exile*, 183.
36 Skelton, *McGee*, 332.
37 PAC, Brown Papers, March 1, 1864.
38 Harvard University, Morse Collection, Howe to his wife, Nov. 22, 1867.
39 PAC, Macdonald Papers, Macdonald to Sidney Smith, Feb. 21, 1861.
40 Watkin, *Canada and the States*, 3.
41 Phelan, 202-3.
42 Watkin, 65.

43 *Ibid.*, 16.
44 *Ibid.*, 496-9.
45 *Ibid.*, 503.
46 Morton, *Critical Years*, 108.
47 *Assembly Debates*, April 17, 1861.
48 *Leader*, April 23, 1861.
49 PAO, Hodgins Papers, Macdonald to Ryerson, March 18, 1861.
50 *Globe*, May 14, 1862.
51 Tassé, 309.
52 Watkin, 95.
53 Queen's University, Mackenzie Papers, Brown to Holton, May 29, 1862.
54 PAC, Newcastle Papers, Monck to Newcastle, August 11, 1862.
55 PAC, Macdonald Papers, Cameron to Macdonald, March 16, 1863.
56 Creighton, *Macdonald*, I, 339-40.
57 Mitchell, "Edward Watkin," *CHR*, XXXIV, 3, 1953, 229.
58 *The Nor'Wester*, Dec. 28, 1859.
59 *Globe*, Jan. 26, 1860.
60 PAC, Macdonald Papers, Brydges to Macdonald, Feb. 24, 1864.
61 *Globe*, March 15, 1864.
62 *La Patrie*, Feb. 18, 1887.
63 De Celles, *Cartier et son Temps*, 97n.
64 UNBL, Tilley Papers, April 1, 1864.
65 *Globe*, June 16, 1864.
66 *Spectator*, June 20, 1864.
67 Morton, *Monck Letters*, 72.
68 *La Minerve*, June 21, 1864.
69 L. Taché, "Sir E.-P. Taché," *RUO*, 1935, 244n.; Taché to F.-A. Quesnel, July 9, 1864.
70 *Morning Telegraph*, August 9, 1864.
71 *Ibid.*, August 6, 1864.
72 Morton, *Monck Letters*, 94.
73 *Morning Telegraph*, September 5, 1864.
74 Tassé, 396-7.
75 Monck, *My Canadian Leaves*, 211.
76 PAC, Brown Papers, George Brown to Anne Brown, Oct. 31, 1864.
77 Tassé, 407-8.
78 *The Times*, Oct. 24, 1864.
79 *New York Herald*, Feb. 9, 1861.
80 Buffalo *Express*, Dec. 30, 1861.
81 *Diplomatic Correspondence*, 1864-65, II, 762; Shippee, 147.
82 *La Minerve*, Dec. 1, Dec. 20, 1864.
83 PAC, *Macdonald Papers*, Wodehouse to Cartier, Nov. 12, 1872; Pennell to Cartier, Nov. 15, 1872; Cartier to Kimberley, Nov. 18, 1872; Cartier to Macdonald, Jan. 23, 1873.
84 *Gazette*, Dec. 20, 1864.
85 Brunet, *Province du Canada*, 281; also Winks, *Canada and the United States: The Civil War Years*.
86 PAC, Macdonald Papers, Macdonald to Cameron, Dec. 19, 1864.
87 *Confederation Debates*, 6 (Feb. 3, 1865).
88 *Ibid.*, 54-5.
89 *Ibid.*, 55.
90 *Ibid.*, 55-6.
91 *Ibid.*, 62.
92 *Ibid.*, 358.
93 ANQ, Papiers Langevin, Gélinas to Langevin, Nov. 8, 1864.
94 *Ibid.*, Rhéaume to Langevin, March 25, 1865.
95 *Sessional Papers*, Charlevoix Election Case, Aug. 8, 1876, 41.
96 Archives de la Chancellerie de l'Archvêché de Montréal, Cazeau to Truteau, Feb. 26, 1865.
97 Morton, *Monck Letters*, 250.
98 Toronto *Empire*, Dec. 31, 1892.
99 Stacey, *Canada and the British Army*, 181.
100 *Ibid.*
101 *Confederation Debates*, Feb. 9, 1865.
102 PAC, Macdonald Papers, Cartier to Macdonald, Sept. 1, 1866.
103 *Journal de Québec*, March 26, 1938.
104 PAC, Brown Papers, George Brown to Anne Brown, Aug. 15, 1864.
105 Halifax *Morning Chronicle*, Jan. 13, 1865.
106 Boyd, 265.
107 PAC, Galt Papers, Galt to his wife, Dec. 21, 1865.
108 M.A. Booker, *Catalogue de la Bibliothèque du feu L'Hon. Sir G.E. Cartier, Baronet*, Montreal, 1873.
109 "Testament de Sir George-Etienne Cartier," *RAQ*, 1960-61, 175.
110 *Ibid.*, 177.
111 *Ibid.*, 179-80.
112 Tassé, 508.
113 *Ibid.*, 515.
114 ANQ, Papiers Langevin, Langevin to his mother, Jan. 24, 1867.
115 PAC, Galt Papers, Galt to his wife, Dec. 19, 1867.
116 ANQ, Papiers Langevin, Belleau to Chapais, March 13, 1867.
117 Tassé, 518-9.

118 PAC, Galt Papers, Galt to his wife, July 2, 1867.

119 Boyd, 284-5.

PART III (All Aboard for the West)

1 Helmcken, *Reminiscences*, V, 67-9.
2 New York *Tribune*, May 28, 1867.
3 Josephson, *Politicos*, 13.
4 *British Parliamentary Papers*, Vol. 27, 321-2.
5 Boyd, 292.
6 Tassé, 599.
7 PAC, Collection Cartier, H. Williams to Cartier, May 7, 1869.
8 Boyd, 295.
9 Morton, *Critical Years*, 234.
10 PAC, Macdonald Papers, Cartier to Macdonald, Nov. 20, 1868.
11 Stacey, *Canada and the British Army*, 210.
12 PAC, Macdonald Papers, Cartier to Macdonald, Dec. 29, 1868.
13 Boyd, 299.
14 Tassé, 606.
15 Boyd, 301.
16 ANQ, Papiers Chapais, Riel to Cartier, Feb. 24, 1865; Stanley, *Riel*, 33 (trans.).
17 Mousseau, *Une Page d'Histoire*, (Montreal, 1887), 11-13; Stanley, 381n. (trans.).
18 St. Boniface Historical Society, *Comte Rendu de ses Activités*; Stanley, 34 (trans.).
19 Morton, *Begg*, 35.
20 Winks, *Civil War Years*, 170.
21 Brebner, *North Atlantic Triangle*, 165.
22 Larsen, *Jay Cooke*, 337-8.
23 Willson, *Friendly Relations*, 181-2.
24 Bowsfield, "James Wickes Taylor," *MRSP*, III, 1968, 51-2; Taylor to Cooper, Nov. 23, 1867.
25 *Ibid.*, 191; June 30, 1865.
26 *Ibid.*, 70-1.
27 *Globe*, Jan. 4, 1869.
28 Rumilly, *Québec*, I, 160.
29 St. Paul *Press*, Nov. 4, 1869.
30 *Sessional Papers*, 1870, v, 12.
31 PAC, Macdonald Papers.
32 *Sessional Papers*, 1870, v, 12.
33 PAC, Macdonald Papers, Nov. 20, 1869.
34 *Ibid.*, Nov. 27, 1869.
35 Morton, *Birth, MRSP*, I, 1965, 90; April 27, 1870.
36 Creighton, *Macdonald*, II, 64.
37 *Report of the Select Committee*, 1874, Taché deposition.
38 Stanley, *Riel*, 81; Willson, *Strathcona*, 42n.
39 Wade, *French Canadians*, I, 400.
40 *The New Nation*, Feb. 18, 1870.
41 PAC, Riel Papers, "Affaire Scott," Riel to Masson.
42 Bowsfield, "Taylor," 125-6.
43 *Report*, Taché deposition.
44 Benoit, *Vie de Mgr. Taché*, II, 75; Taché to Governor General, May 7, 1870.
45 Morton, *Begg*, 128; Jay Cooke to H.D. Cooke, April 14, 1870.
46 Denison, *Struggle for Imperial Unity*, 22.
47 *Globe*, April 7, 1870.
48 Denison, *Struggle*, 26.
49 *Canadian Illustrated News*, April 16, 1870.
50 PAC, Macdonald Papers, Macdonald to Rose, Feb. 23, 1870.
51 Stanley, *Birth of Western Canada*, 119.
52 Boyd, 303.
53 De Celles, 141.
54 Stanley, "Journal de l'Abbé Ritchot," *RHAF*, XVII, 4, 551.
55 *Report*, Ritchot deposition.
56 Rumilly, *Québec*, I, 145.
57 Morton, *Birth*, 95.
58 Boyd, 304.
59 *Report*, June 9, 1870, Young to Granville.
60 *Ibid.*, July 1, 1870, Lynch to Young.
61 Dubuc, "Correspondence de Sir Joseph Dubuc," *RHAF*, XX, 3, 430.
62 *Ibid.*, 431.
63 *Ibid.*, 434.
64 *La Minerve*, July 2, 1870.
65 *Report*, June 18, 1870, Ritchot to Cartier.
66 *The New Nation*, July 1, 1870.
67 Archevêché de Saint-Boniface, Cartier to Taché, July 5, 1870.
68 PAC, Macdonald Papers, Cartier to Macdonald, July 19, 1870.
69 *Report*, Taché deposition.
70 Denison, *Struggle*, 43-4.
71 McDougall, *Red River Rebellion*, 46.
72 *Globe*, July 13, 1870.

73 *Report*, Royal deposition.
74 *RHAF*, XVII, 2, 259.
75 Archevêché de Saint-Boniface, Cartier to Taché, Nov. 2, 1870.
76 *Blackwood's Magazine*, Dec. 1870, 715.
77 Royal Canadian Military Institute, Denison Papers, Frederick Denison to G.T. Denison, March 15, 1871; Stanley, *Riel*, 167.
78 *Report*, Jan. 20, 1872.
79 *Globe*, March 1871; Stanley, *Riel*, 177.
80 Public Archives of Manitoba, Riel Papers, Royal to Riel, Dec. 17, 1870.
81 *Report*, Taché to Cartier, May 6, 1871.
82 *Ibid.*, Taché deposition.
83 *Ibid.*, Taché to Riel and Lépine, Feb. 16, 1872.
84 Smith, *Treaty of Washington*, 16-17.
85 *Ibid.*, 5.
86 Seward, *Cruise to Labrador*, 24.
87 Ireland, "Diary," *BCHQ*, IV, 2, 116.
88 *Ibid.*, 117.
89 *Ibid.*, 118-19.
90 *Ibid.*, 120; my italics.
91 Boyd, 307.
92 Ireland, 117.
93 *Ibid.*, 128.

94 PABC, Crease Papers, Musgrave to Crease, Aug. 8, 1870; Morton, *Critical Years*, 248.
95 *Ibid.*, Helmcken Papers, Trutch to Helmcken, April 17, 1871; Ormsby, 250.
96 Tassé, 700.
97 PAC, Macdonald Papers, Brydges to Macdonald, Nov. 19, 1869.
98 *Ibid.*, Allan to Macdonald, Nov. 23, 1869.
99 *Ibid.*, Brydges to Macdonald, Jan. 25, 1870.
100 *Ibid.*, Macdonald to Brydges, Jan. 25, 1870.
101 Tassé, 656-7.
102 PAC, Macdonald Papers, Macdonald to Rose, March 25, 1870; Feb. 23, 1870.
103 Lockhart, "Macdonald Conservatism," *CHAR*, 1939, 131.
104 PAC, Macdonald Papers, Hincks to Macdonald, Feb. 15, 1871.
105 *Ibid.*, Macdonald to Cartier.
106 *Globe*, May 24, 1871.
107 *Debates*, 34 Vict. 1871, II, 661.
108 *Ibid.*, 662-3.
109 *Ibid.*, 746.
110 *Ibid.*, 749.
111 *Ibid.*, 759.
112 *Ibid.*, 761.

PART IV (Pandora's Box)

1 Keefer, *Philosophy of Railroads*, 337.
2 Currie, *Grand Trunk*, 301.
3 Irwin, *Pacific Railways*, 139.
4 *Ibid.*, 161.
5 *Journals*, 1873, VII, 96.
6 *Ibid.*
7 Hincks' Testimony, "Report of the Royal Commission," *Appendix to Journals*, 1873, VII, 12.
8 *The Manitoban*, July 15, 1871.
9 Irwin, 165.
10 PAC, Macdonald Papers, Macdonald to Rose, Oct. 18, 1872.
11 *Appendix*, 152.
12 *Ibid.*, 106-7.
13 PAC, Macdonald Papers.
14 Irwin, 148.
15 *Ibid.*
16 Stevens, *Canadian National Railways*, II, 408.
17 Hidy, *The House of Baring*, 154.

18 Tassé, 248.
19 Poor, *First International Railway*, 265. (written by J.A. Poor's daughter).
20 *Poor's Railroad Manual*, 1873-74, 618.
21 *Statutes*, 35 Vict. Cap. 90, 1872.
22 Irwin, 143.
23 *Journals*, 96.
24 *La Minerve*, Aug. 9, 1870.
25 *Ibid.*, Sept. 5, 1870.
26 *Appendix*, 101.
27 *Ibid.*, 108.
28 *Ibid.*, 197.
29 *Ibid.*, 138.
30 *Ibid.*, 198.
31 *Ibid.*
32 Rumilly, *Québec*, I, 151.
33 Wade, I, 353; Rumilly, I, 155.
34 Wade, 353.
35 Rumilly, 178.

36 *Canadian Illustrated News*, Feb. 24, 1872.
37 De Celles, 184n.
38 *Appendix*, 197.
39 PAC, Macdonald Papers, Macdonald to Rose, Jan. 11, 1872.
40 *Appendix*, 200.
41 PAC, Macdonald Papers, Brydges to Macpherson, March 11, 1872.
42 *Appendix*, 200.
43 *Ibid.*, 33.
44 *Ibid.*, 201.
45 *Ibid.*
46 PAC, Macdonald Papers, Macdonald to Rose, March 5, 1872.
47 *Ibid.*, March 27, 1872.
48 Irwin, 119.
49 Tassé, 721-2.
50 PAC, Macdonald Papers, Macdonald to Rose, April 17, 1872.
51 Sulte, *Mélanges Historiques*, IV, 61-2.
52 Tassé, 727.
53 Irwin, 178.
54 *Appendix*, 202.
55 Queen's University, Mackenzie Papers, S.J. Watson to Mackenzie, June 24, 1872.
56 *Appendix*, 50-2.
57 *Ibid.*, 193-5.
58 *Ibid.*, 211-12.
59 *Ibid.*, 203.
60 PAC, Macdonald Papers, Allan to Macdonald, July 12, 1872.
61 *Ibid.*, Macpherson to Macdonald, July 27, 1872.
62 *Ibid.*, Allan to Macdonald, July 17, 1872.
63 *Ibid.*, Cartier to Macdonald, July 19, 1872.
64 *Ibid.*, Cartier to Macdonald, July 22, 1872.
65 *Ibid.*, Macdonald to Cartier.
66 *Appendix*, 142.
67 PAC, Macdonald Papers, Macdonald to Dufferin; Glazebrook, 58. Nephritis only affects the mental faculties in secondary ways, such as aggravating a disposition already present. Cartier retained his powers of judgment right up to his death.
68 *Appendix*, 167-8.
69 *Ibid.*, 144.
70 PAC, Macdonald Papers, Allan to Macdonald, July 30, 1872.
71 *Appendix*, 206.
72 *Ibid.*, 147.
73 *Ibid.*, 203.
74 *Ibid.*, 183.
75 *Ibid.*, 214.
76 *Ibid.*, 188; testimony of Thomas White, editor of Montreal *Gazette*.
77 PAC, Macdonald Papers, F.B. McDaniel to Macdonald, Sept. 22, 1873.
78 *Fonds de la Succession Cartier*, p. 73; Hudon to Cartier, Sept. 3, 1872; Best thesis, 575.
79 Tassé, 758.
80 *Ibid.*, 759.
81 PAC, Collection Cartier, Cartier to Grey Campbell, Aug. 6, 1872.
82 *Ibid.*
83 Rumilly, *Québec*, I, 188.
84 Tassé, 761-4.
85 Rumilly, *Québec*, I, 192.
86 Sulte, *Mélanges Historiques*, IV, 65.
87 Boyd, 323.
88 PAC, Macdonald Papers, Macdonald to Lisgar, Sept. 2, 1872.
89 *Ibid.*
90 Denison, *Soldiering in Canada*, 186.
91 ANQ, Papiers Langevin, Sept. 7, 1872.
92 *Ibid.*, Nov. 4, 1872.
93 PAC, Macdonald Papers, Macdonald to Archibald, Sept. 7, 1872.
94 *Ibid.*, Cartier to Macdonald, Sept. 12, 1872.
95 *Report.*
96 Tassé, 768-9.
97 PAC, Macdonald Papers, Macpherson to Macdonald, Sept. 17, 1872.
98 *Appendix*, 203-4.
99 Tassé, 774.
100 *Ibid.*, 775.
101 *Ibid.*, 779.
102 Boyd, 326.
103 PAC, Macdonald Papers, Cartier to Macdonald, Oct. 17, 1872.
104 *Journals*, 98.
105 *Sessional Papers*, No. 5, Vol. 6, 1873; No. 13, 4.
106 *Appendix*, 148.
107 *Ibid.*, 215.
108 *Ibid.*, 204.
109 PAC, Macdonald Papers, Allan to Macdonald, Nov. 13, 1872.
110 *Ibid.*, Foster to Cartier, Nov. 14, 1872.
111 *Sessional Papers*, 32.
112 PAC, Macdonald Papers.
113 *Ibid.*, Collection Cartier, Cartier to Macdonald, Nov. 30, 1872.
114 Boyd, 327.

115 PAC, Macdonald Papers, Macdonald to Cartier, Dec. 23, 1872.
116 *Journals*, 99.
117 Irwin, 196.
118 PAC, Macdonald Papers, Cartier to Macdonald, Jan. 23, 1873.
119 *Ibid.*, Hincks to Macdonald, Feb. 10, 1873.
120 *Ibid.*, Smith to Macdonald, Feb. 20, 1873.
121 *Ibid.*, Macdonald to Rose, Feb. 13, 1873.
122 *Ibid.*, Allan to Macdonald, April 9, 1873.
123 *Debates*, 1877, III, 1789.
124 PAC, Macdonald Papers, Foster to Macdonald, Feb. 3, 1873.

125 *Ibid.*, Abbott to Macdonald, Oct. 1, 1873.
126 *Debates*, March 10, 1873.
127 PAC, Macdonald Papers, Macdonald to W.H. Gibbs, March 23, 1872.
128 *Debates*, April 2, 1873; 36 Vict. 115-16.
129 PAC, Macdonald Papers, Macdonald to Cartier, April 10, 1873.
130 *Ibid.*, Cartier to Macdonald, April 19, 1873.
131 *Ibid.*, Macdonald to Allan, May 2, 1873.
132 Boyd, 334.
133 *Ibid.*, 335.
134 *Ibid.*, 336.
135 *Ibid.*, 338.
136 *Ibid.*, 342.

INDEX

(Due to space limitations, I have not included place names, the names of hotels, steamboats, newspapers, political ridings and less important personalities. I have indexed all references to the Cartier family, but leave it to the reader in the case of George-Etienne.)

"A La Claire Fontaine", 125
Abbott, J.J.C., 81, 155, 253, 256-57, 260, 272-73, 279, 287-89, 304, 311-17
"Aide-toi, le ciel t'aidera", 33.
Allan, Sir Hugh, 78, 228-29, 245, 247-51, 256-57, 259-64, 268-70, 272-76, 279-94, 296, 300-17, 321, 324-25
Allan Line, 131, 175, 245, 250-51, 282, 295, 302, 312, 321
Amnesty, 207-08, 210, 212-15, 217-19
Annexation, 73, 79-81, 83-84, 101, 105, 160, 162, 187, 190, 192-94, 202-03, 211, 227-28, 267, 314
Archibald, Sir A.G. 211, 214-15, 217, 219-20, 222, 246, 248, 299, 311
Association canadienne-française des townships, 65
Atlantic & Pacific Transit & Telegraph Co., 140
"Avant tout je suis canadien", 39
Bagot, Sir Charles, 56, 59
Baldwin, Robert, 56, 59, 64, 77, 82, 169
Banks, General N.P., 191-92, 274
Bank of Montreal, 32, 169, 250-51
Bannatyne, A.G.B., 187, 195, 202, 204
Banque du Peuple, 36
Baring Bros., 85-87, 112, 120, 127, 251, 254, 259, 269, 311
Bayle, Abbé, 28, 297
Belleau, Sir N.-F., 113, 165, 174, 322
Bernard, Susan Agnes (see Lady Macdonald)
Berthelot, Amable, 35, 57
Bétournay, Louis, 300
Black, Judge John, 207, 209
Blake, Edward, 208, 216, 220, 222, 260, 268, 315
Bourget, Bishop Ignace, 65, 265-68, 279, 292, 296-97
Bright, John, 135, 180, 184-86
Bright's Disease, 240, 263, 298, 303, 324
British American League, 79
British American Land Co., 32, 37, 39, 65
British Columbia Act, 225-27, 232, 234, 246, 277
Brockville & Ottawa Railway, 256
Brown, George, 75, 82, 86-90, 106-11, 114-17, 126-28, 133-50, 159-61, 163, 165-68, 184, 187, 205, 272
Brown, Thomas Storrow, 39, 42, 45, 47, 49
Brown-Dorion Ministry, 109, 122
Brydges, Charles John, 141-42, 164, 172, 228-29, 244-46, 251, 254, 261-62, 270-73, 286, 316
Buckingham & Chandos, Duke of, 175, 185
Buffalo-Fort Erie International Bridge, 260, 262
Buller, Charles, 51, 53
Cameron, Capt. D.R., 187, 197, 199, 200
Cameron, John Hillyard, 139, 158, 216
Cameron, Malcolm, 109
Campbell, Alexander, 148, 305
Canada Central Railway, 256-57, 260, 273, 286, 303, 312-13, 323, 326
Canada First Movement, 194, 196-97, 208, 213, 249, 268
Canada Pacific Railway Co., 261, 274, 279, 285, 304, 309-10
Canada Land & Improvement Co., 261
Canadian Pacific Railway, 120, 201, 203, 225-29, 232-34, 239-40, 244-52, 259-61, 263-64, 267, 269, 273-82, 284-94, 298, 302-14, 316, 324-26
Cardwell, Edward, 156, 185
Carleton, Sir Guy, 20-21, 120
Carrall, R.W.W., 225, 227
Cartier, Adèle, 83
——— Antoine-Côme, 40, 172, 294
——— Antoine-Jacques, 27
——— Damien, 27, 36, 51-52, 58, 68, 104
——— François, 18
——— Henri, 47-48, 66-67
——— Hortense (Fabre), 36, 60, 74, 169, 172, 263, 303, 318, 321, 323
——— Hortense II, 61, 171-72, 263, 276, 303, 318-19, 321, 323
——— Jacques, the navigator, 17, 173, 259, 276n, 321
——— Jacques I, 18, 36
——— Jacques II, 19-21, 24, 39, 41
——— Jacques III, 24-28, 38, 40, 44, 56, 70

——— Joseph I, 19-20

——— Joseph II, 24, 51, 59, 169

——— Josephine, 61, 171-72, 263, 276, 303, 314, 317-19, 321, 323

——— Léocadie, 302

——— Louis I, 18

——— Louis II, 294

——— Marguerite (Paradis), 24, 26-27, 65, 171

——— Perrine, 66

——— Reine-Victoria, 88

Cartier & Cartier, 30, 58-59, 73; Fees Book, 9, 58

Cartier, Pominville & Bétournay, 112, 265, 285

Cartier-Macdonald Ministry, 109, 118-19, 123, 133, 137

Cass, Gen. G.W., 247, 259, 273, 283, 292, 301, 304

Cauchon, Joseph, 62, 101, 105, 112, 116, 163, 250, 296, 302-03, 320, 323

Cayley, William, 111, 114-15, 118, 124

Central Pacific Railway, 234, 243, 274

Champlain & St. Lawrence Railway, 70

Chandler, Zachariah, 191, 223

Chapais, Jean-Charles, 105-07, 174

——— Thomas, 165-66

Charlottetown Conference, 148-49

Chauveau, Pierre-Joseph-Olivier, 57, 302

Civil Code of Lower Canada, 112-13

Civil War, American, 83-84, 128-30, 132-33, 142, 151, 153, 180, 198, 242

Clarke, Henry J., 220, 299

Cobden, Richard, 180, 184

Colborne, Sir John, 42, 44, 50-51

Collège de Montréal, 27-28, 67, 169, 187-89, 213, 216

Colonial Office, 82, 84, 119, 127, 151, 182

Colonial Society, 186

Commercial Bank, 263-64

Cooke, Jay, 192, 196, 208, 229-41, 243-52, 259, 261, 263, 267, 269, 272-75, 277, 283, 286, 289, 291, 298, 301-05, 309, 324-26

Coursol, Charles-Joseph, 155-56, 295

Crimean War, 82, 98, 110

Cuvillier, Augustin (Austin), 36, 56, 169, 171

Cuvillier, Luce, 169, 171-72, 174, 275, 321

Cuvillier, Maurice, 169, 171-72, 267

Debartzch, Pierre-Dominique, 40, 45, 57

De Cosmos, Amor, 225, 303

Denison, Lt.-Col. George T., 195, 208-09, 211, 213, 215-16, 298

Dennis, Col. J.S., 199-200

Derbishire, Stewart, 49-50

Dominion Lands Act, 276

Dominion Line, 251, 303

Dorion, Antoine-Aimé, 62, 65, 80, 83, 101, 108-10, 112-14, 116-17, 133, 135-39, 144, 147, 158, 228, 315, 320, 322

Double Shuffle, 119, 121

Doutre, Joseph, 67-69, 189, 228, 266, 322-23

Draper, William, 56, 59-60

Draper-Viger Ministry, 59

Drummond, L.T., 60, 101, 138

Dubuc, Joseph, 213-14, 217, 219-21, 299

Dufferin & Ava, Marquis of, 104, 248, 297, 320, 323-25

Durham, Lord, 41, 48-54, 73, 107

Duvernay, Ludger, 29-31, 33, 36, 38, 43-49, 51, 54-55, 60, 68, 83, 98, 323

Eastern Townships, 32, 39, 65, 73, 84, 112, 252, 256n, 264, 283, 289

Eastern Townships-Vermont Central Railway Ring, 252-53, 309, 312-13, 315

Elgin, Lord, 64, 72-74, 77-79, 82, 84, 89, 95-96, 130

Fabre, Edouard, 35-36, 60, 65-66, 88

——— Hector, 36, 169, 228

Fils de la Liberté (Sons of Liberty), 38-42

Fish, Hamilton, 193-94, 208, 210, 220, 224, 227, 246-47

Fisheries, 223-24, 231

Foley, Michael, 136, 138-39, 145

Foster, Asa Belknap, 228, 241, 253-54, 256-57, 260, 272-73, 306, 309, 312-13, 324-26

Franco-Prussian War, 231, 243, 251

Fréchette, Louis, 190, 228

Futvoye, Major Georges, 9, 209

Galt, Sir, A.T., 65, 81, 87, 115, 117-18, 121, 124, 134, 136-37, 145, 148-49, 163-64, 168, 172-76, 209, 227-28, 230, 233, 251, 254, 256, 262-63, 322

Gauthier, Abel, 118, 165, 321

Girard, Marc, 216-19, 202

Gladstone, W.E., 78, 151, 164, 185, 186, 274, 303

Glyn, Mills & Co., 85-87, 127, 311

Goldie, Civil Secretary, 51-52

Gore, Col. Charles, 44-45, 60

Graham, Cyril, 247

Grand Trunk Railway, 71, 84-90, 111-12, 123-24, 126-28, 130, 136, 138, 140-41, 144, 151, 164, 179, 182-83, 185, 189-90, 202, 228-29, 240, 244-46, 248-51, 254, 256-57, 259-60, 262-64, 267, 269, 273, 275, 279, 284, 302, 307, 311-12, 316-17, 326

Grant, Ulysses S., 165, 193, 208, 219, 223-24, 232, 242, 325

Granville, Earl of, 186, 200-01, 213, 224

Great Western Railway, 71, 75, 123, 186

Guarantee Act, 71

Gzowski, Sir Casimir, 87, 245, 260, 272

Head, Sir Edmund Walker, 96-99, 113, 116-21, 124, 127, 131, 140

Helmcken, Dr. J.S., 180, 225-27

Hincks, Sir Francis, 54-55, 61, 71, 77, 82-91, 96, 221, 224-25, 230-31, 233, 247-49, 251-52, 259, 261, 263, 271, 304, 310, 322

Hincks-Morin Ministry, 84-91

Holton, Luther, 81, 87, 110, 137, 139

Hornby, Sir Edmund, 86-87

House of the Seven Chimneys, 21, 25-26, 45, 56, 65, 164, 169, 275, 294, 322

Howe, Joseph, 97-98, 127, 138, 166, 184, 196-99, 210, 214, 220, 307

Howland, Sir William Pearce, 168, 172, 175, 322

Hudson's Bay Company, 114, 125, 131, 136, 139-41, 174, 182, 184-85, 187-90, 194-95, 199-207, 218-23, 246-47, 251-52, 261-62, 269, 311

Hudson's Bay Company Territory (Rupert's Land; Assiniboia), 108, 115, 142, 179, 184, 186-87, 191, 194, 199, 207, 223, 229, 232-34, 243-44, 277, 283n, 304, 324

Huntington, Lucius Seth, 227-28, 230, 234, 241, 253-54, 257, 267, 293, 309, 313-15, 317, 324, 326

Intercolonial Railway, 120, 122, 128, 138, 142, 145, 149, 156, 164, 248; Loan Act, 174

International Financial Society, 140, 283n

International Pacific Railway, 246, 257, 269

Interoceanic Railway Company of Canada, 263, 279, 285, 301, 303-04, 306, 308-10

Jackson, Andrew, 39, 120

Jetté, L.-A., 267, 292-96

Johnstone, Dr. George, 303, 317-19

Joint Commission of 1871, 224, 227, 230-32, 239

Joly de Lotbinière, H.-G., 160-61

Kansas Central & Kansas Pacific Railways, 244

Keefer, Thomas Coltrin, 72, 240-41

Kittson, Norman, 184, 190, 202, 213

Labelle, Rev. Antoine, 265, 267-68, 333

Laflamme, Rodolphe, 155, 189, 228, 266, 267, 293, 313

LaFontaine, Louis-Hippolyte, 27, 29, 34, 36, 44, 49-50, 53-65, 73-77, 82-83, 96, 142, 176

Langevin, Hector-Louis, 9, 104-06, 112, 118, 123, 148, 162, 172, 174-76, 264, 289, 298, 302, 307, 320

Laparre, Henri, 66-69

Larose, Louis, 47-48

Lépine, Ambrose, 217, 222, 299

Limoilou, 169, 171, 259, 275, 281, 297, 300, 322

Lincoln, Abraham, 120, 133, 142, 151, 155, 157, 191, 193

London money market, 248, 252, 261, 273-74, 291, 311, 314

Lytton, Sir Edward Bulwer, 121, 131, 141

Macdonald, Lady Agnes (Bernard), 174, 212n, 215, 250, 318

Macdonald, Lady Flora, 163, 186

Macdonald, Sir John Alexander, 7, 9, 76, 79, 83, 91, 101, 102-03, 106, 108-10, 113-17, 122-23, 125, 127, 132-39, 142-48, 153, 158-59, 163-65, 168, 172-75, 184, 186-87, 199-203, 205, 207, 209-12, 215-16, 218, 224, 229-32, 240, 244-50, 252, 256, 259-61, 263-64, 268-69, 273-74, 276, 278-81, 286-90, 296-97, 299-304, 306-18, 320, 323-25, 327

Macdonald, John Sandfield, 106, 109, 133, 135-38, 144, 184, 222, 260

Macdonald-Cartier Ministry, 109, 113-14, 119

Macdonald-Dorion Ministry, 109, 138-39, 227-28

Macdonald-Sicotte Ministry, 109, 138, 155, 228

McDougall, William, 109, 132-33, 137, 147-48, 154, 172, 175, 184-85, 187, 194-95, 197-201, 204, 207, 210, 216

McGee, Thomas D'Arcy, 114, 125-26, 137-39, 145, 148-49, 154, 164, 172, 179, 182-83, 286

Mackenzie, Alexander, 182, 208, 210, 216, 220, 233, 268, 279, 298, 313, 315, 320

Mackenzie, William Lyon, 37, 61, 87-88, 101, 108, 130

McMicken, Gilbert, 156, 209, 215

McMullen, George "Washington", 247-48, 259, 261-62, 268, 272-73, 279, 282, 285, 292, 294, 301, 304-06, 308-12, 315, 317, 324, 326

MacNab, Sir Allen, 75-79, 83, 86, 95, 100-01, 134

MacNab-Morin Ministry, 95, 109

MacNab-Taché Ministry, 100-01, 109

Macpherson, David L., 81, 87, 260, 263-64, 270-73, 279-81, 285-87

Mair, Charles, 179, 194-95, 199-200, 204, 208, 213

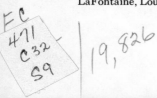

Manifest Destiny, 83, 154, 180, 224, 232
Manitoba Bill, 210, 214, 225, 239, 277
Massawippi Valley Railway, 254, 256
Merchants Bank, 250, 263
Métis, 188, 194-95, 197-98, 200, 202-04, 213, 215, 217, 219, 222, 278, 327
Militia, 185, 212, 231, 259, 277
Militia Bill of 1854, 134-37
Militia Bill of 1868, 182
Militia, Saint-Denis & Verchères (5th Batallion), 19, 24-25, 28, 169
Militia Affairs, Ministry of, 97, 134
Militia & Defence, Ministry of, 175, 182
La Minerve, 29-30, 36, 58, 62, 64, 66, 69, 72, 81, 83, 147, 162, 164, 187, 213-14, 216, 249, 293-94, 296, 298
Monck, Charles Stanley, 4th Viscount, 131-32, 136-38, 144-45, 147, 153-54, 156, 164-65, 173-75
Monck, Frances, 131, 146, 148, 163
Montreal Riding, 114, 133, 139, 266
Montreal East Riding, 155, 264, 266, 268, 275, 282, 293-96, 303
Montreal, Quebec & Occidental Railway, 256n, 323
Montreal & St. Jerome Colonization Railway, 267-68
Montreal & Vermont Junction Railway, 254, 256, 326
Morgan, J.S., 140, 283
Morin, A.-N., 35, 60, 65, 81, 83-84, 88, 90, 100, 164, 228
Nelson, Dr. Wolfred, 39, 42, 44, 47-50, 58-59, 64, 66-67, 69, 75-77, 81
New Brunswick School Bill, 280, 295
New York Central Railway, 241, 244, 262, 303-04
Newcastle, Duke of, 124, 127-28, 138, 140, 232, 244
Ninety-Two Resolutions, 34-35, 80, 169
Norris, George, 312-13
North Shore Railway, 105, 112, 123, 250, 264, 275, 311
Northcote, Sir Stafford, 184, 200-01, 212, 252
Northern Colonization Railway, 248, 250-51, 256, 264, 267-68, 275, 280-82, 285, 293, 311-13, 323
Northern Railway, 71, 123, 261, 303
Northern Pacific Railway, 181, 192-93, 196, 208, 229, 234, 237, 243-49, 252, 254, 257, 273-75, 277, 283, 292-93, 298, 304, 307, 324, 326
Notre Dame Parish (Cathedral), 60, 172, 183, 260, 322
"O Canada, mon pays, mes amours", 28, 33, 149, 187, 321, 328
Oaths Bill, 316-17

O'Callaghan, Dr. E.B., 38-39, 42, 49
O'Donoghue, W.B., 202, 207, 217, 219-20
Ogden, William B., 247-48, 273, 301, 305
Ogdensburg, 254, 257, 313, 326
Ogdensburg & Lake Champlain Railway, 257
Orange Order, 54, 77, 125, 134, 158, 208, 210-11, 216, 220
Oswego Transcontinental Railway Convention, 254
Pacific Scandal, 227, 239-40, 311, 324-25
Papineau, Louis-Joseph, 27, 29, 34-36, 39-44, 49, 55, 59, 61-62, 65-66, 69, 73-76, 130, 169, 228, 265
Parti National, 267, 280, 292-93, 296
Pennsylvania Railroad, 244, 247, 259
Permanent Central Committee, 35, 39, 48
Perrault, Charles-Ovide, 35-36, 45
Peto, Brassey, Jackson & Betts, 85, 87, 90
Philadelphia & Erie Railroad, 247
Pittsburg, Fort Wayne & Chicago Railroad, 247
Place Saint-Jacques, 292-96
Pominville, François-Pierre, 9, 172, 297, 322
Poor, J.A., 228, 256
Portland Maine Bonding Agreement, 60, 98, 147, 160, 164, 232, 241, 245, 248, 320
Prince of Wales, Albert Edward, 124-25, 129, 134, 164
Programme Catholique, 266, 298
Provencher, J.-A.-N., 187, 197, 200
Provisional Government, Métis, 200, 203-07, 220
Quebec Conference, 150, 151, 163, 174
Quebec, Montreal, Ottawa & Occidental Railway, 256n, 323
Ramsey, Alexander, 181, 191, 196, 219, 245
Rebellion of 1837, 7, 36, 39, 41 *passim*, 46 (map), 66, 207, 215, 218, 328
Rebellion Losses Bill, 74-78
Reciprocity, 80, 168, 193, 228-32
Reciprocity Treaty of 1854, 82, 142, 154, 223
Red River Expedition, 211-12, 217, 223
Red River Resistance, 185-214, 226, 249, 327
Representation by Population, 107-09, 132-39, 142, 144, 149
Reynolds, Thomas, 257, 260, 286
Rimouski, Bishop Langevin of, 162, 264, 321
Riel, Louis, 28, 143, 155, 185, 187-92, 195-214, 216-20, 222-24, 228-29, 299
Ritchot, Rev. N.-J., 197-98, 202, 207,

210-16, 218, 224

Rodier, Edouard-Etienne, 29-32, 34-35, 38, 48-49, 51, 53

Roman Catholic Church, 160, 162-63, 168, 185, 260, 264-67, 295

Rose, Sir John, 68, 81, 114, 139, 172, 199-200, 209, 230, 248, 252, 259, 269, 271, 273-74, 276, 300, 311, 320-21

Ross, John J., 90, 121, 131

Royal Commission of 1873, 241, 248, 261, 270, 278, 280, 291, 316-17

Royal, Joseph, 213, 216-17, 219-20, 222, 299-300

Rue Notre-Dame, 57, 61, 96, 275

St. Albans Raid, 154-56

Saint-Antoine, 19, 24-25, 39, 44, 47, 49, 56, 59, 64-65, 67, 171, 294

Saint-Denis, 19-20, 40-47, 51, 59-60, 66, 69, 75

Saint-Germain House, 44-47, 67

Saint-Jean-Baptiste Society, 33, 65, 98, 183

St. Lawrence & Atlantic Railway, 60, 70-71, 84-85, 228

St. Lawrence & Ottawa Railway, 256-57

St. Lawrence International Bridge Co., 257, 312-13, 326

St. Paul & Pacific Railway, 193, 196

de Salaberry, Charles-Michel, 25, 169

de Salaberry, Col. Charles, 202-03, 209

Sault Ste. Marie, 246, 248, 252, 257

Schultz, Dr. John Christian, 194-96, 199-200, 204, 208, 219

Scott, Alfred, 204, 207, 209

Scott, Richard W., 260, 286, 297, 303

Scott, T.A., 244, 247, 259

Scott, Thomas, 204-05, 208-11, 217, 220, 222

Seventy-Two Resolutions, 150, 159

Seward, William Henry, 98, 129, 133-34, 142, 151, 153-57, 180-81, 191, 198, 223-24, 317

Sicotte, Louis-Victor, 89, 105, 110, 113, 122-23, 135-38, 165, 322

Smith, Charles Mather, 247, 261, 270, 272-73, 294, 309, 311

Smith, Donald A., 190, 201-06, 211, 219, 222-23, 246, 261-62, 272-73, 304, 324-25

Smith, J. Gregory, 154, 229, 234, 237, 244-48, 254, 256-57, 267, 274, 283, 286, 293, 309, 312-13, 317, 326

Southeastern Counties Junction Railway, 227, 254, 256

"Un Souvenir de 1837", 328

Standing Committe on Railways, 60, 71, 84, 124, 141, 173, 225-26, 234, 241, 246, 259, 262, 269, 285, 291

Stanstead, Shefford & Chambly Railway, 227, 254, 256, 326

Starnes, Henry, 172, 267

Stephen, George, 251, 262, 324

Stewart, Murdock, 18, 21

Sulpician Order, 27-28, 70, 172, 188, 265, 297

Sulte, Benjamin, 10, 102, 277-78

Sumner, Charles, 153-54, 165, 180, 224, 229, 234

Symes, Clara, 171

Taché, Bishop Alexandre-Antonin, 188, 197, 201-02, 206-08, 214-17, 222, 299, 326

_____ Sir Etienne-Pascal, 86, 100-01, 105-07, 110, 113, 118, 123, 125, 134, 144-47, 155, 159, 162, 164-65, 188

_____ Jean-Charles, 110, 118, 327

Taché-Macdonald Ministry, 101, 109, 145

Taylor, James Wickes, 191-94, 196, 202-03, 205, 207-10, 220, 227, 243-44, 247-48, 275

Ten Resolutions, 37

Thibault, Rev. J.-B., 202-03

Thom, Adam, 41, 50

Tilley, Samuel Leonard, 128, 138, 145, 148, 164, 168, 173, 175, 225, 316

Toronto Rolling Mills, 245, 260

Torrance, Daniel, 262, 303

_____ David, 251, 262, 303

Treaty of Washington, 157, 219-20, 231-32, 274, 276, 308n

Trent Affair, 130, 134, 153

Trutch, Joseph W., 225-27

Tupper, Charles H., 147, 173, 175-76, 184, 187, 202, 224, 234, 325

"La Tuque Bleue", 66-67

Ultramontanism, 265-66, 268

Union Pacific Railway, 243-44, 274

Verchères (Surrey) Riding, 24, 64-65, 84, 88, 100, 114, 216

Vermont Central Railway, 173, 228-29, 234, 244, 252, 254, 256-58, 274, 277, 289, 293, 309, 312-13, 315, 326

Viger, Denis-Benjamin, 36-37, 59-60, 66

Vincent, Thomas, 263, 303, 318

Watkin, Sir Edward, 127-28, 130-32, 137-38, 140-41, 153, 185

Weir, Lt. George, 44-45

Wellbeck St., 303, 317

Westminster Conference, 173-74, 265

Wetherall, Lt.-Col. George, 44-45

Wolseley, Col. Garnet, 206, 216-19

Young, Lt. Bennett, 154, 156

Young, John, 139, 228-29, 253-54, 257, 267, 296, 309, 326

Young, Sir John (Lord Lisgar), 185, 209-13, 215-16, 226, 229, 276, 297-98, 321